THE BEST OF
FOOD&WINE®

AN EXCLUSIVE GIFT EDITION

FROM
BENSON & HEDGES

THE BEST OF
FOOD&WINE

American Express
Publishing Corporation
New York

Cover: Cool Garlic Shrimp with Tomatoes and Croutons (p. 25)

Publisher: Paul D. Wolff
Editorial Director: Susan Crandell
Editor/Designer: Kate Slate
Art Director: Elizabeth G. Woodson
Illustrator: Hong Chow

Published by American Express Publishing Corporation
1120 Avenue of the Americas, New York, New York 10036

Manufactured in the United States of America

ISBN 0-916103-11-0

♟

TABLE OF CONTENTS

FOREWORD

Welcome once again to *The Best of Food & Wine*, our annual collection of the finest recipes from the pages of *Food & Wine* magazine. We believe that the kitchen is the focal point of our lives, the gathering place for friends and family, the room where we convene and entertain as well as cook. These nearly 500 recipes, like *Food & Wine* itself, reflect this contemporary point of view. They are selected for people like us who lead busy, active lives but still yearn for the good life.

Every recipe that appears in the magazine and in this edition of *The Best of Food & Wine* is carefully tested in the *Food & Wine* kitchens until we are sure it will work with home equipment and is as deliciously easy as possible to prepare. As always, you can count on us for food to suit any mood and occasion—from a quick weeknight dinner to a lazy Sunday brunch. But the book also strongly reflects the way we like to entertain and eat right now. You'll find lots of light recipes as well as ideas for bountiful breakfasts—a meal we happily have rediscovered in America. Sophisticated sandwiches, which suit our speeded-up lives, are here in profusion. And complex carbohydrates—which sound much more luscious when described as pastas, grains and breads—are an important part of the book, just as they are of a healthy diet.

Whether the food you sample from these pages is light and modern or rich and old-fashioned, one thing is certain: There will be a big reward in taste and high style. This book is for all of us who are dedicated to living wisely . . . and well.

Ila Stanger
Editor-in-Chief

FOOD & WINE'S VINTAGE RATINGS
1978-1988

COMPILED BY ELIN McCOY & JOHN FREDERICK WALKER

	1978	1979	1980	1981	1982
Red Bordeaux	8 Rich, full, good depth. Start drinking.	8 Fruity & well-balanced. Start drinking.	5 Small-scale, lightweight, pleasant. Drink up.	7½ Full, attractive wines. Start drinking.	9½ Rich, massive. Sample now or wait 4 years.
Sauternes	5 Big, but lacks typical richness. Drink up.	6 Light but has character. Drink up.	7 Attractive, small-scale. Start drinking.	7½ Well-balanced wines. Start drinking.	7 Variable. Best are big, powerful wines. Start drinking.
Red Burgundy	8 Outstanding; excellent balance. Drink now.	6 Soft, supple, appealing. Drink up.	6 Mostly light wines. Drink now.	5½ Variable vintage. Most early maturing.	7 Big, soft wines. Drink now.
White Burgundy	9 Superb; well-balanced. Drink up.	7 Attractive, fruity wines. Drink up.	5 Variable; the best are attractive. Drink up.	8 Attractive wines. Drink up.	8 Big, rich wines. Drink now.
Napa/Sonoma Cabernet Sauvignon	8 Full, rich, soft. Drink now.	7 Uneven quality; some very good. Drink now.	8 Powerful, tannic. Start drinking.	8 Variable. Many attractive. Drink now.	7 Lighter style; some attractive. Drink now.
Napa/Sonoma Chardonnay	8 Powerful, ripe wines. Fading. Drink up.	8 Rich, intense, fading. Drink up.	8½ Balanced but fading. Drink up.	7 Soft, ripe wines. Fading. Drink up.	7½ Variable, light, fading. Drink up.
Barolo & Barbaresco	9 Classic, concentrated & tannic. Start drinking.	8 Elegant, well-balanced wines. Start drinking.	6 Uneven. Best are well-balanced, attractive. Drink now.	7 Firm, solid wines. Start drinking.	8½ Big, powerful wines; very promising. Wait 1-4 years.
Chianti	8 Very good; solid, tannic. Drink up.	7 Attractive, ripe wines. Drink up.	6 Uneven; best are small-scale. Drink up.	7 Good, firm wines. Drink up.	7½ Attractive but early maturing. Drink now.
Germany	6 Lightweight, crisp. Drink up.	7 Good quality & balance. Drink up.	5 Light & lean. Drink up.	7 Well-balanced, attractive. Drink up.	7 Soft, fruity. Drink up.
Vintage Porto	5 Not generally declared. Rich, soft. Try now.	No vintage declared.	7 Light but good. Sample in 1-4 years.	No vintage declared.	7 Soft, well-balanced. Sample in 4-7 years.

The following ratings and comments reflect a variety of opinions, including our own, on the quality and character of various categories of wines from recent vintages. The ratings—0 for the worst, 10 for the best—are averages, and better or worse wine than indicated can be found in each vintage. Assessments of the most current vintages are more predictive and hence less exact than those of older vintages.

Scores are based on a wine's quality at maturity. A lower-rated but mature wine will often be superior to a higher-rated but immature wine. When-to-drink advice is based on how such wines seemed to be developing in mid-1989, and presumes good storage. The earliest date suggested for consumption applies to the lesser wines of the vintage, which will mature faster than the finest examples of the year.

1983	1984	1985	1986	1987	1988
7½ Firm, powerful. Start tasting.	6 Small-scale, firm. Wait 2 years.	8½ Soft, delicious, elegant. Try in 2 years.	8½ Mixed vintage. Some classic tannic wines. Try in 6 years.	6 Flavorsome but lightweight. Wait 3 years.	7½ Good, somewhat tannic wines. Wait.
9 Rich, classic wines. Start drinking.	5½ Mixed quality. Few good. Drink now.	7½ Soft, full, good. Sample now.	8½ Luscious & rich. Sample now.	6 Light, lean; few good wines.	9 Very promising; rich, concentrated.
8½ Variable. Some very good. Start sampling.	6½ Variable, lighter wines. Start drinking.	9½ Glorious, rich & round. Start drinking.	7 Variable; mostly light, soft wines. Sample now.	7 Stylish lighter wines. Sample now.	9 Concentrated, fruity, delicious.
8 Good, rich wines. Start drinking.	7 Crisp wines. Some fine. Start drinking.	8 Big but soft. Start drinking.	9 Crisp, balanced, classic. Start drinking.	7 Light, round, soft. For early drinking.	7½ Good; some very fine.
7 Good, but not great. Start drinking.	8 Big, rich, powerful. Try in 2 years.	9½ Brilliant, deep & elegant. Wait 4 years.	8 Deep, full & powerful. Wait 4 years.	8 Dark, firm, promising. Wait 4 years.	7½ Mixed vintage; some concentrated. Wait.
7 Good moderate year. Drink up.	7 Good full wines. Drink up.	8 Lovely, balanced. Drink now.	9 Crisp, leaner style. Start drinking.	8 Elegant & crisp. Start drinking.	8 Good, fruity wines. Start sampling.
7 Lighter vintage. Start sampling.	5½ Light, variable. For early drinking.	9 Splendid, rich. Wait 3 years.	8 Well-balanced & fruity. Wait 3 years.	8 Round, rich, full. Wait 5 years.	8½ Rich, powerful wines. Wait.
7 Attractive, early maturing. Drink now.	5 Spotty. Drink up.	9½ Superb balance & flavor. Start sampling.	8 Medium-bodied, fine quality. Start drinking.	7 Average quality. Start sampling.	8 Very promising, concentrated, balanced. Wait.
9 Excellent year. Marvelous late-harvest wines. Drink now.	6½ Lean & tart. Drink now.	8½ Excellent. Start drinking.	6 Light, crisp wines. Start drinking.	7 Mostly lean, some fine. Start sampling.	9 Outstanding, full-flavored, fruity. Start sampling.
8 Firm, solid wines. Sample in 5-10 years.	No vintage declared.	9 Marvelous, deep & fruity. Wait 10-12 years.	—	—	—

9

APPETIZERS & FIRST COURSES

GUACAMOLE

Although this was designed as a part of a Mexican-style sandwich called Triple-Decker Tostada (p. 157), it's a good basic guacamole recipe that can be used as a dip or in another sandwich.

——— *Makes About 2 Cups* ———
4 large, ripe avocados, preferably Hass
1 small onion, minced
2 large garlic cloves, minced
2½ tablespoons fresh lemon juice
Salt and freshly ground pepper

In a large bowl, mash the avocado with a fork. Stir in the onion, garlic, lemon juice and salt and pepper to taste. *(This can be made several hours ahead. Squeeze lemon juice over it, place plastic wrap directly on top and refrigerate.)*
—*Marcia Kiesel*

• • •

EGGPLANT CAVIAR

Set this garlicky eggplant dip out with crudités, a bowl of tomato salsa and some chips.

——— *Makes About 2 Cups* ———
3 medium-large eggplants (about 1¼ pounds each)
1 large head of garlic, unpeeled
⅓ cup olive oil
1 medium-large onion, chopped
2 tablespoons fresh lemon juice
1 tablespoon anchovy paste
Salt and freshly ground pepper

1. Preheat the oven to 400°. Prick the eggplants in several places. Place the eggplants and the whole head of garlic in a roasting pan and bake for about 45 minutes, or until the eggplants and garlic feel soft when pressed. (The garlic may take longer than the eggplant.)

2. Deeply score the eggplants in several places. Place in a colander to drain off the bitter liquid, about 1 hour.

3. Meanwhile, cut off the base of the garlic head to expose the flesh. Squeeze the garlic into a medium bowl.

4. When the eggplants have drained, peel them. Add the pulp to the garlic and mash with a fork to combine.

5. In a large heavy skillet, heat the olive oil. Add the onion and cook over moderate heat until translucent, about 6 minutes. Stir in the eggplant and garlic mixture, 1½ tablespoons of the lemon juice and the anchovy paste. Simmer the mixture, stirring frequently, until very thick and dark, about 30 minutes.

6. Season the eggplant caviar with the remaining ½ tablespoon lemon juice and salt and pepper to taste. Transfer to a bowl and refrigerate until chilled. Serve chilled or at room temperature.
—*John Martin Taylor*

• • •

ASPARAGUS WITH GOAT CHEESE DIP

These lightly blanched asparagus tops are picked up by hand and eaten as crudités. They look particularly attractive bunched in one direction and fanned out on a large platter.

——— *50 Appetizer Servings* ———
2 cups cottage cheese
½ pound mild goat cheese, such as Bucheron
1 cup sour cream
¼ to ½ teaspoon cayenne pepper, to taste
1 teaspoon fresh lemon juice
¼ cup dry white wine
6 scallions (white part only), minced
⅓ cup minced fresh chives or scallion greens
10 pounds asparagus

1. In a food processor, combine the cottage cheese, goat cheese, sour cream, cayenne, lemon juice and wine. Process until well blended and smooth, about 15 seconds. Transfer to a medium bowl. Fold in the scallions and chives. Cover and refrigerate. *(The dip can be prepared up to a day ahead.)*

2. Trim the asparagus to leave 3-inch tips. In a large stockpot of boiling salted water, cook the asparagus tips over high heat until crisp-tender, 2 to 3 minutes. (If your pot is not large enough, do in 2 batches.) Drain at once and rinse under cold running water; drain well. Wrap the asparagus in plastic and refrigerate for up to a day, until ready to serve with the goat cheese dip.
—*New York Parties, New York City*

• • •

PICKLED PRAWNS

Tangy pickled shrimp can be served as an hors d'oeuvre with toothpicks or as part of a main-course buffet. Although this recipe will feed a huge crowd, it is easily scaled down.

——— *50 Appetizer Servings* ———
1 cup coarsely chopped Italian flat-leaf parsley
¼ cup mixed pickling spices
2 teaspoons salt
7 pounds medium shrimp, shelled and deveined
1 cup fresh lemon juice
¾ cup white wine vinegar
½ cup extra-virgin olive oil
3 tablespoons capers, rinsed and drained
1 tablespoon coarse (kosher) salt
¼ cup hot pepper sauce
3 medium red onions, thinly sliced
8 bay leaves
8 celery ribs, thinly sliced

1. In a stockpot or large flameproof casserole, bring 3 quarts of water to a boil over high heat. Stir in the parsley, pickling spices and salt. Add the shrimp and cook, stirring occasionally, until barely pink and loosely curled, 2 to 3 minutes. Drain in a large colander and let cool.

2. Meanwhile, make the marinade. In a large bowl, combine the lemon juice, vinegar, olive oil, capers, salt and hot sauce. Add the shrimp, red onions, bay leaves and celery. Toss to mix the ingredients and to coat the shrimp with marinade. Cover and refrigerate for 24 hours, stirring occasionally.

3. When ready to serve, remove and discard the bay leaves. Drain off the marinade and transfer the shrimp with celery and onions to a glass serving bowl.

—*New York Parties, New York City*

• • •

GRAVLAX WITH MUSTARD SAUCE

Gravlax is easy to make at home, though it requires two to three days to cure. Order the salmon well ahead to guarantee the correct size.

——— *50 Appetizer Servings* ———
4 fresh salmon sides (about 3 pounds each), skin on, trimmed and boned
1 cup lemon-flavored vodka
1½ cups coarse (kosher) salt
1 cup sugar
½ cup plus 1 tablespoon coarsely cracked black pepper
2 large bunches of fresh dill
1 large bunch of fresh chives
2 lemons
Dark bread, as accompaniment
Mustard Sauce (recipe follows)

1. Rinse the fish under cold running water; pat dry. Run your fingers over the salmon. If you feel any small bones that have been missed, pull them out with tweezers.

2. Pour ½ cup vodka into each of 2 large nonreactive baking dishes or roast-ing pans. In a medium bowl, toss together the salt, sugar and pepper.

3. Dip the fish into the vodka and turn several times. Lay the fish sides on a flat work surface, skin-side down. Rub the sugar mixture into the fish.

4. Spread 1 bunch of the dill and the chives on top of 2 of the fillets. Cover the 2 herb-topped fish sides with the other 2 sides, sandwiching them flesh-sides together, with the thick end of one fish above the thin end of another.

5. Wrap each pair in cheesecloth and return to the baking dishes. Cover with foil and top with a large wooden board and heavy cans or weights. Refrigerate for 2 to 3 days, turning twice a day.

6. The night before serving, drain off the marinade. Remove and discard the herbs. Place the fish skin-side down on a flat surface. Very thinly slice on the diagonal. Wrap in plastic wrap and refrigerate.

7. Place the gravlax on platters and garnish with the remaining bunch of dill sprigs and with lemon slices. Serve with slices of dark bread and Mustard Sauce.

—*New York Parties, New York City*

• • •

MUSTARD SAUCE

——— *Makes About 4½ Cups* ———
1½ cups grainy mustard, such as Pommery
¼ cup dry mustard
⅔ cup (packed) dark brown sugar
2 cups mayonnaise
1 cup chopped dill

In a food processor, blend the grainy mustard, dry mustard and brown sugar. Add the mayonnaise and process very briefly, until just blended. Transfer to a medium bowl and fold in the dill. Cover and refrigerate overnight.

—*New York Parties, New York City*

• • •

ROAST BEEF AND HORSERADISH SPIRALS

This very simple and delicious hors d'oeuvre actually improves in taste if prepared the night before serving, which makes it a perfect choice for entertaining.
🍷 A spicy, fruity white, such as 1986 Mark West Gewürztraminer, or a peppery, flavorful red such as 1986 Kendall-Jackson Zinfandel

——— *8 to 10 Appetizer Servings* ———
1 package (8 ounces) cream cheese, at room temperature
1 tablespoon prepared white horseradish
2 teaspoons Dijon-style mustard
½ teaspoon salt
¼ teaspoon freshly ground pepper
16 thin slices of roast beef (about 1 pound)

1. In a medium bowl, combine the cream cheese, horseradish, mustard, salt and pepper. Blend well.

2. On a work surface, overlap 2 slices of the roast beef to form a rectangle, about 8 by 4 inches. Spread 2 tablespoons of the horseradish cream over the beef. Beginning with a long side, tightly roll up the beef. Tightly wrap the roll in plastic wrap. Repeat with the remaining roast beef and horseradish cream. Refrigerate the rolls for at least 3 hours or overnight.

3. To serve, trim off the edges of the rolls. Using a sharp knife, slice each roll crosswise on the diagonal ½ to ¾ inch thick and arrange on a plate. Serve with toothpicks.

—*W. Peter Prestcott*

• • •

IMPERIAL SHRIMP ROLLS WITH CORIANDER AND PEANUTS

The shrimp in this Vietnamese dish are soaked in vinegar and then "cooked," seviche style, in a lime marinade. The result is a thoroughly refreshing, tasty appetizer.

──────── *Makes 8 Rolls* ────────

1 pound medium shrimp—shelled, deveined and cut lengthwise in half
½ cup distilled white vinegar
Pinch of salt
1 small onion, thinly sliced
1 garlic clove, minced
¼ teaspoon crushed hot red pepper
¼ teaspoon sugar
2 teaspoons fish sauce (nuoc mam)*
1 tablespoon fresh lime juice
8 rice paper spring roll wrappers,* 8½ inches in diameter
1 tablespoon plus 1 teaspoon finely chopped, unsalted, dry-roasted peanuts
2 tablespoons plus 2 teaspoons chopped fresh coriander
2 tablespoons plus 2 teaspoons chopped fresh mint
Nuoc Cham Dipping Sauce (p. 251)
*Available at Asian markets

1. In a medium bowl, combine the shrimp with the vinegar and salt; let soak for 5 minutes. Remove the shrimp and squeeze to remove excess vinegar. Pour off the vinegar and return the shrimp to the bowl. Add the onion, garlic, hot pepper, sugar, fish sauce and lime juice. Toss to mix well. Cover, refrigerate, and let the shrimp "cook" in the marinade until they are almost opaque throughout, 1½ to 2 hours.

2. When the shrimp are ready, prepare the wrappers. Using a pastry brush, generously brush both sides of each spring roll wrapper with warm water and set aside in a single layer until softened and pliable, about 2 minutes. If any still seem brittle, brush with additional water.

3. Place ⅓ cup of the shrimp mixture along the lower edge of a spring roll wrapper about 1 inch in from the edge. Sprinkle the shrimp with ½ teaspoon of the chopped peanuts and 1 teaspoon each of the coriander and mint. Fold the bottom of the wrapper up snugly over the shrimp and fold in both sides. Roll up into a compact cylinder about 5 inches long. Repeat with the remaining shrimp mixture and wrappers. *(The recipe can be made up to 1 hour in advance and kept covered in the refrigerator.)* Serve with Nuoc Cham Dipping Sauce on the side.
—*Marcia Kiesel*

• • •

OPERA'S STUFFED GRAPE LEAVES

A variety of Middle Eastern flavors—mint, cinnamon, raisin, almond—are combined with couscous and lamb in these delicious stuffed grape leaves.

──────── *Makes 24* ────────

24 brine-packed grape leaves
¼ cup quick-cooking couscous
½ cup extra-virgin olive oil
¼ cup minced onion
1 garlic clove, minced
½ pound ground lamb
2 tablespoons raisins
2 tablespoons sliced almonds
¼ teaspoon cinnamon
1 tablespoon chopped fresh basil plus 24 large whole basil leaves
¼ teaspoon cayenne pepper
¼ teaspoon allspice
¼ teaspoon paprika
1 tablespoon chopped parsley
1 tablespoon chopped fresh mint
¼ teaspoon salt
⅛ teaspoon freshly ground black pepper
Lemon wedges, for garnish

1. In a medium saucepan of boiling water, blanch the grape leaves for 2 minutes. Drain and rinse well. Pat dry.

2. Prepare the couscous according to the package directions; let cool.

3. In a large skillet, heat the olive oil over moderate heat. Add the onion and garlic and cook until softened, about 5 minutes. Add the ground lamb and cook, stirring, until browned, about 4 minutes. Remove from the heat.

4. Stir in the remaining ingredients except for the whole basil leaves and lemon wedges. Stir in the cooked couscous. Season with salt and pepper to taste.

5. Set a basil leaf in the center of each grape leaf. Place 1 tablespoon of the filling on top of each basil leaf. Fold in the sides of the grape leaves, then roll up from the stem ends to completely enclose the filling. Serve with lemon wedges.
—*Opera, Los Angeles*

• • •

CLASSIC NACHOS

These are nachos just like Mom used to make—if Mom ran a Tex-Mex bar. Baked in a single layer and topped with the minimum amounts of refried beans and cheese, these nachos are thin, crisp—and addictive. (If you're from the goopy school of nacho making, just use more beans and cheese.)

──────── *Makes 36* ────────

36 unsalted corn tortilla chips
¾ cup canned refried beans
4 pickled jalapeño peppers, each sliced into 9 rounds
3 to 4 plum tomatoes, diced
2 scallions, thinly sliced
3 ounces medium-sharp Cheddar cheese, grated
3 ounces Monterey Jack cheese, grated

1. Preheat the oven to 475°. Dollop each tortilla chip with 1 teaspoon of the refried beans. Arrange the chips, bean-side up, in a single layer, on two large jelly-roll pans or edged baking sheets.

2. Top each chip with a slice of jalapeño pepper. Sprinkle the tomatoes and scallions evenly over the nachos. In a bowl, combine the grated cheeses and sprinkle evenly on top.

3. Bake on the top rack of the oven, one pan at a time, until the cheese is melted and the nachos are sizzling slightly, about 5 minutes. With a metal spatula, transfer the nachos to a platter and serve at once.

—*Michael McLaughlin*

• • •

SALAD NACHOS VINAIGRETTE

These cold and crunchy nachos are a reconstructed version of those I enjoyed years ago at a now-defunct Boulder, Colorado, restaurant called Tico's. Although they take more fussing to assemble than hot nachos, the oven—and the cook—stays cool. Arrange them on big white platters and, instead of beer or margaritas, drink white or rosé wine.

———— *Makes 36* ————
¾ cup canned refried beans
3 pickled jalapeño peppers, seeded and minced
2 tablespoons fresh lime juice
1 teaspoon Dijon-style mustard
½ teaspoon salt
Freshly ground black pepper
⅓ cup corn oil
1½ ripe avocados, preferably Hass
1 medium Spanish or red onion, finely diced
¼ cup minced fresh coriander
36 unsalted corn tortilla chips
4 ounces medium-sharp Cheddar cheese, grated
1 cup finely shredded inner leaves of romaine lettuce
4 medium radishes, very thinly sliced

1. In a bowl, stir together the refried beans and jalapeño peppers.

2. In another bowl, whisk together the lime juice and mustard. Season with ¼ teaspoon of the salt and black pepper to taste. Gradually whisk in the corn oil. Mix until incorporated and set aside.

3. Halve and pit the avocados. With a spoon, scoop the flesh into a bowl and mash with a fork. Stir in the onion, coriander and remaining ¼ teaspoon salt.

4. Evenly spread 1 teaspoon of the bean mixture on each tortilla chip. Top the bean layer with 1 teaspoon of the avocado mixture. Arrange the nachos on two serving platters as you go along.

5. Sprinkle the cheese evenly over the nachos. Sprinkle the lettuce evenly over the cheese. Sprinkle the radishes evenly over the lettuce. Drizzle the reserved vinaigrette dressing over the nachos and serve at once.

—*Michael McLaughlin*

• • •

CHILI PARLOR NACHOS

The best nachos are the messiest, involving lots of communal scraping and scooping and finger licking. The addition of a ladle of chili con carne insures that this nacho variation will be messy—and delicious—indeed. Have plenty of napkins on hand.

I wish I could recommend a canned chili, but I can't. Make these instead with the leftovers of a batch of homemade chili, or order a bowl to go from your favorite parlor.

———— *6 to 8 Appetizer Servings* ————
1 package (8 ounces) unsalted corn tortilla chips
6 pickled jalapeño peppers, seeded and minced

10 ounces sharp Cheddar cheese, grated
1½ cups chili with beans
2 small onions, finely chopped
⅓ cup sour cream

1. Preheat the oven to 425°. In a 10-inch pie plate, spread half the tortilla chips in a thick layer to the edge (the layer will be about 1½ inches deep). Sprinkle the chips evenly with half of the jalapeño peppers and half of the cheese. Top with the remaining chips, mounding them slightly. Sprinkle the remaining jalapeño peppers and cheese on top.

2. Bake the nachos on the top rack of the oven until the cheese is melted and the chips are lightly browned, 10 to 12 minutes.

3. Meanwhile, bring the chili to a simmer. Ladle the hot chili over the nachos. Sprinkle the onions evenly over the chili and dollop the sour cream all over the top. Serve at once.

—*Michael McLaughlin*

• • •

NACHOS WITH BACON AND ONIONS

Originally the result of a desperate late night's foraging through the refrigerator, these gutsy nachos are worth making on purpose. They are served with sour cream to quell the fire.

———— *Makes 36* ————
½ pound bacon
36 unsalted corn tortilla chips
1 medium Spanish onion, finely chopped
6 pickled jalapeño peppers, seeded and minced
8 ounces Monterey Jack cheese, grated
8 ounces sour cream

1. In a large skillet, cook the bacon over moderate heat until crisp and brown,

10 to 12 minutes. Transfer the bacon to paper towels to drain. Crumble into pieces.

2. Preheat the oven to 475°. Arrange the tortilla chips in a single layer in two large jelly-roll pans or edged baking sheets. Scatter the bacon, onion and jalapeño peppers over the chips. Sprinkle the cheese on top.

3. Bake on the top rack of the oven, one pan at a time, until the cheese is melted and the nachos are sizzling slightly, about 5 minutes. With a metal spatula, transfer the nachos to a platter. Serve at once, with the sour cream alongside.

—*Michael McLaughlin*

• • •

SALMON CAVIAR TOASTS

The firm, dense bread that is used for these toasts is marvelous, but for convenience you can buy a loaf of brioche or firm-textured white bread.

——— *Makes About 48* ———
½ loaf of Toasting Bread (p. 169)
2½ tablespoons unsalted butter, at room temperature
4 ounces salmon caviar
Lemon wedges, as accompaniment

1. Preheat the broiler. Cut the bread into ⅜-inch-thick slices; trim off the crusts. Spread the butter evenly over one side of the bread slices and arrange them, buttered-side up, in a single layer on a cookie sheet.

2. Broil the bread about 4 inches from the heat until light golden brown, about 1 minute. Toast only one side. Cut each piece of toast into 4 triangles. Let cool. *(The bread can be toasted and cut up 2½ hours ahead.)*

3. Shortly before serving, spread about 1 teaspoon of the caviar onto the toasted side and serve with lemon wedges.

—*Lydie Pinoy Marshall*

• • •

SOUTHWESTERN MONTEREY JACK CHEESE SANDWICHES

In a restaurant in Tucson, I once had a pastry tostada that was spread with guacamole and sprinkled with chopped coriander, scallion and jalapeño. It was then covered with *queso blanco*, baked until the cheese melted and served in wedges like a pizza. I don't remember what it was called, but it was rich and very, very good.

——— *1 Appetizer Serving* ———
2 thin lengthwise slices of avocado
⅛ teaspoon salt
⅛ teaspoon freshly ground black pepper
1 fresh lime wedge
2 flour tortillas, 6 inches in diameter
1½ ounces Monterey Jack cheese, thinly sliced
2 teaspoons chopped fresh coriander
1 small scallion, thinly sliced
½ pickled jalapeño pepper, seeded and chopped

1. Preheat a griddle or heavy skillet, preferably cast iron, over moderate heat. Season the avocado with the salt, black pepper and lime juice.

2. Lay the tortillas, one at a time, on the griddle and cook over moderate heat until soft and pliable, about 30 seconds.

3. Arrange one-fourth of the cheese down the middle of each tortilla. Dividing evenly, top each tortilla with the seasoned avocado, the coriander, scallion, jalapeño and the remaining cheese.

4. Fold the bottom flap over the cheese, then fold in both sides of the tortilla. Roll the tortilla over snugly to secure the top. Press lightly to form a slightly flattened rectangular package.

5. Put seam-side down on the griddle and cook until browned, about 4 minutes on each side. Cut in half and serve.

—*Anne Disrude*

• • •

OPEN-FACED GOAT CHEESE TOASTS

This recipe was inspired by an appetizer served by a caterer I worked with years ago. Although they can be offered with the salad course, I also find that slightly expanded portions of both a salad and these goat cheese toasts make a very nice supper.

——— *2 Appetizer Servings* ———
4 tablespoons goat cheese (about 2 ounces)
4 slices of sourdough or coarse peasant bread, cut ½ inch thick and lightly toasted
1 tablespoon fresh thyme leaves, or 1 teaspoon dried
1 teaspoon freshly ground pepper
4 teaspoons extra-virgin olive oil

1. Preheat the broiler. Spread the goat cheese on one side of each slice of toast.

2. In a small bowl, mix the thyme, pepper and olive oil. Spread over the cheese.

3. Broil about 5 inches from the heat for 1 to 2 minutes, until the cheese and oil sizzle.

—*Anne Disrude*

• • •

GOUGERES

These delicious bite-sized puffs of cheese-rich choux pastry can be baked ahead, frozen and then reheated, making them ideal do-ahead party appetizers.

Makes 60 to 65
Bite-Size Gougères

1 cup all-purpose flour
3/4 teaspoon salt
1/2 teaspoon freshly ground black pepper
1/2 teaspoon thyme
Pinch of cayenne pepper
1 cup milk
1 stick (4 ounces) unsalted butter, cut into 1/2-inch cubes
5 extra-large eggs, at room temperature
6 ounces freshly grated Parmesan cheese
1/2 cup grated Gruyère cheese

1. Preheat the oven to 425°. In a medium bowl, combine the flour with the salt, black pepper, thyme and cayenne.

2. In a large heavy saucepan, combine the milk and the butter. Bring to a boil over high heat, stirring as the butter melts. Remove the pan from the heat immediately and add the seasoned flour all at once. With a wooden spoon, stir vigorously just until the dough masses into a ball and does not cling to the sides of the pan.

3. Transfer the dough to a large mixer bowl. On medium speed, beat in the eggs, one at a time, stirring after each addition until the egg has been completely absorbed. Continue this process until 4 of the eggs have been used. The dough should be smooth and satiny and just hold its shape when a small quantity is scooped up on the tip of a spoon. Add the Parmesan and Gruyère cheeses to the dough and beat in thoroughly.

4. Spoon—or pipe out using a pastry bag fitted with a 1/2-inch star tip—2 to 2 1/2 teaspoons of dough about 1 inch in diameter onto buttered baking sheets, setting the gougères about 1 1/2 inches apart. Beat the remaining egg and, with a pastry brush, lightly brush the tops to glaze.

5. Bake for 20 minutes, rotating the baking sheets halfway through, until the gougères reach a rich golden brown. Let cool slightly. Serve warm. *(The gougères can be made ahead and frozen for up to 2 weeks. Before serving, thaw and reheat them in a 350° oven until crisp, about 10 minutes.)*

—Bob Chambers

• • •

HAPPY PANCAKES

When people first sample Vietnamese food, I always insist that they try these crisp, crêpelike cakes, richly flavored with caramelized onions, shrimp, pork and bean sprouts. You can speed things up if you use two skillets at once.

Makes 10

1 3/4 cups rice flour*
1/4 teaspoon turmeric
1 scallion, thinly sliced
3/4 cup plus 2 tablespoons vegetable oil
1 pound boneless pork loin, cut crosswise into very thin slices
1 pound medium shrimp, shelled and deveined
1 small onion, thinly sliced
10 medium mushrooms, sliced
1 1/4 teaspoons salt
1 1/4 teaspoons freshly ground pepper
2 1/2 cups bean sprouts
Nuoc Cham Dipping Sauce (p. 251)
*Available at Asian markets

1. In a medium bowl, whisk together the rice flour and 2 cups of cold water.

Add the turmeric and scallion and mix well.

2. In a large nonstick skillet, heat 1 1/2 tablespoons of the oil over high heat. Add 3 slices of pork, 3 shrimp, a few slices of onion and 1 sliced mushroom. Season with 1/8 teaspoon each of the salt and pepper. Cook for 1 minute.

3. Stir the rice flour mixture again and ladle 1/3 cup into the pan; tilt the pan to evenly distribute the batter. Cover and cook until the sides of the pancake turn deep brown and curl up, about 5 minutes.

4. Scatter 1/4 cup of the bean sprouts over the pancake, fold it in half and slide it onto a warm platter. Keep warm in a low oven while you repeat with the remaining ingredients. Serve the pancakes warm, with Nuoc Cham Dipping Sauce on the side.

—Marcia Kiesel

• • •

CORN AND CRABMEAT FRITTERS

Serve warm as an appetizer or as one of the dishes in an Indonesian rijsttafel. I put out a small bowl of *ketjap manis* (p. 256) for guests to sprinkle over the top of the fritters, if they like.

Makes About 30 Fritters

3 cans (12 ounces each) corn niblets, well drained
1/2 pound lump crabmeat, flaked and picked over to remove any cartilage
5 scallions, thinly sliced
2 garlic cloves, crushed through a press
1/2 teaspoon cumin
1/2 teaspoon salt
1/4 teaspoon freshly ground pepper
1 tablespoon cornstarch
3 eggs, beaten
Peanut or corn oil, for pan frying

1. In a medium bowl, mix together the corn, crabmeat, scallions, garlic, cumin, salt, pepper, cornstarch and eggs.

2. In a large skillet, heat ¼ inch of oil over moderate heat. Spoon the batter into the hot oil in batches, 1 tablespoon at a time. Fry, turning once, until browned on both sides, about 3 minutes. Drain the fritters on paper towels. Serve warm or at room temperature.

—*Copeland Marks*

• • •

CORN AND CHIVE MADELEINES WITH GOLDEN CAVIAR

Here's a wonderfully elegant appetizer for a special occasion. Although the quantity may seem daunting, the madeleines can be baked (and then frozen) up to two weeks in advance, making the actual last-minute preparation quite manageable.

——————*Makes About 100*——————
4 tablespoons unsalted butter, melted
1½ cups all-purpose flour
1 cup yellow cornmeal
2 tablespoons sugar
2 teaspoons baking powder
1 teaspoon salt
¼ teaspoon cayenne pepper
¼ cup cold vegetable shortening
1½ cups milk
2 eggs, lightly beaten
1 tablespoon freeze-dried minced chives
1 cup crème fraîche or sour cream
4 ounces golden caviar

1. Preheat the oven to 400°. With a pastry brush, generously coat as many mini-madeleine pans or mini-muffin pans as you have with the melted butter.

2. In a large bowl, sift together the flour, cornmeal, sugar, baking powder, salt and cayenne. With a pastry cutter or two knives, cut in the shortening until the mixture resembles a coarse meal.

3. Whisk in the milk, eggs and chives until just blended; do not overmix. Spoon 1 teaspoon of the batter into each madeleine or muffin cup to fill about three-quarters full.

4. Bake until golden brown around the edges, 7 to 8 minutes. Tap the madeleines from the pans onto wire racks to cool. Bake in batches until the batter is used up, rebuttering the pans as necessary. *(The madeleines can be prepared up to 2 weeks in advance and frozen. Thaw before using.)*

5. Top each with about ½ teaspoon of crème fraîche and a tiny dab of caviar up to 1 hour before serving.

—*New York Parties, New York City*

• • •

GOAT CHEESE PHYLLO TRIANGLES WITH CARAMELIZED ONIONS AND OREGANO

These phyllo triangles are an irresistible combination of caramelized onions, goat cheese and fresh oregano, which adds a needed bit of pungency to cut the richness of the cheese.

——————*Makes About 16 Pastries*——————
3 tablespoons unsalted butter plus 4 tablespoons unsalted butter, melted
2 large onions, thinly sliced
6 ounces mild goat cheese, such as Bucheron, crumbled
1½ ounces thinly sliced prosciutto, cut crosswise into ¼-inch-wide strips
1 jalapeño pepper, seeded and minced
1 tablespoon chopped fresh oregano
1 package (8 ounces) phyllo dough

1. In a large skillet, heat the 3 tablespoons unmelted butter over moderately high heat. When the foam subsides, add the onions and cook, stirring occasionally, until the onions begin to brown, about 10 minutes.

2. Reduce the heat to low and cook until very soft, about 12 minutes. Transfer to a medium bowl and let cool.

3. Stir in the goat cheese, prosciutto, jalapeño pepper and oregano.

4. Preheat the oven to 350°. Place one sheet of phyllo dough on a work surface with a short end facing you. Brush it lightly with some of the melted butter. (Keep the remaining sheets of phyllo covered with a damp cloth to prevent them from drying out.) Place another sheet of phyllo over the first and brush that with some more melted butter. Top with 1 more sheet of phyllo.

5. Cut the layered phyllo in half lengthwise. Spoon 2 tablespoons of the onion mixture onto the bottom left-hand corner of 1 of the phyllo strips. Fold the bottom left-hand corner up, aligning the bottom and right-hand edges of the phyllo to create a triangle shape. Fold the triangle up and over, aligning the right-hand edges and making another triangle, in classic flag-folding fashion. Fold 2 more times in this way, and fold the extra phyllo down over the larger triangle. Continue this procedure with the remaining phyllo sheets and filling. Place the pastries, seam-side down, on 2 baking sheets. Brush the tops with melted butter. *(The pastries can be made up to 1 week ahead and frozen; do not thaw before baking.)*

6. Bake about 12 minutes, until golden brown all over.

—*Marcia Kiesel*

• • •

FRIED CALAMARI WITH CURRY-CORIANDER DIPPING SAUCE

Squid is one of my favorite foods, and I wish more people felt the same way. The best way to get someone to try squid is, first, to call it calamari and, second, serve it deep-fried. Instead of the usual tomato or tartar sauce accompaniment, I've come up with a coriander-curry dip that provides a provocative change.

——— *4 to 6 Appetizer Servings* ———
3 cups plus 1 tablespoon vegetable oil
2 teaspoons whole coriander seeds, crushed
2 garlic cloves, minced
2 teaspoons curry powder
½ teaspoon soy sauce
1 tablespoon plus 1 teaspoon hoisin sauce*
1 tablespoon fresh lemon juice
2 pounds calamari, cut into rings, large tentacles cut in half, dried well
1 cup rice flour*
2 tablespoons chopped fresh coriander
*Available at Asian markets and health food stores

1. In a small heavy saucepan, heat 1 tablespoon of the oil over low heat. Add the coriander seeds, garlic and curry powder. Cook, stirring occasionally, until the garlic is translucent and the spices are fragrant, about 3 minutes.

2. Increase the heat to high and add ⅓ cup of water. Boil until the mixture is reduced slightly, about 2 minutes.

3. Stir in the soy sauce, hoisin sauce and lemon juice. Return to a boil. Remove from the heat and strain the sauce through a fine-mesh sieve into a small bowl. Set aside to cool.

4. Meanwhile, in a wok or large saucepan, heat the remaining 3 cups oil over high heat until it reaches 375°.

5. In batches, place handfuls of calamari into a sieve and toss with some of the rice flour, until the calamari are completely coated. Drop the calamari into the hot oil and fry, stirring occasionally, until golden brown and tender, about 2 minutes. Remove with a slotted spoon and drain on paper towels. Repeat with the remaining calamari. Keep the fried calamari warm in a 300° oven while you fry the remaining batches.

6. Stir the chopped coriander into the cooled sauce. Serve the fried calamari hot with the sauce on the side.

—*Marcia Kiesel*

• • •

FRIED CHICKEN DRUMETTES WITH LEMON GRASS

If your market does not carry chicken wing sections labeled drumettes, buy 4 pounds of chicken wings. Cut off the meaty joints farthest from the tips; these are the drumettes. Reserve the remainder of the wings for stock.

——— *4 to 6 Appetizer Servings* ———
2 pounds chicken drumettes
1 tablespoon dark soy sauce*
1½ teaspoons salt
2 stalks of lemon grass* (bottom third only), finely minced
2 tablespoons dry sherry
1 tablespoon all-purpose flour
1 tablespoon cornstarch
2 teaspoons freshly ground black pepper
1 teaspoon crushed hot red pepper
¼ cup minced fresh coriander
2 cups peanut oil
Lemon Grass Dipping Sauce (p. 250)
*Available at Asian markets

1. In a medium bowl, combine the chicken, soy sauce and salt. Toss to coat. Let marinate at room temperature, tossing occasionally, for 1 hour.

2. Put the lemon grass and sherry in a small heatproof bowl. Set in a steamer or on a rack in a saucepan over boiling water, cover and steam for 15 minutes.

3. Combine the flour, cornstarch, black pepper, hot pepper and coriander. Toss to mix well. Add the seasoned flour and the lemon grass and sherry to the chicken. Toss well to coat evenly.

4. In a large skillet or wok, heat the oil to 375°. Add the chicken in batches without crowding and fry until golden brown, 5 to 7 minutes. Drain on paper towels and serve hot, with a bowl of Lemon Grass Dipping Sauce on the side.

—*Bruce Cost*

• • •

VIETNAMESE STUFFED CHICKEN WINGS

It may be a surprise to you that the wings are put into room-temperature oil to fry, but they absorb a minimum of oil and will be very crisp.

——— *Makes About 12* ———
2 pounds chicken wings (about 12)
1 pound skinless, boneless chicken breasts, thinly sliced crosswise
¼ teaspoon freshly ground white pepper
2 teaspoons cornstarch
½ teaspoon baking powder
¼ teaspoon sugar
1 tablespoon fish sauce (nuoc mam)*
1½ teaspoons vegetable oil, plus about 1 quart for deep-frying
1 large scallion, thinly sliced
¼ pound mushrooms, finely chopped
Nuoc Cham Dipping Sauce (p. 251)
*Available at Asian markets

19

APPETIZERS & FIRST COURSES

1. Cut off the "drumstick" joint of the wing and reserve for another use. With a small sharp knife, scrape around the exposed second joint of the chicken wings to loosen the meat. With your hand, work the meat down the double bone, squeezing and pushing, to separate the skin and meat from the bones. Snap the double bones off at the joint. *(The wings can be boned up to a day ahead, wrapped and refrigerated.)*

2. In a medium bowl, combine the chicken breast slices, white pepper, cornstarch, baking powder, sugar, fish sauce and 1½ teaspoons vegetable oil; mix to blend well. Cover and freeze until very firm, about 15 minutes.

3. In a food processor, puree the chicken breast mixture, scraping down the bowl once or twice, until very smooth and stiff, about 1 minute. Return the mixture to the bowl and stir in the scallion and mushrooms.

4. With oiled hands, hold a boned chicken wing in one hand and push the stuffing into the pocket, packing it in firmly and stuffing it generously. Repeat, using all the filling and chicken wings. The wings should be slightly overstuffed.

5. Put 6 of the chicken wings into a large saucepan set over high heat. Add enough vegetable oil to cover and cook, stirring occasionally, until the wings are golden brown and crisp, about 20 minutes. Remove the wings with tongs to drain on paper towels. Keep warm in a low oven, if desired, while you fry the remaining wings.

6. Reduce the heat to moderate, add the remaining stuffed chicken wings to the hot oil and cook until golden brown and crisp, about 15 minutes. Serve at once with Nuoc Cham Dipping Sauce on the side.

—*Marcia Kiesel*

• • •

BEEF GRILLED IN LA-LOT LEAVES

These are great served by themselves as an appetizer. If the la-lot leaves are not available, jarred grape leaves make a fine substitute. The pulverized dried lemon grass has an intense lemon perfume that will add a fascinating flavor to any marinade, but if you can't find it, substitute one teaspoon of grated lemon zest for a still flavorful but slightly different result.

——— *4 to 6 Appetizer Servings* ———
1-ounce package dried sliced lemon grass*
½ pound trimmed eye of beef round, very thinly sliced against the grain
2 garlic cloves, crushed through a press
2 tablespoons sugar
2 tablespoons soy sauce
2 teaspoons medium-dry sherry
½ teaspoon vegetable oil
¼ teaspoon Oriental sesame oil
¼ teaspoon freshly ground pepper
30 fresh la-lot leaves* or grape leaves in brine, well rinsed
*Available at Asian markets

1. In a spice mill or blender, grind the lemon grass to a powder. Measure out 1 teaspoon. Reserve the remainder for future use.

2. In a medium bowl, combine the beef with the 1 teaspoon ground lemon grass and all the remaining ingredients except the leaves. Mix well, cover and marinate in the refrigerator for at least 2 and up to 24 hours.

3. Soak 6 long wooden skewers in a bowl of cold water for at least 30 minutes.

4. Meanwhile, wrap each piece of beef by placing it on one large leaf or 2 smaller leaves and folding the top and bottom up to cover; the sides remain open. Thread 5 packets of wrapped beef onto each wooden skewer.

5. Preheat the broiler or light a grill. Broil or grill the skewer about 5 inches from the heat until the leaves are crisp and brown on one side, about 3 minutes. Turn the skewers over and broil for about 3 minutes longer, until lightly browned all over. Serve hot.

—*Marcia Kiesel*

• • •

MUSHROOM TOASTS

In Italy, this recipe is done with the succulent wild mushrooms called *porcini* (*cèpes* in France, *Steinpilz* in Germany). A good substitute for those expensive delicacies is Italian *cremini* or fresh *shiitake*, both of which are beginning to appear in supermarkets in the United States. The dish is still quite flavorful when made partially or entirely with ordinary white mushrooms.

——— *4 to 6 First-Course Servings* ———
3 tablespoons unsalted butter
1½ tablespoons olive oil
¾ pound firm fresh mushrooms— porcini, cremini or shiitake— coarsely chopped
1 garlic clove, minced
2 tablespoons chopped parsley
½ teaspoon salt
Freshly ground pepper
2 tablespoons dry Marsala
1 tablespoon heavy cream
12 to 16 slices of Italian bread, toasted

1. In a large skillet, melt the butter in the oil over high heat. Add the mushrooms, garlic and parsley. Sauté, stirring, until the mushrooms absorb the fat, 1 to 2 minutes. Reduce the heat to low and season with the salt and several grindings of pepper. Cook, stirring, until the mushrooms begin to release their juices. Increase the heat to moderate and cook, stirring occasionally, until the juices evaporate, about 6 minutes.

2. Add the Marsala to the pan and cook until reduced to about 1 tablespoon, scraping up any browned bits from the bottom of the pan.

3. Transfer the mushrooms and any remaining liquid to a food processor and puree to a paste, about 1 minute. With the machine on, gradually add the cream. Taste for salt and pepper. (It should be slightly oversalted while still warm.) Transfer the mushroom puree to a bowl and let cool completely. *(The mushroom puree can be made up to 1 day in advance. Cover and refrigerate. Let return to room temperature before serving.)*

4. When ready to serve, generously spread the mushroom puree over the toasted Italian bread.

—*Tom Maresca & Diane Darrow*

• • •

MARINATED MUSHROOMS WITH ROASTED RED PEPPERS AND MARJORAM

You can use all white button mushrooms if you wish, but fresh *shiitake*—or other fleshy wild mushrooms—add a more earthy flavor and varied texture.

—— 4 to 6 First-Course Servings ——
- *⅓ cup extra-virgin olive oil*
- *3 large shallots, minced*
- *2 large garlic cloves, minced*
- *1 pound medium white button mushrooms, quartered*
- *1 pound medium fresh shiitake mushrooms, stemmed and quartered*
- *¼ cup balsamic vinegar*
- *2 large red bell peppers*
- *1 tablespoon chopped fresh marjoram*
- *1 teaspoon freshly ground black pepper*
- *1 teaspoon salt*
- *1 large ripe avocado, preferably Hass, peeled and cut into 1-inch cubes*
- *1 bunch of arugula*

1. In a large heavy skillet, heat the olive oil over moderate heat. Add the shallots and garlic and reduce the heat to low. Cook the mixture, stirring occasionally, until softened but not browned, about 5 minutes.

2. Increase the heat to moderately high and add the button and the *shiitake* mushrooms, stirring well to combine. Cover and cook, stirring once, until the mushrooms are slightly softened, about 4 minutes.

3. Uncover, increase the heat to high, add the balsamic vinegar and cook for 1 minute. Spoon the mixture into a large bowl and let it cool to room temperature, stirring occasionally.

4. Meanwhile, roast the red peppers directly over a gas flame or under the broiler as close to the heat as possible, turning until charred all over. Enclose the peppers in a paper bag and set aside for 10 minutes to steam. When cool enough to handle, peel the peppers and remove the core, seeds and ribs. Slice the peppers lengthwise into ⅜-inch-thick strips.

5. Combine the roasted peppers with the mushrooms. Stir in the marjoram, black pepper and salt. Refrigerate the mixture until ready to serve. *(The recipe can be prepared to this point 1 day ahead and kept covered in the refrigerator.)*

6. To serve, fold the avocado cubes into the mushroom mixture. Arrange the arugula leaves on a large serving plate and place the mushroom salad on top. Serve chilled or at room temperature.

—*Marcia Kiesel*

• • •

PORK AND JICAMA ROLLS WITH ZINFANDEL BARBECUE SAUCE

The sauce of this fiery, full-flavored dish works best when you cook it in a very large pan that will heat the Zinfandel quickly.

🍷 A rich, young Zinfandel with pronounced berry flavors will stand up to the chiles here. Try the 1986 Rosenblum Cellars Sonoma Valley or the 1986 Lytton Springs Sonoma County.

—— 6 First-Course Servings ——
- *2 to 3 fresh jalapeño peppers, to taste*
- *4 pounds pork spareribs, trimmed of excess fat*
- *2 garlic cloves, crushed through a press*
- *½ teaspoon salt*
- *¼ teaspoon freshly ground black pepper*
- *¾ cup chili sauce*
- *2 tablespoons cider vinegar*
- *¾ teaspoon chili powder*
- *6 tablespoons robust young Zinfandel*
- *24 wide, soft lettuce leaves, such as Boston*
- *6 large scallions, cut into julienne strips (about 1 cup)*
- *3 ounces jicama, cut into thin julienne strips (about 1 cup)*
- *36 fresh coriander leaves (1 small bunch)*

1. Preheat the broiler. Place the jalapeño peppers on a broiler tray and broil about 4 inches from the heat, turning frequently, until blackened all over, about 5 minutes. Put the peppers in a paper bag for 10 minutes to loosen the skins. Rinse off the blackened skins under cold running water. Discard the stems, ribs and seeds; finely chop the peppers.

2. Rub the spareribs with the garlic. Season with the salt and black pepper. Place the ribs on a rack and broil about 4 inches from the heat with the oven door slightly ajar, turning every 5 minutes until evenly browned, about 20 minutes. Drain on paper towels. Let cool.

3. Meanwhile, in a heavy nonreactive saucepan, combine the chopped jalapeños, chili sauce, cider vinegar and chili powder. Bring to a boil over high heat. Reduce the heat to low and simmer until thick, about 5 minutes. Stir in the Zinfandel and cook until hot but not boiling. Remove the barbecue sauce from the heat.

4. Cut the meat off the ribs, discarding any fat and gristle. Cut into long ¼-inch-wide strips.

5. Lay 12 of the lettuce leaves on a work surface. Generously brush 1 side with the barbecue sauce. Divide the meat, scallions, jicama and coriander evenly among the lettuce leaves. Roll up each leaf to enclose the filling. Then place each roll, seam-side down, inside a second lettuce leaf. Roll up and serve 2 per person.

—David Rosengarten

• • •

POBLANOS RELLENOS WITH CORIANDER-CORN SAUCE

These stuffed chiles require a bit of work, but they're well worth the effort. The large, deep-green poblano peppers are incredibly sweet and only mildly hot. Brie works well as a filling because it melts easily, and its nutty, buttery flavor remains even when the cheese is heated.

8 First-Course or
——— **4 Main-Course Servings** ———
8 large poblano peppers, stems
*   intact*
1 tablespoon unsalted butter
1 small onion, chopped
1 cup corn kernels, fresh or frozen
½ cup heavy cream

2 tablespoons sour cream
1 large tomato, seeded and diced
¼ cup plus 2 teaspoons chopped
*   fresh coriander*
½ teaspoon salt
¼ teaspoon freshly ground black
*   pepper*
1 pound Brie cheese, chilled
3 eggs, separated
½ cup corn oil
½ cup all-purpose flour
2 tablespoons toasted pine nuts
Coriander leaves, for garnish

1. Roast the peppers directly over a gas flame or under the broiler as close to the heat as possible, turning, until charred all over. Place the peppers in a paper bag to steam for 5 minutes. Gently remove the blackened skin without tearing the pepper or removing the stem. Rinse briefly under cold water. Using kitchen scissors, cut a slit lengthwise to the core on one side of each pepper. Cut the seed core from the base of the stem, keeping the pepper intact. Remove and rinse all seeds from the cavity. Pat the peppers dry.

2. In a medium saucepan, melt the butter over low heat. Add the onion and corn and cook, stirring occasionally, until the onion is tender, about 5 minutes.

3. Stir in the heavy cream and increase the heat to moderate. Bring to a boil and cook until the cream is thickened and slightly reduced, about 3 minutes.

4. Remove from the heat and stir in the sour cream, tomato, 2 tablespoons of the chopped coriander and the salt and black pepper. Remove from the heat; set the sauce aside.

5. Cut the rind off the Brie and divide the cheese into 8 equal pieces. Place a piece of cheese plus 1 teaspoon of the remaining chopped coriander inside each pepper and gently press it closed.

6. In a medium bowl, beat the egg whites with a pinch of salt until stiff. Beat in the egg yolks until well blended.

7. In a large skillet, heat the corn oil over high heat until it begins to shimmer. Dredge the stuffed peppers in the flour; shake off any excess. Beat the eggs again briefly. One at a time, dip the peppers into the egg, coating them all over. Fry 4 peppers at a time over high heat until brown on one side, about 2 minutes. Turn the peppers over and cook until the cheese is melted and the peppers are browned on the other side, about 2 minutes. Drain on paper towels.

8. Briefly warm the sauce over moderate heat. Pour onto a large platter or individual serving plates. Place the peppers on the sauce, sprinkle the pine nuts and coriander leaves on top and serve.

—Marcia Kiesel

• • •

RAW SALMON MARINATED IN AMONTILLADO SHERRY

This adaptation of gravlax uses the first spring asparagus. A touch of sweetness works wonders with the salty character of this cured salmon, which is marinated two days before serving.

❦ Since amontillado sherry figures prominently in this dish, a glass of Harvey's medium dry Amontillado or Savory & James deluxe medium Amontillado is a lovely accompaniment.

——— **4 First-Course Servings** ———
1 thick salmon fillet (½ pound)
3 tablespoons plus 2 teaspoons
*   medium-dry Amontillado sherry*
1 teaspoon sugar
1 tablespoon coarse (kosher) salt
¼ teaspoon freshly ground pepper
1 cup (loosely packed) fresh
*   tarragon or 1 tablespoon dried*

16 thin asparagus (½ pound),
  trimmed and peeled
1 egg yolk
¼ cup sunflower or safflower oil
1 tablespoon walnut oil
1½ teaspoons Dijon-style mustard

1. Place the salmon fillet on a plate, skin-side down. Rub 2 teaspoons of the sherry into the fish. With a mortar and pestle lightly grind the sugar, salt and pepper. Coat the top of the salmon with the seasonings. Strew the tarragon evenly over the surface. Cover the salmon with plastic wrap, then place a board on top and a 5-pound weight (use canned goods) on top of that. Refrigerate for 48 hours, basting the salmon once with the liquid that accumulates on the plate.

2. Shortly before serving, in a large skillet of boiling salted water, cook the asparagus over moderately high heat until just tender, 2 to 3 minutes. Rinse under cold water; drain well.

3. In a small double boiler over simmering water, combine the remaining 3 tablespoons sherry with the egg yolk. Whisk constantly until thick enough to coat the back of a spoon, 4 to 6 minutes. Do not let the egg scramble; adjust the heat as necessary.

4. Transfer the sherry-egg mixture to a blender or food processor. With the machine on, pour in the sunflower oil and walnut oil in a thin stream. Blend just until smooth, 5 to 10 seconds. Add the mustard and blend briefly to combine.

5. Unwrap the salmon and scrape off the tarragon. Rinse the fish under cold water and pat dry with paper towels. With a very sharp knife, cut the salmon on the diagonal into broad, thin slices.

6. Place the salmon on 4 dinner plates. Arrange the asparagus decoratively on top. Spoon a little of the sauce alongside the salmon and sprinkle with freshly ground pepper.

—David Rosengarten

• • •

MOROCCAN SOLE RAGOUT WITH ORANGES AND BASIL

This spicy stew is light and tasty. The flavor is best if the sauce is made the day before—later, steam the fish on top.
❦ Because of the eclectic ingredients here—chick-peas, bacon, basil, oranges—a rich but not powerful white with some depth of flavor, such as 1985 Hogue Cellars Sémillon Reserve or 1985 Inglenook Sémillon, is ideal.

—— **6 First-Course Servings** ——
3 tablespoons extra-virgin olive oil
1½ teaspoons ground coriander
1¼ teaspoons imported sweet
  paprika
¼ teaspoon cayenne pepper
2 large red bell peppers, thickly
  sliced
1 medium onion, thinly sliced
3 garlic cloves, minced
3 ounces lean, smoked slab bacon,
  cut into ¼-inch dice (about ⅓ cup)
½ cup dry white wine
18 ounces sole fillets, cut into
  6 equal pieces
½ teaspoon salt
¼ teaspoon freshly ground black
  pepper
⅔ cup cooked or canned chick-peas
2 large navel oranges, peeled and cut
  into sections
½ cup finely shredded fresh basil

1. In a large flameproof casserole, heat the olive oil over moderately high heat. Add the coriander, paprika and cayenne. Cook, stirring, until fragrant, about 1 minute. Reduce the heat to low and add the bell peppers, onion and garlic. Cover and cook until the vegetables are softened but not browned, about 10 minutes.

2. Meanwhile, blanch the bacon in a small saucepan of boiling water for 2 minutes. Drain and set aside.

3. Add the blanched bacon, wine and 1½ cups of water to the casserole. Cover and cook for 20 minutes.

4. Uncover, increase the heat to moderately high and boil for about 3 minutes. Cover and set aside. *(The recipe can be prepared to this point up to 1 day in advance. Let cool, then refrigerate the sauce.)*

5. Fold each piece of fish in thirds like a letter, to form small bundles. About 10 minutes before serving, bring the sauce to a boil over moderate heat. Reduce the heat to low, stir in the salt, black pepper, chick-peas, orange sections and basil. Arrange the fish bundles on top, cover and simmer until the fish is just opaque throughout and separates when lightly touched, about 5 minutes.

6. To serve, spoon equal amounts of the sauce and vegetables into shallow soup plates and top with a piece of fish.

—Marcia Kiesel

• • •

CITRUS'S CRAB COLESLAW

The crab and cabbage mixture is rolled in blanched cabbage and then sliced into smaller sections that resemble sushi rolls.

—— **6 First-Course Servings** ——
1 small head of savoy cabbage
½ cup mayonnaise
2 tablespoons white wine vinegar
1 teaspoon minced fresh tarragon or
  ½ teaspoon dried
2 tablespoons ketchup
1 teaspoon grainy mustard
2 dashes of hot pepper sauce
¼ teaspoon curry powder
¼ teaspoon freshly ground black
  pepper
½ pound lump crabmeat, flaked and
  picked over to remove any
  cartilage
½ cup diced (¼-inch) bell peppers—
  red, yellow and/or green, for
  garnish

1. Bring a large pot of salted water to a boil over high heat. Remove 6 of the large dark green outer leaves of the cabbage. Plunge them into the boiling water and blanch until softened, about 3 minutes. Drain and rinse under cold water. Pat dry.

2. Quarter and core the remaining cabbage and shred enough to make 1 packed cup. Place in a medium bowl. Reserve the remaining cabbage for another use.

3. In a medium bowl, whisk together the mayonnaise and vinegar until smooth. Stir in the tarragon, ketchup, mustard, hot sauce, curry powder and black pepper until well blended. Add the shredded cabbage and toss until well coated. Add the crabmeat and toss again.

4. Remove the cores of the blanched cabbage leaves. Lay the leaves on a flat surface with the stem ends facing you. Fill each leaf with ¼ cup of the crab mixture. Roll up the leaves to enclose the filling. Using a serrated knife, cut each roll into 4 pieces. Stand 4 pieces on end in a row in the center of each plate. Garnish with the diced bell peppers.

—Michel Richard, Citrus, Los Angeles

• • •

MUSSELS MARINARA

At Amerigo's in the Bronx, this Neapolitan classic is served with *friselle*, a hard hot pepper biscuit, for dipping into the sauce.

❦ The full flavor and character of the sauce call for a medium-bodied Italian red with good fruit such as 1985 Nozzole Chianti Classico.

──────── **4 First-Course Servings** ────────
⅓ cup extra-virgin olive oil
4 large garlic cloves
3 dozen mussels, scrubbed and
debearded
1 can (35 ounces) crushed Italian
plum tomatoes
1 tablespoon minced parsley

1 tablespoon minced fresh oregano
or 1 teaspoon dried
Salt and freshly ground pepper

1. In a large flameproof casserole, heat the oil. Add the garlic and cook over moderate heat until lightly browned, 3 to 5 minutes.

2. Add the mussels, tomatoes, parsley and oregano. Bring to a boil. Reduce the heat to moderate, cover and simmer, stirring occasionally, until the mussels open, 5 to 7 minutes.

3. Using a slotted spoon, transfer the mussels to soup bowls. Discard any that do not open. Season the sauce with salt and pepper to taste. Ladle the sauce over the mussels and serve hot.

—Amerigo's, New York City

• • •

SCALLOPS VENETIAN STYLE

In Italy this dish is matchless when prepared with the large sea scallops that are sold with their crimson roe attached—a seasonal treat. It is still fine prepared without the roe as long as the sea scallops are very fresh.

──────── **4 First-Course Servings** ────────
5 tablespoons unsalted butter
3 tablespoons minced shallots
1 pound sea scallops, with roe if
available, cut horizontally into
thirds
¼ cup dry white wine
4 slices of firm-textured white bread,
toasted and quartered on the
diagonal into triangles

1. In a large nonreactive skillet, melt 3 tablespoons of the butter over low heat. Add the shallots and cook until softened but not browned, about 3 minutes.

2. Increase the heat to moderately high, add the scallops and cook, stirring constantly (and gently if the roe is attached), for 1 minute. Add the wine and ¼ cup of water. Reduce the heat to low, cover and cook until the scallops are barely opaque throughout, about 2 minutes.

3. Using a slotted spoon, transfer the scallops to a warm plate and cover with foil to keep warm. Over high heat, quickly boil down the liquid in the pan until it is reduced to a thick syrup, about 2 minutes. Remove from the heat and stir in the remaining 2 tablespoons butter to make a creamy sauce.

4. Divide the scallops among 4 plates, distribute the sauce over them, garnish with the toast points and serve at once.

—Tom Maresca & Diane Darrow

• • •

72 MARKET ST.'S SAUTEED
SEA SCALLOPS

The key to the flavor of this light seafood salad is in the sweetness of the Hawaiian Maui onion, available in the spring. Other juicy sweet onions such as Vidalia and Walla Walla can be substituted.

──────── **2 First-Course Servings** ────────
2 cups (loosely packed) arugula,
large stems removed
3 tablespoons extra-virgin olive oil
2 teaspoons fresh lemon juice
½ teaspoon salt
¼ teaspoon freshly ground pepper
¾ cup thinly sliced Maui or other
sweet onion
¼ pound sea scallops, sliced
horizontally ¼ inch thick
1 tablespoon balsamic vinegar

1. In a medium bowl, toss the arugula with 2 tablespoons of the olive oil, the lemon juice, ¼ teaspoon of the salt and ⅛ teaspoon of the pepper. Divide between 2 large plates and set aside.

2. In a large skillet, heat the remaining 1 tablespoon olive oil over moderately high heat. Add the onion and sauté, stirring constantly, until it just begins to soften, about 1 minute.

3. Add the scallops and cook, tossing, until barely opaque, 2 to 3 minutes. Stir in the balsamic vinegar and the remaining ¼ teaspoon salt and ⅛ teaspoon pepper. Remove from the heat.

4. Spoon the scallop mixture onto the arugula and serve at once.

—*Leonard Schwartz,*
72 Market St., Los Angeles

• • •

BARBECUED BACON-WRAPPED SHRIMP

Tangy and sweet-sour with a thick, spicy marinade that clings after grilling, these shrimp work as an appetizer or main course.

6 First-Course or
—— **3 to 4 Main-Course Servings** ——
9 thin slices of lean smoked bacon (about ½ pound)
2 teaspoons imported sweet paprika
½ teaspoon cayenne pepper
½ teaspoon curry powder
½ teaspoon ground cumin
½ teaspoon ground coriander
½ teaspoon salt
½ teaspoon freshly ground black pepper
1 tablespoon olive oil
2 tablespoons sugar
2 tablespoons fresh lemon juice
18 jumbo shrimp (2 pounds), shelled and deveined

1. Cut the slices of bacon in half. In a large heavy skillet, partially cook the bacon over moderate heat to render some of the fat without allowing the pieces to crisp, about 1 minute on each side. Remove the slices as they are done and drain on paper towels.

2. In a medium bowl, combine the paprika, cayenne, curry powder, cumin, coriander, salt and black pepper; stir in the olive oil, sugar and lemon juice. Add the shrimp. Toss well to coat; let marinate at room temperature for 30 to 60 minutes.

3. Meanwhile, light a charcoal fire. Remove the shrimp from the marinade, reserving the marinade. Wrap a slice of bacon around each shrimp and secure with a toothpick to hold both ends of the bacon. Toss in the marinade to coat.

4. Set a grill rack about 5 inches from the glowing coals for 5 minutes. Put all the shrimp on the grill and brush half the remaining marinade over them. Grill for 4 minutes; turn, brush with the remaining marinade and grill for about 4 minutes longer, or until the shrimp are just opaque throughout. Serve hot or warm.

—*Jim Fobel*

• • •

COOL GARLIC SHRIMP WITH TOMATOES AND CROUTONS

The shrimp in this recipe marinate overnight, so plan accordingly.

❦ The piquant, acidic flavor of tomato needs an equally sharp white wine that can add a lemonlike accent to the shrimp. Try a crisp California Sauvignon Blanc, such as 1987 Iron Horse or 1986 Viansa.

—— **6 First-Course Servings** ——
1 pound medium shrimp, peeled and deveined
⅓ cup plus 3 tablespoons extra-virgin olive oil
5 large garlic cloves—4 peeled and crushed, 1 minced
1 tablespoon capers
2 tablespoons vinegar from the capers or white wine vinegar
½ cup chopped fresh basil
½ teaspoon salt
¾ teaspoon freshly ground pepper
4 slices of coarse white bread, crusts trimmed, cut into ½-inch cubes
3 medium tomatoes, cut into 8 wedges each

1. In a large saucepan of boiling water, poach the shrimp until just cooked through, about 2 minutes. Drain and rinse under cold water. Place the shrimp in a medium bowl, cover and refrigerate.

2. In a small bowl, combine ⅓ cup of the olive oil, the crushed garlic, capers, caper vinegar, basil, salt and pepper. Pour over the shrimp and toss. Cover and refrigerate overnight, tossing occasionally.

3. Preheat the oven to 400°. In a small bowl, mix together the minced garlic and the remaining 3 tablespoons olive oil. Arrange the bread cubes on a baking sheet and drizzle with the garlic oil. Toss to coat. Bake, tossing occasionally, until the croutons are golden brown, about 10 minutes. *(The croutons can be made up to 6 hours ahead. Let cool and store in an airtight container.)*

4. Remove the shrimp from the refrigerator about 30 minutes before serving and divide evenly among 6 salad plates. Garnish with 4 tomato wedges, top with the garlic croutons and serve.

—*Marcia Kiesel*

• • •

SOUPS

AU PIED DE COCHON'S ONION SOUP

Is there any place in Paris that's better known for its onion soup than the 24-hour bistro Au Pied de Cochon? Almost all of us who love Paris have at one time or another made the ritualistic late-night trip to this restaurant in Les Halles, the former French food market, to indulge in this Parisian gastronomic pastime.

▼ Serve a fruity, direct, refreshing red, such as the 1987 Jaffelin Beaujolais-Villages, or an off-dry white, such as the 1987 Kenwood Chenin Blanc, as a contrast to the mélange of savory flavors in this classic soup.

——————— *6 Servings* ———————
*1 pound white or other sweet onion
   (about 2 large), thinly sliced*
*2 cups dry white wine, such as
   Muscadet or Mâcon-Villages*
2 tablespoons unsalted butter
*6 cups unsalted beef stock, or 3 cans
   (13¾ ounces each) beef broth
   diluted with 1 cup water*
*6 slices of French or Italian bread,
   cut ½ inch thick, preferably stale*
*2 cups freshly grated imported
   French Gruyère cheese (about ½
   pound)*

1. Preheat the oven to 425°. Combine the onions, white wine and butter in a medium flameproof gratin dish. Cook, uncovered in the hot oven, stirring once or twice, until the onions are very soft and most of the liquid is evaporated, about 1 hour. Remove from the oven and set the onions aside.

2. Preheat the broiler with the rack set about 6 inches from the heat. In a large saucepan, bring the stock to a simmer over high heat.

3. Arrange 6 deep ovenproof soup bowls on a baking sheet. Evenly distribute the cooked onions among the bowls and ladle the simmering stock over the onions. Place a round of bread on top of each. Sprinkle the grated cheese over all.

4. Place the baking sheet under the broiler and cook for 2 to 3 minutes, until the cheese is just melted and lightly browned. Serve hot.

—*Patricia Wells*

• • •

FRESH PIMIENTO BISQUE

In the South, sweet red peppers are called pimientos, and the word *bisque* is applied to a rather formal first-course soup for a special dinner. This is one of my family's favorite fancy soups. It is strained, very smooth and creamy and served in the most elegant bouillon cups one can muster. Mother's were white French Havilland with a scalloped gold border. When I was a child, I always judged the importance of our guests by whether the Havilland was brought out or not.

——————— *6 to 8 Servings* ———————
¼ cup rice
*4 large red bell peppers, coarsely
   chopped*
1 small onion, chopped
2 cups chicken stock or canned broth
2 cups milk
½ cup heavy cream
¼ teaspoon cayenne pepper
¼ teaspoon imported sweet paprika
*⅛ teaspoon freshly ground white
   pepper*
Salt

1. Place the rice in a small saucepan with 2 cups of water. Bring to a boil, reduce the heat to low and simmer uncovered until the rice is overcooked and mushy and the water has almost boiled away, about 40 minutes.

2. In a medium saucepan, combine the red peppers, onion and 2 cups of water. Boil over moderate heat until the peppers are tender but still bright red, about 10 minutes. Drain at once.

3. Put the rice, red peppers, onion and 1 cup of the chicken stock into a blender or food processor. Puree until smooth.

4. Strain the puree into a medium saucepan, add the milk and the remaining 1 cup chicken stock. Simmer over low heat for 5 minutes to thicken slightly.

5. Stir in the cream, cayenne, paprika and white pepper. Season with salt to taste. Cover the bisque and set aside for 1 hour to blend the flavors. Rewarm over low heat before serving.

—*Camille Glenn*

• • •

GREEN PEA SOUP

Buttermilk adds both richness and zest to this smooth pea soup.

——————— *6 Servings* ———————
*4 medium leeks (white part only)—
   trimmed, washed and cut into thin
   julienne strips*
4 tablespoons unsalted butter
*1 large head of lettuce, outer leaves
   and core removed, shredded*
6 fresh whole mint leaves
*4 cups fresh shelled green peas or 2
   packages (10 ounces each) frozen
   peas*

1 tablespoon salt
½ teaspoon freshly ground white
    pepper
2 teaspoons fresh lemon juice
1½ cups chicken stock or canned
    broth
½ cup buttermilk

1. In a steamer, cook the leeks until almost tender, about 7 minutes.

2. In a large heavy saucepan, melt the butter over moderate heat. Add the lettuce, mint, peas, salt, pepper and the leeks and stir to combine. Increase the heat to moderately high and cook, stirring, for 4 minutes. Reduce the heat to low, cover and cook until the peas are soft, 10 to 13 minutes.

3. Transfer the cooked vegetables to a food processor. Add the lemon juice and puree until smooth.

4. Return the puree to the pot. Add the stock and bring to a simmer over moderate heat. Stir in the buttermilk and heat through but do not boil. Serve hot.

—Lee Bailey

• • •

TOMATO-CARROT SOUP WITH CHERVIL

This soothing tomato and carrot soup can be served hot, as here, or it can be made well in advance and served chilled or at room temperature.

──────── *6 Servings* ────────
1 small sweet potato (about 6
    ounces)
3½ pounds ripe plum tomatoes
2 tablespoons unsalted butter
2 tablespoons olive oil
1 medium onion, coarsely chopped
1 garlic clove, minced
½ cup (loosely packed) fresh chervil,
    coarsely chopped, plus 6 sprigs for
    garnish

¼ cup (loosely packed) parsley,
    coarsely chopped
3 medium carrots, cut into ½-inch
    slices
1 teaspoon sugar
2 teaspoons salt
¼ teaspoon freshly ground white
    pepper
4 cups chicken stock or canned
    low sodium broth
Crème fraîche, for garnish

1. Pierce the sweet potato with a fork. Wrap in a paper towel and microwave on high for 4 to 6 minutes; let stand, wrapped, for 5 minutes. Or bake in a 375° oven for 45 minutes, until tender. Peel the sweet potato and cut into 1-inch cubes.

2. Preheat the broiler. Arrange the tomatoes on a baking sheet or in a shallow roasting pan and broil as close to the heat as possible for 6 minutes, turning frequently, until the skins are blackened. Transfer the tomatoes to a medium bowl and set aside for 30 minutes. Peel and core the tomatoes.

3. In a large nonreactive skillet or flameproof casserole, melt the butter in the oil over moderate heat. Add the onion and sauté until softened but not browned, about 5 minutes. Add the tomatoes with any accumulated juices and the garlic and simmer for 15 minutes.

4. Add the chervil, parsley, carrots, sugar, salt and white pepper. Reduce the heat to low, cover and cook until the carrots are tender, 15 to 20 minutes.

5. Transfer the cooked vegetables to a food processor and add the cubed sweet potato. Puree, in 2 batches, if necessary, until smooth, about 30 seconds.

6. Return the puree to the skillet. Add the stock and cook over moderately high heat, stirring occasionally, until warmed through, about 5 minutes. Serve immediately, garnished with a sprig of fresh chervil and a dollop of crème fraîche.

—Lee Bailey

• • •

CREAM OF CARROT AND LEMON SOUP

This is my favorite vegetable soup. It has a wonderfully vibrant taste and looks beautiful as well.

──────── *6 to 8 Servings* ────────
6 tablespoons unsalted butter
1 large onion, chopped
1 large garlic clove, sliced
1½ pounds carrots, peeled and
    sliced
3 tomatoes, chopped
1 baking potato, peeled and sliced
¼ cup shredded fresh basil or Italian
    flat-leaf parsley
4 cups Rich Chicken Stock (p. 246)
    or Goose Stock (p. 247) or 3 cups
    canned chicken broth diluted with
    1 cup water
1½ teaspoons salt
¼ teaspoon freshly ground pepper
1 cup crème fraîche
¼ teaspoon hot pepper sauce
¼ cup fresh lemon juice
Carrot curls, crème fraîche and
    Italian flat-leaf parsley, for
    garnish

1. In a large saucepan or flameproof casserole, melt 4 tablespoons of the butter. Add the onion and garlic, cover and cook over low heat until softened but not browned, about 5 minutes.

2. Add the carrots, tomatoes, potato, basil, stock, salt, pepper and remaining 2 tablespoons butter. Bring to a boil over high heat, reduce the heat to moderately low and simmer, covered, for 45 minutes.

3. Strain the soup, reserving the broth and the vegetables. Puree the vegetables in a food processor until smooth. Return the puree and the broth to the pan. Add the crème fraîche and hot sauce. Simmer, uncovered, for 15 minutes. *(The recipe can be made to this point up to 1 day ahead. Cover and refrigerate.)*

4. Before serving, reheat the soup and stir in the lemon juice. Ladle the soup into individual soup bowls. Garnish each serving with a carrot curl, a dollop of crème fraîche and a leaf of parsley.

—*Lydie Pinoy Marshall*

• • •

HOT AND SOUR LEMON GRASS SOUP WITH SHRIMP AND STRAW MUSHROOMS

This is a very easy soup to make. The lime leaves and lemon grass add a special, pleasing citrus taste. If you can't find the lime leaves and lemon grass, make the soup with just the lime juice, but grate some of the zest and add it in Step 2.

———— **6 Servings** ————

¾ *pound medium shrimp, shelled and deveined, shells reserved*
3 *stalks of fresh lemon grass—green tops trimmed off and reserved, white bulb pounded flat and cut into 1-inch lengths*
1 *can (15 ounces) Oriental straw mushrooms,* * *drained*
5 *lime leaves,* * *fresh or frozen (optional)*
1 *small tomato, cut into wedges*
1 *large scallion, thinly sliced*
1½ *cups bean sprouts*
3 *tablespoons plus 1 teaspoon fresh lime juice*
¼ *teaspoon freshly ground black pepper*
¼ *cup fish sauce (nuoc mam)* *
¼ *teaspoon crushed hot red pepper*
½ *teaspoon hot Chinese chili oil,* * *or more to taste*
* *Available at Asian markets*

1. In a medium saucepan, cover the reserved shrimp shells with 4 cups of water. Add the reserved lemon grass tops and bring to a boil over high heat. Remove from the heat, strain the stock and return it to the saucepan.

2. Add the straw mushrooms, lime leaves, lemon grass bulb and tomato wedges to the stock. Bring the stock to a boil, reduce the heat and simmer for 4 minutes.

3. Add the shrimp and simmer until loosely curled and opaque throughout, about 2 minutes.

4. Remove from the heat and pour the soup into a tureen. Stir in the scallion, bean sprouts, lime juice, black pepper, fish sauce, hot pepper and chili oil. Serve at once.

—*Marcia Kiesel*

• • •

GREENPORT SOUP

This soup is named after the little village where I spend my weekends and vacations, but I love to serve it to friends in my city apartment as well.

———— **6 Servings** ————

4 *cans (13¾ ounces each) chicken broth*
1 *package (10 ounces) frozen tiny peas*
1 *head of leafy lettuce (about ½ pound), shredded*
½ *cup chopped scallions*
½ *cup (packed) Italian flat-leaf parsley*
4 *tablespoons unsalted butter*
3 *tablespoons all-purpose flour*
¼ *cup dry sherry*
½ *cup sour cream*
Salt and freshly ground pepper
Parmesan Croutons (p. 173)

1. In a large heavy saucepan, combine the chicken broth, peas, lettuce, scallions and parsley. Bring to a boil over moderate heat. Reduce the heat to low and simmer for 15 minutes.

2. In a blender or food processor, puree the soup in batches until very smooth.

3. In a large saucepan, melt the butter over low heat. Add the flour and cook, stirring, for 2 to 3 minutes without letting the roux color. Whisk in the pureed soup and the sherry. Bring to a simmer over moderate heat. Cook for 5 minutes to blend the flavors. Remove from the heat. *(The recipe can be prepared to this point up to 1 day ahead. Let cool, cover and refrigerate. Reheat before proceeding.)*

4. Stir the sour cream into the hot soup. Season with salt and pepper to taste. Serve with the Parmesan Croutons.
—*W. Peter Prestcott*

• • •

VEAL SHANK SOUP

Obviously this has its inspiration in the traditional Milanese dish osso buco—hearty and satisfying.

—————— *6 Servings* ——————
¼ cup extra-virgin olive oil
1 medium onion, finely chopped
1 medium carrot, finely chopped
1 large celery rib, finely chopped
6 small veal shanks (about 5 pounds total), trimmed of excess fat and cut through the bone by the butcher into pieces 1 to 1½ inches thick
½ teaspoon salt
¼ teaspoon freshly ground pepper
2 tablespoons all-purpose flour
4 tablespoons unsalted butter
1½ cups dry white wine
3½ cups beef stock or chicken stock or canned beef or chicken broth
2 teaspoons minced fresh sage
2 teaspoons minced fresh rosemary
1 garlic clove, crushed through a press
1½ cups cooked basmati or long-grain white rice, as accompaniment
Grated zest of 1 lemon
12 large pitted green olives, quartered
1 tablespoon drained capers

1. In a large skillet, heat 2 tablespoons of the oil. Add the onion, carrot and celery and sauté over moderately low heat, stirring, until softened but not browned, about 5 minutes. Transfer to a large flameproof casserole. Wipe the skillet.

STICK-TO-THE-RIBS SOUP DINNER

Lee Bailey's general rule for his "soup meals" is, the colder the weather, the heartier the soup. The centerpiece for this winter dinner is based on osso buco, and consists of generous hunks of veal shanks cooked with lots of strong herbs. Serves 4.

Veal Shank Soup (p. 31)

Crusty Garlic Rolls (p. 170)

🍷 *Wine or Beer*

Green Salad with Stilton Cheese (p. 141)

Blackberry Jam Tart (p. 228)

Coffee

---

2. Pat the pieces of veal shank dry on paper towels and tie with kitchen string to secure the meat to the bone. In a small bowl, combine the salt, pepper and flour. Dredge the veal shanks in the seasoned flour to coat; shake off any excess.

3. In the skillet, melt the butter in the remaining 2 tablespoons olive oil over moderate heat. Add the veal without crowding and sauté, turning, until golden brown, about 4 minutes on each side. Drain on paper towels.

4. Wipe out any excess fat from the skillet. Pour in ¾ cup of the wine. Bring to a boil over moderate heat, scraping up any browned bits from the bottom. Boil until the wine is reduced to about ¼ cup,

---

4 to 5 minutes. Pour over the vegetables in the casserole and put the veal on top.

5. Add the remaining ¾ cup wine, the stock, sage, rosemary, garlic and 2¼ cups of water to the casserole. Bring to a boil over moderately high heat. Reduce the heat to low and simmer, uncovered, for 1½ hours, or until the veal is tender when pierced with a knife.

6. To serve, spoon about ¼ cup of rice into 6 deep soup bowls. Cut the string off the veal and put 3 or 4 pieces in each bowl. Divide the soup among the bowls. Combine the lemon zest, olives and capers. Sprinkle on top for garnish.
—*Lee Bailey*

• • •

DOUBLE CHICKEN SOUP

Finally, a chicken soup that tastes the way chicken soup used to taste—like chicken. This version is so rich, you won't be able to put down your spoon.

—————— *4 Servings* ——————
1 whole free-range chicken (about 4½ pounds), rinsed and patted dry
5 carrots, quartered lengthwise
4 leeks (white and tender green), quartered lengthwise
4 celery ribs, cut into 2-inch pieces
3 parsnips, quartered lengthwise
2 imported bay leaves, crumbled
1 teaspoon salt
½ teaspoon whole black peppercorns
Rich Free-Range Chicken Stock, chilled (p. 247)
Freshly ground black pepper

1. In a large heavy saucepan or stockpot, place the chicken, carrots, leeks, celery, parsnips, bay leaves, salt and peppercorns. Add the chicken stock and 4

cups of water. Bring slowly to a boil over moderately low heat. Reduce the heat to a simmer and cook, uncovered, skimming off the foam and fat occasionally, until the chicken is tender, about 1 hour.

2. Strain the soup and transfer the chicken and vegetables to a warm platter. Cover loosely with foil.

3. Return the broth to the pan and bring to a boil over high heat. Boil until reduced to 6 cups, 30 to 40 minutes. Season with additional salt and freshly ground pepper to taste.

4. To serve, carve the chicken. In 4 warmed soup bowls, place slices of white and dark meat, carrots, leeks, celery and parsnips. Ladle on the broth and serve hot.

—Molly O'Neill

• • •

COLLARD GREENS AND BLACK-EYED-PEA SOUP WITH CORNMEAL CROUSTADES

In the South greens are traditionally simmered with smoked pork and spices. In this recipe the side dish is turned into a soup simply by using more liquid. Cooking time for the greens is about one hour, two to three hours less than down-home cooked greens. The shorter cooking time preserves the texture, flavor and color of the greens; cooked longer, they tend to become a rather soft, gray-green mass that only a southerner can love.

The soup improves if made a day in advance and can be frozen and reheated in a microwave oven.

——— *6 to 8 Servings* ———
¾ pound smoked ham hocks, hog jowls or pork knuckles

4 carrots, halved crosswise
4 celery ribs, halved crosswise
15 to 20 sprigs of parsley, tied in a bundle with kitchen string
1 teaspoon salt
4 whole cloves
4 medium onions
10 garlic cloves, unpeeled
8 whole black peppercorns
6 small dried hot red peppers
2½ teaspoons thyme
2 imported bay leaves
2 cups dry white wine
½ pound dried black-eyed peas, rinsed and picked over
1½ pounds collard greens
12 to 16 thin slices of Cornmeal Yeast Bread (p. 166)
½ cup finely grated Cheddar cheese
Cider vinegar or hot pepper sauce, as accompaniment

1. In a large stockpot, place the ham hocks, carrots, celery, parsley and salt. Stick a clove into each onion and add to the pot. Thread the garlic cloves onto toothpicks or short wooden skewers (for easy removal when the soup is done) and add to the pot. Tie the peppercorns, hot peppers, thyme and bay leaves in a double thickness of cheesecloth and add to the pot. Add the wine and 5 quarts of hot water. Bring to a boil over high heat. Reduce the heat to a simmer and cook, partially covered, for 1 hour, skimming the surface occasionally.

2. Meanwhile, place the black-eyed peas in a large saucepan and add cold water to cover by at least 2 inches. Bring to a boil over moderately high heat and boil for 2 minutes. Remove from the heat, cover and let stand for 1 hour; drain.

3. Wash the collard greens and discard any large, coarse stems. Stack the greens and cut into ½-inch-wide strips. Cut across the strips to make ½-inch squares.

4. When the broth has simmered for 1 hour, add the greens and simmer, partial-

ly covered, until wilted, about 15 minutes. Add the black-eyed peas and simmer, uncovered, until the peas are tender but not mushy, about 45 minutes.

5. With a slotted spoon, remove the ham hocks, carrots, celery, onions and garlic from the soup and set aside. Remove the herb bouquet and the parsley bundle and discard. Remove the cloves from the onions and discard the cloves.

6. Place the carrots, celery and onions in a food processor. Remove the garlic cloves from the toothpicks and squeeze the garlic into the food processor, discarding the skins. Puree the vegetables with ½ cup of the broth until smooth, about 30 seconds. Return the puree to the soup.

7. Preheat the broiler. Pick over the ham hocks to remove any meat. Crumble the lean pieces with your fingers and return them to the soup. Season with additional salt to taste.

8. Place the slices of Cornmeal Yeast Bread on a baking sheet and broil 4 inches from the heat for about 1 minute on each side, until lightly browned and crisp. Sprinkle each slice with the cheese and broil for about 20 seconds, until melted and bubbly.

9. To serve, ladle the soup into bowls and float 2 croustades on top of each. Pass a cruet of vinegar and a bottle of hot sauce on the side.

—Sarah Belk

• • •

Top, Nachos with Bacon and Onions (p. 15); bottom, Classic Nachos (p. 14).

**Above: top, Pickled Prawns (p. 12); bottom, Asparagus
with Goat Cheese Dip (p. 12). Right: Corn and
Shrimp Chowder with Tomatoes and Herbs (p. 37).**

CHIU CHOW RICE NOODLE SOUP WITH SHRIMP, SCALLOPS AND SNOW PEAS

Chiu Chow cuisine from the region of Swatow along the China coast, north of Hong Kong, is very rich and heavily dependent upon seafood. Cooks from this region use a thin, salty fish sauce, which they add to most of their dishes. They are particularly known for their soups, such as this one. The gin used here is a substitute for a potent Chinese sorghum liquor called *fen chiew*.

♟ Match the intensity of this dish with a classic pairing—soup with sherry—and complement the seafood with a crisp, tartly dry fino sherry, such as Tio Pepe, Pando or La Iña.

——————— *6 Servings* ———————

½ pound dried rice noodles,* rice sticks* or fresh linguine

4½ cups chicken stock or 2¼ cups canned broth diluted with 2¼ cups water

1 tablespoon light fish sauce,* preferably Chinese, or light soy sauce

1-inch piece of fresh ginger

2 garlic cloves, thinly sliced

1 tablespoon minced Szechuan pickle*

2 tablespoons peanut oil

1½ teaspoons Oriental sesame oil

2 teaspoons gin

½ pound large shrimp (12), shelled and deveined

¼ pound sea scallops, each cut horizontally into 3 medallions

¼ pound snow peas, each cut diagonally into 3 pieces

2 tablespoons minced scallion

2 tablespoons chopped fresh coriander

*Available at Asian markets

1. In a large pot of boiling water, cook the noodles, loosening them so that they won't stick together, until just pliable, about 1½ minutes. Turn off the heat, run cold water into the pot and drain. Rinse and drain twice more. Drain well and set aside.

2. Place the chicken stock in a large pot. Add the fish sauce, ginger, garlic, Szechuan pickle, peanut oil, sesame oil and gin. Cover and bring to a boil over high heat. Reduce the heat to low and simmer for 2 minutes.

3. Increase the heat to high and add the shrimp, scallops, snow peas and minced scallion. Add the reserved noodles and bring to a boil. Remove from the heat. Add the coriander and serve.

—*Eileen Yin-Fei Lo*

• • •

BACK PORCH SUPPER

Sit-down suppers needn't be dressy. In fact, this supper would be perfect for the back porch or a backyard picnic table. The chowder recipe makes quite a lot, but it also will keep nicely for reheating later. Serves 8 to 10.

Corn and Shrimp Chowder with Tomatoes and Herbs (p. 37)

Baking Powder Biscuits

Chiffonade of Lettuce with Chives and Buttermilk Dressing

♟ *Amber Beer*

Blueberry Pie (p. 225) with French Vanilla Ice Cream

Open-Faced Goat Cheese Toasts (p. 16).

CORN AND SHRIMP CHOWDER WITH TOMATOES AND HERBS

This creamy chowder is made without flour or cream, but it has a rich flavor. Serve it as part of a summer supper, either as a main course or as an appetizer before barbecued meats, fish or poultry. This recipe makes enough chowder for a crowd, so you may want to cut the ingredients in half. Serve with oyster crackers or other plain biscuits.

♟ Bacon, shrimp, tomato and herbs give this dish a pungent richness best echoed by a round-textured, deep-flavored white, such as 1986 Rosemount Hunter Valley Sémillon or 1985 Inglenook Napa Valley Sémillon.

——————— *16 Servings* ———————

11 ears of corn

2 teaspoons vegetable oil

12 ounces thickly sliced bacon, cut crosswise into ½-inch strips

3 large onions, coarsely chopped

5 slender carrots, sliced on the diagonal ¼ inch thick

3 celery ribs, sliced on the diagonal ¼ inch thick

1 pound new or small boiling potatoes—peeled and cut ½ inch thick

3¾ cups chicken stock or 2½ cans (13 to 14 ounces each) canned broth

3 sprigs of fresh thyme or ½ teaspoon dried

3 cups milk

1¼ pounds medium shrimp, shelled and deveined

½ teaspoon salt

¼ teaspoon freshly ground pepper

3 dashes of hot pepper sauce

3 large tomatoes—peeled, seeded and cut into ½-inch dice

3 tablespoons fresh chives, cut into ½-inch lengths

1. Using a sharp knife, slice the corn kernels off the cobs. Scrape the cobs with

the dull side of the knife to release any milky corn juice (you should have 7 cups of corn and juice). Cut 4 of the scraped corn cobs in half and set aside.

2. In a large heavy saucepan or flame-proof casserole, heat the oil over moderate heat. Add the bacon and cook, stirring frequently, until lightly golden but not yet crisp, 10 to 15 minutes. Drain on paper towels and pour off all but 2 tablespoons of fat from the pan.

3. Add the onions, carrots and celery to the pan and cook, stirring frequently, until softened, about 5 minutes.

4. Add the potatoes, chicken stock, thyme and reserved corn cobs. Reduce the heat to low, cover and simmer, skimming occasionally, until the potatoes are tender but still hold their shape, about 15 minutes. Discard the cobs.

5. Uncover the soup and stir in the corn kernels and juices. Simmer until just tender, about 3 minutes. Using a slotted spoon, transfer about 3½ cups of the solids to a blender or food processor and puree coarsely. Return the puree to the soup, add the milk and simmer over low heat until warm, about 5 minutes. *(The chowder can be made to this point up to 2 days ahead. Store the soup and cooked bacon separately in the refrigerator; return to a simmer before proceeding.)*

6. Stir the reserved bacon into the chowder and add the shrimp. Cover and simmer over low heat until the shrimp are opaque throughout, about 3 minutes. Season with the salt, pepper and hot pepper sauce.

7. Stir in the tomatoes and half of the chives. Cook over low heat until the tomatoes are warm, about 1 minute. (If the soup is too thick, add a little milk or water.) Ladle the chowder into shallow soup plates and garnish each with the remaining chives.

—*Richard Sax*

• • •

OYSTER STEW WITH SPRING PEAS AND SAVORY

This soup is rich tasting but light on the tongue. It uses milk instead of cream. For a smoky flavor, substitute *andouille* sausage for part or all of the pancetta. Cook the diced sausage in a dry skillet over moderate heat until light brown, then add it to the soup with the potato and peas.

———— *6 to 8 Servings* ————
3 dozen oysters in their shells or 3 dozen freshly shucked oysters with their liquor
½ cup dry white wine
2 cups shelled peas (from about 3 pounds of pods) or 1 package (10 ounces) thawed frozen baby peas
1 large Idaho potato, peeled and cut into ½-inch dice
½ pound lean pancetta or slab bacon, cut into ¼-inch dice
4 tablespoons unsalted butter
1 large onion, chopped
2 tablespoons all-purpose flour
1½ quarts milk
2 tablespoons minced winter savory
1 teaspoon salt
1 teaspoon freshly ground pepper

1. Place a fine-mesh sieve over a medium bowl. Open each oyster over the sieve to allow the oyster liquor to drain into the bowl. Lift the sieve of oysters from the bowl. One by one, dip each oyster into the liquor and rub lightly to get rid of any sand or grit. Place the oysters in a clean bowl and refrigerate.

2. Slowly strain the oyster liquor through 2 or 3 layers of cheesecloth into a small nonreactive saucepan, stopping just before you get to the settled grit on the bottom of the bowl. Add the white wine. Boil over moderately high heat, skimming the surface occasionally, until reduced to ½ cup, about 10 minutes. Set aside.

3. Meanwhile, in a medium saucepan of boiling water, cook the fresh peas until tender, about 4 minutes. With a slotted spoon, remove the peas to a bowl and set aside.

4. Cook the potato in the same water until tender, about 6 minutes. With a slotted spoon, remove the potato to a bowl and set aside.

5. Add the pancetta to the same pan and when the water returns to a rolling boil, strain and set aside.

6. In a large heavy saucepan or flame-proof casserole, melt the butter over moderate heat. Add the onion, reduce the heat to low and cook, stirring occasionally, until soft, about 12 minutes.

7. Add the reserved pancetta and cook for 2 minutes. Whisk in the flour and increase the heat to high. Whisking constantly, add the milk, 1 cup at a time. Bring to a boil, then reduce the heat to low and simmer, stirring occasionally, until slightly thickened and the taste of raw flour is gone, about 10 minutes.

8. Add the cooked or frozen peas, potato, oysters and wine reduction to the stew. Increase the heat to moderate and simmer until the oysters just begin to curl around the edges, about 2 minutes. Remove from the heat and stir in the savory, salt and pepper. Serve hot.

—*Marcia Kiesel*

• • •

FISH & SHELLFISH

SAUTEED PECAN FLOUNDER

The chopped pecans give this pan-fried flounder a marvelous, rich-tasting crust.
♟ Crisp light white, such as 1987 Antinori Galestro

——————— 6 Servings ———————
1½ cups shelled pecans, coarsely chopped
1½ cups fresh bread crumbs
½ teaspoon salt
¼ teaspoon freshly ground pepper
1 cup all-purpose flour
2 eggs, lightly beaten
2 tablespoons milk
6 flounder fillets (about 2¼ pounds total)
3 tablespoons unsalted butter
3 tablespoons safflower oil
Golden Tomato, Pepper and Onion Sauce (p. 253)

1. In a small bowl, combine the pecans, bread crumbs, salt and pepper. Pour onto a sheet of waxed paper or a large plate. Pour the flour out onto another sheet of waxed paper or large plate. In a large bowl, whisk together the eggs and milk until blended.

2. Pat the flounder dry and dredge, one piece at a time, in the flour, making sure to coat evenly. Shake off any excess. Dip each fillet in the egg mixture and allow any excess liquid to drain off. Coat the fillets in the pecan/bread crumb mixture, patting gently to help the coating adhere. Shake off any excess.

3. In a large skillet, melt 1½ tablespoons of the butter in 1½ tablespoons of the oil over moderate heat. Add 3 of the fillets and sauté over moderate heat until golden brown on the bottom, about 3 minutes. Turn and sauté until golden brown on the other side, about 3 minutes. Transfer the fish to a warm platter and cover loosely with foil. Repeat with the remaining butter, oil and flounder fillets.

Serve hot, with the Golden Tomato, Pepper and Onion Sauce on top or on the side.

—Lee Bailey

• • •

BROILED FLUKE WITH MEXICAN PEPPERS AND ONIONS

If the fluke is not available, substitute any mild white fish fillets, such as flounder or sole.

——————— 6 Servings ———————
1 tablespoon safflower oil
6 fluke fillets (about 1¾ pounds total)
2 tablespoons light soy sauce
1¼ cup coarsely chopped scallions
1½ tablespoons coarsely chopped Italian flat-leaf parsley
1½ tablespoons coarsely chopped dill
2 tablespoons fresh lemon juice
Freshly ground pepper
2 tablespoons unsalted butter
Lemon wedges, for garnish
Mexican Peppers and Onions (p. 121)

1. Preheat the broiler. Line a 10-by-15-inch shallow pan with aluminum foil. Spread the oil evenly over the foil. Place the fillets in the pan, turn to coat both sides with oil. Rub both sides of the fillets with the soy sauce. Sprinkle with the scallions, parsley, dill and lemon juice. Season with pepper and dot with butter.

2. Broil the fish about 4 inches from the heat, about 4 minutes, without turning, until the thickest part of the fish just flakes. With a large spatula, place the fillets on 6 warmed plates. Garnish with lemon wedges and serve with the Mexican Peppers and Onions.

—Lee Bailey

• • •

IRRESISTIBLE FISH DINNER

Even those guests normally unenthusiastic about fish will be seduced by the combination of mild-flavored flounder and a rich, crunchy pecan coating in this menu from Lee Bailey. Serves 6.

Sautéed Pecan Flounder (p. 40)

Golden Tomato, Pepper and Onion Sauce (p. 253)

Buttered New Potatoes (p. 122)

♟ Crisp Light White, such as 1987 Antinori Galestro

Gingered Peaches (p. 213)

Brown Sugar Shortbread (p. 240)

Coffee

GRILLED HERB-STUFFED SNAPPER WITH EGGPLANT-TOMATO COMPOTE

At Max's Place in Miami, this dish is made with local yellowtail snapper cooked outdoors over a hardwood fire to crisp the skin. The Eggplant-Tomato Compote is a robust accompaniment for the simply cooked fish.
♟ The play of many herbs in the fish and compote recipes is best matched with a crisp, elegant white such as 1986 Mastroberardino Fiano di Avellino.

——————— 4 Servings ———————
¼ cup extra-virgin olive oil
1 teaspoon fresh lime juice
⅛ teaspoon crushed hot red pepper
14 large fresh basil leaves
4 whole red snappers (1¼ to 1½ pounds each), gutted and cleaned
4 sprigs of fresh thyme

4 sprigs of fresh oregano
4 sprigs of fresh tarragon
4 sprigs of Italian flat-leaf parsley
1 teaspoon coarse (kosher) salt
Eggplant-Tomato Compote (p. 120)

1. In a small saucepan, warm the olive oil until barely hot to the touch. Add the lime juice, hot pepper and 6 of the basil leaves. Remove from the heat and let steep for 30 minutes. Strain.

2. Preheat the oven to 500°. Brush a large, rimmed baking sheet or shallow roasting pan with some of the basil olive oil. Stuff each snapper with 1 sprig each of the thyme, oregano, tarragon and parsley and 2 of the basil leaves.

3. Arrange the fish on the baking sheet. Brush with the remaining basil oil and sprinkle with the salt. Roast for about 15 minutes, until nicely browned and just opaque throughout. Serve with the Eggplant-Tomato Compote.

—Max's Place, Miami

• • •

HALIBUT IN CAPERED BASIL MARINARA

At Giovanni's in Cleveland, this dish is prepared with whole yellow pike. Any firm-fleshed white fish such as striped bass or whiting can also be used. Serve the remaining sauce over spaghetti to accompany the fish.

——————— 4 Servings ———————
1 medium onion, chopped
3 tablespoons olive oil
1 can (28 ounces) crushed tomatoes
1 tablespoon capers, rinsed if salted
½ teaspoon salt
½ teaspoon freshly ground pepper
1 teaspoon sugar
¼ cup (packed) shredded fresh basil
4 halibut steaks (8 ounces each),
   about 1 inch thick

1. Preheat the oven to 350°. In a medium nonreactive saucepan, sauté the on-

ion in the olive oil over moderate heat until softened but not browned, about 5 minutes.

2. Add the tomatoes, capers, salt, pepper and sugar. Bring to a boil. Stir in the basil and simmer until the sauce is reduced by one-third, about 10 minutes.

3. Pour the sauce into a nonreactive baking dish just large enough to hold the fish in a single layer. Add the fish steaks and baste with the sauce. Cover and bake for 15 minutes, or until the fish is just opaque throughout.

4. Transfer the fish to plates or a platter and spoon some of the sauce over it.

—Carl Quagliata,
Giovanni's, Cleveland

• • •

GRILLED RED SNAPPER WITH RETSINA BEURRE BLANC

This dish will work with other wine, but only the pointed pine scent of retsina creates such a memorable harmony with the olives and the oregano. Fresh oregano blends better with the wine than dried.
❦ As for the drink of choice, try the Achaia retsina if you like strong piny flavors; try the Boutari retsina if you like your retsina milder.

——————— 4 Servings ———————
1 whole red snapper (2½ pounds),
   gutted and cleaned
¾ teaspoon salt
½ teaspoon freshly ground pepper
1 tablespoon olive oil, plus more for
   basting
1 pound plum tomatoes—peeled,
   seeded and cut into ¼-inch dice
¼ cup plus ½ teaspoon fresh lemon
   juice
3 tablespoons minced fresh oregano,
   or 1 teaspoon dried
¼ teaspoon crushed garlic
6 large Calamata olives, pitted and
   finely chopped

3 sticks (12 ounces) plus 4
   tablespoons cold unsalted butter,
   cut into tablespoons
10 medium shallots, minced
1¼ cups plus 2 tablespoons retsina
Fresh oregano leaves or dried
   oregano branches, for garnish

1. Season the cavity and the outside of the fish with ¼ teaspoon each of the salt and pepper. Rub 2 teaspoons of the olive oil over the skin and inside the cavity. Set the fish on a tray and refrigerate.

2. In a small bowl, combine the tomatoes with ½ teaspoon of the lemon juice, 2 teaspoons of the fresh oregano (or ¼ teaspoon of the dried) and the crushed garlic. Stir in the remaining ½ teaspoon salt and ¼ teaspoon pepper.

3. In another small bowl, combine the olives, 1 teaspoon of the fresh oregano (or ¼ teaspoon dried) and the remaining 1 teaspoon olive oil. Stir to mix well; set aside.

4. Preheat a grill or the broiler. In a heavy saucepan, melt 4 tablespoons of the butter over moderate heat. Add the shallots and the remaining 2 tablespoons oregano (or ½ teaspoon dried). Cook until the shallots are softened, but not browned, about 5 minutes.

5. Add the remaining ¼ cup lemon juice and 1 cup of the retsina. Boil over high heat until the liquid is reduced to 1 tablespoon, about 10 minutes.

6. Add ¼ cup of the retsina, stir well and reduce the heat to low. Whisk in the remaining 3 sticks of butter, 1 tablespoon at a time, to form a thick, creamy sauce. (Move the pan on and off the heat to prevent the butter from melting too quickly and separating.)

7. Strain the sauce into a clean saucepan. Whisk in the remaining 2 tablespoons retsina to thin the sauce slightly. Keep warm in a pan of warm water.

8. Meanwhile, drain the reserved tomato mixture in a sieve and discard the liquid.

9. Grill or broil the red snapper 6 to 8 inches from the heat, turning once, until the skin is lightly browned and the fish is just cooked through, 5 to 10 minutes per side, depending on the intensity of the heat. Baste occasionally with olive oil.

10. Divide the snapper into 4 fillet portions. Set a piece of fish in the center of each of 4 warmed dinner plates. Surround with 3 mounds of the reserved tomatoes. Nestle a small amount of the reserved olive mixture on top.

11. Reheat the sauce, if necessary, over moderate heat, stirring (be careful not to get the sauce too hot or it will break). Pour the sauce around the fish, tomatoes and olives. Garnish each serving with a few oregano leaves.

—David Rosengarten

• • •

FENNEL'S SALMON WITH VEGETABLES

In this recipe the salmon is cooked only on one side, so that the top third remains uncooked. If you like your salmon cooked through, either reduce the heat and continue cooking until the surface loses its translucency or flip the fillets and cook them on the other side.

🍷 Simply prepared salmon calls for a classic match of rich, full-bodied Chardonnay, such as 1986 Clos du Bois Calcaire or 1987 Beringer Private Reserve.

6 Servings

¾ cup plus 3 tablespoons olive oil
1 medium zucchini—halved lengthwise, seeded and cut into ¼-inch dice
1 medium red bell pepper, cut into ¼-inch dice
1 medium yellow bell pepper, cut into ¼-inch dice
1 small fennel bulb—trimmed, cored and cut into ¼-inch dice
Salt and freshly ground black pepper
¼ cup fish stock or chicken broth
2 tablespoons fresh lemon juice
1 large tomato—peeled, seeded and cut into ¼-inch dice
⅓ cup chopped parsley
6 center-cut salmon fillets (6 ounces each), skin intact

1. In a large skillet, heat 1 tablespoon of the olive oil over moderate heat. Add the zucchini, the red and yellow bell peppers and the fennel. Cook until the vegetables are softened but still bright in color, about 5 minutes. Remove from the heat and season lightly with salt and pepper.

2. Meanwhile, in a small nonreactive saucepan, bring the fish stock to a boil over high heat. Reduce the heat to low and stir in the lemon juice. Gradually whisk in ¾ cup of the olive oil in a thin stream. Add the tomato and parsley. Season with salt and pepper to taste.

3. In a large skillet, heat the remaining 2 tablespoons olive oil over moderate heat. Add the salmon fillets, skin-side down. Cook without turning until the skin is crisp, the bottom two-thirds of the salmon is opaque and the top third is still raw, about 7 minutes. Remove the skin from the salmon and cut it into thin strips.

4. To assemble the dish, reheat the vegetables over high heat. Reheat the sauce over moderate heat if necessary. Spoon the vegetables onto 6 serving plates. Top each mound of vegetables with a salmon fillet and garnish with the strips of salmon skin. Spoon the sauce around the salmon and vegetables.

—Jean-Pierre Bose, Fennel, Los Angeles

• • •

SALMON IN CUCUMBER SAUCE

Salmon and cucumber are by now a classic duo on elegant tables. In this main-course version, the cucumber, though warmed through, retains its crunchiness—a delicious contrast to the creamy sauce and the silken texture of the fish.

🍷 Rich, dry white, such as 1986 Frog's Leap Chardonnay or 1986 Louis Latour Chardonnay

4 Servings

2 tablespoons unsalted butter
1 medium onion, minced
1 garlic clove, minced
1 cup heavy cream
1 cup dry white wine
¼ cup brandy
2 teaspoons white wine vinegar
2 tablespoons Dijon-style mustard
½ teaspoon salt
¼ teaspoon freshly ground pepper
2 large cucumbers—peeled, halved lengthwise and seeded
⅓ cup minced parsley
⅓ cup minced fresh dill
4 salmon steaks (6 to 8 ounces each), 1 inch thick
1 teaspoon olive oil
1 tablespoon fresh lemon juice

1. In a large skillet, melt the butter over moderately high heat. Add the onion and garlic. Cook, stirring, until softened but not browned, about 2 minutes. Reduce the heat to low, cover and cook until the onions are very soft, about 6 minutes.

2. Add the cream, wine, brandy, vinegar, mustard, salt and pepper. Increase the heat to moderately high and boil, uncovered, whisking occasionally, until thickened, about 8 minutes.

3. Meanwhile, with a melon baller, cut out as many half-spheres as possible from the two cucumbers.

4. Add the cucumber pieces to the sauce, reduce the heat to low and cook, stirring occasionally, until the cucumber is slightly soft, about 5 minutes. Stir in all but 1 tablespoon each of the parsley and dill. Remove from the heat and cover to keep warm.

5. Heat the oven to 400°. Pat the salmon steaks dry with paper towels. In a large ovenproof skillet, heat the olive oil over high heat until smoking slightly. Add the salmon to the pan and sauté for 1 minute on each side, until browned. Transfer the skillet to the oven and bake until the salmon is just opaque throughout, checking for doneness around the center bone, about 7 minutes.

6. Remove the salmon from the oven and drizzle the lemon juice over the top. Spoon the reserved sauce onto a large, warm serving platter and put the fish on top. Sprinkle the remaining 1 tablespoon each parsley and dill over the salmon.

—*W. Peter Prestcott*

• • •

HEARTY ELEGANCE FOR FOUR

This Italian-inspired menu is filled with dishes that combine hearty, definite flavors—goat cheese, porcini mushrooms, oregano, espresso coffee, toasted sesame seeds—with a certain restraint and elegance. Serves 4.

🍷 *Bellinis*

Open-Faced Goat Cheese Toasts (p. 16)

Striped Bass with Potatoes and Porcini Mushrooms (p. 43)

Braised Belgian Endive

🍷 *Dry White Wine*

Coffee Granita (p. 209)

Toasted Sesame Seed Biscotti (p. 243)

Espresso

STRIPED BASS WITH POTATOES AND PORCINI MUSHROOMS

At once rustic and elegant, this recipe from Pazzia in Los Angeles counterpoints the delicate fish with earthy porcini and oven-crisped potatoes.

——————— *4 Servings* ———————
2 ounces dried porcini mushrooms
1 cup boiling water
6 tablespoons unsalted butter
2 medium all-purpose potatoes, sliced ⅛ inch thick
2 tablespoons extra-virgin olive oil
1 large garlic clove, minced
1 tablespoon minced fresh oregano or ¾ teaspoon dried
2 teaspoons minced parsley
½ teaspoon salt
½ teaspoon freshly ground pepper
2 whole striped bass (2 pounds each) —filleted, skinned and cut diagonally into ½-inch strips
2 tablespoons fresh lemon juice

1. Preheat the oven to 400°. In a small heatproof bowl, cover the dried mushrooms with the boiling water and let soak for 20 minutes.

2. In a small saucepan, melt the butter. Rinse the potato slices in cool water, drain in a colander and pat dry with paper towels. Place the potatoes in a medium bowl and toss with the melted butter. Arrange the potatoes on a large baking sheet, overlapping them only slightly. Bake on the lowest rack of the oven for 25 to 30 minutes, until browned and crisp.

3. Meanwhile, drain the mushrooms. Strain the soaking liquid through a sieve lined with a double thickness of cheesecloth and reserve it. Rinse the mushrooms well to remove any grit. Cut off and discard any tough bits.

4. In a medium skillet, heat 1 tablespoon of the oil. Add the garlic and cook over moderate heat until golden, 2 to 3 minutes. Add the mushrooms, ¼ cup of the reserved soaking liquid, 1 teaspoon of the fresh oregano (or ¼ teaspoon dried) and the parsley, salt and pepper. Cook until the liquid has evaporated, about 3 minutes.

5. Meanwhile, brush a baking sheet with the remaining 1 tablespoon oil. Arrange the fish strips on the sheet about 1 inch apart. Drizzle on the lemon juice and season with the remaining 2 teaspoons fresh oregano (½ teaspoon dried). Bake for 2 to 3 minutes, until the fish is just cooked through.

6. Mound the porcini on 4 warmed plates. Arrange the fish and overlapping potato slices attractively around the mushrooms and serve immediately.

—*Pazzia, Los Angeles*

• • •

TROUT EN PAPILLOTE

In this recipe, trout fillets are stuffed with aromatics, moistened with a little white wine and then sealed in parchment paper before baking. The fish cooks in its own steam and arrives on the plate fragrant and gift wrapped. Parchment paper is readily available at most supermarkets these days. The packages can be assembled several hours ahead and refrigerated until cooking time.

🍷 Although trout is a mild, sweet-fleshed fish, garlic, mushrooms and scallions add deeper flavor and suggest a sharp, earthy white, such as 1987 Maître d'Estournel Bordeaux Blanc or Preston Cuvée de Fumé from California.

——————— *4 Servings* ———————
4 tablespoons unsalted butter
1 tablespoon vegetable oil
1 large garlic clove, coarsely chopped
1 medium carrot, coarsely chopped
1 celery rib, coarsely chopped

1 small onion, coarsely chopped
2 tablespoons minced dill
1 cup coarsely chopped mushrooms
   (about 4 ounces)
½ teaspoon salt
⅛ teaspoon freshly ground pepper
2 teaspoons fresh lemon juice
8 scallions, green tops trimmed to 1
   inch
1½-inch piece of fresh ginger, peeled
   and cut into thin matchsticks
4 trout (10 ounces each), filleted
¼ cup dry white wine

1. Preheat the oven to 450°. In a medium nonreactive skillet, melt the butter in 1 teaspoon of the oil over low heat. Add the garlic, carrot, celery, onion and dill. Mix well, cover and cook until the vegetables are tender, about 10 minutes.

2. Meanwhile, wrap the mushrooms in the corner of a kitchen towel and squeeze to remove as much liquid as possible.

3. Add the mushrooms, salt, pepper and lemon juice to the vegetables. Increase the heat to high and cook for 1 minute, stirring constantly. Remove from the heat, cover and set aside.

4. Cut 4 pieces of parchment paper into 12-by-15-inch rectangles. With the short ends of the paper facing you, brush the bottom half of each sheet with oil, using a total of 1½ teaspoons. Place 2 scallions next to each other on the diagonal over each oiled area. Sprinkle the fresh ginger around the scallions. Top with the trout fillets, skin-side down.

5. Evenly distribute the reserved vegetable and mushroom mixture over the fillets. Cover with another trout fillet, skin-side up. Moisten each fish with 1 tablespoon of the wine.

6. Fold the parchment paper in half over the trout. Crimp the edges by making tight folds every inch or so all around to seal completely. Brush the remaining ½ teaspoon of oil over a baking sheet and set the 4 packages on top.

7. Bake the trout for 8 minutes. Transfer the packages immediately to warmed plates. Cut a deep cross in the top of each package and serve.

—*W. Peter Prestcott*

• • •

FENNEL-SCENTED GRILLED TROUT

At Providence's Al Forno restaurant, the trout and fennel are grilled over a medium-hot charcoal fire.

——————— *4 Servings* ———————
2 medium fennel bulbs (about 1
   pound each), trimmed, feathery
   tops reserved
About 3 tablespoons fruity extra-
   virgin olive oil
2 teaspoons coarse (kosher) salt
4 whole trout (10 to 12 ounces each),
   cleaned
2 teaspoons Ricard or other anise-
   flavored liqueur
Lemon wedges, for serving

1. Prepare a charcoal fire or preheat the broiler. Slice the fennel bulbs lengthwise ¼ inch thick. Brush lightly with oil and sprinkle with 1 teaspoon of the salt.

2. Brush the trout inside and out with oil and sprinkle all over with the remaining 1 teaspoon salt. Drizzle ½ teaspoon of the Ricard into each cavity, then stuff each fish with the reserved fennel tops.

3. Grill or broil the trout and fennel for about 4 minutes a side, until the fish is browned outside and just flakes and the fennel is tender. Drizzle each fish with ½ teaspoon of the oil and serve with the lemon wedges.

—*Johanne Killeen, Al Forno,
Providence, Rhode Island*

• • •

TURBOT IN CIDER VINEGAR SAUCE

Odile Engel, one of Normandy's best-known cooks, has a simple, homey style. She's passionate about fish, and in this dish from her small village restaurant Le Pavé d'Auge in Beuvron-en-Auge, she flavors it with Normandy's rich local butter and the region's apple cider vinegar.
♟ Crisp white, such as 1987 Beringer Sauvignon Blanc or 1987 Dry Creek Fumé Blanc.

——————— *4 Servings* ———————
1 pound flatfish fillets—turbot, brill,
   sole or flounder
¼ cup best-quality apple cider
   vinegar
1½ sticks (6 ounces) cold unsalted
   butter, cut into small pieces
Salt and freshly ground pepper

1. In the bottom of a steamer or fish poacher, bring 2 cups of water to a boil over high heat. Place the fish fillets on a rack in the steamer, reduce the heat to moderate, cover and cook until they are just opaque throughout, 4 to 5 minutes.

2. Meanwhile, in a small nonreactive saucepan, bring the cider to a boil over moderately high heat. Add the butter, a few pieces at a time, whisking constantly after each addition and moving the pan on and off the heat as necessary, until the sauce is smooth and creamy. Season to taste with salt and pepper.

3. To serve, place the fish fillets on warmed dinner plates and spoon the sauce over the top.

—*Patricia Wells*

• • •

AROMATIC SWORDFISH STEAKS

Fresh coriander and parsley add fragrance and flavor to the swordfish.

❦ A dense, meaty fish like this is nicely set off by a rich, oak-aged Chardonnay, such as 1987 Joseph Phelps from Napa Valley or Rosemount from Hunter Valley.

──────── *4 Servings* ────────

4 swordfish steaks (about ½ pound each), 1 inch thick
¼ cup chopped fresh coriander
¼ cup chopped parsley
1 garlic clove, coarsely chopped
1½ teaspoons paprika
½ teaspoon ground coriander
¼ teaspoon ground cumin
Pinch of cayenne pepper
2 tablespoons fresh lime or lemon juice
3 tablespoons olive oil
Salt

1. Pat the swordfish steaks dry. In a food processor, make a marinade paste by combining the fresh coriander, parsley, garlic, paprika, ground coriander, cumin, cayenne and lime juice. With the machine on, add the olive oil.

2. In a large plastic bag or in a bowl, layer the swordfish steaks with the marinade, putting some between each steak. Seal tightly and marinate in the refrigerator for 1 to 2 hours.

3. Light a charcoal fire. Remove the swordfish from the marinade and season lightly with salt. Grill the steaks over glowing hot charcoal for 4 to 5 minutes per side, until just opaque throughout.

—*Jim Fobel*

• • •

LE CHARDONNAY'S SAUERKRAUT WITH SMOKED FISH

If you can't find the variety of smoked fish called for in this recipe, just use a bit more of whichever kinds you do find.

❦ Dry Alsace Riesling, such as 1986 Domaine Weinbach or Léon Beyer

──────── *6 Servings* ────────

1 stick (4 ounces) plus 2 tablespoons cold unsalted butter, cut into tablespoons
1 medium onion, chopped
2 large garlic cloves, minced
2 imported bay leaves
2 pounds fresh sauerkraut, rinsed and well drained
2 cups Johannisberg Riesling
6 ounces skinless smoked trout fillets, cut into pieces
6 ounces smoked salmon, cut into pieces
4 ounces skinless smoked sturgeon fillets, cut into pieces
5 ounces skinless smoked eel, cut into pieces
6 smoked mussels
2 tablespoons heavy cream
⅛ teaspoon freshly ground white pepper
Pinch of cayenne pepper
2 tablespoons minced chives

1. Preheat the oven to 325°. In a heavy medium casserole, melt 2 tablespoons of the butter over moderately low heat. Add the onion and cook until softened, about 5 minutes.

2. Stir in the garlic, bay leaves, sauerkraut and 1½ cups of the Riesling. Increase the heat to moderately high and bring to a boil. Cover the casserole and transfer to the oven. Bake for 1 hour.

3. Remove the casserole from the oven. Stir the sauerkraut mixture. Gently fold in the smoked trout, salmon, sturgeon, eel and mussels. Cover and bake for 15 minutes or until the fish is warmed through and the flavors have blended.

4. Meanwhile, in a medium nonreactive saucepan, combine the remaining ½ cup Riesling and the heavy cream. Bring to a boil over moderately high heat and boil until reduced to about ⅓ cup, about 3 minutes.

5. Remove from the heat and whisk in the remaining stick of butter, 1 tablespoon at a time. Whisk in the white pepper and cayenne.

6. Gently mound the sauerkraut and fish mixture on warm plates and sprinkle with the chives. Pass the butter sauce separately.

—*Claude Alviry, Le Chardonnay, Los Angeles*

• • •

OLLA BOUILLABAISSE WITH SALSA FRESCA

If you have a Mexican *olla*, a big earthenware pot with a glazed interior, use it to cook and serve this seafood stew.

──────── *12 Servings* ────────

¼ cup olive oil
2 Spanish onions, coarsely chopped
8 large tomatoes, peeled and chopped (about 8 cups)
6 garlic cloves, chopped
¼ cup plus 2 tablespoons minced Italian flat-leaf parsley
6 large sprigs of fresh thyme or 2 teaspoons dried
2 bay leaves
1 tablespoon salt
2 tablespoons plus 2 teaspoons finely crushed hot red pepper or chile caribe
2 dozen littleneck clams (or other medium, 2- to 3-inch clams)
2 pounds monkfish or swordfish, cut into bite-size pieces

2 pounds mild firm-fleshed fish
  fillets, such as hake, halibut or
  cod, cut into bite-size pieces
2 pounds bay scallops or quartered
  sea scallops
¼ cup golden tequila, such as José
  Cuervo
¼ cup fresh orange juice
¼ cup fresh lime juice
Grated zest of 1 orange
½ cup coarsely chopped fresh
  coriander (optional)
6 limes, quartered
Salsa Fresca (p. 252)

1. In a large heavy pot, heat the olive oil over moderate heat. Add the onions and cook until softened and translucent, 6 to 8 minutes.

2. Add the tomatoes, garlic, ¼ cup of the parsley, the thyme, bay leaves, salt and 2 teaspoons of the hot pepper. Cook over moderately high heat, stirring frequently, for 15 minutes. Add 4 cups of water and bring the sauce to a simmer. *(The recipe can be prepared to this point up to 1 day ahead. Let cool, then cover and refrigerate. Reheat the sauce before proceeding.)*

3. Meanwhile, put the clams in a large saucepan with ¼ cup of water. Cover and cook over high heat until the clams open, about 5 minutes. Remove to a bowl. Strain and reserve the cooking liquid.

4. To the sauce, add all the fish, scallops, tequila, orange juice, lime juice and orange zest. Cover and cook over moderately high heat until the fish is opaque throughout, about 5 minutes. Remove from the heat and stir in the clam liquid.

5. Ladle the bouillabaisse into large shallow bowls, placing 2 clams on top of each serving. Sprinkle with the remaining 2 tablespoons parsley and the coriander if desired. Serve with lime quarters and pass the Salsa Fresca and remaining hot pepper on the side.

—*Jane Butel*

• • •

MODERN SOUTHERN LUNCHEON

Good ol' crab cakes go uptown for this updated southern luncheon. The crab cakes are served warm with a sweet red pepper remoulade and a salad of vinaigrette-dressed shrimp, radicchio and Belgian endive. Serves 4.

Crab Cakes with Shrimp-Radicchio Salad and Sweet Red Pepper Remoulade (p. 46)

Angel Biscuits (p. 170)

Iced Tea

Peach and Ginger Trifle (p. 202)

CRAB CAKES WITH SHRIMP-RADICCHIO SALAD AND SWEET RED PEPPER REMOULADE

This is adapted from an appetizer served at Savannah's 45 South Restaurant and makes a lovely luncheon dish.

――――――― **4 Servings** ―――――――
1 pound lump crabmeat, picked over
  to remove any cartilage and flaked
Sweet Red Pepper Remoulade
  (p. 251)
½ cup minced onion
¼ cup minced red bell pepper
1 egg
¼ cup fresh lemon juice
About 2 tablespoons fresh bread
  crumbs
1 teaspoon Dijon-style mustard
¾ teaspoon salt
⅜ teaspoon cayenne pepper
2 tablespoons tiny (nonpareil)
  capers

1 medium celery rib (including leafy
  top), thinly sliced
½ pound medium shrimp (about
  18), shelled and deveined
5 tablespoons extra-virgin olive oil
2 teaspoons balsamic vinegar
2 teaspoons minced shallots
2 tablespoons minced fresh dill
½ cup all-purpose flour, for
  dredging
1 tablespoon unsalted butter
1 small head of radicchio—halved,
  cored and sliced crosswise ¼ inch
  thick
1 large Belgian endive, sliced
  crosswise ¼ inch thick
1 medium tomato—cored, seeded
  and cut into small dice, for
  garnish
Italian flat-leaf parsley, for garnish

1. In a large bowl, combine the crab and ¼ cup of the Sweet Red Pepper Remoulade. Add the onion, red bell pepper, egg, ½ teaspoon of the lemon juice, 2 tablespoons of bread crumbs, the mustard, ¼ teaspoon of the salt and ¼ teaspoon of the cayenne. Refrigerate up to 4 hours.

2. Combine the remaining Sweet Red Pepper Remoulade and the capers in a bowl. Set the remoulade sauce aside.

3. In a large heavy saucepan, bring 1 quart of water, 3 more tablespoons of the lemon juice and the celery to a boil over high heat. Add the shrimp and cook, uncovered, until just pink and loosely curled, about 1 minute. Drain well.

4. In a large mixing bowl, combine 3 tablespoons of the olive oil, the vinegar, shallots, dill and the remaining 2½ teaspoons lemon juice, ½ teaspoon salt and ⅛ teaspoon cayenne. Add the shrimp, toss and set aside at room temperature.

5. Meanwhile, place the flour in a pie plate. Scoop up ¼ cup of the crab mixture in a measuring cup, invert it into the flour and pat it into a cake about ½ inch thick and 2 inches across. Continue with the remaining mixture to form 12 small crab cakes. *(NOTE: The crab mixture will be quite loose. It will come together as you shape it in the flour, and the cakes will be nice and light. If the cakes do not hold together well, simply mix in a few more bread crumbs, then shape.)*

6. In a large heavy skillet, melt the butter in the remaining 2 tablespoons olive oil over high heat. Fry the crab cakes in 2 or 3 batches without crowding, cooking them until browned outside and just set throughout, about 1 to 1½ minutes per side. Immediately transfer to paper towels to drain. Keep warm in a low oven while cooking the remaining cakes.

7. To serve, add the radicchio and endive to the shrimp and toss well. Divide the shrimp mixture evenly among 4 heated plates and surround with 3 crab cakes. Top each crab cake with about 1½ tablespoons of the reserved remoulade sauce. Garnish with the diced tomato and parsley leaves. Serve warm.

—Sandy Hollander, 45 South Restaurant, Savannah

• • •

LOBSTER FRICASSEE WITH ARTICHOKES

This luscious lobster dish is from one of Manhattan's most innovative Italian restaurants, San Domenico. There, it is made with quartered baby artichokes that are added to the pan with the carrots and onions right at the start.

❦ The lobster and mild butter sauce call for a rich, complex white such as 1985 Edoardo Valentini Trebbiano d'Abruzzo or, if you prefer, a white Burgundy or California Chardonnay.

─────── *4 Servings* ───────
4 large artichokes
2 ounces pancetta, minced
1 stick (4 ounces) plus 2½ tablespoons cold unsalted butter, cut into tablespoons
1 large onion, halved lengthwise and thinly sliced
2 medium carrots, thinly sliced
2 parsley sprigs plus 1 tablespoon minced parsley
2 tablespoons fresh lemon juice
2 boiled lobsters (1½ pounds each), meat removed and cut into 1-inch chunks (about 1½ cups of meat weighing approximately ½ pound)
1 tablespoon chopped fresh tarragon
¼ teaspoon salt
½ teaspoon freshly ground pepper

1. Trim off the stems of the artichokes. In a large steamer basket, steam the artichokes until tender, about 20 minutes. Let cool.

2. In a large saucepan, sauté the pancetta in 2½ tablespoons of the butter over moderately high heat until the fat begins to render, about 2 minutes. Reduce the heat to moderately low and cook until the pancetta is browned, about 7 minutes longer.

3. Add the onion, carrots and parsley sprigs and cook until the onion has softened, about 10 minutes.

4. Meanwhile, remove the leaves from the artichokes and reserve for another use. Scoop out the hairy chokes. Cut the bottoms into 1-inch chunks and add to the onion and carrot mixture with 1 cup of water. Bring to a simmer over moderate heat and cook until the carrots are tender, about 10 minutes longer.

5. Strain, reserving the vegetables and liquid. Discard the parsley sprigs. Set the liquid aside for 10 minutes, then skim off as much fat as possible.

6. Pour the liquid into a medium nonreactive saucepan and add the lemon juice. Bring to a boil over moderately high heat and boil until reduced to ¼ cup, about 5 minutes. Reduce the heat to low and whisk in the remaining stick of butter, 1 tablespoon at a time, until it is thoroughly incorporated and the sauce is creamy.

7. Add the reserved onion and carrots and the lobster, artichokes, minced parsley, tarragon, salt and pepper. Warm just until heated through. Serve in heated soup plates.

—San Domenico, New York City

• • •

CHESAPEAKE SCALLOPED OYSTERS

Scalloped oysters should be prepared just before baking; otherwise the crushed crackers will lose their crispness. To save time, drain the oysters, season the cream and toast the bread crumbs. With this procedure, the oysters can be prepared very quickly.

─────── *6 to 8 Servings* ───────
1 cup crushed saltine crackers
1 pint shucked oysters (about 24), drained
½ cup heavy cream
½ teaspoon salt
¼ teaspoon cayenne pepper
½ cup fresh bread crumbs, lightly toasted
4 tablespoons unsalted butter, cut into small pieces

1. Preheat the oven to 400°. Sprinkle ¾ cup of the crushed saltines into a large shallow baking dish. Add the oysters in a single layer.

2. In a small bowl, season the cream with the salt and cayenne and drizzle the cream evenly over the oysters.

3. Toss the remaining ¼ cup crushed saltines with the toasted bread crumbs and sprinkle them over the entire dish. Dot with the butter.

4. Bake in the middle of the oven until the oysters are plumped and the crumb topping is light golden brown, about 20 minutes.

—Camille Glenn

• • •

RAGOUT OF SCALLOPS AND SHRIMP

This elegant shellfish ragout is designed as a first course, but would also do nicely as a main course for lunch or supper.

12 First-Course
—— *or 6 Main-Course Servings* ——
1½ pounds medium shrimp, shelled and deveined, shells reserved
1½ pounds sea scallops
2 cups rich fish stock or 2 bottles (8 ounces each) clam juice
5 tablespoons olive oil
2 medium onions, chopped
3 celery ribs, chopped
2 garlic cloves, crushed through a press
¼ cup thinly sliced carrot
1 can (35 ounces) Italian peeled tomatoes, with their juice
2 teaspoons lemon juice
⅛ teaspoon cayenne pepper
1 cup heavy cream
2 tablespoons Cognac or other brandy
¼ cup minced fresh chives
Thyme Croutons (p. 173), as accompaniment

1. Slice the shrimp in half lengthwise. Cover tightly with plastic wrap and refrigerate. Slice the scallops horizontally into ¼-inch-thick medallions. Cover tightly with plastic wrap, pierce the plastic several times with a skewer and refrigerate. *(The shellfish can be prepared to this point up to 1 day in advance.)*

2. In a medium saucepan, bring the stock to a boil. Add the reserved shrimp shells. Reduce the heat to moderately low and simmer for 8 to 10 minutes, stirring occasionally. Strain the liquid and reserve, discarding the shells.

3. In a large flameproof casserole, heat 2 tablespoons of the olive oil. Add the onions and sauté over moderately high heat until the onions are softened and just beginning to brown, about 5 minutes.

4. Add the celery, garlic and carrot. Cook the vegetables for 1 minute. Add the tomatoes and their juice, the lemon juice and reserved fish stock. Bring just to a boil and cook for 30 minutes, or until reduced to 5 cups.

5. Puree the vegetables and stock in a blender or food processor until smooth. Strain through a fine-mesh sieve for finer texture, pressing to extract all the liquid; discard the vegetable pulp. *(The pureed base can be prepared to this point up to 1 day in advance. Cover and refrigerate.)*

6. In a medium saucepan, combine the pureed base with the cayenne, cream and Cognac. Warm the tomato cream sauce over moderately low heat.

7. Meanwhile, in a large flameproof casserole, heat the remaining 3 tablespoons oil over high heat. Add the shrimp and scallops and reduce the heat to moderately high. Sauté, stirring frequently, until the shrimp are pink and loosely curled and the scallops are firm, 3 to 4 minutes.

8. With a slotted spoon, transfer the cooked seafood to 12 warmed ramekins or a large gratin. Pour any pan juices from the casserole into the tomato cream sauce. Season with additional salt and pepper to taste and pour the sauce over the scallops and shrimp. Garnish with the chives. Pass the croutons separately.

—*Bob Chambers*

• • •

LOW COUNTRY SHRIMP

One of the dinner specialties at Jilich's on East Bay in Charleston, this sauté of shrimp and country ham with the added surprise of kiwi typifies new southern cooking at its best. Serve with rice.
❦ Rich Chardonnay, such as 1986 Clos Pegase or 1986 Ste. Chapelle Reserve

—— *4 Servings* ——
2 tablespoons olive oil
1½ ounces (about 4 to 5 thin slices) Smithfield ham or prosciutto, cut into thin julienne strips
⅓ cup minced shallots
½ teaspoon crushed hot red pepper
½ cup dry white wine
1 pound (16 to 20) medium-large shrimp, shelled and deveined
2 kiwis, peeled and cut into ¼-inch dice
1 cup heavy cream
¼ teaspoon salt
⅛ teaspoon freshly ground black pepper

1. In a large heavy skillet, heat the oil over high heat for 1 minute. Add the ham, shallots and hot red pepper. Sauté for 30 seconds.

2. Add the wine and boil until reduced by half, 2 to 3 minutes. Add the shrimp, kiwis and cream. Reduce the heat to moderately low and cook uncovered, stirring occasionally, until the shrimp are pink and loosely curled, 5 to 6 minutes. With a slotted spoon, transfer the shrimp to a plate.

3. Boil the liquid in the skillet over high heat until it is the consistency of a thin white sauce, 2½ to 3 minutes. Season with the salt and pepper. Return the shrimp to the skillet and cook, stirring, until heated through, about 1 minute.

—*Jilich's on East Bay,
Charleston, South Carolina*

• • •

SOUTHERN CURRIED SHRIMP AND CHICKEN

This is a home version of Elizabeth Terry's lightened country captain, which is an old Savannah classic. It's perfect for a party because it's baked in a single casserole that can go from oven to buffet or dinner table.

🍷 Fruity soft white, such as 1987 Mirassou Monterey Riesling

────── *6 to 8 Servings* ──────

1 cup converted rice
1 tablespoon curry powder
1½ teaspoons minced fresh ginger
1½ teaspoons grated orange zest
1¼ teaspoons salt
¼ teaspoon cayenne pepper
2½ tablespoons dried currants
1½ pounds skinless, boneless chicken breasts
⅛ teaspoon freshly ground black pepper
2 Granny Smith apples (about ¾ pound), cored and cut into ½-inch dice but not peeled
1 medium onion, minced
1 medium green bell pepper, minced
1 can (14 ounces) Italian peeled tomatoes, well drained and coarsely chopped
1 tablespoon minced garlic
¾ cup rich chicken stock or 1 can (13¾ ounces) chicken broth, reduced to ¾ cup
1½ pounds (30 to 40) medium shrimp, shelled and deveined
½ cup coarsely chopped pecans, lightly toasted

1. Preheat the oven to 400°. In a heavy medium saucepan, combine the rice, curry powder, ginger, orange zest, ¾ teaspoon of the salt and the cayenne. Stir in 2 cups of water and bring to a boil over high heat. Boil gently, uncovered, until all the liquid is absorbed and the rice is al dente, about 20 minutes.

2. Meanwhile, in a small bowl, soak the currants in 2 tablespoons hot water for about 10 minutes.

3. Cut the chicken breasts crosswise and on an angle into strips about 1½ inches wide and arrange in a single layer in a generously buttered medium flameproof casserole. Season with the remaining ½ teaspoon salt and the black pepper.

4. Layer on the apples, onion, green pepper, tomatoes, currants with their soaking liquid and the garlic. Pour the chicken stock evenly over all. Spoon the curried rice on top of the casserole, fully covering the ingredients underneath.

5. Cover the casserole securely with heavy-duty aluminum foil and bring to a boil over moderate heat, about 5 minutes. Transfer the casserole to the oven and bake until the chicken is cooked through (white throughout but still moist), about 20 minutes.

6. Stir the casserole well, arrange the shrimp on top, re-cover with aluminum foil and bake just until the shrimp are pink and loosely curled, about 5 to 7 minutes longer.

7. Remove the casserole from the oven and let stand, covered, for 15 minutes. Stir well; then scatter the toasted pecans on top.

—Elizabeth Terry,
Elizabeth on 37th, Savannah
• • •

FROGMORE STEW

This specialty of South Carolina Low Country is not really a "stew." As with a New England boiled dinner, the main ingredients are boiled in a broth and then drained and served hot. The recipe can be adjusted to serve any number—just allow 2 teaspoons of "boil" per quart of water and ½ pound shrimp, ¼ pound sausage and 1½ ears of corn per person.

────── *8 Servings* ──────

¼ cup Seafood Boil (p. 248) or commercial shrimp boil with 3 tablespoons coarse (kosher) salt added
2 pounds hot smoked sausage links, cut into 2-inch pieces (see Note)
12 ears freshly shucked corn, broken into 3- to 4-inch pieces
4 pounds large shrimp in their shells

In a stockpot, combine the Seafood Boil with 6 quarts of water and bring to a boil. Add the sausage and boil for 5 minutes. Add the corn and cook for 5

FOURTH-OF-JULY FEAST

Serving Frogmore Stew—a Low Country shrimp boil—is a marvelous way to show off the fresh shrimp and corn of summer and a great way to celebrate the Fourth of July. John Martin Taylor fleshes out this holiday feast with appetizers, several salads and a quintessentially southern peach ice cream for dessert. Serves 8.

Eggplant Caviar (p. 12)

Crudités

Tomato Salsa

Chips

────────

Frogmore Stew (p. 49)

Crab Hoppin' John (p. 135)

Green Bean and Benne Salad (p. 144)

────────

Fresh Peach Ice Cream (p. 206)

minutes longer. Add the shrimp to the pot and cook until pink and firm and the corn is crisp-tender, about 3 minutes. Drain immediately and serve.

NOTE: If you can't find hot smoked sausage, use another smoked sausage such as kielbasa and add ½ teaspoon crushed hot pepper per serving to the pot.

—John Martin Taylor

• • •

SHRIMP CURRY GRANT

Even Gunga Din would love this mild, fresh-tasting curry with shrimp. Serve it over basmati rice or our homegrown Tex-mati variety.

———— *6 Servings* ————
1 tablespoon unsalted butter
2 tablespoons vegetable oil
1 large red bell pepper, cut into
  ½-inch squares
1 large green bell pepper, cut into
  ½-inch squares
1 large onion, chopped
2 large celery ribs, chopped
1 tablespoon plus 1 teaspoon curry
  powder
1½ medium cucumbers—peeled,
  seeded and diced
1¼ cups plum tomatoes—peeled,
  seeded and chopped—or 1 can
  (14 ounces) Italian peeled
  tomatoes, with their juice,
  chopped
1¼ cups chicken stock or canned
  broth
1½ pounds medium shrimp, shelled
  and deveined
¼ cup unsweetened grated coconut*
1 tablespoon fresh lime juice
½ teaspoon salt
½ teaspoon freshly ground black
  pepper
*Available at health food stores

1. In a large skillet, melt the butter in the oil over moderately high heat. Add the red and green peppers, onion and celery, and sauté until the vegetables are slightly softened, about 4 minutes.

2. Add the curry powder, reduce the heat to moderate and cook, stirring frequently, about 2 minutes, or until fragrant. Stir in the cucumbers and cook, stirring, until the mixture becomes bright green, 2 to 3 minutes.

3. Add the tomatoes (and juice if canned) and the stock. Bring to a boil over moderate heat and add the shrimp. Cook until the shrimp are opaque throughout, 2 to 3 minutes.

4. Remove from the heat and stir in the coconut, lime juice, salt and pepper.

—F&W

• • •

SHRIMP WITH BLACK BEANS

Garlic lovers will find this simple stir-fry absolutely irresistible. Serve it with steamed white rice.

❧ This substantial dish needs a refreshing but characterful white wine to underscore, rather than compete with, its depth of flavors. A 1987 Marqués de Riscal Rueda or 1987 Kendall-Jackson Sauvignon Blanc would play that role well.

———— *4 Servings* ————
2 tablespoons light soy sauce
1½ tablespoons oyster sauce*
1 tablespoon dry white wine
1 tablespoon Oriental sesame oil
1 teaspoon ginger juice (1½ inches
  fresh ginger crushed through a
  garlic press)
1 tablespoon cornstarch
1 teaspoon sugar
½ teaspoon salt
Pinch of white pepper
1½ pounds medium shrimp, shelled
  and deveined
¼ cup Chinese salted black beans,*
  rinsed 3 times and drained
6 garlic cloves, crushed through a
  press
3½ tablespoons peanut oil
Sprigs of fresh coriander, for
  garnish
*Available at Asian markets and
  some supermarkets

1. In a large bowl, combine the soy sauce, oyster sauce, white wine, sesame oil, ginger juice, cornstarch, sugar, salt and white pepper. Add the shrimp and toss to coat. Set aside to marinate at room temperature for 30 to 60 minutes.

2. Meanwhile, in a small bowl, mash the black beans and the garlic into a paste. Set aside.

3. In a wok or large skillet, heat the peanut oil over high heat until it begins to smoke. Add the black bean and garlic paste. Cook, stirring, until the garlic turns light brown, about 1 minute.

4. Reserving the marinade, remove the shrimp with a slotted spoon, add to the wok and spread them quickly into a single layer. Then stir with the paste.

5. Add the marinade to the wok and continue to stir-fry until the shrimp are curled and opaque throughout, about 5 minutes. Remove the shrimp from the wok, garnish with coriander sprigs and serve hot.

—Eileen Yin-Fei Lo

• • •

MEAT

MEAT

VEAL ROASTED WITH COGNAC-SHALLOT BUTTER

The butter in the veal helps keep the meat moist and creates rich pan juices that are reduced to a deeply flavored sauce. This simple method of roasting produces juicier, more tender results with fresh rather than frozen veal.

♥ Complement the rich yet mild flavor of the veal with a deeply fruity red wine with some acidity, such as 1984 Trefethen Pinot Noir or 1984 Belvedere Carneros Pinot Noir, served slightly cool.

—————— 6 Servings ——————
6 tablespoons unsalted butter, softened to room temperature
1 shallot, chopped
1 tablespoon chopped parsley
2 teaspoons chopped fresh thyme or ¾ teaspoon dried
2 tablespoons Cognac or Calvados
1½ teaspoons Dijon-style mustard
½ teaspoon salt
¾ teaspoon freshly ground pepper
3-pound veal shoulder roast, rolled and tied
¼ cup dry white wine

1. In a food processor, combine the butter, shallot, parsley, thyme, 1 tablespoon of the Cognac, the mustard, ¼ teaspoon of the salt and ½ teaspoon of the pepper. Process for about 30 seconds to blend well.

2. Using a rubber spatula, scrape the butter onto a large piece of plastic wrap. Shape into a log 1 inch in diameter. Wrap and refrigerate until firm, about 1 hour. *(The butter can be made up to a week in advance and frozen. Thaw until soft enough to cut before using.)* Unwrap the butter, cut it into 12 equal pieces and refrigerate.

A SIMPLY STYLISH DINNER FOR SIX

In the spirit of informality that characterizes entertaining today, this menu from Marcia Kiesel treats good food as simply as possible. And to make life even easier for the host/ess, the recipes are designed with plenty of do-ahead options. Serves 6.

Cool Garlic Shrimp with Tomatoes and Croutons (p. 25)

♥ *Crisp California Sauvignon Blanc, such as 1987 Iron Horse or 1986 Viansa*

Veal Roasted with Cognac-Shallot Butter (p. 52)

Pappardelle with Carrot and Zucchini Ribbons (p. 105)

♥ *Light Red, such as 1985 Peppoli Chianti Classico*

Frozen Lemon-Anise Cream (p. 208)

3. Using a sharp knife, make 12 long, thin cuts in the veal roast at equal intervals. Insert a piece of butter into each cut. (Don't worry if the butter becomes soft or spreads over the meat.) Wrap the roast in plastic wrap and refrigerate until the butter firms up again, about 2 hours. *(The roast can be prepared to this point up to 1 day in advance. Remove the meat from the refrigerator about 30 minutes before roasting.)*

4. Preheat the oven to 450°. Unwrap the meat, place it in a small roasting pan and roast for 10 minutes. Reduce the oven temperature to 325° and pour the wine into the bottom of the pan. Continue to roast the meat until the internal temperature reaches 145° to 150° on a meat thermometer, about 1 hour and 20 minutes. Remove the roast to a warm serving platter and cover with aluminum foil.

5. Pour off any grease from the roasting pan and place the pan over high heat. When the pan begins to smoke, add 1 cup of water and stir, scraping up the browned bits from the bottom of the pan. Stir in the remaining 1 tablespoon Cognac and boil, stirring, until the pan juices are reduced to about ½ cup, about 3 minutes. Season the sauce with the remaining ¼ teaspoon each of salt and pepper.

6. Carve the roast into ¼-inch-thick slices and pour any accumulated juices into the sauce. Serve at once with the sauce on the side.

—Marcia Kiesel

• • •

VEAL CHOPS WITH WINE AND SHALLOTS

In this recipe, veal chops are cooked until rosy pink in the center and then topped with a delicate wine and shallot reduction and crowned with brandied mushroom caps. I like to accompany this dish with saffron rice and a green vegetable.

♥ Rich Chardonnay, such as 1987 Edna Valley from California or 1987 Rothbury Estate Reserve from Australia

—————— 4 Servings ——————
3 tablespoons all-purpose flour, for dredging
4 veal chops, cut ¾ inch thick

4 tablespoons unsalted butter
3 tablespoons vegetable oil
12 medium mushroom caps
½ teaspoon fresh lemon juice
2 teaspoons Cognac or other brandy
¼ pound shallots, thinly sliced
1 teaspoon minced fresh rosemary or
    ½ teaspoon dried
½ cup dry white wine
½ teaspoon salt
¼ teaspoon freshly ground pepper
1 tablespoon minced parsley
1 teaspoon grated lemon zest

1. Preheat the oven to 250°. Lightly flour the veal chops; shake off any excess.

2. In a large heavy skillet, melt 3 tablespoons of the butter in 1½ tablespoons of the oil over moderately high heat. Add the chops and cook until medium rare, about 3 minutes on each side. Transfer the chops to a heatproof platter, cover loosely with foil and keep warm in the oven. Set the skillet aside.

3. In a medium nonreactive skillet, heat the remaining 1½ tablespoons oil and 1 tablespoon butter over high heat until the fat is lightly browned, about 1 minute. Add the mushroom caps, rounded-side down, and cook, shaking the pan occasionally, until browned, 2 to 3 minutes. Turn the mushrooms over and cook until softened, about 2 minutes longer. Stir in the lemon juice and Cognac and remove from the heat. Cover with foil to keep warm.

4. Add the shallots and rosemary to the fat remaining in the skillet used for the chops and cook over moderate heat, stirring and scraping the bottom with a wooden spoon, until the shallots are softened, about 5 minutes.

5. Add the wine and simmer, stirring constantly, until slightly reduced, about 3 minutes. Season with the salt and pepper.

6. In a small bowl, combine the parsley and lemon zest. Place the chops on warmed serving plates. Pour the sauce over the chops and top each one with three mushroom caps. Sprinkle on the parsley and lemon mixture and serve.

—*W. Peter Prestcott*

• • •

MEDITERRANEAN TENDERLOIN OF BEEF

The pure flavors of impeccable olive oil, sun-dried tomatoes, black olives and parsley make a perfect sauce to accompany the pasta and beef. Complete the meal with a selection of cheeses.

🍷 A bright-flavored Piedmontese red, such as 1985 Pio Cesare Barbera d'Alba or 1985 Renato Ratti Nebbiolo d'Alba, would be set off perfectly by this beef dish, with its Mediterranean grace notes of olives and tomatoes.

———— 4 Servings ————

2 teaspoons coriander seeds
½ teaspoon black peppercorns
¼ teaspoon coarse (kosher) salt
½ cup plus 2 tablespoons extra-
    virgin olive oil
2-pound piece of beef tenderloin,
    trimmed of excess fat
2 large shallots, thinly sliced
1 large garlic clove, thinly sliced
½ cup thinly sliced oil-packed sun-
    dried tomatoes
⅓ cup pitted and quartered brine-
    cured black olives, preferably
    Calamata
⅓ cup chopped Italian flat-leaf
    parsley
¾ pound tubular pasta, such as
    penne
¼ teaspoon freshly ground pepper

1. Preheat the oven to 425°. With a mortar and pestle or in an electric mill, coarsely grind the coriander, peppercorns and salt. Stir in 2 tablespoons of the olive oil to make a paste.

2. Place the beef in a small roasting pan. Rub the spice paste all over the meat and set aside.

3. In a medium saucepan, heat 1 tablespoon of the olive oil over low heat. Add the shallots and garlic and cook until they are softened but not browned, about 5 minutes.

4. Stir in the sun-dried tomatoes, olives, parsley and remaining 7 tablespoons olive oil. Heat, stirring, until warmed through. Cover to keep warm and set aside.

5. Cook the meat until medium-rare and the internal temperature reaches 125°, about 20 minutes. Remove the meat to a carving board, cover loosely with foil and let rest for 10 minutes. Strain the roasting juices into the sun-dried tomato sauce.

6. Meanwhile, in a large pot of boiling salted water, cook the pasta until tender but firm, about 12 minutes. Drain, return the pasta to the pot and stir in the sun-dried tomato sauce. Season with the pepper and cover to keep warm.

7. To serve, carve the meat against the grain into ¼-inch-thick slices and arrange on a serving platter. Transfer the pasta to a serving bowl and serve the two together. Pour any meat juices from carving over the tenderloin.

—*Nora Carey*

• • •

PEPPER-RUBBED VEAL LOIN CHOPS WITH MADEIRA GLAZE

The chops are rubbed with a dry pepper marinade and refrigerated overnight. A touch of sugar in the mixture caramelizes to help seal the juices in the chops when they are seared.

♥ Rosé Champagne, such as 1982 Bollinger or 1979 Dom Ruinart

───────── *12 Servings* ─────────
2 teaspoons black peppercorns
1½ teaspoons white peppercorns
1½ teaspoons pink peppercorns
4 teaspoons thyme
2 teaspoons salt
4 teaspoons sugar
12 veal loin chops, cut 1 inch thick
    (6 to 8 ounces each)
6 tablespoons olive oil
2 medium onions, finely chopped
3 medium carrots, thinly sliced
2 celery ribs, sliced
4 garlic cloves, unpeeled
4 cups veal or chicken stock or 3 cans
    (10½ ounces each) low-sodium
    chicken broth
3 tablespoons tomato paste
¼ cup dry Madeira
1½ teaspoons arrowroot or
    cornstarch dissolved in 1
    tablespoon of water

1. Combine 1½ teaspoons of the black peppercorns with the white and pink peppercorns, the thyme, salt and sugar. Coarsely grind with a mortar and pestle or in an electric spice grinder.

2. Rub the seasoning evenly into both sides of the chops. Cover with plastic wrap and refrigerate overnight.

3. Place 2 roasting pans or baking sheets, each large enough to hold 6 veal chops, in the freezer.

4. In a large flameproof casserole, heat 3 tablespoons of the olive oil over high heat. Add the chops, 3 at a time, and sauté, turning once, until browned, about 2 minutes on each side. As they are browned, set the chops on the cold pans in the freezer. Chill for 25 minutes; then remove from the freezer, cover tightly with plastic wrap and refrigerate for at least 2 hours or overnight.

5. Meanwhile, in the pan where the chops were browned, heat the remaining 3 tablespoons olive oil. Add the onions, carrots, celery, garlic and remaining ½ teaspoon black peppercorns. Sauté over moderate heat until the onions are softened but not browned, about 5 minutes.

6. Add the stock and tomato paste. Bring to a boil, reduce the heat to moderately high and simmer, uncovered, for 30 minutes.

7. Strain the stock through a fine-mesh sieve, pressing gently to extract all the liquid; discard the vegetables. If there is more than 2 cups of stock, boil to reduce. If there is less, add water.

8. In a small saucepan, return the stock to a boil. Add the Madeira and the arrowroot mixture. Cook, whisking constantly to prevent lumps, until the sauce thickens and returns to a boil. Remove from the heat and cover tightly. *(The recipe can be prepared to this point up to 1 day ahead. Let the sauce cool, cover tightly and refrigerate.)*

9. About 20 minutes before serving, preheat the oven to 500°. Place the baking sheets with the chops on the upper and lower shelves of the oven for 8 minutes. Switch the positions of the pans and bake for 8 inutes longer, or until a meat thermometer inserted in the thickest part reads 130° and the center is nicely pink.

SPARKLING CHAMPAGNE DINNER FOR 12

The trick in designing an ambitious menu such as this New Year's celebration from Bob Chambers, is figuring out how to prepare the food and enjoy your company too. In the following menu, this is made possible by recipes that can be prepared totally or in part well ahead of the event. Serves 12.

Gougères (p. 17)

♥ *A Light Stylish 1983 Billecart-Salmon Blanc de Blancs or 1984 Gloria Ferrer Royal Cuvée*

Ragout of Scallops and Shrimp (p. 48)

♥ *Rich 1982 Ayala Brut or 1984 Iron Horse Brut*

Pepper-Rubbed Veal Loin Chops with Madeira Glaze (p. 54)

Red Cabbage with Granny Smith Apples (p. 118)

Sage-Glazed Carrots (p. 119)

Parslied Potato Cakes (p. 123)

♥ *Deep Round 1982 Bollinger Rosé Grande Année or Domaine Chandon Blanc de Noirs*

Mixed Green Salad with Soured Cream and Blue Cheese Dressing (p. 141)

Rosé Champagne Sorbet (p. 208)

Double Cranberry Mousse in Tulip Cups (p. 199)

♥ *Fruity, Delicately Sweet Lanson Ivory Label Demi-Sec or Schramsberg Crémant*

10. Meanwhile, reheat the reserved Madeira glaze over moderate heat until hot. Let the chops rest for about 2 minutes out of the oven, covered lightly with aluminum foil, then serve with the glaze.

—*Bob Chambers*

• • •

BLAZING BURRITOS

Here the abundance of browned onions adds a slightly sweet note to these tangy burritos.

—————— *Makes 8 Burritos* ——————
2 tablespoons unsalted butter
1 tablespoon vegetable oil
2 pounds red onions, thinly sliced
1½-pound boneless sirloin steak, about 1¼ inches thick
¾ teaspoon salt
¾ teaspoon freshly ground pepper
8 flour tortillas
½ cup taco sauce

1. In a large skillet, melt the butter in the oil over moderate heat. Add the onions and cook over moderately low heat, stirring occasionally, until softened and browned, about 40 minutes. Set aside.

2. Preheat the broiler. Season the steak on both sides with ½ teaspoon of the salt and ½ teaspoon of the pepper. Broil 4 to 5 inches from the heat for about 5 minutes on each side for medium-rare. Let the meat stand for about 20 minutes.

3. Halve the steak lengthwise and cut diagonally across the grain into very thin strips, about ¼ inch thick.

4. If the tortillas are not very pliable, warm them in the oven for about 15 seconds. Spread 1 tablespoon of the taco sauce over the middle of each tortilla. Put a layer of meat on top of the taco sauce and then a layer of the browned onions. Season with the remaining salt and pepper. Fold in one side of the tortillas over the filling. Bring up the bottom and roll snugly. Wrap each burrito separately in a 12-inch square of aluminum foil. *(The recipe can be prepared to this point up to 3 hours ahead.)*

5. When ready to serve, preheat the oven to 500°. Put the burritos on a baking sheet and bake for 5 minutes, or until just heated through.

—*F&W*

• • •

BEEFSTEAK RANCHERO WITH FRESH TOMATO SALSA

These tasty steaks, which marinate overnight, are good with hot corn tortillas, fresh tomato salsa, a pot of pinto beans and corn on the cob.
♟ Ice-cold imported beer, such as Ringnes or Carlsberg

——————— *2 to 3 Servings* ———————
1 small onion, thinly sliced
1 large garlic clove, thinly sliced
½ cup chopped fresh coriander
1 fresh jalapeño pepper, seeded and thinly sliced
1 medium tomato, thinly sliced
2 large trimmed shell steaks, about 1 inch thick
½ teaspoon salt
Fresh Tomato Salsa (recipe follows)

1. In a shallow glass dish, layer half the onion, garlic, coriander, jalapeño and tomato. Season the steaks on both sides with the salt and place in the dish. Cover with the remaining onion, garlic, coriander, jalapeño and tomato. Cover and refrigerate for 12 hours or overnight.

2. Light a charcoal fire. Place a grill about 5 inches over the glowing coals and heat for 5 minutes. Remove the steaks from the dish, brushing off any vegetables that cling. Grill the steaks, turning with tongs every 3 minutes, to the desired degree of doneness: if the meat is chilled, the steaks will take 10 to 12 minutes for medium-rare. Serve with Fresh Tomato Salsa on the side.

—*Jim Fobel*

• • •

FRESH TOMATO SALSA

————— *Makes About 1½ Cups* —————
2 large juicy tomatoes, about ½ pound each
¼ cup chopped fresh coriander
2 tablespoons minced onion, preferably white
1 small fresh jalapeño pepper, seeded and minced
2 tablespoons olive oil
½ teaspoon salt
¼ teaspoon freshly ground black pepper

Cut the tomatoes into ½-inch dice and put them in a medium bowl. Stir in the coriander, onion, jalapeño pepper, olive oil, salt and black pepper. Set aside at room temperature for up to 2 hours or cover and refrigerate. Let return to room temperature before serving.

—*Jim Fobel*

• • •

STUFFED FLANK STEAK

This is very good when made one day ahead, refrigerated and reheated or served at room temperature for lunch the next day.

——————— **6 to 8 Servings** ———————

¾ pound bulk breakfast sausage
2 flank steaks (1½ pounds each), trimmed of excess fat
1¼ teaspoons salt
¾ teaspoon freshly ground pepper
½ teaspoon thyme
1 teaspoon paprika
2 garlic cloves, crushed through a press
2 tablespoons safflower or corn oil
2 medium green bell peppers, cut into ¼-inch strips
4 small onions—2 halved and thinly sliced, 2 chopped
1 tablespoon juniper berries, finely crushed
2 tablespoons olive oil
2 medium carrots, cut into ½-inch slices
2 medium celery ribs, chopped
1 tablespoon minced parsley
1 can (28 ounces) Italian peeled tomatoes, drained
1½ cups dry red wine
½ cup beef stock or canned low-sodium broth diluted with water

1. In a large heavy skillet, cook the sausage over moderately high heat until brown and crumbly, 5 to 7 minutes. Remove with a slotted spoon and transfer to a medium bowl. Discard any fat and wipe out the skillet.

BACK-TO-BASICS STEAK DINNER

Forgoing fancier cuts of beef, such as tournedos, Lee Bailey prefers basic cuts, such as the flank steak in this menu. The steak is rolled around a sausage, green pepper and onion stuffing and then oven-braised in a red wine and tomato sauce. Serves 6 to 8.

Stuffed Flank Steak (p. 56)

Mashed Turnips and Potatoes (p. 127)

Warm Broccoli Salad (p. 142)

❦ Dry Red Wine

Natchez Lemon Cake (p. 236)

Coffee

---

2. Meanwhile, pound the steaks with the coarse side of a metal meat tenderizer for about 30 seconds on each side. In a small bowl, combine 1 teaspoon of the salt, ½ teaspoon of the pepper, the thyme, paprika and garlic, and rub into 1 side of each steak.

3. In the skillet, heat the safflower oil over moderately high heat. Add the green peppers and sliced onions, cover and cook, stirring occasionally, until the vegetables are wilted and softened, about 10 minutes.

4. Add the juniper berries to the sausage and mix well with your hands, breaking up any large pieces of meat. Spread half the sausage mixture evenly over each steak and press down gently. Distribute the cooked peppers and onions on top.

5. Roll the steaks, starting from a long side, jelly-roll style, being careful not to squeeze the sausage out. Secure each steak roll with kitchen string tied at 2-inch intervals.

6. Preheat the oven to 300°. In a large flameproof casserole, heat the olive oil over high heat. Add the steak rolls, leaving space between them, and cook, turning, until browned all over, about 5 minutes. Remove from the pan and season with the remaining ¼ teaspoon each salt and pepper.

7. Pour out any oil from the pan and add the chopped onions, the carrots, celery and parsley. Arrange the meat on top. Add the tomatoes, wine and stock. Bring to a boil and remove from the heat. Cover tightly, transfer to the oven and braise, turning once, for 2 hours.

8. Remove from the oven. Take off the strings and set the steak rolls aside on a platter. Strain the liquid from the pan, reserving the vegetables. In a food processor, puree the vegetables and return to the pan with the liquid; stir to combine. Add the meat to the sauce. Let cool for at least 30 minutes to allow the meat to absorb the juices, or cover and refrigerate overnight. Thinly slice and serve with the sauce on the side.

—*Lee Bailey*

• • •

KOREAN BEEF RIBS

For their beef ribs, Korean-American butchers traditionally slice three or four ribs across the bone ½ inch thick. The result is thin pieces of meat with three or four pieces of bone in them. Alternatively, you can use boneless meat cut from meaty short ribs (also called chuck cross ribs).

Serve these with spicy pickled vegetables, especially Korean *kim chee* if you can find it, lightly cooked spinach tossed with sesame oil and rice. The marinade is also delicious with chicken and pork. Plan on marinating the ribs the night before you cook them.

─────── **6 Servings** ───────

5 pounds flanken-style beef ribs, sawed across the bones into ½-inch-wide strips
⅓ cup sake
¼ cup granulated sugar
1 cup soy sauce
7 large garlic cloves, minced
4 scallions (white and 2 inches of green), minced
3 tablespoons (packed) dark brown sugar
½ teaspoon Oriental sesame oil
2 tablespoons vegetable oil
¼ teaspoon freshly ground pepper

1. Rub the ribs on both sides with the sake and granulated sugar and place them in a large glass baking dish or enameled roasting pan. Cover and let stand for 10 to 15 minutes.

2. Meanwhile, in a medium bowl, combine the soy sauce, garlic, scallions, brown sugar and sesame oil. Add 1⅓ cups water and stir until the sugar dissolves. Stir in the vegetable oil and pepper. Pour this marinade over the ribs and turn to coat evenly. Cover and refrigerate overnight. Let the ribs return to room temperature before cooking.

3. Light the grill or preheat the boiler. Grill the ribs over a hot fire: First sear the ribs on each side for 30 seconds, then adjust the rack further from the coals and grill until tender, about 5 minutes per side. Alternatively, broil the ribs about 3 inches from the heat until browned and medium well done, 2 to 3 minutes on each side.

—*Linda Burum & Linda Merinoff*

• • •

INDONESIAN CURRIED BEEF RIBS

These ribs will blacken on the outside because of the sugar in the marinade. The beef ribs marinate for at least 2 (and up to 8) hours, so plan accordingly.

─────── **6 Servings** ───────

6 pounds beef short ribs, trimmed of fat
2-inch cube of tamarind pulp*
12 garlic cloves
1 large onion, coarsely chopped
2 tablespoons chopped fresh ginger
4 small fresh hot chile peppers, seeded (optional)
2 tablespoons curry powder
½ cup ketjap manis*, preferably homemade (p. 255) or 2 tablespoons brown sugar mixed with 6 tablespoons soy sauce
2 teaspoons freshly ground black pepper
*Available at Indonesian or Middle Eastern markets

1. Arrange the ribs in a single layer in a large glass or enameled baking dish.

2. In a small bowl, soak the tamarind pulp in ½ cup of hot water for 30 minutes. Strain through a fine sieve, pressing on the pulp to release as much liquid as possible.

3. In a blender or food processor, combine the tamarind liquid with the garlic, onion, ginger, chiles, curry powder, *ketjap manis* and black pepper. Puree until smooth.

4. Rub the curry mixture into the ribs. Cover and let marinate at room temperature for 2 to 4 hours or refrigerate for up to 8 hours. Let return to room temperature before cooking.

5. Light the grill or preheat the oven to 450°. Grill the ribs, turning frequently, until tender and lightly charred, 45 to 60 minutes. Alternatively, bake the ribs in a single layer on a rack set in a roasting pan for 35 minutes. Turn the ribs over and continue to cook until dark brown and crisp, about 10 minutes longer.

—*Linda Burum & Linda Merinoff*

• • •

ANISE SHORT RIBS OF BEEF

This rich, aromatic dish is even better when prepared two days in advance and refrigerated, or two weeks ahead and frozen. The fat can then be removed easily, and the dish rewarmed before serving.

❡ Dry rosé, such as 1986 Domaines Ott Bandol Rosé, or 1986 Simi Rosé of Cabernet Sauvignon

─────── **12 Servings** ───────

4 pounds beef short ribs, cut into 3-inch pieces and trimmed of excess fat
4 garlic cloves, sliced
1 medium onion, thinly sliced
1-inch piece of fresh ginger, peeled and thinly sliced
1 teaspoon crushed hot red pepper
⅓ cup ketjap manis,* preferably homemade (p. 256)
2 salam leaves*
2 slices of laos root (galingale)*
½ teaspoon (3 or 4 lobes) star anise*
2 tablespoons (packed) brown sugar
3 tablespoons cider vinegar
*Available at Asian markets

1. Put the beef ribs, garlic, onion, ginger and hot pepper into a large flameproof casserole. Cook, stirring, over moderate heat until the beef is no longer pink, about 3 minutes.

2. Add the *ketjap manis*, salam leaves, laos root, star anise, brown sugar, vinegar and 3½ cups of water. Bring to a boil, reduce the heat to moderately low and simmer, covered, for 2 hours, or until the beef is tender and the sauce has thickened. (Should the liquid evaporate too quickly, add another ½ cup of water. If the meat is cooked and the sauce is still thin, boil until the liquid is reduced to a light coating consistency.) Skim any fat from the surface. Serve warm.

—Copeland Marks

• • •

COMMANDER'S PALACE CHOPPED SIRLOIN STANLEY

Emeril Lagasse, executive chef of Commander's Palace in New Orleans, on the subject of the horseradish sauce and sautéed bananas he serves with this chopped sirloin dish at the restaurant: "The combination is unusual. I remember when I first read about it in an old cookbook, I thought, My God, who is going to eat this thing? But then after you taste the bananas that have absorbed the horseradish sauce, you see it is an excellent combination."

——— **5 Generous Servings** ———
2 tablespoons unsalted butter
5 bananas, split lengthwise and
*   halved crosswise*
3 pounds freshly ground lean beef
*   sirloin*
1 shallot, minced
2 garlic cloves, minced
¼ cup minced red onion
½ cup minced red bell pepper
¼ cup chopped parsley
½ teaspoon salt

¼ teaspoon freshly ground white
*   pepper*
2 eggs
¼ cup Worcestershire sauce
½ cup fresh bread crumbs
Creamy Horseradish Sauce
*   (p. 251), warm*

1. Preheat the broiler. Meanwhile, in a large heavy skillet, melt 1 tablespoon of the butter over high heat. When the foam subsides, place half the bananas in the pan and cook, turning once, until they are brown and crusty all over, about 5 minutes. Remove to a plate and cover loosely with foil to keep warm. Repeat with the remaining butter and bananas.

2. In a large bowl, place the ground beef, shallot, garlic, onion, bell pepper, parsley, salt, white pepper, eggs, Worcestershire sauce and bread crumbs. Toss the mixture together with a fork until well mixed without mashing the meat. Shape into 5 round patties 1-inch-thick.

3. Place the patties on a baking sheet and broil 4 inches from the heat until nicely browned, 4 minutes on the first side and 3 minutes on the second side for medium-rare.

4. For each serving, spread about ⅓ cup of the Creamy Horseradish Sauce on a dinner plate, place the hamburger on one side of the sauce and fan out 4 pieces of sautéed banana on the other side.

—Commander's Palace, New Orleans

• • •

JEAN-LOUIS PALLADIN'S STEAK AND EGG BURGERS

Jean-Louis Palladin, French-born chef of Jean-Louis Restaurant in Washington, D.C., prefers to make his hamburgers with sirloin. "I also like what you Americans call the flank because it is really tasty. I cook the hamburgers in the pan with extra-virgin olive oil. In the same pan I sauté an egg, which I serve on top of the hamburger. My mother does that, and I love it."

——— **2 Servings** ———
10 ounces freshly ground beef sirloin
½ cup minced shallots (about 3)
½ teaspoon salt
¼ teaspoon freshly ground pepper
1 tablespoon extra-virgin olive oil
2 slices of pumpernickel bread
2 eggs

1. In a medium bowl, place the ground beef, shallots, salt and pepper. Toss with a fork until well mixed. Shape into 2 round patties ¾-inch-thick.

2. Brush a large cast-iron skillet with about ½ teaspoon of the oil. Preheat the pan over moderately high heat until the pan is very hot, about 5 minutes.

3. Place the hamburgers in the pan and cook until nicely browned, 3 minutes on each side for medium-rare. Remove the pan from the heat and place each burger on a slice of pumpernickel bread.

4. Add the remaining 2½ teaspoons oil to the pan and reduce the heat to moderately low. Crack the eggs into the pan and cook sunnyside up until the white is set, 1 to 2 minutes. Place the eggs on top of the burgers and serve at once.

—Jean-Louis Palladin, Jean-Louis
*   Restaurant, Washington, D.C.*

• • •

'21' CLUB HAMBURGER

At the '21' Club, a piece of frozen herb butter is buried in the hamburger meat to keep it as moist as possible. Besides giving flavor, the frozen piece of butter prevents the burger from overcooking, and when it melts it makes the hamburger juicier.

——— *1 Generous Serving* ———
4 thin slices of tomato
2 thin slices of red onion
2 teaspoons fresh lemon juice
3 tablespoons olive oil
1 tablespoon finely chopped fresh basil
⅜ teaspoon salt
⅜ teaspoon freshly ground pepper
2 large slices of Italian peasant bread, cut about ½ inch thick
12 ounces freshly ground beef sirloin or chuck (22 percent fat)
1 tablespoon Herb Butter, frozen (p. 252)

1. Preheat the broiler. Put the tomato and red onion slices in a small bowl. Drizzle the lemon juice and 2 tablespoons of the olive oil over the vegetables. Sprinkle on the basil, ⅛ teaspoon each of the salt and pepper and toss.

2. Brush the bread slices on one side with the remaining 1 tablespoon olive oil. Broil about 4 inches from the heat, turning once, until lightly toasted, about 1 minute on each side.

3. Handling the meat as little as possible, shape it into a round ball, and with your finger, press an indentation into the middle. Place 1 tablespoon of the frozen Herb Butter into the hole and enclose with the meat. Flatten each ball into a ¾-inch-thick patty and season both sides with the remaining ¼ teaspoon each salt and pepper.

ELEGANT HAMBURGER DINNER

These days elegant food has gone casual and vice versa. It would be hard to find a food more casual than the hamburger, or an ingredient more elegant than a truffle, making this dinner menu ever-so au courant. Serves 4.

🍷 *Kirs*

Belgian Endive Spears with Sour Cream and Caviar

Black-Truffled Hamburgers (p. 59)

Pan-Roasted Potatoes with Lemon and Marjoram (p. 122)

Steamed Green Beans Tossed with Olive Oil, Cracked Pepper and Coarse Salt

🍷 *Red Burgundy, such as La Tâche, or California Zinfandel, such as Fetzer*

Chicory and Dandelion Salad with a Light Vinaigrette

Melon Tart with Muscat de Beaumes de Venise (p. 228)

🍷 *Muscat de Beaumes de Venise*

Café Filtre

4. Broil the hamburger about 4 inches from the heat, turning once, until it is nicely browned, 4 minutes on the first side and 3 minutes on the second side for medium-rare.

5. Sandwich the hamburger between the toasted bread slices and serve the sliced tomato and onion on the side of the plate.

— *'21' Club, New York City*

• • •

BLACK-TRUFFLED HAMBURGERS

For cooking on an outdoor grill, I use beef that has 22 percent fat; for an indoor griddle, 18 percent. On a charcoal grill the fat sort of vaporizes, and you need a little bit more. Whereas on a griddle, the fat doesn't render out as much. I use chuck or sirloin. I think it's a waste to use a very expensive cut. There isn't much flavor.
🍷 The fitting drink with this sandwich is a luscious, old-fashioned, deep red, rich and powerful Burgundy—a La Tâche, any wine made by Roumier (his own or Comte de Vogüé) or a Morey-Saint-Denis. Use a balloon glass, so the perfume of the wine and the truffled beef hits your brain at the same time.

——— *4 Servings* ———
2 pounds freshly ground beef sirloin or chuck
2 ounces fresh black truffle, finely chopped
¼ cup Lemon Mayonnaise (p. 251)
2 teaspoons salt
1 teaspoon freshly ground pepper
3 tablespoons unsalted butter
4 English muffins, split

1. In a large bowl, place the ground beef, truffle, Lemon Mayonnaise, salt and pepper. Toss the ingredients together with a fork until well mixed. Cover and set aside at room temperature to blend the flavors, about 2 hours.

2. Preheat the broiler. Shape the mixture into 4 round patties 1-inch-thick and place them on a baking sheet.

3. Broil the hamburgers 4 inches from the heat until nicely browned, 4 minutes on the first side and 3 minutes on the second side, for medium-rare.

4. Meanwhile, toast and butter the English muffins. Serve the truffled hamburgers between the toasted muffins.

— *Jeremiah Tower*

• • •

JULIA CHILD'S SOUR CREAM BURGER

I like meat that has at least 20 percent fat. You've got to have fat in it, or it doesn't have the taste. The hamburger shouldn't be patted. It should be loosely formed, just enough to hold it together.

❦ California Zinfandel, such as 1986 Fetzer

——————— 1 Serving ———————

5 ounces freshly ground beef chuck
    (20 percent fat)
1 tablespoon sour cream
1 large pinch of thyme
1 teaspoon grated onion
¼ teaspoon salt
⅛ teaspoon freshly ground pepper
French bread roll or 2 large slices of
    crusty French bread or a toasted
    English muffin
Unsalted butter

1. In a medium bowl, place the ground beef, sour cream, thyme, onion, salt and pepper. Toss the ingredients together with a fork until well mixed, without mashing the meat, and shape into a round 1-inch-thick patty.

2. Set a ridged iron skillet or grill pan over moderately high heat and preheat for 5 minutes.

3. Place the patty in the pan and cook until nicely browned, 3 minutes. Turn the patty and cook for 2 minutes on the second side for medium-rare.

4. Meanwhile, toast and butter the French bread. Serve the hamburger on the toasted bread.

—Julia Child

• • •

NO-APOLOGIES MEAT LOAF

This is basic beef loaf, with a touch of onion and green pepper, topped with strips of bacon. I think of it as the instantly recognizable truck stop/diner/hash house standard American meat loaf. Of course, it's good made at home too, particularly if you follow the advice of one diner cook I asked, who confided that the secret of her recipe was "ketchup in and ketchup on."

❦ A soft, rich red wine, such as an Australian Shiraz, would echo the direct, appealing flavors here. Either the 1984 Wolf Blass Bilyara Cellars or 1984 Chateau Tahbilk would be excellent.

——————— 6 to 8 Servings ———————

3 tablespoons unsalted butter
1 large onion, finely diced
1 medium green bell pepper, finely
    diced
1 large celery rib, finely diced
1 teaspoon thyme
2 pounds lean ground beef,
    preferably sirloin
½ cup old-fashioned rolled oats
⅔ cup ketchup
2 eggs, lightly beaten
2 teaspoons salt
1½ teaspoons freshly ground pepper
3 slices of bacon, halved crosswise

1. In a large skillet, melt the butter over moderate heat. Add the onion, green pepper, celery and thyme, reduce the heat to low and cook, covered, stirring once or twice, until the vegetables are very soft, about 20 minutes. Remove from the heat; cool to room temperature.

2. Preheat the oven to 350°. In a large bowl, combine the cooked vegetables and the beef. Add the oats, ⅓ cup of the ketchup and the eggs, salt and pepper; mix well.

3. Spoon the meat mixture into a large shallow baking dish. Form the meat into a flat loaf about 2 inches high and smooth the top with the back of a spoon. Spread the remaining ⅓ cup ketchup over the loaf; arrange the bacon strips on top.

4. Bake the meat loaf for 1 hour, or until it is just cooked through and shows no trace of pink. (A thermometer will register 145° in the center of the loaf.) Let the meat loaf stand for about 10 minutes before slicing and serving.

—Michael McLaughlin

• • •

BEEF, SAUSAGE AND SPINACH LOAF WITH TOMATO-OLIVE SAUCE

If you think this sounds rather like a large meatball, sliced, you're right. It's good served with a steamed or sautéed green vegetable and mashed potatoes flavored with a hearty handful of grated Parmesan cheese. Reheated leftovers make splendid hero sandwiches, especially when topped with the last of the tomato sauce and a bit of melted mozzarella.

❦ This peppery meat loaf, with its highly seasoned tomato and olive sauce, needs a straightforward gutsy red, such as 1985 Corvo or Torres Coronas, to match.

——————— 8 to 10 Servings ———————

⅓ cup olive oil
1 large onion, finely diced
4 garlic cloves, minced
1 teaspoon basil
1 teaspoon oregano
1 teaspoon thyme
1 teaspoon crushed hot red pepper
2 packages (10 ounces each) frozen
    spinach—thawed, squeezed dry
    and finely chopped
2 pounds lean ground beef,
    preferably sirloin
1 pound Italian-style sweet sausage,
    removed from its casing and
    crumbled

¾ *cup fine dry bread crumbs*
3 *eggs, lightly beaten*
⅓ *cup freshly grated Parmesan*
 cheese
1½ *teaspoons salt*
Tomato-Olive Sauce (p. 249)

1. In a large skillet, heat the olive oil over high heat. Add the onion, garlic, basil, oregano, thyme and hot pepper. Reduce the heat to low and cook, covered, stirring once or twice, until the onion is very tender, about 20 minutes.

2. Uncover, add the spinach and cook, stirring to break up any clumps, for 3 minutes. Let cool to room temperature.

3. Preheat the oven to 350°. In a large bowl, combine the beef and sausage. Stir in the spinach mixture, bread crumbs, eggs, Parmesan cheese and salt; mix well. In a large shallow baking dish, form the meat into a rounded loaf and smooth the top with the back of a spoon.

4. Bake the meat loaf for about 1½ hours, or until it is well browned. (A thermometer will register 160° to 165° in the center of the loaf.)

5. Let the meat loaf stand for about 10 minutes before slicing and serving. Pass the Tomato-Olive Sauce on the side.

—*Michael McLaughlin*

• • •

DOUBLE-MUSHROOM PORK AND VEAL LOAF WITH THYME

Two kinds of mushrooms and pork and veal combine in a rich, subtle meat loaf that is as hearty and reassuring as comfort cooking should be. The plainest of potato preparations and the simplest of green vegetables are all this dish needs by way of accompaniment.

♟ The earthy flavors of mushroom and thyme call for a wine with comparable pungency, such as a stylish California Pinot Noir—preferably a 1986 Acacia Carneros "St. Clair," Saintsbury Carneros or Monterey Vineyard.

DELUXE DINER DINNER

This menu pays homage to an all-American institution, although this thyme-scented pork and veal loaf with wild mushrooms is only a kissing cousin to the traditional ketchup-covered diner offering. Serves 6.

♟ *Cocktails*

Spiced Almonds

Double-Mushroom Pork and Veal Loaf with Thyme (p. 61)

Diner Home Fries (p. 122)

Modern Mixed Veggies (p. 129)

♟ *Australian Shiraz, such as 1984 Wolf Blass Bilyara Cellars or 1984 Chateau Tahbilk*

Star Glazed Apples (p. 214) with Crème Fraîche

Espresso

Calvados

---

6 to 8 Servings

1½ *cups chicken stock or canned*
 broth
1 *ounce (about 1 cup) dried wild*
 mushrooms, such as porcini or
 shiitake, rinsed
¼ *cup rice*
½ *pound fresh mushrooms*
6 *tablespoons unsalted butter*
1 *medium onion, chopped*
½ *cup heavy cream*
3 *tablespoons minced fresh thyme or*
 2 *teaspoons dried*

---

2 *garlic cloves, minced*
2 *teaspoons salt*
1 *teaspoon freshly ground pepper*
1½ *pounds ground veal*
1 *pound ground pork (about 20*
 percent fat)
2 *eggs, lightly beaten*

1. In a small saucepan, bring the chicken stock to a boil. Put the dried mushrooms in a small heatproof bowl and pour on the stock. Let stand, covered, until softened, about 30 minutes.

2. Meanwhile, in a small saucepan, bring 1½ cups of water to a boil, add the rice, cover and cook over low heat until softened, about 12 minutes. Drain and set aside.

3. Remove the soaked mushrooms, reserving the liquid. Strain the stock through a fine sieve or several layers of dampened cheesecloth. In a food processor, combine the soaked mushrooms and fresh mushrooms; finely chop.

4. In a large skillet, melt the butter over high heat. Add the onion and the chopped mushrooms and cook, stirring frequently, until lightly browned, about 8 minutes.

5. Stir in the reserved stock, the cream, cooked rice, thyme and garlic. Cook, stirring frequently, until the mixture is reduced and very thick, about 5 minutes. Remove from the heat, stir in the salt and pepper and let cool to room temperature.

6. Preheat the oven to 350°. In a large bowl, combine the veal and pork. Add the mushroom mixture and the eggs and mix well. Transfer to a large shallow baking dish and form into a flat loaf.

7. Bake the meat loaf until a thermometer inserted in the center registers 160°, about 1 hour and 10 minutes. Let the loaf rest on a rack for about 10 minutes before slicing and serving.

—*Michael McLaughlin*

• • •

MEAT

SOUTHWESTERN CHILI-CHEESE MEAT LOAF

The goal here is a meat loaf as intensely flavored and spicy as a bowl of good chili. Instead of the usual potato/vegetable accompaniment, serve cilantro-spiked white rice and a crisp green salad.

——————— *6 to 8 Servings* ———————
¼ cup olive oil
1 medium onion, finely diced
1 red bell pepper, finely diced
4 garlic cloves, minced
2 fresh jalapeño peppers, minced
2 tablespoons plain (unseasoned, unblended) chili powder
2 teaspoons salt
2 teaspoons oregano
2 teaspoons ground cumin
1 can (28 ounces) Italian peeled tomatoes, crushed and well drained
1½ pounds lean ground beef, preferably sirloin
½ pound lean ground pork
1 cup fine dry bread crumbs
2 eggs, lightly beaten
1 cup corn kernels, canned or frozen
3 scallions, thinly sliced
½ pound sharp Cheddar cheese, grated

1. In a large skillet, heat the olive oil over high heat. Add the onion, bell pepper, garlic, jalapeño peppers, chili powder, salt, oregano and cumin. Cover, reduce the heat to low and cook, stirring once or twice, until the vegetables are soft, about 10 minutes.

2. Add the tomatoes and cook, covered, stirring once or twice, for 10 minutes longer. Remove from the heat and let cool to room temperature.

3. Preheat the oven to 350°. In a large bowl, combine the beef and pork. Add the tomato mixture, bread crumbs and eggs; mix well. Add the corn and scallions and mix to distribute evenly. Transfer the meat mixture to a shallow baking dish and form into a flat loaf.

4. Bake until a thermometer inserted in the center registers 160°, about 1 hour. Pour off any grease or pan juices. Sprinkle the cheese evenly over the loaf and return it to the oven until the cheese is just melted, about 4 minutes.

—*Michael McLaughlin*

• • •

PRETTY-MUCH PATE

Though differences in technique, ingredients and finished product abound, there is an essential spicy, meaty richness common to both meat loaf and pâté. Here I've linked the two by emphasizing traditional pâté seasonings—thyme, shallots, nutmeg and bay—and by the chicken livers in the center. Serve this meat loaf hot with sweet and sour cabbage and a gratin of potatoes, or offer it cold with coleslaw, potato salad and a beer.

——————— *8 to 10 Servings* ———————
4 tablespoons unsalted butter
1 medium onion, chopped
1 large leek (white part only), finely chopped
3 shallots, minced
4 garlic cloves, minced
1 tablespoon thyme
3 bay leaves
½ teaspoon freshly grated nutmeg
1 pound lean ground beef, preferably sirloin
1 pound lean ground veal
1 pound ground pork
3 eggs, lightly beaten
½ cup fine dry bread crumbs
½ cup minced Italian flat-leaf parsley
1 tablespoon salt
1½ teaspoons freshly ground pepper
½ pound chicken livers, trimmed and cut into ½-inch chunks

1. In a large skillet, melt the butter over moderate heat. Add the onion, leek, shallots, garlic, thyme, bay leaves and nutmeg. Reduce the heat to low, cover and cook, stirring once or twice, until very tender, about 20 minutes. Remove from the heat and let cool to room temperature. Remove the bay leaves.

2. Preheat the oven to 350°. In a large bowl, combine the beef, veal and pork. Stir in the leek mixture, the eggs, bread crumbs, parsley, salt and pepper; mix well.

3. Place half the meat mixture in a large oval gratin or baking dish. Arrange the chicken livers down the center of the meat. Put the remaining meat mixture on top and press to shape into a loaf and enclose the chicken livers.

4. Bake the meat loaf until a thermometer registers 165° in the center of the loaf, about 1 hour and 10 minutes. Let the meat loaf stand for 10 minutes before slicing and serving.

—*Michael McLaughlin*

• • •

HOT-SWEET MEATBALLS WITH SHRIMP AND SNOW PEAS

The slight sweetness of this spicy dish is typically Indonesian.

12 Servings
——————— *(with other dishes)* ———————
1 pound ground beef
1 egg, beaten
½ teaspoon salt
1 medium onion, sliced
2 garlic cloves, sliced
1 to 2 teaspoons sliced fresh hot chile pepper, or 1 teaspoon crushed hot red pepper

1½ cups homemade coconut milk, or
¾ cup canned unsweetened
coconut milk* diluted with ¾ cup
water
2 tablespoons corn or peanut oil
1 salam leaf*
1 slice of laos root (galingale)*
¼ teaspoon shrimp paste*
½ pound fresh medium shrimp,
shelled and deveined
2 teaspoons brown sugar
¼ pound snow peas
1 medium tomato, cut into
½-inch cubes
*Available at Asian markets

1. Mix the beef, egg and salt together.
Shape into small meatballs about ½ inch
in diameter.

2. Steam the meatballs on a heatproof
dish for 10 minutes in a Chinese-style
steamer or on a rack in a covered saucepan. Remove the meatballs from the
steamer and set aside. *(The recipe can be
prepared to this point up to 6 hours ahead
and refrigerated.)*

3. In a food processor, combine the
onion, garlic, hot pepper and ¼ cup of the
coconut milk. Process to a smooth paste,
about 30 seconds.

4. In a large skillet, heat the oil over
moderate heat. Add the spice paste and
stir-fry until almost dry, about 2 minutes.
Add the salam leaf, laos root, shrimp
paste, fresh shrimp and brown sugar. Stir-
fry until the shrimp are pink and loosely
curled, 2 to 3 minutes.

5. Add the remaining 1¼ cups coconut
milk and bring to a boil. Add the meatballs and simmer for 10 minutes, turning
and basting frequently.

6. Add the snow peas and tomato and
cook until the snow peas are bright green
and just tender, about 2 minutes.
—*Copeland Marks*
• • •

INDONESIAN RIJSSTAFEL

A *rijsstafel* is a traditional Indonesian
meal in which rice (*rijsstafel* means
rice table) and at least five other dishes
are served buffet style. This example
from Copeland Marks will serve 12.

SMOKY BLACK BEAN CHILI

I prefer the small, thin-skinned black, or
turtle, beans in chili rather than the usual
kidney beans. A splash of bourbon gives
this deep-flavored chili a richer taste.

———— *Makes About 4 Cups* ————
½ ounce dried whole chile such as
ancho, pasilla or green (see Note)
¼ cup plus 2 tablespoons olive oil
1 pound pork shoulder stew meat,
cut into small dice
1 pound beef chuck, cut into small
dice
5 large garlic cloves, chopped
1 large Spanish onion, chopped
¼ pound andouille sausage, peeled
and cut into medium dice
1 tablespoon ground cumin
2 tablespoons ground chiles, such as
ancho or pasilla (see Note)
1 can (35 ounces) Italian peeled
tomatoes, chopped, liquid
reserved
¼ cup bourbon
1 tablespoon oregano, preferably
Mexican or Greek
1 can (15 ounces) black beans,
drained
¼ cup tomato paste
Salt and freshly ground black pepper

1. Soak the whole dried chile in ½ cup
of hot water until soft, about 20 minutes.
Chop the chile and reserve the liquid.

2. Meanwhile, in a large flameproof
casserole, heat ¼ cup of the olive oil over
high heat. Add the pork and beef in small
batches and cook, turning once, until
browned all over, about 3 minutes a side.
Using a slotted spoon, remove the meat to
a plate or a bowl as it is cooked.

3. Reduce the heat to low and add the
remaining 2 tablespoons olive oil to the
casserole. Add the garlic, onion and sausage and cook, stirring occasionally, until
the onion is soft, about 10 minutes.

4. Increase the heat to moderate and

add the cumin and ground chiles. Cook, stirring occasionally, for 5 minutes.

5. Stir in the tomatoes and their liquid, the chile and its soaking liquid, the browned meat, bourbon and oregano. Reduce the heat to low, cover and simmer, stirring occasionally, for 1½ hours.

6. Stir in the black beans and tomato paste and salt and black pepper to taste. Simmer briefly to blend the flavors, 3 to 4 minutes. Remove from the heat.

NOTE: Dried chiles and ground chiles are available at Latin American and specialty food stores. You may also order them by mail from The Chile Shop, 109 E. Water St., Santa Fe, NM 87501; 505-983-6080 or Aphrodisia Products, 282 Bleecker St., New York, NY 10014; 212-989-6440.

—*Marcia Kiesel*

• • •

PORK ROAST WITH GARLIC AND FENNEL

Author John Mariani's wife, Galina, who is French and Russian, prepares this traditional Italian roast with a double dose of garlic—half of it is crushed, seasoned and spread over the roast as a marinade, half is cooked whole and eaten along with the meat.

──────── *4 to 6 Servings* ────────
12 garlic cloves—6 peeled, 6 unpeeled
1½ teaspoons coarse (kosher) salt
1 teaspoon freshly ground pepper
1 teaspoon fennel seeds, crushed
1½ tablespoons olive oil
2½ pounds boneless pork loin roast, trimmed of excess fat and tied

1. In a mortar, crush the 6 peeled garlic cloves with a pestle. Add the salt, pepper, fennel seeds and olive oil. Crush to a paste.

2. Score the pork roast ¼ inch deep at 1½-inch intervals. Rub the garlic paste over the entire surface. Cover with plastic wrap and refrigerate for at least 4 hours, or overnight.

3. Remove the roast from the refrigerator and let it return to room temperature, about 1½ hours. Meanwhile, preheat the oven to 375°.

4. Place the roast in a lightly oiled, large roasting pan. Roast until the meat reaches an internal temperature of 160°, about 1 hour and 15 minutes. (Do not overcook, or the meat will toughen.)

5. Meanwhile, in a small saucepan of boiling water, cook the remaining 6 unpeeled garlic cloves for 10 minutes. Drain and set aside. Let the roast sit for 5 minutes, then carve into slices and serve with the whole garlic cloves in their skins.

—*Galina Mariani*

• • •

ITALIAN HOME-STYLE MENU

Here's a nice, straightforward meat-and-potatoes meal, Italian style. If you are a fan of broccoli rabe, you could sauté some in olive oil, perhaps with some slivered pancetta, and serve it in place of, or in addition to, the zucchini. Serves 4 to 6.

🍷 *Campari and Sodas*
Assorted Olives
────────────
Pork Roast with Garlic and Fennel (p. 64)

Grated Zucchini with Tomatoes (p. 128)

Oven-Roasted Potatoes

🍷 *Robust Red, such as 1986 Corvo or 1986 Frescobaldi Chianti*
────────────
Cappuccino Crème Caramel (p. 201)

Espresso

CHINESE ROAST PORK

This marinated and highly flavored roast pork can be shredded and used in a variety of dishes, including noodle dishes, stir-fries, or even sandwiches. Note that the pork must marinate for a minimum of 4 hours.

──────── *6 to 8 Servings* ────────
2 pounds boneless pork loin, trimmed of excess fat
3 tablespoons oyster sauce*
3 tablespoons hoisin sauce*
3 tablespoons honey
2½ tablespoons dark soy sauce*
2½ tablespoons light soy sauce
2 tablespoons blended whiskey
1 teaspoon five-spice powder*
½ teaspoon salt (optional)
Pinch of white pepper
*Available at Asian markets

1. Quarter the pork lengthwise into 4 large strips. With the tip of a small knife, pierce the meat at ½-inch intervals.

2. In a medium bowl, whisk together the oyster sauce, hoisin sauce, honey, dark soy sauce, light soy sauce, whiskey, five-spice powder, salt and white pepper.

3. Line a roasting pan with heavy-duty aluminum foil. Arrange the pork strips on the foil in a single layer. Pour the oyster sauce marinade over the meat and let marinate for at least 4 hours, or overnight, in the refrigerator.

4. Preheat the oven to 500°. Roast the pork in the top third of the oven, basting occasionally with the marinade in the pan, for about 45 minutes, until white throughout and caramelized on the outside. If not using at once, let the meat cool, then wrap and refrigerate for up to 5 days or freeze for up to 1 month.

—*Eileen Yin-Fei Lo*

• • •

PORK TENDERLOIN WITH TENDER FENNEL AND GARLIC

The fennel in this recipe is transformed into a meltingly delicious and mild-flavored vegetable. Serve a salad of thinly sliced sweet red peppers, watercress and shallots as a first course.

❦ Echo the spicy flavors in this pork dish with a Pinot Noir that has enough crispness to cut across the unctuousness of the meat. Look for top California examples, such as 1986 Robert Stemmler or 1986 Sinskey.

——————— *4 Servings* ———————
1 teaspoon grated lemon zest
2 large fennel bulbs, quartered and partially cored, plus 2 tablespoons chopped fennel leaves
5 tablespoons extra-virgin olive oil
1 pound pork tenderloin, cut into ¼-inch-thick slices
8 garlic cloves, unpeeled
1 teaspoon salt
¼ cup dry white wine
1 tablespoon fresh lemon juice
2 tablespoons unsalted butter
¼ teaspoon freshly ground pepper

1. In a large shallow baking dish, mix together the lemon zest, 1 tablespoon of the fennel leaves and 2 tablespoons of the olive oil. Toss the pork slices in the marinade and set aside.

2. In a large skillet, heat 2 tablespoons of the olive oil over moderately high heat. Add the fennel bulbs and cook, turning occasionally, until lightly browned all over, about 8 minutes.

3. Add the garlic, ½ teaspoon of the salt and ¼ cup of water. Bring to a boil, cover, reduce the heat to low and simmer until the fennel and garlic are very tender, about 20 minutes.

4. Meanwhile, remove the pork from the marinade and season with the remaining ½ teaspoon salt. In a large skillet, heat the remaining 1 tablespoon oil over moderately high heat. Add the pork to the skillet and cook, in two batches if necessary, until well browned, about 2 minutes on each side. Transfer the meat to a warmed serving platter. Set aside, covered loosely with foil to keep warm.

5. Drain the excess fat from the pan. Add the wine and bring to a boil over high heat, scraping up any brown bits from the bottom of the pan. Boil until reduced by half, about 2 minutes. Whisk in the lemon juice, butter and pepper and remove from the heat. Pour any cooking juices from the fennel into the sauce.

6. To serve, arrange the fennel, garlic and pork on the platter and spoon the sauce over them. Garnish with the remaining 1 tablespoon chopped fennel leaves.

—*Nora Carey*

• • •

PHILIPPINE RIBS ADOBONG

Adobo refers to the method of braising foods in soy sauce, vinegar and garlic. While these ribs are not exactly authentic, we find that the marinade suits them perfectly.

——————— *6 Servings* ———————
4½ to 5 pounds country-style pork loin spareribs
1½ cups distilled white vinegar
⅓ cup soy sauce
2 tablespoons minced garlic
2 imported bay leaves
1 teaspoon salt
¾ teaspoon whole black peppercorns
¾ cup thick unsweetened coconut milk (sometimes called coconut cream)*
*Available at Southeast Asian and Indian markets

1. Cut the exterior fat from the ribs. In a large glass baking dish or enameled roasting pan, combine the vinegar, soy sauce, garlic, bay leaves, salt, peppercorns and ⅓ cup of water. Add the ribs and turn to coat on all sides. Cover and marinate at room temperature for 2 hours, turning the ribs several times.

2. Drain the marinade into 2 large nonreactive skillets. Bring to a boil and add half the ribs to each pan. Cover and simmer over low heat, turning once, until the ribs are barely tender, about 1 hour.

3. Add the coconut milk to the skillets and simmer, covered, until the ribs are tender and cooked through, about 15 minutes longer. Remove the ribs and set aside.

4. Pour all the cooking liquid into one skillet and boil over high heat until reduced to 1 cup, about 20 minutes. Strain the sauce through a fine sieve.

5. Light the grill or preheat the broiler. Give the sauce a stir. When the coals are very hot, brush the ribs with the sauce and grill, turning and basting once, until slightly crisp on the outside, 1 to 3 minutes on each side. Alternatively, brush the ribs with the sauce and broil about 4 inches from the heat until slightly crisp, about 1½ minutes on each side.

—*Linda Burum & Linda Merinoff*

• • •

CHINESE RIBS

These ribs are juicier when cooked in slabs, but if you like your ribs really crisp, you can cut them into individual pieces.

❦ Fruity, spicy white, such as 1986 Gundlach-Bundschu Gewürztraminer or 1987 Clos du Bois Early Harvest Gewürztraminer

——————— *6 Servings* ———————
½ cup soy sauce
⅓ cup plus 1 tablespoon honey
¼ cup hoisin sauce*
6 garlic cloves, minced
3 tablespoons mirin (sweet rice wine)* or dry sherry

¾ teaspoon five-spice powder*
5 pounds pork spareribs
*Available at Asian markets

1. In a small bowl, mix together the soy sauce, honey, hoisin sauce, garlic, *mirin* and five-spice powder.

2. Pour half of this marinade into a large glass baking dish or enameled roasting pan. Add half of the ribs and turn to coat. Place the remaining ribs on top of the first batch and pour on the remaining marinade. Turn the second batch of ribs to coat. Cover and marinate the ribs for 2 to 3 hours at room temperature or overnight in the refrigerator. Let return to room temperature before cooking.

3. Light the grill or preheat the oven to 400°. Grill the ribs, turning and basting occasionally with any remaining marinade, until tender and cooked through, about 45 minutes. Alternatively, spread the ribs on a rack set in a roasting pan and bake for 30 minutes, basting occasionally with the marinade. Reduce the heat to 350° and cook until tender, about 40 minutes longer.

—*Linda Burum & Linda Merinoff*

• • •

THAI LEMON GRASS PORK RIBS

While these ribs can be baked, they are much better grilled because the smoky taste is almost essential. The ribs must marinate for a minimum of 4 hours, so plan accordingly.

——— *6 Servings* ———
4 large stalks of fresh lemon grass*
or ¼ cup dried lemon grass* plus
¼ teaspoon grated lemon zest
5 pounds of baby-back pork ribs in
slabs
2 tablespoons plus 1 teaspoon
minced garlic
4 shallots, minced
3 small fresh green chiles,
preferably serrano, seeded

⅓ cup distilled white vinegar
3 tablespoons fish sauce (nuoc
mam)*
2 tablespoons Oriental sesame oil
2 tablespoons sugar
½ teaspoon salt
Thai Basil Dipping Sauce (p. 250)
*Available at Asian markets

1. If using fresh lemon grass, mince the white bulb and tender part of the stalk. Discard the tops. If using dried lemon grass, soak it with the lemon zest in ⅔ cup of boiling water in a small saucepan for 3 hours. Then simmer over moderate heat until all the liquid is evaporated, about 35 minutes.

2. Score the membrane on the bony side of the ribs in a crosshatch fashion.

3. In a food processor, combine the lemon grass, garlic, shallots, chiles, vinegar, fish sauce, sesame oil, sugar and salt. Puree to a fine paste.

4. In a large glass baking dish or an enameled roasting pan, spread the paste evenly over both sides of the ribs. Drizzle any excess liquid over the slabs. Cover the ribs with plastic wrap and weigh down with heavy cans. Let marinate for 4 to 6 hours at room temperature or overnight in the refrigerator. Let return to room temperature before cooking.

5. Light the grill or preheat the oven to 500°. Grill the ribs, turning often so that they cook evenly, until medium well done and no trace of pink remains near the bone, about 45 minutes. Baste occasionally with any liquid remaining in the baking dish. Alternatively, place the ribs on a rack set in a roasting pan and bake until medium-well done and slightly charred, about 40 minutes.

6. Cut the ribs apart and serve them with individual dishes of Thai Basil Dipping Sauce.

—*Linda Burum & Linda Merinoff*

• • •

PORK TAMALES WITH HOMINY

Felipe Rojas-Lombardi remembers his mother, Judith Lombardi Pedresche, bringing *tamales cusqueños* to the table as huge packages, baked in banana leaves.

——— *8 Servings* ———
1 tablespoon coarse (kosher) salt
1½ pounds lean pork shoulder, cut
into 8 pieces
½ cup plus 2 tablespoons (5 ounces)
lard or rendered bacon fat
2 garlic cloves, minced
½ cup paprika
¼ teaspoon freshly ground white
pepper
2 teaspoons ground cumin
3 cans (16 ounces each) hominy,
rinsed and drained (about 6 cups)
4 eggs—2 raw, 2 hard cooked and
chopped
3 tablespoons light rum
1 teaspoon baking powder
24 dry corn husks (see Note)

1. In a saucepan, combine 4 cups of water with the salt. Add the pork and simmer over moderate heat for 25 minutes. Remove to a plate and set aside. Reserve the cooking liquid.

2. In a large skillet, heat 2 tablespoons of the lard over moderate heat. Add the pork and sauté, turning, until golden brown, 15 to 20 minutes.

3. Add the garlic, paprika, white pepper and cumin. Cook, stirring, for 1 minute. Add the reserved cooking liquid from the pork and cook over low heat just until the pork is fork-tender and the liquid is reduced to ¾ cup, 35 to 40 minutes. Drain the pork, reserving the cooking liquid.

4. In a food processor, combine the hominy with the remaining ½ cup lard, the 2 raw eggs, the rum, baking powder and the ¾ cup cooking liquid. Process until just mixed. Transfer to a bowl and knead into a smooth dough.

5. Prepare the dry corn husks by dipping them quickly into boiling water to soften them. Place 2 corn husks on a flat surface and overlap the 2 short sides by a few inches to form a rectangle. Lay a third husk in the same direction over the juncture for reinforcement.

6. Spoon 3 tablespoons of the dough in the center of the husks and place 1 piece of the pork and 1 heaping tablespoon of chopped hard-cooked egg on top. Cover with another 3 tablespoons of the dough, making sure the filling is totally sealed between the 2 layers of dough.

7. Folding the husks as you would wrapping paper, fold 1 of the long sides of the husks over the dough to cover it completely. Then fold the opposite side up and over. Fold each of the short ends toward the center to overlap and form a neat, compact rectangular package. Place in the middle of a long piece of string and tie as you would a package. Knot the string in the center. Repeat with the remaining corn husks and filling.

8. Place the tamales in a steamer over plenty of boiling water and steam, tightly covered, until heated through, about 45 minutes. Remove from the steamer. Cut and discard the string. Divide among 8 plates and serve the tamales at once in their steaming husks.

NOTE: Corn husks are available at Latin American and specialty food stores or by mail from Dean & DeLuca, 560 Broadway, New York, NY 10012.

—*Felipe Rojas-Lombardi*

• • •

CASUAL BUFFET FOR A CROWD

The philosophy of this menu from W. Peter Prestcott is that the food should be in abundance, and that as much of it as possible should be store bought. The appetizer, for instance, is commercial tortellini that are cooked and then tossed with grated Parmesan and crushed hot pepper. Serves 12.

Spiced Tortellini

Curried Walnuts

Sherried Olives

Ham and Potato Gratin (p. 67)

🍷 *Blush Wine or Fruity Red, such as 1987 Georges Duboeuf Beaujolais-Villages*

Tomato and Watercress Salad

Semifreddo Rapido (p. 208)

Sugar Cookies

HAM AND POTATO GRATIN

I like this hearty, straightforward dish for its ease of preparation and comforting, homey flavors.

🍷 The somewhat sharper, saltier flavors in this menu—particularly in the olives and ham—suggest a soft, fruity refreshing white, such as a dry 1987 Buehler White Zinfandel or 1986 Clos du Bois Fleur d'Alexandra blend, as a foil.

--- *12 Servings* ---

6 tablespoons unsalted butter
⅓ cup all-purpose flour
3 cups milk
3 eggs, lightly beaten
3 cups grated sharp Cheddar cheese (about ¾ pound)
1 tablespoon Dijon-style mustard
½ teaspoon freshly grated nutmeg
¼ teaspoon freshly ground pepper
2 pounds boiling potatoes, peeled and sliced ¼ inch thick
3 tablespoons olive oil
3 medium onions, thinly sliced
1 cup Madeira
1 package (10 ounces) frozen chopped spinach, thawed and squeezed dry
1½ pounds thinly sliced baked ham
½ cup freshly grated Parmesan cheese

1. In a medium saucepan, melt the butter over low heat. Add the flour and cook, stirring constantly, for 2 to 3 minutes without letting the roux color. Gradually whisk in the milk until smooth. Bring to a boil over moderate heat, whisking constantly. Reduce the heat to low and simmer for 10 minutes, whisking occasionally.

2. Remove from the heat and whisk in the eggs, one at a time. Stir in the Cheddar cheese, mustard, nutmeg and pepper until thoroughly blended. Press a piece of plastic wrap directly onto the surface of the cheese sauce.

3. In a large saucepan of boiling salted water, cook the potatoes until tender, 12 to 15 minutes. Drain and pat dry.

4. Meanwhile, in a large skillet, heat the olive oil. Add the onions and cook over low heat, stirring occasionally, until they are softened but not browned, about 10 minutes.

5. Add the Madeira, increase the heat to high and boil until only 2 tablespoons of liquid remain, about 7 minutes. Stir in the spinach and set aside.

6. Preheat the oven to 350°. Lightly butter a shallow 3-quart gratin or baking dish. Layer one-third of the ham slices

67

evenly over the bottom of the dish. Top with half of the cooked potatoes and spread one-third of the cheese sauce evenly over the top. Cover with all the onion and spinach mixture. Repeat layering with half of the remaining ham, all the remaining potatoes and half of the remaining cheese sauce. Top with the remaining ham and cheese sauce and sprinkle the Parmesan cheese evenly over the top of the gratin.

7. Bake the gratin for 30 minutes, or until heated through. To brown the top, broil about 4 inches from the heat until browned and bubbly, 2 to 3 minutes. Let cool for 10 minutes before serving.

—*W. Peter Prestcott*

• • •

STUFFED HEAD OF CABBAGE WITH TOMATO SAUCE

This makes a very pleasing presentation. I like to use a spaghetti cooker with an insert to cook the stuffed cabbage. But if you use this method, be sure to check the pot from time to time; because of the long steaming, you may have to add more water if it evaporates.

Stuffed cabbage is also good with uncooked tomato salsa, if you can get your hands on ripe tomatoes.

——— *6 to 8 Servings* ———
1 large head of cabbage
¾ pound bulk breakfast sausage
1 tablespoon unsalted butter
¾ pound cooked ham, fat and rind removed, coarsely ground in a food processor
2 tablespoons safflower oil
1 medium onion, coarsely chopped
2 celery ribs, coarsely chopped
½ cup rice
1 large garlic clove, crushed through a press
¼ cup toasted pine nuts
⅛ teaspoon thyme

COMFORTING MIDWINTER MEAL

Unlike most stuffed cabbage recipes, this one from Lee Bailey is a whole head stuffed with sausage, ham, onions, rice and pine nuts. To serve the cabbage, give each guest a wedge of cabbage and spoon out the stuffing separately. Serves 6 to 8.

Stuffed Head of Cabbage with Tomato Sauce (p. 68)

Baked Buttery Sweet Potato Chips (p. 125)

🍷 *Dry Red Wine*

Chocolate Peanut Butter Pie (p. 226)

Coffee

¼ teaspoon freshly ground black pepper
⅛ teaspoon cayenne pepper
2 tablespoons minced parsley
2 eggs, lightly beaten
Tomato Sauce (p. 248)

1. Carefully remove 4 of the outside cabbage leaves, rinse and reserve. Using a large sharp knife, cut 1 inch off the root end of the cabbage. With a small sharp knife, cut a deep "X" in the bottom, then cut around the "X" to make a circular hole. Lift out the cabbage pieces and discard. Hollow out the inside of the cabbage, using short, slashing, crosshatch motions, and leaving about 1 inch of cabbage wall. Immerse the hollowed-out cabbage in salted cold water for 10 minutes. Drain on paper towels, open-end down.

2. Meanwhile, in a large skillet, fry the sausage over moderate heat, breaking up any lumps with a spoon. Cook, turning, until well browned, with a dark crisp outer crust, about 8 minutes. Drain, transfer the sausage to a large mixing bowl and set aside.

3. Wipe out the skillet with paper towels and add the butter. Melt over moderate heat. Add the ham and cook until most of the liquid evaporates, 4 to 5 minutes. Transfer to the mixing bowl containing the sausage.

4. Wipe out the skillet again and add the oil. Add the onions and celery and cook over moderate heat until just wilted but not browned, about 5 minutes. Add to the ham and sausage.

5. In a small pot of boiling salted water, cook the rice for 7 minutes. Drain and rinse with hot water.

6. Add the rice, garlic, pine nuts, thyme, black pepper, cayenne and parsley to the meat and sautéed vegetables. Toss, then add the eggs and mix well.

7. Fill the cabbage shell with the ham and sausage stuffing, mounding it slightly on top if necessary. Lay one of the reserved leaves over the opening. Wrap the cabbage in a large sheet of cheesecloth. Gather the ends together and tie securely with kitchen string. Put the cabbage in a steamer, cut-side up, and steam until the cabbage is tender but not mushy and the rice is tender, about 1¼ hours.

8. Transfer the cabbage to a warm platter. Pour off any liquid that exudes. Surround with the reserved leaves for garnish. Serve hot, with the Tomato Sauce on the side.

—*Lee Bailey*

• • •

Mediterranean Tenderloin of Beef (p. 53).

Left, Chicken Breasts with Toasted Mustard Seed Sauce (p. 84) and Calamata-Stuffed Tomatoes (p. 127). Above, Grilled Lamb Tenderloin with Mesclun and Gigondas Vinaigrette (p. 79).

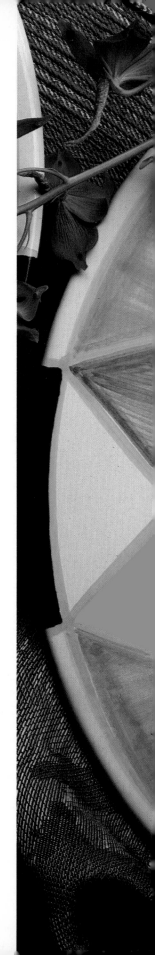

Above, Shrimp with Black Beans (p. 50). Right, Veal Roasted with Cognac-Shallot Butter (p. 52).

Far left, Roasted Chicken
with Achiote and Garlic
Sauce (p. 82). Near left,
Pork Tenderloin with Tender
Fennel and Garlic (p. 65).
Above, Roasted Rack of
Lamb (p. 79).

SWEET MUSTARD-GLAZED HAM AND PORK LOAF

This meat loaf comes pretty much unaltered from my grandmother Millie's handwritten recipe book. The simple list of ingredients says to me that it's a Depression-era dish; it's also the supper my mother prepares for my first meal when I'm home for a visit.

❡ The homespun mustard and pork flavors and the saltiness of the ham find their natural complement in the sweet but bitter notes of a rich ale, such as Anchor Steam Liberty Ale or a traditional English ale, such as Bass.

——————— 6 to 8 Servings ———————
1 pound firm and smoky baked ham, trimmed of any tough outer rind
1½ pounds ground pork
1 cup finely crushed saltine crackers (about 30)
1 cup milk
1 teaspoon freshly ground pepper
Sweet Mustard Glaze (recipe follows)

1. Preheat the oven to 350°. In a food processor, finely chop the ham. In a large bowl, stir together the ham and pork. Add the cracker crumbs, milk and pepper; mix thoroughly. Transfer to a large shallow baking dish and form into a flat loaf.

2. Bake the meat loaf for 30 minutes. Spread one-third of the Sweet Mustard Glaze over the loaf and bake for 15 minutes. Spread half the remaining glaze over the loaf and bake for 15 minutes. Spread the last of the glaze over the loaf and bake for 15 to 20 minutes, or until the loaf is

Lemon Chicken with Capers and Pine Nuts (p. 83).

glazed and brown and a thermometer inserted in the center registers at least 165°.

3. Let cool slightly, then transfer the loaf to a serving platter. Let stand for 10 minutes before slicing and serving.

—*Michael McLaughlin*

• • •

SWEET MUSTARD GLAZE

——————— Makes About 1 Cup ———————
1 cup (packed) light brown sugar
⅓ cup cider vinegar
¼ cup Dijon-style mustard

In a small, heavy, nonreactive saucepan, whisk together the brown sugar, vinegar, mustard and ⅓ cup of water over moderate heat. Bring to a boil, reduce the heat to low and simmer, stirring frequently, for 20 minutes. Let cool to room temperature.

—*Michael McLaughlin*

• • •

REBECCA'S CHILES EN NOGADA

Although these chiles—stuffed with a savory pork filling, lightly fried and served with a creamy walnut sauce—take time to put together, don't be daunted. Every bite proves they're worth it.

❡ The welter of flavors in the chiles and piccadillo filling calls for a spicy white that can bridge the varied tastes and refresh the palate as well. Choose a tart Gewürztraminer, such as 1988 Fetzer from California or 1985 Muré Clos St-Landelin from Alsace.

——————— 4 Servings ———————
1 pound ground pork
¼ cup minced white onion
2 teaspoons minced garlic
1 can (35 ounces) Italian peeled tomatoes, drained and chopped
¼ cup raisins
8 green olives, pitted and minced

1 teaspoon ground cumin
⅓ cup red wine vinegar
3 cups vegetable oil, for frying
8 medium Anaheim or other long, mild chiles
1 cup flour
3 eggs, lightly beaten
Walnut Sauce (recipe follows)
⅓ cup chopped walnuts
2 tablespoons pomegranate seeds (optional)
3 tablespoons coarsely chopped fresh coriander

1. In a large skillet, cook the pork over moderately high heat for 2 minutes, stirring to break up the meat. Add the onion and garlic and cook until the pork is browned and crumbly, about 6 minutes.

2. Stir in the tomatoes, raisins, olives, cumin and vinegar. Bring to a boil, reduce the heat to low and simmer until the mixture is almost dry, about 10 minutes.

3. In a deep skillet or a large saucepan, heat the oil until almost smoking (about 350°). Add the whole chiles and fry, turning once, until the skins are blistered, about 2 minutes.

4. Drain the chiles on paper towels. Let cool, then scrape off the skins with a small sharp knife. Leaving the stems intact, make a lengthwise slit down one side of each chile. Using a small spoon, carefully scoop out the cores and seeds. Fill the chiles with the pork mixture.

5. Reheat the oil in the skillet to 350°. Dredge the chiles in the flour. Dip them in the beaten eggs, then fry in the hot oil, turning, until golden brown all over, about 5 minutes. Drain on paper towels.

6. Place the chiles on individual plates or a platter and ladle the Walnut Sauce over them. Sprinkle with the walnuts, pomegranate seeds and coriander.

—*David Millen,
Rebecca's, Los Angeles*

• • •

MEAT

WALNUT SAUCE

——— *Makes About 1½ Cups* ———
⅓ cup chopped walnuts
½ cup sour cream
3 ounces queso ranchero (Mexican soft cheese) or fresh goat cheese
½ cup milk

In a blender, combine the walnuts, the sour cream and cheese. Puree, gradually adding the milk. The mixture will thicken as it blends.

—*David Millen,*
Rebecca's, Los Angeles

• • •

SAUTEED CALF'S LIVER AND ONIONS

Venice produces many versions of this classic combination of calf's liver and onions, but the underlying principle of all of them is that the better the liver, the less you have to do with it.

——— *4 Servings* ———
1 pound calf's liver—trimmed, thinly sliced and cut into ½-inch-thick strips
1 cup milk
3 tablespoons unsalted butter
3 tablespoons olive oil
1 pound sweet onions (such as Bermudas or Vidalias), thinly sliced
½ teaspoon salt
¼ teaspoon freshly ground pepper
2 tablespoons minced parsley
Lemon wedges, for garnish

1. Place the liver in a large, shallow bowl or glass pie pan, pour on the milk and set aside for 1 to 3 hours.

2. In a large skillet, melt the butter in the oil over low heat. Add the onions and cook, stirring occasionally, until very soft and light golden, about 30 minutes.

3. Drain the strips of liver, pat dry and add to the skillet. Increase the heat to moderately high and sauté, stirring constantly, until the liver is browned outside, but still supple and rosy inside, about 3 minutes.

4. Add the salt, pepper and parsley and toss to combine. Serve at once, garnished with lemon wedges.

—*Tom Maresca & Diane Darrow*

• • •

VENETIAN FALL WINE DINNER

This fall menu from Tom Maresca and Diane Darrow matches seasonal Venetian dishes with special red wines of the region. Serves 4.

Mushroom Toasts (p. 20)
🍷 *1985 Loredan Venegazzù della Casa or Pio Cesara Barbera*

———

Risotto with Fennel (p. 116)

———

Sautéed Calf's Liver and Onions (p. 78)

Grilled Radicchio with Anchovy-Mustard Sauce (p. 126)
🍷 *1985 Maculan Cabernet Fratta or Antinori Chianti Classico Riserva*

———

Sand Tart (p. 230)
🍷 *1987 Anselmi Recioto di Soave or Livio Felluga Picolit or Malvasia della Lipari*

LOIN LAMB CHOPS WITH FRESH SPINACH AND MUSHROOMS

You may feel that you're doing a bit of a juggling act trying to coordinate the rapid cooking of the elements in this dish. However, the combined flavors and visual effects of the green spinach and rosy lamb are well worth it. Serve a beet, Belgian endive and chive salad as a first course. Have the butcher tie the lamb chops to hold them together.

🍷 Lamb chops have a special affinity for Cabernet Sauvignon and Merlot. The tannin in these wines contrasts with the richness of the meat, and their herbal qualities accent the taste. Both 1984 Buena Vista Carneros Estate or 1986 Firestone Merlot are admirable choices.

——— *4 Servings* ———
8 boneless loin lamb chops, cut 1 inch thick (about 2 pounds total), trimmed of excess fat and tied
¼ cup extra-virgin olive oil
1½ teaspoons salt
½ teaspoon minced rosemary, preferably fresh
1 pound mushrooms, sliced ¼ inch thick
1 pound fresh spinach, stemmed and rinsed
½ cup dry red wine
3 tablespoons unsalted butter

1. Preheat the broiler. Rub the chops all over with 2 tablespoons of the olive oil, ½ teaspoon of the salt and ¼ teaspoon of the rosemary. Set the chops aside.

2. In a large heavy skillet, heat 1 tablespoon of the olive oil over high heat. Add the mushrooms, ½ teaspoon salt and the remaining ¼ teaspoon rosemary. Cook, stirring occasionally, until they are golden brown, about 5 minutes. Remove the skillet from the heat and set aside.

3. Broil the lamb chops about 5 inches from the heat for 3 to 4 minutes on each side, or until golden brown on the outside and rosy pink in the center. Remove the string from each chop. Reheat the mushrooms briefly over moderate heat and arrange neatly down the center of a warmed serving platter. Put the chops on top of the mushrooms.

4. In the large nonreactive skillet, heat the remaining 1 tablespoon olive oil over moderately high heat. Add the spinach and the remaining ½ teaspoon salt. Cook, stirring frequently, until wilted and tender but still bright green, about 4 minutes. Spoon the spinach around the chops. Cover to keep warm.

5. Add the wine to the pan and cook over high heat until it is reduced to ¼ cup, about 4 minutes. Reduce the heat to low and whisk in the butter. Pour over the chops and serve.

—*Nora Carey*

• • •

GRILLED LAMB TENDERLOIN WITH MESCLUN AND GIGONDAS VINAIGRETTE

There are several keys to this dish. The selection of greens is very important. The blend of young greens called *mesclun* is ideal. But an assortment of something crisp (like romaine), something tender (like Boston lettuce), something bitter (like Italian chicory) and a small proportion of something spicy (like arugula or watercress) will work beautifully. The lamb loin is expensive, but its buttery texture is worth every penny.

🍷 Select a robust young Gigondas (about 2 years old) for the full dose of peppery flavor that this wine can offer. The 1985 Domaine Les Pallières will stand up beautifully to this dish. Other French reds made from the Syrah grape—such as Guigal's great 1985 Côte Rôtie—can be substituted.

———*4 Servings*———
1 small garlic clove, minced
1 teaspoon salt
1¼ teaspoons coarsely ground pepper
¾ pound boneless lamb loin from a 2½-pound rack of lamb
¼ cup Gigondas, Côte Rôtie or Crozes-Hermitage
1 tablespoon plus 2 teaspoons red wine vinegar or raspberry vinegar
2 tablespoons plus 2 teaspoons sunflower or safflower oil
8 cups of mixed greens (see headnote)

1. In a small bowl, combine the garlic, ¾ teaspoon of the salt and 1 teaspoon of the pepper. Rub evenly over the lamb. Prepare a hot outdoor grill or preheat the broiler. Grill or broil the lamb, 6 inches from the heat for about 6 minutes, until charred on all sides. The lamb will be extremely rare. Let stand for 15 minutes before carving.

2. Combine the Gigondas and the vinegar in a small bowl. Gradually whisk in the oil. Season with the remaining ¼ teaspoon each salt and pepper.

3. When ready to serve, pour all but 4 teaspoons of the vinaigrette over the greens. Toss well. Divide the greens among 4 dinner plates. Slice the lamb into very thin slices. Arrange the lamb on top of each salad. Drizzle the remaining 4 teaspoons vinaigrette over the lamb.

—*David Rosengarten*

• • •

ROASTED RACK OF LAMB

Ask your butcher to french the racks of lamb, leaving only the ribs cleaned back to the eye. This eye, a perfect morsel, is the only meat that remains. Almost all the fat should be trimmed off.

🍷 California Pinot Noir, such as 1986 B.V. Carneros, or 1985 Burgundy, such as Prosper Maufoux Santenay

———*4 to 5 Servings*———
2 racks of young lamb, 8 chops each, at room temperature
4 garlic cloves, crushed through a press
½ teaspoon salt
½ teaspoon freshly ground pepper

1. Preheat the oven to 500°. Smear the garlic generously over the lamb and season with the salt and pepper. Wrap the exposed bones with aluminum foil.

2. Arrange the lamb, meat-side up, on a baking sheet and put in the upper third of the oven. Roast for 25 minutes, or until lightly charred on the outside, pink on the inside. Remove and let stand for 5 minutes before carving into individual chops.

—*Lee Bailey*

• • •

GARLIC-OREGANO LAMB SKEWERED WITH VEGETABLES

This skewered lamb is a traditional preparation using oregano and yogurt. If you've never marinated lamb in yogurt, you'll discover that the yogurt tenderizes the meat while creating a delectable crust as it broils. Other good choices for vegetables to broil with the lamb are broccoli florets, blanched sweet potato chunks and cherry tomatoes. The lamb must marinate overnight, so plan accordingly.

———*6 Servings*———
¼ cup plain yogurt
2 tablespoons chopped fresh oregano

2 garlic cloves, minced
2 pounds lean lamb, shoulder or leg,
    cut into 2-inch cubes
12 shallots, peeled
18 shiitake mushrooms (about 1
    pound), stems removed
1 large red bell pepper, cut into
    1-inch pieces
1 medium zucchini, sliced crosswise
    ¼ inch thick
1 large lemon, sliced crosswise into
    12 slices
¼ cup extra-virgin olive oil
1½ teaspoons salt
1½ teaspoons freshly ground pepper
Olive-Oregano Relish (p. 257)

1. In a large bowl, mix the yogurt, oregano and garlic. Add the lamb cubes and stir to coat the meat well. Cover and refrigerate overnight.

2. In a small saucepan of boiling water, cook the shallots over moderate heat until tender but still firm, about 10 minutes. Drain well.

3. In a large bowl, combine the shallots, shiitake mushrooms, red pepper, zucchini and lemon slices. Toss the vegetables with the olive oil and ¾ teaspoon each of the salt and pepper.

4. Preheat the broiler. Season the lamb with the remaining ¾ teaspoon each of the salt and pepper.

5. Divide the lamb cubes into 6 equal portions. Divide the shallots, mushrooms, pepper pieces, zucchini slices and lemon slices into 6 equal portions. On each of 6 long metal skewers, alternate the lamb cubes with the vegetables and lemon slices.

6. On a large baking sheet, arrange the skewers close together but not touching. Broil about 5 inches from the heat for 5 minutes, until the lamb is crusty and medium-done. Serve with the Olive-Oregano Relish.

—*Marcia Kiesel*

• • •

LAMB BARBECUE ON A STICK

If you prefer beef to lamb, substitute an equal amount of tender sirloin or filet mignon, cut into one-inch cubes. For this recipe, you'll need 20 wooden skewers, soaked in water for at least one hour to prevent burning.

——————— *12 Servings* ———————
2 tablespoons tamarind paste,
    dissolved in ¼ cup water and
    strained
2 teaspoons ground cumin
4 shallots, sliced
2 garlic cloves, sliced
2 teaspoons sugar
1 teaspoon salt
1 teaspoon crushed hot red pepper
2 tablespoons soy sauce
2 tablespoons corn or peanut oil
2 pounds trimmed boneless leg of
    lamb, cut into ½-inch cubes
Peanut Dipping Sauce (p. 251)

1. In a food processor, combine the tamarind liquid, cumin, shallots, garlic, sugar, salt, hot pepper, soy sauce and oil. Process to a smooth paste.

2. In a bowl, combine the lamb and the soy marinade and toss to coat. Let stand at room temperature for 1 hour.

3. Preheat the broiler. Thread 4 cubes of lamb onto each of 20 wooden skewers that have been soaked in water for at least 1 hour. Place on an oiled broiler pan. Broil about 4 inches from the heat, turning, until browned all over, about 5 minutes. Serve warm with Peanut Dipping Sauce.

—*Copeland Marks*

• • •

FRAGRANT LAMB SHISH KEBABS WITH CUCUMBER-YOGURT SAUCE

Serve these tender, tasty lamb kebabs with a rice pilaf with toasted pine nuts and sliced tomatoes. Be sure to allow a day or two for the meat to marinate.

❦ The richness of grilled lamb and the tartness of the Cucumber-Yogurt Sauce require a red that won't be overwhelmed by the sharp flavors. A gutsy but balanced young Zinfandel, such as 1986 Cuvaison or Caymus, is the answer.

——————— *6 Servings* ———————
1 cup plain yogurt
2 shallots, finely chopped
2 large garlic cloves, crushed
    through a press
1 tablespoon rosemary, crumbled
1½ teaspoons oregano, crumbled
2 pounds trimmed boneless leg of
    lamb, cut into 1½-inch cubes
Cucumber-Yogurt Sauce (p. 252)

1. In a large bowl, combine the yogurt, shallots, garlic, rosemary and oregano. Mix to blend well. Add the lamb and toss to coat. Cover and marinate in the refrigerator for 1 to 2 days.

2. Light a charcoal fire. Remove the lamb from the marinade and thread onto 6 long metal skewers. Grill the lamb over glowing hot charcoal, turning once or twice, for about 10 minutes for medium-rare or until cooked to your taste. Serve with the Cucumber-Yogurt Sauce.

—*Jim Fobel*

• • •

POULTRY

A GOOD ROAST CHICKEN

This recipe is deceptively simple. The roast chicken, perfumed with rosemary and basted with sweet butter, can be the mainstay of a superb family dinner or can serve as the centerpiece of the most elegant dinner party. If you want crisp skin, turn the oven up to 375° for the last 10 minutes of roasting.

❦ Choose a light red that will not overwhelm the mildness of the chicken, such as 1985 Caymus Special Selection or 1986 Carneros Creek Pinot Noir.

——— *4 Servings* ———
1 whole free-range chicken (4½ to
 5½ pounds), rinsed and patted dry
3 sprigs of fresh rosemary or
 1½ teaspoons dried
4 tablespoons unsalted butter, cut
 into 4 pieces, at room temperature
2 teaspoons coarse (kosher) salt
1 teaspoon coarsely ground pepper

1. Preheat the oven to 325°. Loosen the breast skin from the meat. Place 1 sprig of the rosemary (or ¼ teaspoon dried) and 1 tablespoon of butter under the skin on each side of the breast. Place the remaining sprig of rosemary (or 1 teaspoon dried) in the cavity. Truss the bird. Rub the remaining 2 tablespoons butter over the chicken and sprinkle all over with the salt and pepper.

2. Place the chicken, breast-side up, in a roasting pan. Roast for 45 minutes. Baste and continue roasting, basting every 15 minutes, until the bird is golden brown, the juices run clear and the internal temperature of the thigh reaches 170°, about 1 hour longer.

3. Transfer the chicken to a warm platter, cover loosely with foil and let rest for about 15 minutes before carving.
— *Molly O'Neill*

• • •

ROASTED CHICKEN WITH ACHIOTE AND GARLIC SAUCE

Robert Del Grande, chef and co-owner at Cafe Annie in Houston, likes to serve this dish with a watercress salad dressed in walnut oil.

❦ Although roasted chicken is normally amenable to just about any wine match, the garlic sauce here tunes the dish toward an herbaceous, crisp Sauvignon Blanc, such as 1987 Iron Horse or 1987 Silverado, to match the pungency.

——— *4 Servings* ———
4 cups chicken stock or canned broth
¾ cup orange juice
½ cup achiote seeds (annato seed)*
1 whole chicken (about 3½ pounds)
5 garlic cloves, peeled, plus 2 heads
 of garlic, unpeeled
1 tablespoon paprika
1¼ teaspoons salt
2 medium onions, sliced
2 large sweet potatoes (about 1
 pound each), peeled and
 quartered
2 tablespoons unsalted butter,
 melted
1 tablespoon fresh lime juice
1 teaspoon coarsely cracked pepper
*Available at Latin American
 markets

1. In a medium saucepan, combine 1 cup of the chicken stock, the orange juice, achiote seeds and 1 cup of water. Bring to a boil over moderate heat. Cook until the achiote seeds are soft and the liquid is almost entirely evaporated, about 25 minutes.

2. Meanwhile, using a sharp heavy knife, cut the chicken along both sides of the backbone; remove and discard. Pushing down with both hands, press the chicken flat. Remove and discard any excess fat and large protruding bones. Turn the chicken over. Make a small incision through the skin between the leg and the lower end of the breast on each side. Slide the ends of the drumsticks through the holes to secure the legs in place.

3. Transfer the achiote mixture to a blender and add the 5 peeled garlic cloves, the paprika, ¼ teaspoon of the salt and 1 more cup of the chicken stock. Puree the achiote marinade until smooth, about 1 minute.

4. Preheat the oven to 350°. Separate the heads of garlic into cloves. Butter the bottom of a large roasting pan. Cover the bottom of the pan with the onion slices and the unpeeled garlic cloves. Place the chicken, skin-side up, on top of the onion and garlic.

5. Brush the chicken liberally with the achiote marinade. Arrange the sweet potatoes around the chicken. Roast, basting with the melted butter and pan juices every 15 minutes, until the chicken is browned outside and the juices run clear when the thickest part of the thigh is pricked, about 1 hour and 15 minutes.

6. Transfer the chicken and sweet potatoes to a carving board and cover with foil to keep warm.

7. Squeeze the roasted garlic cloves into a blender, discarding the skins. Add the roasted onions, any juices from the roasting pan, the remaining 2 cups chicken stock and the lime juice. Puree until smooth. (Add a little water to thin if desired.)

8. Transfer the sauce to a medium saucepan and stir in the remaining 1 teaspoon salt and the cracked pepper. Rewarm the sauce over low heat, stirring, until heated through.

9. Quarter the chicken and divide among 4 warm dinner plates. Serve with the sweet potatoes and garlic sauce.
— *Robert Del Grande,*
Cafe Annie, Houston

• • •

BAKED CHICKEN BREASTS WITH SCALLIONS AND LIME

The three greens of the scallions, parsley and lime zest make for a pretty presentation as well as a lively flavor. In the Veneto, this combination is used on fish—mainly on *triglia*, a kind of mullet, though we've tried it successfully on bluefish, sardines and smelts. But our nicest discovery was how well this treatment works with chicken breasts.

4 Servings

4 skinless, boneless chicken breast halves (about 5 ounces each)
½ cup all-purpose flour, for dredging
5 tablespoons unsalted butter
⅔ cup minced scallions (white and tender green)
1 large garlic clove, minced
½ cup dry white wine
¼ teaspoon salt
¼ teaspoon freshly ground pepper
1 tablespoon fresh lime juice
2 teaspoons minced lime zest
1 tablespoon chopped parsley
1 tablespoon fine, dry bread crumbs

1. Preheat the oven to 400°. Trim off any fat or membranes from the chicken breasts. Pound the thicker ends lightly to flatten to an even thickness.

2. Dredge the chicken breasts in the flour; shake off any excess. In a large nonreactive skillet, melt 4 tablespoons of the butter over moderately high heat. Add the chicken and sauté, turning once, until golden brown, about 3 minutes on each side. Remove to a plate.

3. Reduce the heat to low and add the scallions and garlic. Cook until softened, about 5 minutes. Increase the heat to moderately high, add the wine and boil, scraping up any browned bits, until reduced by half, 2 to 3 minutes.

4. Spread half the scallion sauce in a buttered baking dish just large enough to

hold the chicken in a single layer. Add the chicken and season with the salt and pepper. Drizzle on the lime juice. Cover with the remaining sauce. Sprinkle on the lime zest, parsley and bread crumbs. Dot with the remaining 1 tablespoon butter.

5. Bake the chicken in the top third of the oven for 15 minutes, or until the chicken is white throughout but still juicy. Serve at once.

—*Tom Maresca & Diane Darrow*

• • •

ITALIAN SPRING DINNER

Not only do Italians change their eating habits with the seasons, they also change their wines. In this spring menu from Tom Maresca and Diane Darrow, the wines of choice are white, to complement the meal's shellfish and chicken dishes. Serves 4.

Scallops Venetian Style (p. 24)

🍷 *1987 Gradnik Sauvignon Blanc or Bolini Pinot Grigio*

Rice with Peas (p. 115)

Baked Chicken Breasts with Scallions and Lime (p. 83)

Buttered Asparagus

🍷 *Jermann Vintage Tunina or 1987 La Scolca Gavi*

Strawberries with Lemon and Sugar (p. 212)

Biscotti

Espresso

LEMON CHICKEN WITH CAPERS AND PINE NUTS

Serve this with steamed broccoli and drizzle it with some of the sauce from the pan.
🍷 A tart, zesty dish like this is nicely contrasted by a rich, round Chardonnay with its own lemony overtones, such as 1986 Girard or 1987 De Loach.

4 Servings

¼ cup pine nuts
2 whole chicken breasts (10 ounces each), boned and split in half, with skin attached
½ teaspoon salt
½ teaspoon freshly ground pepper
1 tablespoon extra-virgin olive oil
½ cup dry white wine
1½ tablespoons fresh lemon juice
1 tablespoon capers
3 tablespoons unsalted butter

1. Preheat the oven to 400°. Spread the pine nuts on a baking sheet and toast in the oven until golden brown, about 4 minutes. Set aside to cool.

2. Gently pound each boneless chicken breast half between 2 sheets of waxed paper until flattened to an even ¼ inch. Season with the salt and pepper.

3. In a large skillet, heat the olive oil over moderately high heat until almost smoking. Add the chicken breasts, skinside down, and cook until golden brown, about 5 minutes. Turn the breasts over and cook until white throughout but still moist, about 3 minutes. Arrange the chicken on a large warmed platter. Cover loosely with foil to keep warm. Pour off the fat from the skillet.

4. Add the wine to the skillet and bring to a boil, scraping up any brown bits from the bottom of the pan. Cook over high heat until reduced by half, about 3 minutes.

5. Add the lemon juice and capers. Remove from the heat and whisk in the

butter, one tablespoon at a time. Pour any accumulated juices from the chicken platter into the sauce. Pour the sauce over the meat and sprinkle with the pine nuts.

—*Nora Carey*

• • •

GRILLED MARINATED CHICKEN BREASTS

Although there is some marination time (about 3 hours) required, this grilled chicken dish is nearly effortless.

——— 6 Servings ———
¾ cup fresh lemon juice
¾ cup vegetable oil
¼ cup minced onion
1½ teaspoons salt
¼ teaspoon thyme
2 tablespoons green peppercorn mustard
12 skinless, boneless chicken breast halves (4 to 5 ounces each)

1. In a medium bowl, whisk together the lemon juice, oil, onion, salt, thyme and mustard.

2. With a sharp knife, score both sides of each breast in a cross-hatch pattern about ⅛ inch deep. Pour one-third of the marinade into a shallow glass bowl. Add half the chicken in a single layer and cover with another third of the marinade. Put the remaining breasts in a layer on top and pour on the remaining marinade. Cover with plastic wrap and refrigerate for 2 hours, turning occasionally. Remove from the refrigerator for 1 hour before cooking to bring to room temperature.

3. Meanwhile, preheat the broiler. Arrange the chicken on a broiler rack and grill about 4 inches from the heat for 3 minutes. Turn and grill for another 3 minutes, or until the juices run clear

when pierced with a sharp knife. Make sure not to overcook. Transfer to a warmed platter and cover loosely with foil until ready to serve.

—*Lee Bailey*

• • •

CHICKEN BREASTS WITH TOASTED MUSTARD SEED SAUCE

♟ To match the delicacy of the chicken, try a dry Chenin Blanc with its faint peachy flavor. Look for 1986 Chappellet or Villa Mt. Eden.

——— 6 Servings ———
2 cups heavy cream
3 tablespoons Dijon-style mustard
¾ teaspoon salt
1 teaspoon freshly ground pepper
1½ tablespoons yellow mustard seeds
6 boneless chicken breast halves, with skin on (about 6 ounces each)
2 teaspoons fresh lemon juice
3 large scallions, thinly sliced

1. In a heavy medium saucepan, bring the cream to a boil over high heat. Reduce the heat to low and cook, stirring occasionally until the cream is slightly thickened and reduced to 1¼ cups, about 10 minutes.

2. Remove the cream from the heat and whisk in the mustard, ¼ teaspoon of the salt and ½ teaspoon of the pepper. *(The sauce can be made ahead to this point up to 4 hours in advance. Whisk it occasionally to keep a skin from forming.)*

3. Meanwhile, in a small skillet, toast the mustard seeds over moderately high heat, shaking the pan until they are lightly browned and begin to pop. Immediately transfer the seeds to a plate to cool.

4. Preheat the oven to 500°. Place the chicken breasts on a broiling pan, skin-side up, and season with the remaining ½ teaspoon salt and ½ teaspoon pepper. Bake on the top rack of the oven until the

A SUNNY, SAVORY MEDITERRANEAN MEAL

The impressive titles of the recipes in this menu from Marcia Kiesel belie the dishes' simplicity and ease of preparation. Of course, you needn't let your guests in on this secret. Serves 6.

Moroccan Sole Ragout with Oranges and Basil (p. 23)

♟ *1985 Hogue Cellars Sémillon Reserve or 1985 Inglenook Sémillon*

Chicken Breasts with Toasted Mustard Seed Sauce (p. 84)

Calamata-Stuffed Tomatoes (p. 127)

♟ *Dry California Chenin Blanc, such as 1986 Chappellet or Villa Mt. Eden*

Almond Cream Sundae with Fresh Fruit and Hot Chocolate (p. 217)

chicken has only a trace of pink in the center, about 12 minutes.

5. Turn the broiler on and broil the chicken until the skin is browned and crisp, about 1 minute. Let the chicken stand for 2 to 3 minutes while you reheat the sauce over low heat. Stir the lemon juice, scallions and mustard seeds into the sauce.

6. To serve, arrange a chicken breast on each of 6 dinner plates. Spoon the sauce on top.

—*Marcia Kiesel*

• • •

SESAME OAT CHICKEN

Ground oats make a crunchy coating for boneless chicken breasts. They can be applied equally well to fish fillets. Sesame seeds, which provide more fiber, add a nice texture and flavor to chicken. Thyme is a delicious seasoning for either fowl or fish, but feel free to substitute any dried herb.

——————— *4 Servings* ———————
⅔ cup old-fashioned rolled oats
6 tablespoons olive, sunflower or
*   safflower oil*
1 teaspoon thyme
½ teaspoon freshly ground white
*   pepper*
1 tablespoon sesame seeds
1½ pounds skinless, boneless
*   chicken breasts or thin white fish*
*   fillets*
Salt (optional)
Lemon wedges, for garnish

1. In a food processor, process the rolled oats until finely ground.

2. In a large heavy skillet, preferably cast iron, heat about 3 tablespoons of the oil (the amount will depend on the size of the pan) over moderately high heat until hot but not smoking.

3. Meanwhile, on a plate or in a pie pan, toss together the ground oats, thyme, white pepper and sesame seeds. Dredge the chicken or fish in the oat mixture, pressing to coat well.

4. Place half of the chicken breasts or fish fillets in the hot pan and fry until browned, 3 to 4 minutes per side for the chicken, and 1 to 2 minutes per side for the fish. Drain on paper towels and blot lightly. Keep warm in a low oven. Repeat with the remaining oil and chicken or fish. Serve with a sprinkling of salt if desired and the lemon wedges.

—Tracey Seaman

• • •

SPICY GRILLED CITRUS CHICKEN

In a sense, the zesty marinade used to flavor the chicken breasts is related to Mexican *sangrita* because tomato, orange and lime are combined to make a luscious barbecue sauce with a kick of hot pepper and a lick of honey. The chicken must marinate for about 12 hours, so plan accordingly.

——————— *6 Servings* ———————
1 can (6 ounces) frozen orange juice
*   concentrate, thawed*
½ cup canned tomato puree
¼ cup honey
1 teaspoon minced orange zest
1 teaspoon minced lemon zest
1 teaspoon minced lime zest
3 tablespoons fresh lemon juice
3 tablespoons fresh lime juice
4 garlic cloves, crushed through a
*   press*
1 teaspoon thyme leaves
¾ teaspoon cayenne pepper
¾ teaspoon freshly ground black
*   pepper*
1 teaspoon salt
6 chicken breast halves with skin
*   and bones (about ½ pound each)*

1. In a large bowl, combine the orange juice concentrate, tomato puree, honey, orange zest, lemon zest, lime zest, lemon juice, lime juice, garlic, thyme, cayenne, black pepper and salt. Mix to blend well.

2. Add the chicken and turn to coat. Cover and refrigerate for 12 hours, or overnight.

3. Light a charcoal fire. When the coals are glowing, place a lightly oiled grill about 5 inches above the fire and heat for 5 minutes. Remove the chicken from the marinade; reserve the marinade. Place the chicken, bone-side down, on the grill. Cook for 5 minutes.

4. Meanwhile, pour the marinade into a small nonreactive saucepan and bring to a boil over moderate heat. Boil for 1 minute. After the chicken has cooked for

5 minutes, spoon some of the marinade over each piece and turn. Grill, basting with the marinade and turning every 5 minutes, for 20 to 30 minutes, until the chicken is white throughout but still juicy.

—Jim Fobel

• • •

SAUTEED GEWURZTRAMINER CHICKEN WITH CABBAGE AND LEEKS

The chicken thighs for this dish are marinated for 24 hours, so plan accordingly.
❦ This dish requires a fragrant Alsace Gewürztraminer with good acidity to cut through the richness of bacon and sautéed cabbage. Look for less ripe vintages such as the 1984 Zind-Humbrecht or the 1986 Willm. Do not use the sweeter versions labeled either Vendange Tardive or Sélection de Grains Nobles.

——————— *4 Servings* ———————
8 chicken thighs, boned
¾ teaspoon salt
¾ teaspoon freshly ground pepper
2 cups plus 4 teaspoons young Alsace
*   Gewürztraminer*
7 slices of smoked bacon
2 garlic cloves, minced
2 medium leeks (white part only),
*   cut into thin julienne strips*
3 pounds savoy, Napa or Chinese
*   cabbage (1 large head), shredded*
¼ teaspoon freshly grated nutmeg
1 cup all-purpose flour, for dredging
7 tablespoons unsalted butter
1 cup chicken stock or canned broth
1 tablespoon chopped parsley

1. Season the chicken thighs with ½ teaspoon of the salt and ¼ teaspoon of the pepper. Place in a shallow nonreactive dish just large enough to hold the thighs. Pour in enough Gerwürztraminer to cover, approximately 2 cups. Cover with plastic wrap and refrigerate for 24 hours.

2. Remove the chicken from the marinade, reserving the liquid. Pat dry with paper towels. Cut eight 2-inch-long pieces of bacon from the bacon slices. Tuck 1 piece under the skin of each thigh. Cut the remaining bacon crosswise into ½-inch pieces. Season the thighs with the remaining ¼ teaspoon salt and ¼ teaspoon of the pepper.

3. In a large heavy skillet, preferably cast iron, cook the bacon pieces over moderate heat until crisp, 5 to 7 minutes. Remove the bacon with a slotted spoon and drain on paper towels. Pour off all but 1 tablespoon of the fat and return the skillet to the heat.

4. Add the garlic and leeks to the skillet and cook over moderately low heat until softened but not browned, about 5 minutes.

5. Increase the heat to high and add the cabbage and nutmeg. Cook, tossing well, until wilted, about 3 minutes. (Add ¼ cup of water to the skillet if it seems dry.)

6. Stir in the remaining 4 teaspoons wine and ¼ teaspoon pepper; remove from the heat. Transfer the cabbage to a bowl. Add the reserved bacon and toss well. Cover and keep warm.

7. Wipe out the skillet with a paper towel. Place the flour in a shallow dish. Dredge the chicken thighs in the flour, shaking off the excess. Add 3 tablespoons of the butter to the skillet and melt over moderately high heat until foaming. Add the chicken, skin-side down. Cook over high heat until browned, about 5 minutes. Turn and brown the other side, 3 to 4 minutes longer. Remove and drain on paper towels. Cover the chicken with foil to keep warm while preparing the sauce.

8. In a small nonreactive skillet, boil the stock over high heat until reduced by half, about 3 minutes. Add ½ cup of the reserved Gewürztraminer marinade and bring just to a boil. Remove from the heat. Whisk in the remaining 4 table-spoons butter, 1 tablespoon at a time, moving the pan on and off the heat until the butter is absorbed by the sauce.

9. To serve, divide the cabbage among 4 dinner plates. Nestle 2 chicken thighs on top of each mound of cabbage. Pour the sauce over the chicken and cabbage and sprinkle the parsley on top.
—*David Rosengarten*

• • •

DRUMSTICKS ALONG THE MOHAWK

These drumsticks can be baked several hours ahead and reheated under the broiler just before serving. They are also good at room temperature, but the skin won't be as crisp. The chicken must be marinated for a minimum of 2 hours, but it can also marinate for up to 2 days.

🍷 Spicy white, such as 1987 Mirassou Gewürztraminer

4 Servings

⅓ cup Dijon-style mustard
2 garlic cloves, crushed through a press
1 tablespoon Worcestershire sauce
1 tablespoon vegetable oil
1½ teaspoons hot pepper sauce
1 teaspoon paprika
8 chicken drumsticks, skin slashed at ½-inch intervals

1. In a small bowl, combine the mustard, garlic, Worcestershire sauce, oil, hot sauce and paprika; mix well.

2. Dip each drumstick in the sauce and arrange in a shallow glass dish. Pour any extra sauce over the chicken. Cover with plastic wrap and marinate in the refrigerator for at least 2 or up to 48 hours. Let the chicken return to room temperature before cooking.

3. Preheat the oven to 375°. Bake the chicken for about 35 minutes, or until the outside is browned and the juices run clear when the thickest part is pricked to the bone.

4. Preheat the broiler. Broil the drumsticks 4 inches from the heat for about 2 minutes on each side to crisp the skin. Serve warm.
—*F&W*

• • •

SPICY BAKED SPINACH CHICKEN

Although free-range chickens have more flavor and leaner meat, this dish can certainly be made with a regular, supermarket-variety chicken. Just be sure to remove and discard any excess fat from the chicken before baking.

4 to 6 Servings

5 tablespoons unsalted butter, at room temperature
¼ cup crumbled feta cheese
1 package (10 ounces) frozen chopped spinach, thawed and squeezed dry
½ teaspoon minced fresh jalapeño
1 whole free-range chicken (4½ to 5½ pounds), thighs and legs separated, breast quartered
¼ cup Dijon-style mustard
1 cup fresh bread crumbs
½ teaspoon salt
¼ teaspoon freshly ground pepper

1. In a food processor, combine 3 tablespoons of the butter, the feta cheese, spinach and jalapeño pepper. Puree until smooth. Transfer to a small bowl and refrigerate until firm, about 10 minutes.

2. Wipe the chicken pieces. Carefully separate the skin from the meat and stuff 1 tablespoon of the spinach mixture under the skin of each piece of chicken. Pat the skin in place. Slather the chicken with mustard and place skin-side up on a baking sheet. Refrigerate for 30 minutes. Meanwhile, preheat the oven to 350°.

3. Season the bread crumbs with the salt and pepper. Place in a shallow bowl and roll each piece of mustard chicken in the crumbs. Return the chicken to the baking sheet. Dab each piece with the remaining 2 tablespoons butter. Bake in the preheated oven for 1½ hours, or until the skin is golden and crisp and the meat is falling from the bones.

—*Molly O'Neill*

• • •

SHERRIED CHICKEN WITH STICKY-LICK-IT BARBECUE SAUCE

The sherry marinade brings depth of flavor to the chicken and is then used to make a sticky barbecue sauce. The chicken must marinate for about 6 hours, so plan accordingly.

♟ Chilled rosé, such as 1988 McDowell Zinfandel Blanc or 1987 Simi Rosé of Cabernet Sauvignon

———— *4 Servings* ————
2 cups dry sherry
¼ cup fresh lemon juice
2 bay leaves
2 large garlic cloves, crushed through a press
1 small onion, finely chopped
1 whole chicken (about 4 pounds), cut into 8 pieces
1 can (15 ounces) tomato puree
¼ cup honey
3 tablespoons light molasses
1 teaspoon salt
½ teaspoon cayenne pepper
½ teaspoon thyme
¼ teaspoon freshly ground black pepper
2 tablespoons white wine vinegar

1. In a large bowl, combine the sherry, lemon juice, bay leaves, garlic and onion.

AFTER-WORK DINNER PARTY

The dishes in this dinner menu from W. Peter Prestcott were designed with the working cook in mind. For the most part, shopping for the dinner can be done all in one place, on the way home from work. Even better, of course, would be to make this on the weekend when you have plenty of time. Serves 6.

Roast Beef and Horseradish Spirals (p. 13)

Smoked Trout on Sliced Apples

Three Types of Brined Olives

———

Greenport Soup (p. 30)

Parmesan Croutons (p. 173)

———

Orange and Coriander Chicken with Rice (p. 87)

Glazed Carrots

♟ *California Chardonnay, such as 1986 Rodney Strong "Chalk Hill" or 1986 Viansa*

———

Mixed Green Salad

St. André Cheese

French Bread

———

Baked Nebraskas (p. 203)

Add the chicken and toss well. Cover and marinate in the refrigerator for 6 hours, or overnight.

2. Drain the chicken, reserving the marinade. In a heavy, medium nonreactive saucepan, combine the reserved marinade with the tomato puree, honey, molasses, salt, cayenne, thyme and black pepper. Bring to a boil over moderate heat. Reduce the heat to moderately low

and cook, stirring occasionally, until the sauce is thick and rich and reduced to 2 cups, 35 to 45 minutes. Remove from the heat and stir in the vinegar. Remove the bay leaves.

3. Light a charcoal fire. Grill the chicken over glowing hot coals for 10 minutes, turning 2 or 3 times. Spoon some of the sauce over the pieces and continue grilling, basting liberally with sauce and turning every 5 minutes, until cooked through, 20 to 30 minutes longer.

—*Jim Fobel*

• • •

ORANGE AND CORIANDER CHICKEN WITH RICE

This flavorsome combination makes a great dish for last-minute entertaining. I've substituted leftover roast pork for the chicken with great results.

♟ California Chardonnay, such as 1986 Rodney Strong "Chalk Hill" or 1986 Viansa

———— *6 Servings* ————
⅓ cup fresh lemon juice
3 tablespoons tamari or soy sauce
2 teaspoons grated fresh ginger
2 dashes of hot pepper sauce
2 broiled chickens, cut into 6 serving pieces each
3 tablespoons olive oil
1 medium onion, thinly sliced
1 garlic clove, minced
¾ pound mushrooms, thinly sliced
½ teaspoon ground ginger
½ teaspoon salt
⅛ teaspoon freshly ground pepper
2 cups rice
2 cups canned chicken broth
1 cup dry white wine
½ cup minced fresh coriander
1 tablespoon grated orange zest

1. In a large bowl, combine the lemon juice, tamari, grated ginger and hot pep-

POULTRY

per sauce. Add the chicken pieces and toss well to coat.

2. Preheat the oven to 375°. In a large flameproof casserole, heat the oil. Add the onion and garlic and cook over moderate heat until softened, about 5 minutes.

3. Add the mushrooms and cook, stirring, until softened, about 5 minutes. Stir in the ground ginger, salt and pepper.

4. Add the rice to the casserole and increase the heat to moderately high. Cook, stirring constantly, until the rice is translucent, about 3 minutes. Stir in the chicken broth, wine and ½ cup of water. Bring to a boil and stir well. Cover tightly and bake for 10 minutes.

5. Uncover and arrange the chicken pieces on top of the rice. Pour on any remaining marinade and sprinkle with the coriander and orange zest. Cover and bake until the chicken is heated through and the rice is tender, about 10 minutes.

—W. Peter Prestcott

• • •

GRILLED CHICKEN IN A SPECIAL SAUCE

This is one of Indonesia's finest chicken preparations. The key is the balanced combination of spices and seasonings that are simmered in coconut milk until reduced to a thick paste.

———— **12 Servings** ————
2 whole chickens (3 pounds each)
12 macadamia nuts
8 shallots, sliced
3 garlic cloves, sliced
1-inch piece of fresh ginger, peeled and sliced
2 teaspoons salt
¼ teaspoon turmeric
1 tablespoon brown sugar
1 to 2 teaspoons crushed hot red pepper, to taste
3 cups homemade coconut milk, or 1½ cups canned unsweetened* mixed with 1½ cups water

A CROWD-PLEASING POLENTA

Lee Bailey admits that he came up with the flavorful chicken and sausage dish for this menu just so he could have something to go with polenta, the Italian cousin of two of his southern childhood favorites—grits and corn bread. Serves 6.

Green Pea Soup (p. 28)

Grilled Polenta (p. 130)

Chicken, Sausage, Sweet Peppers and Olives (p. 88)

♟ *Dry Red Wine*

Mixed Green Salad

Fresh Pineapple Mousse (p. 199)

Coffee

1 tablespoon corn oil
3 slices of laos root (galingale)*
2 slices of lemon
*Available at Asian markets

1. Cut the backbone off both chickens. Cut each bird into 10 serving pieces: separate the drumsticks and thighs and the wings; cut each breast crosswise into 2 pieces. Pull off all the skin you can and trim off any excess fat.

2. Light a charcoal grill or preheat the broiler. Grill the chicken pieces over charcoal or broil about 4 inches from the heat, turning once, for 3 minutes on each side to sear the outside. Set aside.

3. In a food processor, grind the macadamia nuts to a smooth paste. Add the shallots, garlic, ginger, salt, turmeric, brown sugar, hot pepper and ½ cup of the coconut milk. Puree the spice paste until smooth.

4. In a large flameproof casserole, heat the oil. Add the coconut spice paste and

stir-fry over moderate heat until the liquid evaporates, about 2 minutes. Add the remaining 2½ cups coconut milk, the laos root and the lemon. Boil until reduced by one-third, about 5 minutes.

5. Add the chicken, reduce the heat to moderately low and simmer, uncovered, until the chicken is tender, about 30 minutes. Boil until the liquid in the pan is reduced to a thick sauce, about 10 minutes. *(The recipe can be prepared up to 2 days ahead and refrigerated. Reheat before serving.)* Serve warm.

—Copeland Marks

• • •

CHICKEN, SAUSAGE, SWEET PEPPERS AND OLIVES

The chicken must marinate for at least 6 hours before cooking, so plan accordingly. Serve alongside Grilled Polenta (p. 130).

———— **6 Servings** ————
4 skinless, boneless chicken breast halves (1¼ pounds total), cut lengthwise into ½-inch strips
1 cup milk
¼ cup hot pepper sauce, preferably Louisiana hot sauce
1¼ pounds bulk pork sausage
2 large garlic cloves, halved and crushed
1 cup dry red wine
1 can (28 ounces) Italian peeled tomatoes, drained and coarsely chopped
½ cup beef stock or canned broth
2 tablespoons olive oil
4 medium yellow bell peppers, cut into ½-inch dice
24 oil-cured black olives, halved

1. In a medium bowl, combine the chicken, milk and hot sauce. Cover and refrigerate for 6 hours or overnight.

2. Form the sausage meat into 18 patties. In a large nonreactive skillet, fry the sausage patties over high heat, turning once, until very brown, 2 to 3 minutes on each side. Drain on paper towels.

3. Pour out the fat. Return the sausage pattties to the pan. Add the garlic and wine. Cover and simmer over moderate heat, turning the patties once, until the liquid is reduced to ¼ cup, about 12 minutes.

4. Add the tomatoes and stock and simmer, uncovered, for 5 minutes.

5. Meanwhile, in a large heavy skillet, heat 1 tablespoon of the olive oil over high heat. Add the yellow peppers and toss to coat well. Sauté, stirring occasionally, until lightly browned and crisp-tender, about 5 minutes. Add the peppers to the sausage patties. Cover and set aside.

6. Drain the chicken and pat dry with paper towels. Discard the marinade. In the large skillet used to fry the peppers, heat the remaining 1 tablespoon olive oil. Add the chicken and cook over high heat, turning constantly, until just white throughout, 3 to 5 minutes. Using a slotted spoon, add the chicken to the sausage patties and peppers. Add the olives and stir to combine.

—*Lee Bailey*

• • •

RAGOUT OF CHICKEN WITH BLACK OLIVES AND ONION JAM

Braised on the bone with browned onions and olives, free-range chicken stays moist and picks up a heady aroma. Serve this dish with buttered egg noodles.

❦ Light California red, such as 1986 Sinskey or Mark West Pinot Noir

———————— *8 Servings* ————————
2 whole free-range chickens (4½ to 5½ pounds each)
2 cups all-purpose flour
1 teaspoon salt
½ teaspoon freshly ground pepper
6 tablespoons unsalted butter
4 pounds large white onions, thickly sliced

2 cups (about 1 pound) oil-cured black olives, pitted (see Note)
4 cups Rich Free-Range Chicken Stock (p. 247)
½ cup dry sherry
2 tablespoons grated lemon zest
2 teaspoons thyme

1. Cut off the wing tips from the chickens. Cut each chicken into 8 pieces: Cut off the legs and separate the drumsticks and thighs. Cut out the backbone and separate the two breasts on the bone with the wings attached. Using a heavy sharp knife, cut crosswise through the bone of each breast to cut into 2 pieces. Rinse the chicken pieces and pat dry.

2. Preheat the oven to 325°. In a medium bowl, combine the flour, salt and pepper. Dredge the chicken pieces in the seasoned flour. In a large flameproof casserole, melt 4 tablespoons of the butter over moderately high heat. Add the coated chicken in 3 batches and cook, turning, until browned, about 4 minutes on each side. As the chicken is cooked, transfer it to a bowl. Wipe out the casserole with paper towels.

3. In the casserole, melt the remaining 2 tablespoons butter over moderate heat. Add the onions, cover and cook until softened, about 15 minutes. Uncover and cook, stirring occasionally, until caramelized to a golden brown, about 25 minutes.

4. Add the olives, chicken stock, sherry, lemon zest and thyme and bring to a boil. Add the chicken pieces. Cover and transfer to the oven. Bake, stirring occasionally, until the chicken is tender, about 1 hour and 15 minutes.

5. Remove the chicken and boil the liquid until the sauce thickens slightly, 5 to 10 minutes. Season with additional salt and pepper to taste. Return the chicken to the casserole.

NOTE: Oil-cured olives can be very salty and may need to be blanched: Place

the olives in a medium saucepan, cover with cold water and bring to a boil over high heat. Drain and rinse under cold water. If still too salty, repeat.

—*Molly O'Neill*

• • •

CHICKEN STEW WITH CORIANDER AND CUMIN

This is my version of a traditional Colombian dish, which was taught to me by a friend from Bogotá. Start the meal with a spinach and bacon salad tossed with sherry vinegar dressing and accompany the chicken with steamed potatoes.

❦ The mildness of chicken means that the zesty spices provide the dominant flavor. Complexity would be wasted, so choose a strong but straightforward white, such as 1987 Hogue Cellars Fumé Blanc or 1986 Columbia Crest Chardonnay.

———————— *4 Servings* ————————
1 tablespoon olive oil
8 chicken thighs (about 2 pounds)
1 teaspoon salt
1 cup dry white wine
½ cup chicken stock or canned broth
1 cup heavy cream
1 tablespoon ground cumin
1 pound carrots, quartered lengthwise, cut into 1-inch-long pieces
1 package (10 ounces) frozen corn kernels
¼ cup chopped fresh coriander
¼ teaspoon freshly ground pepper

1. In a large heavy skillet, heat the olive oil over moderately high heat. Season the chicken with the salt and add to the pan, skin-side down. Sauté until golden brown on the bottom, about 5 to 6 minutes. Turn and cook until browned on the other side, about 5 minutes longer. Drain the chicken on paper towels. Transfer to a large flameproof casserole.

2. Pour off the fat from the skillet. Add the wine and bring to a boil over moderately high heat, scraping up the brown bits from the bottom of the pan. Boil until the wine is reduced by half, about 4 minutes.

3. Stir in the chicken stock, cream and cumin. Pour the liquid into the casserole and bring to a boil over moderate heat. Cover, reduce the heat to low and simmer for 15 minutes.

4. Meanwhile, in a medium saucepan of boiling salted water, cook the carrots until tender, about 15 minutes. Drain.

5. Add the carrots and the frozen corn to the casserole and continue to cook until the corn is heated through, 5 to 7 minutes. Stir in the coriander and pepper and serve.

—*Nora Carey*

• • •

CHICKEN ENCHILADA CASSEROLE WITH SALSA VERDE

You can make this up to three months ahead and freeze it or up to three days ahead and refrigerate it.

———————— **6 Servings** ————————
1 whole roasting chicken (3½ to 4½ pounds)
1 medium carrot, coarsely chopped
2 thick slices of Spanish onion
2 garlic cloves, coarsely chopped
1 teaspoon salt
4 cups corn oil
12 corn tortillas
1 cup heavy cream
½ cup sour cream (see Note)
Salsa Verde (p. 252)
1 cup chopped scallions (white and tender green)
1½ cups coarsely grated Monterey Jack cheese (about 6 ounces)
1½ cups coarsely grated sharp Cheddar cheese (about 6 ounces)
6 lettuce leaves and 6 radish roses, for garnish

1. Put the chicken in a large heavy stockpot or flameproof casserole. Add the carrot, onion, garlic, salt and enough water to cover and bring to a boil. Reduce the heat to a simmer, cover and cook until the chicken is very tender, about 1½ hours.

2. Remove the pot from the heat, uncover and let the chicken cool in the poaching liquid for 1 hour.

3. Pull the chicken off the bones; discard the bones and skin. Tear the meat into ½-by-2-inch strips. Reserve the chicken broth for another use.

4. In a deep-fryer, heat the oil to 375°. Quickly fry the tortillas in the hot oil, 2 or 3 at a time, until crisp. Drain well on paper towels.

5. Preheat the oven to 375°. Lightly oil the bottom of a large shallow baking dish. In a small bowl, combine the heavy cream and sour cream and blend well.

6. Spread ½ cup of the Salsa Verde over the bottom of the baking dish and cover with 6 of the tortillas. Drizzle the tortillas with ½ cup of the salsa and arrange the chicken on top. Spread half the sour cream mixture over the chicken and sprinkle with half the scallions and 1 cup of each cheese. Arrange the remaining 6 tortillas on top and cover with the remaining salsa and cheese. Pour the remaining sour cream mixture on top and sprinkle with the remaining scallions. *(The dish can be prepared ahead to this point. Cover well with plastic wrap and refrigerate for up to 3 days or freeze for up to 3 months. Return to room temperature before baking.)*

7. Bake, uncovered, for 30 to 35 minutes, until the casserole is heated through and the cheese is melted. Garnish each dish with a lettuce leaf and radish rose.

NOTE: If you make the hotter all-chile version of the Salsa Verde, increase the amount of sour cream to 1 cup to tame the heat of the chiles.

—*Jane Butel*

• • •

CHICKEN PANCAKES

It's best not to make these too large. They cook quickly, so it's not a chore.

———— *Makes 24 Small Pancakes* ————
6 medium chicken thighs (1¾ pounds total)
1¼ teaspoons salt
¾ teaspoon freshly ground pepper
1 medium Idaho potato
1 small onion, coarsely grated
2 tablespoons all-purpose flour
2 dashes of hot pepper sauce
3 eggs, lightly beaten
2 tablespoons unsalted butter
2 tablespoons safflower oil
Pear Salsa (p. 253)

1. Preheat the oven to 375°. Season the chicken with ½ teaspoon each salt and pepper. Put the thighs snugly, skin-side

---

SUPPER FOR A FEW CLOSE FRIENDS

As an antidote to elaborate parties and holiday entertaining, Lee Bailey likes to plan a number of small, laid-back dinners in which everything can be prepared ahead. He also recommends having a store-bought dessert if there is the slightest chance that the cook will be pressed for time. Serves 6.

Chicken Pancakes (p. 90) with Pear Salsa (p. 253)

Green Bean and Potato Puree (p. 118)

❦ *Dry Red Wine*

———————————————

Honey-Pepper Grapefruit with Cinnamon Strips (p. 212)

Coffee

up with the skin stretched out, in a baking dish. Bake for 35 minutes, or until the juices run clear when pricked with a knife. Turn off the heat and leave the chicken in the oven for another 45 minutes without opening the door.

2. When the chicken is cool enough to handle, remove the skin and bones and discard. Chop the chicken coarsely. *(The recipe can be done to this point up to 1 day ahead. Cover and refrigerate.)*

3. Peel the potato, grate it and squeeze out as much liquid as possible. In a medium bowl, combine the potato, onion, flour, hot sauce, remaining ¾ teaspoon salt and ¼ teaspoon pepper. Mix to blend well. Add the chicken and eggs and mix.

4. In a large nonstick skillet, melt the butter in the oil over moderate heat until hot but not smoking. Drop rounded tablespoons of the batter into the skillet, allowing room for them to spread. Cook over moderately high heat, until golden on the bottom and set, about 4 minutes. Turn over, flatten slightly with a spatula and cook until golden on the bottom, about 2 minutes longer. Serve the pancakes on a warmed platter with the Pear Salsa on the side.

—Lee Bailey

• • •

TERIYAKI CORNISH HENS

I love the big taste of these little birds, especially after they are marinated in the refrigerator for a day. Don't be alarmed by the large quantity of ginger. It contributes great taste.

——————— *4 Servings* ———————
4 Cornish game hens (about 1½ pounds each)
¾ cup chopped, peeled fresh ginger (about 4 ounces)
2 tablespoons minced garlic
½ cup sugar
1 cup sake
½ cup soy sauce

1. The day before you want to grill the game hens, rinse them under cool water and pat dry. Cut along each side of the spine to free the backbones and discard. Flatten the birds slightly with a mallet or side of a cleaver or with the bottom of a cast-iron skillet.

2. In a blender or food processor, combine the ginger, garlic, sugar, sake and soy sauce. Puree until smooth. Pour the marinade into a large nonreactive baking dish. Add the hens and turn. Marinate in the refrigerator for at least 24 hours, turning occasionally.

3. Light a charcoal fire. When the coals are glowing but covered in gray ash, drain the hens and put them bone-side down on the grill, about 5 inches from the heat. Grill, turning every 5 minutes or so, until the thigh juices run clear when the meat is pricked and the skin is well browned, 18 to 25 minutes.

—Jim Fobel

• • •

CITRUS CORNISH HENS

These succulent little birds are glamorized by the addition of sweet-tart grapefruit. For best success, choose juicy grapefruits that feel heavy for their size. I like to serve the hens with a simple rice pilaf or wild rice and a buttered green vegetable, such as broccoli or peas.
🍷 Alsace Riesling, such as 1986 Trimbach or Zind-Humbrecht

——————— *4 Servings* ———————
4 Cornish game hens (about 1 pound each)
4 large pink grapefruits
4 tablespoons unsalted butter, softened to room temperature
1 cup Madeira
Salt and freshly ground pepper

½ cup chopped pistachio nuts (about 2½ ounces)

1. Preheat the oven to 375°. Rinse the Cornish hens inside and out and pat them dry with paper towels.

2. Grate the yellow zest from 2 of the grapefruits, leaving the bitter white pith. In a small heatproof bowl, pour boiling water over the grated zest and let stand for 1 minute. Drain well.

3. In a small bowl, combine the grapefruit zest with the butter. Blend well. Spread 1 tablespoon of grapefruit butter under the breast skin of each hen.

4. Using a sharp knife, peel and section all 4 grapefruits, cutting in between the membranes. Squeeze the membranes over a bowl and set aside ¼ cup of the grapefruit juice.

5. Stuff the cavities of the hens with half of the grapefruit sections. Reserve the remaining sections for garnish.

6. Truss the hens and place in a medium roasting pan. Baste the birds with the reserved grapefruit juice and bake for 1 hour, basting every 15 minutes. The hens are done when the juices run clear when a thigh is pricked. Transfer the birds to a warmed platter and cover loosely with aluminum foil.

7. Using a bulb baster, remove any fat from the juices in the roasting pan. Set the pan over moderate heat, add the Madeira and bring to a boil. Reduce to a simmer and cook, stirring, until the sauce is thickened, 3 to 4 minutes. Strain the sauce and season with salt and pepper to taste.

8. Remove the trussing strings from the hens. Halve each bird lengthwise and discard the grapefruit sections. Arrange the hens on a serving platter or on individual plates. Garnish with the reserved fresh grapefruit sections and sprinkle the pistachio nuts on top. Pass the sauce separately.

—W. Peter Prestcott

• • •

THANKSGIVING TURKEY WITH MUSHROOM GRAVY

You may want to have the butcher remove the wishbone to facilitate stuffing the turkey and carving it after roasting.

❦ Though turkey goes with a wide variety of wines, the many side dishes Thanksgiving turkeys are ordinarily served with require a simple, fruity light red, such as a 1987 Duboeuf Beaujolais-Villages or 1987 Beaulieu Vineyard Gamay Beaujolais, which will bridge the different tastes and match the festive mood. A fruity sparkling wine, such as Korbel Brut Rosé, would make a delightful alternative.

────── 6 to 8 Servings ──────
1 fresh turkey (10 to 12 pounds), at room temperature, neck reserved
½ lemon
Corn Bread Dressing (recipe follows)
Chestnut Dressing (p. 93)
¾ teaspoon salt
¾ teaspoon freshly ground white pepper
1 stick (4 ounces) plus 1½ tablespoons unsalted butter, softened to room temperature
½ pound mushrooms, sliced
3 tablespoons all-purpose flour
3 cups chicken stock or canned broth
1 tablespoon finely chopped parsley

1. Preheat the oven to 425°. Rinse the turkey thoroughly with cold water inside and out. Dry the turkey with paper towels. Rub the inside of the bird with the lemon half.

2. Spoon about 7 cups of the Corn Bread Dressing into the large tail cavity of the turkey to stuff it loosely. Stuff the smaller neck cavity loosely with some of the Chestnut Dressing; cover with the skin flap. (Place the extra stuffing in a baking dish and bake during the last 15 minutes the turkey roasts and while it rests.) To truss the turkey, close the tail

SOUTHERN THANKSGIVING DINNER

As is clear from the following line-up, southerners do not take Thanksgiving dinner lightly. Camille Glenn, southerner and author of the menu, puts it this way: "It is our favorite holiday . . . We are not overly frugal. We admire elegance, and we love frills." Serves 6 to 8.

cavity after stuffing by securing it with twine. Tie the wings close to the body and tie the legs together.

3. Season the turkey with ¼ teaspoon each of the salt and white pepper. Rub 4 tablespoons of the butter into the skin. Set the turkey on its side in a large roasting pan.

4. Roast the turkey until the top side is brown, about 30 minutes. Turn the turkey onto its other side and roast until brown, about 30 minutes longer. Meanwhile, melt 4 tablespoons of the butter. Dampen and thoroughly wring out a 14-by-24-inch piece of cheesecloth. Put it in a small bowl and pour the melted butter over it, turning to coat the cloth evenly.

5. When both sides of the turkey are brown, turn it on its back. Cover it with the buttered cheesecloth. Add the neck to the pan.

6. Reduce the oven temperature to 325°. Baste the turkey breast thoroughly with the pan drippings, using a large bulb baster. Roast the turkey, basting whenever the cheesecloth dries out, for 1½ hours.

7. Carefully remove the cheesecloth and roast, basting every 15 minutes, until the turkey is browned, the juices in the thickest part of the thigh run clear when pricked and a thermometer thrust into the thick part of the bird's thigh registers between 165° and 170°, 60 to 70 minutes longer. Allow the turkey to rest for 15 to 20 minutes before carving.

8. Meanwhile in a large skillet, melt the remaining 1½ tablespoons butter over high heat. Add the mushrooms and cook, stirring occasionally, until the mushrooms are tender and any liquid evaporates, about 3 minutes. Set aside.

9. Transfer the turkey to a carving board. Discard all but ¼ cup fat from the roasting pan. Place the pan over 2 burners set on moderate heat. Add the flour to the fat. Cook, stirring, for 1 to 2 minutes. Whisk in the chicken stock. Bring to a boil, whisking until the sauce is thickened and smooth, about 4 minutes.

10. Add the sautéed mushrooms, the remaining ½ teaspoon each salt and pepper and the parsley. Cook for 1 to 2 minutes to blend the flavors. Serve in a warm sauceboat with the carved turkey.

—*Camille Glenn*

• • •

CORN BREAD DRESSING

Half of this dressing recipe is enough to stuff the cavity of a 10- to 12-pound turkey. Spoon the second half into a baking dish and bake for about 25 minutes in a preheated 350° oven, or until golden brown. This second method makes a drier stuffing than the one inside the turkey.

——— *Makes About 14 Cups* ———
Corn Bread for Thanksgiving
 Dressing (recipe follows),
 coarsely crumbled (about 12 cups)
1 pound bulk pork sausage
4 medium onions, finely chopped
4 tender pale celery ribs, finely
 chopped
1¼ teaspoons thyme
½ teaspoon sage
½ teaspoon baking powder
1¾ teaspoons salt
1¼ teaspoons freshly ground pepper
2 eggs, lightly beaten
½ cup chicken broth or water

1. Put the crumbled corn bread in a large bowl.

2. Form the sausage into 2-inch flat patties and cook in a heavy skillet over moderate heat, turning, until light brown, about 5 minutes per side. Drain the sausage on paper towels and let cool; then break into small pieces. Add to the corn bread.

3. In a medium saucepan, combine the onions and celery. Add cold water to cover. Bring to a boil over high heat and cook until the vegetables are tender but still crisp, about 3 minutes. Drain well. Add to the corn bread and sausage.

4. Sprinkle the thyme, sage, baking powder, salt and pepper over the dressing. Add the eggs and broth and mix the dressing thoroughly with a large cooking fork to moisten evenly without packing the dressing.

—*Camille Glenn*

• • •

CHESTNUT DRESSING

Only a portion of this dressing is used to stuff Thanksgiving Turkey with Mushroom Gravy (p. 92). Bake the remainder separately in a baking dish.

——— *Makes About 11 Cups* ———
2 pounds large chestnuts in the shell
2 cups chicken stock or low-sodium
 canned broth
1½ sticks (6 ounces) unsalted butter
6 tender pale celery ribs, finely
 chopped
2 medium onions, finely chopped
10 cups coarse fresh bread crumbs
 (from 1 pound 5 ounces firm-
 textured white bread)
2 teaspoons marjoram
1 teaspoon thyme
2 teaspoons salt
1 teaspoon freshly ground pepper

1. Slash the brown shells of the chestnuts on both sides. Drop the chestnuts into a large saucepan of boiling water and cook for 5 minutes. Drain and remove the shells and brown skins while the chestnuts are hot so that they will peel off easily. Cut the chestnuts in half.

2. In a medium saucepan, bring the chicken stock to a simmer over moderate heat. Add the peeled chestnuts and cook until just tender but still firm, about 8 minutes. Drain, reserving the stock. (*The chestnuts can be prepared up to 2 days in advance. Refrigerate covered.*)

3. In a large saucepan, melt 1 stick of the butter. Add the celery, onions and 1½ cups of the reserved stock. Cook over moderately high heat until the broth has boiled away, about 15 minutes. Do not allow the butter to sizzle the least bit or the celery and onions to brown.

4. Melt the remaining 4 tablespoons butter in a small saucepan over moderately low heat or in a heatproof glass bowl in a microwave oven.

5. In a large bowl, combine the celery, onions, bread crumbs and reserved chestnuts. Add the melted butter, marjoram, thyme, salt and pepper. Mix well with a large fork. If the dressing is too crumbly or dry, add the remaining stock. The dressing should be pleasingly moist but not wet.

—*Camille Glenn*

• • •

CORN BREAD FOR THANKSGIVING DRESSING

This recipe combines flour and cornmeal to make an exceptionally light corn bread for poultry stuffing.

Makes About 12 Cups
——— *Crumbled Corn Bread* ———
4 eggs
1½ cups milk
1½ cups white cornmeal (not stone-
 ground)
1½ cups all-purpose flour
1½ sticks (6 ounces) unsalted
 butter, melted
1 tablespoon plus 1 teaspoon baking
 powder
1½ teaspoons salt
1½ teaspoons sugar

1. Preheat the oven to 450°. Lightly grease two 9-inch round cake pans. In a large bowl, combine the eggs and milk. Whisk lightly to blend.

2. In a medium bowl, mix together the cornmeal and flour. Add to the eggs and

milk, whisking to blend well. Add the butter, baking powder, salt and sugar. Mix thoroughly. Spoon the batter into the prepared pans.

3. Bake the corn bread in the center of the oven for 20 minutes, or until it is golden brown on top and a cake tester inserted in the center comes out clean.

4. Invert the corn bread onto a rack to cool. Crumble coarsely. Spread out on a baking sheet to dry completely. *(It's a good idea to do this a day in advance. The corn bread can be baked, cooled, wrapped in aluminum foil and frozen up to 2 weeks in advance.)*

—*Camille Glenn*

• • •

TURKEY BREASTS WITH GRAPEFRUIT SAUCE

If your turkey breasts look a little ragged when you serve them, placing some sprigs of parsley or watercress around them will work wonders.

————— **6 Servings** —————

1½ cups chicken stock or canned low-sodium broth
2 tablespoons juniper berries, coarsely crushed
½ cup all-purpose flour, for dredging
½ teaspoon salt
½ teaspoon freshly ground black pepper
12 slices of uncooked turkey breast (3 ounces each)
½ cup olive oil
2 medium shallots, peeled and thinly sliced
¾ cup fresh grapefruit juice
½ cup frozen apple juice concentrate, thawed
½ teaspoon thyme
½ teaspoon freshly ground white pepper
¼ teaspoon cayenne pepper
Pinch of cumin

2 tablespoons unsalted butter
Peeled grapefruit slices, for garnish

1. In a small saucepan, combine the chicken stock and the juniper berries. Bring to a boil over moderate heat. Reduce the heat to low and simmer for 5 minutes.

2. Meanwhile, in a pie pan or other shallow dish, toss together the flour, salt and black pepper. Dredge the turkey slices in the seasoned flour and shake off any excess.

3. In a large skillet, heat 2 tablespoons of the olive oil over moderately high heat. Add 3 turkey cutlets and sauté until golden brown, firm and white throughout, about 2 minutes per side. Transfer to a warm platter. Repeat the process with the remaining olive oil and turkey slices, cover and set aside.

4. Reduce the heat to moderately low and add the shallots to the skillet. Sauté, stirring constantly, for about 3 minutes, until they begin to soften. Add the grapefruit juice and apple juice. Increase the heat to moderately high and bring to a boil, scraping up any brown bits from the bottom of the pan.

5. Strain the chicken stock and juniper berry sauce into the pan. Discard the juniper berries. Add the thyme, white pepper, cayenne and cumin. Boil until the liquid is reduced to about 2 cups, about 5 minutes.

6. Return the cooked turkey cutlets to the pan and cook just until heated through, about 2 minutes. Transfer the turkey to a large, warm serving platter.

7. Whisk the butter into the sauce in the pan and season with additional salt and white pepper to taste. Pour the sauce over the turkey cutlets and garnish with the grapefruit slices.

—*Lee Bailey*

• • •

LET'S TALK TURKEY

Turkey provides a wonderful foil for the tart, fresh taste of grapefruit in this menu from Lee Bailey. For those guests who might not be avid citrus fans, substitute raspberry or currant jam for the marmalade in the dessert. Serves 6.

Turkey Breasts with Grapefruit Sauce (p. 94)

Parsley Rice Soufflé (p. 116)

Green and Wax Beans with Parmesan Cheese (p. 118)

❦ *Dry Red Wine*

Cold Marmalade Custard (p. 201)

Coffee

GRILLED LEMON DUCK

Although most Asian markets carry both fresh and dried lemon grass, if you can only find the dried version, soak it for 15 minutes or so in warm water to cover. Then add it, and the soaking water, in Step 3.

————— **4 Servings** —————

1 whole duck (4½ to 5 pounds), excess fat removed
2 tablespoons peanut oil
2 dried hot red peppers
1½ tablespoons grated lemon zest
2 stalks of fresh lemon grass* (bottom third only), thinly sliced on the diagonal
4 garlic cloves, smashed
6 slices of fresh ginger, peeled and smashed
¼ cup plus 2 tablespoons fresh lemon juice
⅔ cup (packed) brown sugar

2 tablespoons Thai or Vietnamese
  fish sauce (nuoc mam)*
2 tablespoons dark soy sauce*
1 teaspoon salt
½ teaspoon freshly ground white
  pepper
½ cup chopped fresh coriander
*Available at Asian markets

1. Rinse the duck and pat dry. With a chef's knife or poultry shears, cut along both sides of the backbone and remove it. Spread the duck on a work surface and press on the breastbone to flatten it.

2. In a large flameproof casserole, heat the oil over moderately high heat. Add the hot peppers, lemon zest, lemon grass, garlic and ginger. Stir-fry just until fragrant, about 30 seconds.

3. Add 2 quarts of water and bring to a boil. Add the duck and return to a boil. Reduce the heat to moderately low. Add the lemon juice, brown sugar, fish sauce, soy sauce and salt. Cover and simmer, turning once or twice, for 40 minutes.

4. Remove the duck to a rack. Skim the fat from the surface of the duck cooking liquid. Boil over high heat until the liquid is reduced to about 1½ cups of thin syrup, about 20 minutes. Pour the syrup into a bowl and let cool slightly.

5. With a basting brush, paint the duck all over with some of the syrup. Set aside, uncovered, in a cool, airy place and let stand for 1 hour. Paint the duck again. Season all over with the white pepper.

6. Preheat the oven to 450°. Place the duck on a rack in a roasting pan, skin-side up. Roast for 15 minutes; baste with more of the syrup. Continue to roast until the duck is tender and the skin is browned and crisp, about 20 minutes longer.

7. Remove the duck to a carving board. With a heavy cleaver, chop the duck into 10 pieces. Transfer to a serving platter. Sprinkle the chopped coriander over the duck. Reheat the remaining syrup and serve as a sauce for dipping.

—*Bruce Cost*

• • •

DUCK WITH SPICY EGGPLANT

The fermented, spiced bean curd adds a savory flavor and lovely bronze hue to the duck. If you can't find red bean curd, substitute about one teaspoon bean paste with garlic and/or chiles. The duck must marinate for a minimum of 2 hours (and up to 24), so plan accordingly.

❡ Despite the spiciness of this dish, the richness of the duck and pungency of the eggplant can be matched with peppery, gutsy reds, such as 1985 Mirassou Petite Sirah or 1985 Quivira Zinfandel.

————— 4 Servings —————

1 whole duck (about 4½ pounds) or
  2 whole boneless duck breasts,
  skin on
6 garlic cloves, crushed through a
  press
1 tablespoon sugar
¼ teaspoon freshly ground pepper
2 square (1-inch) pieces of red bean
  curd*
2 teaspoons medium-dry sherry
¼ cup vegetable oil
2 large eggplants (about 3 pounds
  each)
2 large scallions, thinly sliced
¼ cup plus 2 tablespoons Nuoc Cham
  Dipping Sauce (p. 251)
Cherry tomatoes, for garnish
*Available at Asian markets

1. If using a whole duck, carve the breast meat from each side of the bone in one piece, leaving the skin intact. Remove the legs and thighs. Set skin-side down and, with a small sharp knife, cut down the center of the leg to the bone. Scrape against the bone and pull the meat away to remove it in one piece, severing

the connections around the knuckle. Remove as many tendons as possible. If using duck breasts, divide each in half. Place the duck pieces in a shallow dish large enough to hold them in a single layer. Reserve any remaining duck for stock.

2. In a small bowl, mash 4 of the crushed garlic cloves with the sugar and pepper to make a paste. Stir in the bean curd, sherry and 2 tablespoons of the oil. Rub the paste evenly over the duck pieces and let stand, covered, at room temperature for 2 hours or in the refrigerator for up to 24 hours.

3. Preheat the oven to 450°. Place the eggplants on a baking sheet and pierce in 2 or 3 places. Roast in the oven for about 45 minutes, turning once, until very soft and charred all over. Let cool slightly, then cut off the stem end and peel off the skin (it should come off easily in large pieces); leave the eggplants as whole as possible. Set aside.

4. Preheat the broiler. Place the duck pieces, skin-side down, on a baking sheet and broil about 8 inches from the heat for about 5 minutes, until the meat is deep brown on the outside. Turn and cook until the skin is dark brown and the meat is tender but still rosy, about 5 minutes longer.

5. Meanwhile, heat the remaining 2 tablespoons oil in a large skillet over high heat. Add the remaining 2 crushed garlic cloves and the scallions and cook, stirring, until fragrant, about 1 minute.

6. Add the eggplants and cook, stirring and separating into long pieces with chopsticks or 2 forks until softened to a creamy consistency, about 5 minutes. Then stir in the Nuoc Cham Dipping Sauce, bring to a boil and remove from the heat.

7. To serve, place the eggplant on a large platter. Top with the broiled duck pieces. Garnish with cherry tomatoes.

—*Marcia Kiesel*

• • •

ROASTED DUCK BREASTS AND TURNIPS WITH CRANBERRY MARMALADE

The fat from the duck imparts a wonderful flavor to the roasted turnips. Parboiled carrots, potatoes or small whole onions can also be added to the roasting pan at the same time as the turnips. For an added touch of sophistication, on each plate fan the slices of duck on one side and the turnips on the other.

❦ This rich duck dish combines the earthiness of turnips with the tartness of cranberries, which points to a hearty red as the best match. Either a 1985 Guigal Côtes du Rhône or a 1986 Barbi Rosso di Montalcino would be ideal here.

――――――― **6 Servings** ―――――――
1 tablespoon olive oil
1 small onion, thinly sliced
*2½ cups (8 ounces) fresh or frozen
    cranberries*
½ cup unsweetened apple juice
2 tablespoons fresh lemon juice
1 tablespoon soy sauce
⅓ cup sugar
*2 pounds small turnips, peeled and
    quartered*
*2 whole duck breasts, boned and
    split, skin removed and reserved*
1 teaspoon salt
Watercress, for garnish

1. Preheat the oven to 450°. In a medium nonreactive saucepan, heat the olive oil over moderate heat. Add the onion and sauté until softened but not browned, about 5 minutes.

2. Add the cranberries, apple juice, lemon juice, soy sauce and sugar. Bring to a boil, cover, reduce the heat to low and simmer until the cranberries begin to burst, 5 to 10 minutes.

3. Meanwhile, in a large saucepan of boiling salted water, cook the turnips until tender, 8 to 10 minutes. Drain and set aside.

4. Put the duck skin in a large roasting pan, and put in the oven. Cook until about ¼ cup of fat has been rendered, about 5 minutes. Discard the skin.

5. Add the turnips and duck breasts to the pan in an even layer and season with the salt. Roast for 15 minutes, or until the turnips are browned and the duck is just slightly pink in the center. Transfer the duck to a carving board, cover loosely with aluminum foil and let rest for 5 minutes. Turn off the oven and leave the turnips in the roasting pan until ready to serve.

6. Warm the cranberry sauce over moderately low heat. Slice the breasts into thin slices. Transfer any meat juices to the sauce.

7. To serve, divide the duck slices and turnips among 6 warmed plates. Spoon the sauce in between the meat and vegetables and garnish with watercress.

—*Nora Carey*

• • •

ALLARD'S ROAST DUCK WITH OLIVES

Allard, one of Paris's longtime popular bistros, has had this dish on their menu for decades. The recipe comes from the notebooks of Marthe Allard, the restaurant's first cook.

❦ With this, sample a fruity red, such as a Cru Beaujolais Fleurie.

――――――― **4 Servings** ―――――――
*2 tablespoons chicken fat, or 1
    tablespoon oil and 1 tablespoon
    unsalted butter*
*2 pounds chicken wings or backs, cut
    up*
*1 whole duck (about 4½ pounds),
    trussed, neck and gizzard
    reserved*
3 onions, minced
1½ tablespoons all-purpose flour
2 cups dry white wine
*2 quarts chicken stock, or 2 cans
    (13¾ ounces each) chicken broth
    plus 1 quart water*
*Bouquet garni: 12 parsley stems, 8
    peppercorns, ¼ teaspoon thyme,
    ¼ teaspoon fennel seeds and 1
    imported bay leaf tied in a double
    thickness of cheesecloth*
⅓ cup tomato paste
*½ pound brine-cured green olives,
    pitted*
*2 tablespoons unsalted butter, at
    room temperature*

1. In a large stockpot or flameproof casserole, melt the chicken fat over moderate heat. Add the chicken wings and reserved duck neck and gizzards. Cook, stirring over moderately high heat, until golden, about 8 minutes.

2. Add the onions and cook until softened but not browned, about 5 minutes. Sprinkle the flour on top and cook, stirring, for 1 minute.

3. Add the white wine, stock, bouquet garni and tomato paste. Simmer, uncovered, over low heat for 2 hours, stirring occasionally. Strain the sauce through a fine sieve.

4. In a medium saucepan, bring 4 cups of water to a boil. Add the olives and boil over high heat for 2 minutes; drain and rinse under cold running water; drain well. Taste an olive; if still very salty, repeat this blanching.

5. Transfer the olives to a large nonreactive saucepan and cover them with the strained sauce. Simmer, uncovered, over low heat until the sauce is just thick enough to coat a spoon, 1 to 1½ hours.

6. Meanwhile, preheat the oven to 425°. Pierce the duck skin all over with a knife and rub with the butter. Place the bird, breast-side down, on a rack in a roasting pan and roast for 30 minutes. Reduce the oven temperature to 350°, turn the duck breast-side up and roast until the juices run clear when the thigh is pierced with a skewer, about 1 hour.

7. To serve, carve the duck, place on a large deep platter and surround it with the green olives and their sauce.

—*Patricia Wells*

• • •

ROASTED GOOSE WITH CHICKEN LIVER STUFFING

If at all possible, buy a goose that has not been frozen. For six people, one goose is ideal if you learn how to carve it properly (see Note, below). Since goose has a lot of fat, render it and use it to make the Rich Chicken Liver Stuffing, or save it to make delicious confits or roast potatoes.

🍷 Bordeaux, such as 1978 Château Gruaud-Larose

6 Servings
10-pound goose, preferably fresh, gizzard and liver reserved for the stuffing
1 tablespoon minced garlic
1 tablespoon thyme
1 tablespoon coarse (kosher) salt
Rich Chicken Liver Stuffing (p. 98)
3½ cups Goose Stock (p. 247)
4 tablespoons unsalted butter
Freshly ground pepper

1. Trim the goose: Remove the wishbone by cutting off the membrane around the wishbone. With your fingers, loosen the bone and with a small sharp knife, pry the bone loose from the breast meat, breaking it off on both sides of the wings.

INTIMATE CHRISTMAS DINNER FOR SIX

The flavors and the style of this Christmas dinner menu from cooking teacher Lydie Pinoy Marshall are decidedly and deliciously French. Although the roster of dishes may sound imposing, a good deal of the work can be done days and even weeks ahead of time. Serves 6.

Salmon Caviar Toasts (p. 16)

🍷 *Veuve Clicquot or Billecart-Salmon Champagne*

Cream of Carrot and Lemon Soup (p. 29)

Roasted Goose with Chicken Liver Stuffing (p. 97)

Candied Quinces (p. 126)

Flageolets with Garlic Cloves (p. 129)

🍷 *Jaboulet Côte Rôtie or Faraud Gigondas*

Salad of Watercress, Arugula and Fennel (p. 140)

Cheese Platter: Stilton, Chèvre and Brie

🍷 *Joseph Swan Zinfandel*

Ali Baba (p. 237)

🍷 *Château d'Yquem*

French Macaroons with Chocolate Cream Filling (p. 241)

Café Filtre

Reserve the wishbone and the neck for the goose stock. Cut off the wing tip and the second joint of the wings and reserve them for the goose stock. Remove all the loose fat from the cavity. Rinse the cavity of the bird and pat dry. *(The goose can be prepared to this point up to 2 days in advance. Wrap in aluminum foil and refrigerate.)*

2. The day before you roast the goose, combine the minced garlic, thyme and salt. Rub this dry marinade all over the breast, thighs and legs of the goose. Wrap and refrigerate until ready to roast. Remove the bird from the refrigerator 1 to 2 hours before roasting to let it come to room temperature.

3. Preheat the oven to 425°. Prick the skin of the goose all over. Spoon the Rich Chicken Liver Stuffing into the cavity of the goose and sew it up. Put the goose, breast-side down, in a gratin dish or a roasting pan just large enough to hold the bird. Pour 1 cup of stock into the pan.

4. Roast the goose for 15 minutes. Baste the goose with the pan drippings. Reduce the oven temperature to 350° and continue to roast, basting every 10 minutes, for 1 hour.

5. Remove the goose from the oven. Carefully loosen the goose from the pan and transfer it to a board. Drain all the fat from the pan into a large heatproof glass bowl. Return the goose to the roasting pan, breast-side up; add another ½ cup of the goose stock to the pan. Continue roasting for 30 minutes, basting with the pan drippings every 10 minutes.

6. Remove the goose from the oven and again drain the fat into the bowl. Return the goose to the oven, still breast-side up. Add another ½ cup of the stock and roast for 30 minutes longer, or until the goose is golden brown and tender.

Transfer the goose to a carving board and let rest, covered loosely with aluminum foil, for about 20 minutes before carving.

7. Meanwhile, drain the fat from the roasting pan into the bowl. There will be 4 to 6 cups of fat. At the bottom of the fat in the glass bowl, you will see the drippings from the roast. Use a gravy separator or just pour and skim off the fat (if you want to save the flavorful fat for a future use, strain it into a container; it freezes well). Reserve the goose drippings in the bottom of the bowl.

8. Pour the reserved drippings into the roasting pan. Add the remaining 1½ cups goose stock to the pan and bring to a boil over high heat, scraping up the browned bits from the bottom of the pan. Boil until the liquid is reduced to 1 cup.

9. Strain the stock into a clean saucepan and whisk in the butter. Season the sauce with additional salt and pepper to taste. Carve the goose (see Note) and pass the sauce in a gravy boat on the side.

NOTE: To carve a goose: Cut through the shoulder joints to separate the first joint of the wings from the body. Then cut the skin between the legs and the body and push down on the legs to expose the thigh joints; cut through the joints. With the skin-side down, cut through the leg to separate into drumstick and thigh. With a long thin carving knife held parallel to the breast (an electric knife is great for this), cut the breast meat into thin slices.

—Lydie Pinoy Marshall
• • •

RICH CHICKEN LIVER STUFFING

Because it is so rich and moist, this stuffing tastes almost like a mousse.

——— Makes About 3¼ Cups ———
*4 tablespoons rendered goose fat or
    unsalted butter*
2 onions, finely chopped
*3 cups fresh bread crumbs (from 4 to
    5 slices of firm-textured white
    bread, crusts removed)*
½ cup chopped parsley
¾ pound chicken livers, trimmed
*1 goose gizzard and liver (reserved
    from Roasted Goose, p. 97)*
2 teaspoons salt
1 teaspoon oregano
2 eggs, lightly beaten

1. In a large skillet, melt the goose fat over moderate heat. Add the onions and cook, stirring, until softened but not browned, about 10 minutes.

2. Add the bread crumbs and parsley. Cook, stirring occasionally, until lightly toasted, about 5 minutes. Remove from the heat and let cool for 15 minutes.

3. Put the chicken livers and the reserved turkey liver in a food processor. Add the bread and onion mixture, salt, oregano, eggs and reserved gizzard. Turn the machine quickly on and off 10 to 12 times to chop finely. *(The stuffing can be prepared 2 days ahead. Store covered and refrigerated.)*

—Lydie Pinoy Marshall
• • •

PASTA & RICE

PASTA & RICE

ORZO WITH ONIONS AND BLACK OLIVES

This is a simple and comforting dish made with the small rice-shaped pasta called orzo.

───────── 6 Servings ─────────
4 tablespoons unsalted butter
2 cups coarsely chopped onions
1 cup brine-cured black olives, such as Calamata, pitted and coarsely chopped
2 cups orzo (about 12 ounces)
Salt and freshly ground pepper

1. In a large saucepan, melt the butter over moderately low heat. Add the onions and sauté until softened but not browned, about 5 minutes. Toss in the olives and set aside.

2. In a medium saucepan of boiling salted water, cook the orzo until tender but firm, about 10 minutes; drain well.

3. Reheat the onions and olives over low heat and toss in the orzo. Season with salt and pepper to taste.

—*Lee Bailey*

• • •

PASTA WITH TOMATO AND BLACK OLIVE SAUCE WITH ARUGULA

Imported canned tomatoes are the tomatoes of choice when good fresh ones are not available. Quick cooking keeps the flavor of this sauce lively.

───────── 4 to 6 Servings ─────────
¼ cup extra-virgin olive oil
3 garlic cloves, minced
½ teaspoon crushed hot red pepper
1 can (35 ounces) Italian peeled tomatoes, drained and chopped
½ cup Calamata olives, pitted and quartered
¼ teaspoon salt
¼ teaspoon freshly ground black pepper

2 bunches of arugula, trimmed and coarsely chopped (about 2 cups)
1 pound rigatoni or gnochetti rigati
Freshly grated Parmesan cheese, as accompaniment

1. In a large nonreactive skillet, combine the oil, garlic and hot pepper. Cook over low heat until the garlic is softened and fragrant, about 3 minutes.

2. Add the tomatoes, olives, salt and black pepper. Increase the heat to moderately high and simmer until the juices thicken to form a sauce, about 10 minutes.

3. Meanwhile, place the arugula in a pasta serving bowl. Cook the rigatoni in a large pot of boiling salted water until tender but still firm, about 10 minutes. Drain well and toss with the arugula. Add the sauce and toss. Serve with a bowl of Parmesan cheese on the side.

—*Viana La Place & Evan Kleiman*

• • •

COUNTRY-STYLE PASTA WITH RICOTTA

Adding some of the pasta cooking water to ricotta creates a sauce that is less rich than cream, yet clings nicely to the pasta. Bits of bacon and savory onion contribute additional flavor.

🍷 This creamy pasta dish, with its mild, complementary flavors of cheese, bacon and onion, makes a perfect foil for fruity but refined Italian reds, such as 1985 Antinori Pèppoli Chianti Classico or 1985 Frescobaldi Tenuta di Pomino.

───────── 4 to 6 Servings ─────────
2 thick slices of bacon, coarsely chopped
¼ cup extra-virgin olive oil
1 medium onion, chopped
1 pound part-skim ricotta cheese
¼ cup coarsely chopped Italian flat-leaf parsley
¼ cup coarsely chopped fresh basil

1 tablespoon finely chopped scallion green
1⅓ cups freshly grated Parmesan cheese
½ teaspoon salt
½ teaspoon freshly ground pepper
1 pound penne rigate

1. In a large heavy skillet, cook the bacon over moderate heat, stirring occasionally, until it is lightly browned and the fat is rendered, about 5 minutes.

2. Add the oil and onion. Reduce the heat to low and cook until the onion is softened and translucent, about 8 minutes. Remove from the heat and set aside.

SUMMER PASTA DINNER

Grilled vegetables are one of the delicious benefits of the summer season; not only is the weather cooperative, but the variety of fresh vegetables makes firing up the grill worth the effort. Summer is also a good time to make a delicious fresh berry dessert called summer pudding. Serves 6 to 8.

Portuguese Roasted Garlic Pâté (p. 256)

Whole-Grain Toast Points

Fusilli with Grilled Vegetables (p. 101)

🍷 *Fruity White, such as Robert Mondavi 1987 Johannisberg Riesling*

Chardenoux's Salad of Blue Cheese, Nuts and Belgian Endive (p. 141)

Summer Pudding (p. 217)

Iced Espresso

3. In a medium bowl, beat together the ricotta, parsley, basil, scallion green and ⅓ cup of the Parmesan cheese with a wooden spoon. Add to the cooked onion and bacon and season with the salt and pepper. Mix well.

4. Cook the pasta in a large pot of boiling salted water until tender but still firm, about 10 minutes. Meanwhile, add ¼ to ½ cup of the pasta cooking water to the ricotta sauce. Mix well.

5. Drain the cooked pasta and immediately transfer to a shallow pasta serving bowl. Quickly reheat the ricotta sauce if necessary, add to the pasta and toss to mix. Pass the remaining 1 cup Parmesan cheese on the side.

—Viana La Place & Evan Kleiman

• • •

FUSILLI WITH GRILLED VEGETABLES

This recipe can be varied according to the vegetables in season and the amount of time you wish to spend cooking. If you do not have a charcoal grill, you can broil the vegetables instead: Brush them with oil, spread in a single layer on baking sheets and broil about 4 inches from the heat. The cooking times will be a few minutes longer than those given in Steps 2 through 5, below.

❦ Fruity white, such as Robert Mondavi 1987 Johannisberg Riesling

———— *6 to 8 Servings* ————
4 small zucchini, cut lengthwise into thin slices
4 small, narrow Asian eggplants, trimmed and halved lengthwise
2 medium red onions, cut crosswise into ½-inch slices
3 Belgian endives, halved lengthwise
¾ cup extra-virgin olive oil
2 tablespoons balsamic vinegar
1 tablespoon fresh lemon juice
4 garlic cloves, minced
3 tablespoons shredded fresh basil
½ cup coarsely chopped Italian flat-leaf parsley
1 tablespoon minced fresh thyme or ½ teaspoon dried
12 oil-packed sun-dried tomatoes, cut into thin strips
¾ teaspoon salt
¼ teaspoon freshly ground pepper
1 pound fusilli or spaghetti
Freshly grated Parmesan cheese, as accompaniment

1. Light a charcoal grill. Lightly brush the zucchini, eggplants, red onions and Belgian endives with some of the olive oil.

2. When the coals are hot, grill the zucchini, turning once, for about 1 minute on each side, until lightly browned but still slightly firm. Transfer to a large shallow bowl.

3. Grill the eggplants, cut-side toward the heat, for about 2 minutes, until well browned. Turn and grill on the other side, just until the eggplants soften. Place them in the bowl with the zucchini.

4. Grill the onion slices, turning once, for about 5 minutes, until soft and translucent. Add to the other vegetables.

5. Grill the Belgian endives, turning, for about 4 minutes, until lightly browned all over and just wilted. Transfer to the bowl with the other vegetables.

6. When the grilled vegetables are cool enough to handle, cut the zucchini, eggplants and endives crosswise into thin strips. Cut the onion slices in half. Return the vegetables to the bowl and toss gently to mix.

7. In a small bowl, combine the remaining olive oil with the vinegar, lemon juice and garlic. Add the dressing to the grilled vegetables and toss gently to coat.

8. Add the basil, parsley, thyme, sun-dried tomatoes, salt and pepper to the grilled vegetables and again toss gently.

Set aside to marinate at room temperature for at least 1 hour.

9. When ready to serve, cook the fusilli in a large pot of boiling salted water until tender but still firm, about 10 minutes. Drain well and add to the vegetables. Toss gently to mix. Pass a bowl of Parmesan cheese on the side.

—Viana La Place & Evan Kleiman

• • •

PASTA WITH UNCOOKED PUTTANESCA SAUCE

This is an uncooked version of one of the most loved of all Roman sauces. In our recipe the tomato turns dark red and develops a rich flavor after marinating with the olives and anchovies.

❦ The capers, garlic and anchovies in this rich red sauce contribute the sort of zesty flavors that only an assertive, spicy red can match. Look for a peppery California Zinfandel, such as 1986 Ravenswood Sonoma or 1986 Villa Mt. Eden.

———— *4 to 6 Servings* ————
2 pounds plum tomatoes—peeled, seeded and cut into ½-inch dice
4 flat anchovies, chopped to a paste
½ cup oil-cured black olives, coarsely chopped
3 tablespoons drained small capers
½ cup chopped Italian flat-leaf parsley
2 garlic cloves, minced
½ teaspoon crushed hot red pepper
¼ teaspoon salt
½ cup extra-virgin olive oil
1 pound cavatappi or fusilli
Freshly grated Parmesan cheese, as accompaniment

1. In a medium bowl, combine the tomatoes, anchovies, olives, capers, parsley, garlic, hot pepper, salt and olive oil. Stir gently to combine. Cover with a towel and let the sauce marinate at room temperature for 30 to 60 minutes.

2. Cook the pasta in a large pot of boiling salted water until tender but still firm, about 10 minutes. Quickly drain and toss with the sauce in a shallow pasta bowl. Serve at once, with a bowl of Parmesan cheese on the side.

—Viana La Place & Evan Kleiman

• • •

CAPELLINI WITH CALAMARI AND SHRIMP

Chopped walnuts and hot red pepper add a delightful dimension to this light pasta from Tony's in Houston.

❢ The simple, pure flavors of the shrimp and squid marry very well with a light, uncomplicated red wine such as 1986 Bertani's Bardolino.

——————— *4 Servings* ———————
¼ cup chopped walnuts
¼ cup extra-virgin olive oil
2 large garlic cloves, minced
1½ cups chicken stock or canned broth
1 can (14 ounces) Italian peeled tomatoes, drained and chopped
¼ cup dry white wine
¼ cup chopped Italian flat-leaf parsley
1½ teaspoons oregano
½ teaspoon salt
¼ teaspoon freshly ground black pepper
¾ pound capellini
10 ounces cleaned squid, sliced into thin rings
½ pound large shrimp—shelled, deveined and cut into thirds
¼ teaspoon crushed hot red pepper

1. Preheat the oven to 325°. Place the walnuts on a baking sheet and bake for 10 minutes, or until lightly toasted. Let cool.

2. In a large nonreactive skillet, heat the olive oil. Add the garlic and cook over moderate heat until beginning to brown, about 2 minutes. Stir in the chicken stock, tomatoes, wine, parsley, oregano,

salt and black pepper. Bring to a boil. Reduce the heat to moderate and simmer until reduced by half, about 8 minutes.

3. In a large pot of boiling salted water, cook the capellini until tender but still firm, about 3 minutes.

4. Meanwhile, add the squid and shrimp to the sauce and simmer until the seafood is just barely cooked through, about 2 minutes.

5. Drain the pasta in a colander and transfer to a large serving bowl. Add the seafood sauce and toss well. Sprinkle with the hot pepper flakes and toasted walnuts. Serve immediately.

—Tony's, Houston

• • •

ANGELI CAFFE'S SPAGHETTI ALLA FANTASIA

In this pasta, the pepper's sweetness is reinforced by onion and basil, and the salty tang of Gorgonzola is a perfect foil.

❢ Pair the mix of vegetables, Gorgonzola and mildly sweet peppers with a fruity-crisp Sauvignon Blanc, such as 1986 Clos du Val from California or 1986 Hunters from New Zealand.

——————— *4 to 6 Servings* ———————
¼ cup extra-virgin olive oil
4 orange bell peppers, cut into ¼-inch strips
1 medium onion, minced
8 to 10 large fresh basil leaves, finely shredded
½ teaspoon salt
½ teaspoon freshly ground black pepper
1 pound spaghetti
½ pound Gorgonzola dolcelatte cheese, crumbled
Freshly grated Parmesan cheese, as accompaniment

1. In a large skillet, heat the oil. Add the peppers and onion and cook over

moderately low heat until tender, 7 to 8 minutes. Add the basil, salt and pepper toward the end of cooking. Cover and keep warm.

2. Meanwhile, cook the spaghetti in a large saucepan of boiling salted water until tender but still firm, 8 to 10 minutes. Drain well. Place the pasta in a shallow serving bowl. Add the Gorgonzola and toss gently until the cheese melts.

3. Add the pepper mixture and toss again. Pass a bowl of Parmesan cheese on the side.

—Evan Kleiman, Angeli Caffè, Los Angeles

• • •

LINGUINE WITH SARDINIAN CLAM SAUCE

This spicy clam sauce is from Alghero, Sardinia. The presence of green olives indicates a Spanish influence.

❢ Pair this salty dish with its accent of olives with a crisp Sauvignon Blanc, such as 1987 Beringer, or a weightier white with similar tartness, such as 1986 Buehler Napa Valley Pinot Blanc.

——————— *4 to 6 Servings* ———————
2 pounds hard-shelled clams, such as cherrystones or littlenecks
½ cup extra-virgin olive oil
4 garlic cloves, minced
½ teaspoon crushed hot red pepper
1 can (28 ounces) Italian peeled tomatoes, drained and chopped
¼ cup pitted green olives, quartered lengthwise
2 tablespoons coarsely chopped fresh oregano or 1 teaspoon dried
2 tablespoons coarsely chopped Italian flat-leaf parsley
1 cup dry white wine
1 pound linguine

1. To clean the clams, soak them in a sink full of lightly salted cold water for 30 minutes; scrub them, if necessary, to remove any sand from the shell. Rinse the clams under cold running water and place them in a bowl. Clean the sink thoroughly of all sand and fill again with cold salted water. Add the clams to the water and let soak for another 30 minutes.

2. Lift the clams out of the water and rinse under cold water. Place the cleaned clams in a bowl, discarding any that are open and do not close to the touch, any with cracked shells and any that seem too heavy (they are probably filled with mud). Set the clams aside in the refrigerator for up to 3 hours, until needed.

3. In a large nonreactive skillet or flameproof casserole, heat the oil over moderate heat. Add the garlic and hot pepper and cook until the garlic is fragrant, about 1 minute. Add the chopped tomatoes, olives, oregano and 1 tablespoon of the parsley. Cover and cook just until the tomatoes begin to break down, 3 to 5 minutes.

4. Add the clams and the wine to the tomato sauce. Cover, increase the heat to high and cook, shaking the pan occasionally to make sure each clam has contact with the heat, just until they open up, 3 to 5 minutes. (Discard any clams that refuse to open.) With a slotted spoon, quickly transfer all the clams to a bowl and cover to keep warm.

5. Meanwhile, cook the pasta in a large pot of boiling salted water until barely tender and still quite firm, 8 to 9 minutes; drain.

6. Add the pasta to the skillet with the tomato-clam sauce and toss over high heat to allow the pasta to absorb some of the sauce, and cook until tender but still firm, about 1 minute.

7. With tongs, transfer the pasta immediately to a large shallow serving bowl. Place the cooked clams in the shell all over the top of the pasta. Pour any juices left in the skillet over the clams. Sprinkle with the remaining 1 tablespoon chopped parsley.

—*Viana La Place & Evan Kleiman*

• • •

PASTA PRESTO

The main course for this pasta dinner can be put together in just half an hour, and the rest of the dishes can be made ahead of time. Serves 4 to 6.

Marinated Mushrooms with Roasted Red Peppers and Marjoram (p. 21)

Whole-Wheat Sourdough Bread

Pasta with Fresh Tuna (p. 103)

🍷 *Full-Bodied Chardonnay, such as 1986 Charles Shaw or 1986 Navarro*

Berry Fruit Salad (p. 151) with Lemon Sherbet

Pine Nut Wafers (p. 241)

PASTA WITH FRESH TUNA

Here is our fast version of a Sicilian dish in which a chunk of fresh tuna is stuffed with mint and garlic before being braised in tomato sauce. In our recipe the tuna is diced and quickly sautéed, then added to the sauce to finish cooking.

🍷 Full-bodied Chardonnay, such as 1986 Charles Shaw or 1986 Navarro

4 to 6 Servings

1/4 cup plus 2 tablespoons extra-virgin olive oil
1 large onion, cut into 1/2-inch dice
1 can (35 ounces) Italian peeled tomatoes, drained and coarsely chopped
3/4 teaspoon salt
1/2 teaspoon freshly ground pepper
1 pound fresh tuna, cut into 1/2-inch dice
1/2 cup chopped fresh mint
3 garlic cloves, thinly sliced
1 pound spaghetti or linguine

1. Place 1/4 cup of the oil and the onion in a large nonreactive skillet. Cook over low heat, stirring occasionally, until the onion is very soft, 10 to 12 minutes.

2. Add the tomatoes, 1/2 teaspoon of the salt and 1/4 teaspoon of the pepper. Cook over moderate heat, partially covered, until the juices thicken to form a sauce, about 5 minutes. Remove from the heat and set aside.

3. Season the tuna with the remaining 1/4 teaspoon each salt and pepper. In a medium skillet, heat the remaining 2 tablespoons oil. Add the tuna and cook over moderate heat, tossing occasionally, until the tuna is cooked on the surface but still raw in the center, about 4 minutes.

4. Add the tuna, mint and garlic to the tomato sauce and cook over moderate heat, stirring, until the tuna is just barely opaque throughout, 2 to 3 minutes.

5. Meanwhile, cook the spaghetti in a large pot of boiling salted water until tender but still firm, about 9 minutes. Drain well and transfer to a large shallow serving bowl.

6. Pour the hot sauce over the pasta and toss quickly to mix. Serve at once.

—*Viana La Place & Evan Kleiman*

• • •

BUCKWHEAT PASTA WITH KALE AND GOAT CHEESE

There is a classic Italian dish that combines buckwheat pasta with cabbage or spinach and Fontina cheese. This American variation uses kale and goat cheese for a flavorful dish that is perfect on cold winter nights.

🍷 Crisp savory white, such as 1986 Jepson Sauvignon Blanc, or 1986 Groth Sauvignon Blanc

4 Servings

2 pounds kale or collard greens,
tough stems removed
3 tablespoons unsalted butter
¼ cup minced shallots
2 ounces very thinly sliced
Smithfield ham or prosciutto,
trimmed of fat and cut into ¾-inch
squares
1¾ cups heavy cream
¼ pound mild goat cheese, such as
Montrachet or Bucheron
¾ cup freshly grated Parmesan
cheese
1 pound buckwheat pasta or whole
wheat fettuccine, broken into
3-inch pieces
½ teaspoon freshly ground pepper

1. Wash the kale well. Stack the leaves and cut into ⅜-inch-wide strips.

2. In a large pot of boiling salted water, blanch the kale until just tender, about 2 minutes. Drain thoroughly; squeeze dry and set aside.

3. In a large skillet, melt the butter over low heat. Add the shallots and cook, stirring frequently, to soften slightly, about 2 minutes. Add the ham and cook, stirring frequently, until the shallots are tender, 2 to 3 minutes. Add 1 cup of the cream and set aside.

4. In a small bowl, mash the goat cheese with the remaining ¾ cup cream until smooth. Add to the sauce in the skillet along with ¼ cup of the Parmesan cheese and the kale.

5. Cook the pasta according to package directions. Drain thoroughly.

6. Simmer the sauce, stirring frequently, until very slightly thickened, 1 to 2 minutes. (Do not cook too long or the cream will reduce too much and the sauce will be cloying.) Add the pasta to the sauce and toss well. Season with the pepper. Pass the remaining Parmesan cheese on the side.

—Sarah Belk

• • •

OATMEAL AND PEPPER PAPPARDELLE

Pasta dough made with ground rolled oats and durum wheat is rich in protein and fiber. The flavor stands up to highly seasoned sauces, but these tasty noodles are equally good when simply tossed with butter and a sprinkling of Parmesan cheese.

You will need a pasta machine to roll out the dough. (Of course, you can make other noodles, such as fettuccine, besides pappardelle. In Step 7, simply reset the pasta machine to the desired setting and run the pasta dough through to cut the noodles, instead of cutting by hand.)

Makes About 1½ Pounds

2 cups old-fashioned rolled oats
1½ cups durum wheat flour*
1 tablespoon coarsely ground pepper
3 eggs, lightly beaten
3 tablespoons extra-virgin olive oil
Cornmeal, for dusting
*Available at Italian and specialty
food markets

1. In a food processor, process the rolled oats until finely ground. Measure 1½ cups ground oats (save any extra for another use). Combine with the durum wheat flour and pepper in the food processor and process briefly to mix.

2. Whisk together the eggs, olive oil and 2 tablespoons of warm water. Add to the food processor and process, scraping down once, until the dough comes together in pea-size crumbs, about 20 seconds; do not overprocess.

3. Transfer the dough to a lightly floured surface and knead until smooth and elastic, about 6 minutes. Dust with additional flour (up to ⅓ cup) as necessary. Cover the dough with a kitchen towel and let rest for at least 30 minutes, or wrap in plastic and refrigerate overnight (in which case, let the dough stand at room temperature for 30 minutes before rolling).

4. Cut the dough into 6 equal pieces. Work 1 piece at a time, keeping the remaining dough covered. Dust a piece of the dough with flour, flatten it with the heel of your hand and brush off the excess flour with a pastry brush.

5. Set a pasta machine on the widest notch and roll the dough through. Fold the dough into thirds, as you would a business letter. Press lightly to seal. Dust with flour again (brushing off the excess), if necessary, to prevent sticking. Return the dough to the machine and roll through again. Continue rolling through consecutively narrower settings up to the third- or second-to-last setting, dusting with flour as necessary.

6. Set the sheet of dough on a clean, dry towel and let rest for 10 minutes. Meanwhile, continue with the remaining pieces of dough. (If a piece of dough becomes very long and unwieldy, cut it in half crosswise and continue with each half separately.)

7. Using a serrated pastry wheel or sharp knife and a 12-inch ruler as a guide, cut the sheets of dough into 1-inch-wide strips (or use the pasta machine as directed in the headnote). Lightly dust the strips with cornmeal, set on towels and let dry for about 20 minutes (or coil the strips into nests and let dry completely for later use).

8. In a large pot, bring 5 quarts of well-salted water to a boil over high heat. Reduce the heat to moderately high and add the pasta, swirling with a wooden spoon to prevent sticking. Cook until tender but still firm, about 3 minutes. Drain well in a large colander. Serve immediately with your favorite sauce.

—Tracey Seaman

• • •

PAPPARDELLE WITH CARROT AND ZUCCHINI RIBBONS

Colorful strands of carrot and zucchini heighten this pasta side dish.
♥ Rich white, such as 1987 Rosemount Sémillon or 1985 Rutherford Hill Chardonnay Reserve

6 Servings

2 large carrots, peeled
4 small zucchini
¼ pound thinly sliced prosciutto
2½ cups heavy cream
1 teaspoon freshly ground pepper
¾ teaspoon salt
½ teaspoon freshly grated nutmeg
½ pound pappardelle (wide Italian noodles) or fettuccine
½ cup plus 3 tablespoons freshly grated Parmesan cheese

1. Using a vegetable peeler, peel a few lengthwise strips from one side of each carrot to create a flat surface. Turn the carrots onto their flat side and continue peeling thin strips, making them as long as possible.

2. Peel strips from all 4 sides of the zucchini, but discard the inner core of seeds.

3. In a medium saucepan of boiling salted water, blanch the carrot strips until crisp-tender, about 2 minutes. Using a slotted spoon, transfer the carrot strips to a colander and rinse under cold running water. Drain well and set aside.

4. Blanch the zucchini in the same boiling water until bright green and barely tender, about 30 seconds. Drain, refresh, drain well and add to the carrots. *(The recipe can be prepared to this point up to 1 day in advance. Cover and refrigerate until ready to use.)*

5. Freeze the prosciutto slices until hard, about 20 minutes. Stack the frozen slices and cut them into ¼-inch-wide strips. Separate the strips and set aside.

6. In a large saucepan, bring the heavy cream to a boil, stirring, over high heat. Reduce the heat to low. Add the carrot, zucchini, prosciutto, pepper, salt and nutmeg. Cover and remove from the heat. *(The recipe can be prepared to this point up to 1 hour in advance.)*

7. In a large saucepan of boiling salted water, cook the pasta until tender but still firm, about 6 minutes for the pappardelle, 8 to 10 for the fettuccine; drain.

8. Add the pasta and 3 tablespoons of the Parmesan cheese to the cream sauce. Toss gently. Serve at once. Pass the remaining Parmesan cheese on the side.

—*Marcia Kiesel*

• • •

SPAGHETTI AND POTATOES WITH GARLIC AND OIL

One of my favorite garlic recipes is this family spaghetti dish from my childhood.

4 Servings

1 large all-purpose potato
12 ounces spaghetti
1 cup extra-virgin olive oil
12 garlic cloves, coarsely chopped
1 dried hot red pepper
¾ teaspoon salt
¼ teaspoon freshly ground pepper
¼ cup chopped parsley

1. Preheat the oven to 400°. Bake the potato for 40 to 50 minutes, until tender. When it is cool enough to handle, cut it crosswise into ¼-inch slices.

2. In a large pot of boiling salted water, cook the spaghetti until tender but still firm, 8 to 10 minutes.

3. Meanwhile, in a large saucepan, heat the olive oil until very hot. Add the garlic, hot pepper and potato; reduce the heat to moderate and cook, stirring frequently, until the ingredients are light golden, about 5 minutes.

4. In a colander, thoroughly drain the spaghetti as soon as it is cooked and add it to the saucepan with the potato. Mix well over moderate heat. Season with the salt and pepper.

5. Divide the pasta among 4 heated bowls, pouring any oil remaining in the saucepan over the top. Sprinkle each serving with the chopped parsley and additional salt and pepper to taste.

—*John Mariani*

• • •

PASTA FRITTATA

Use a well-seasoned cast-iron, or ovenproof nonstick skillet for this frittata. Any type of leftover cooked pasta will work well in the recipe.

6 to 8 Servings

½ ounce dried porcini mushrooms (about ½ cup)
½ cup uncooked elbow macaroni or 1¼ cups cooked pasta
2 teaspoons olive oil
2½ tablespoons unsalted butter
1 large onion, chopped
10 eggs
4 large plum tomatoes—peeled, seeded and chopped
2 tablespoons heavy cream
1 teaspoon salt
1 teaspoon freshly ground pepper
1 tablespoon chopped fresh marjoram
4 ounces Gruyère cheese, grated (about 1¼ cups)
Marjoram leaves, for garnish

1. Preheat the oven to 400°. In a small bowl, soak the dried mushrooms in ½ cup of boiling water until soft, about 20 minutes. Squeeze dry, discard any tough stems and chop coarsely. Set aside.

105

2. Meanwhile, cook the macaroni in a medium saucepan of boiling salted water until tender but firm, about 8 minutes. Drain, toss with the oil and set aside.

3. In a large ovenproof skillet, melt 1½ tablespoons of the butter over moderate heat. Add the onion, reduce the heat to low and cook, stirring occasionally, until golden and soft, about 12 minutes.

4. Meanwhile, in a large bowl, beat the eggs very lightly just to break the yolks. Stir in the tomatoes, reserved mushrooms, heavy cream, salt, pepper and chopped marjoram. Beat the mixture briefly to blend the ingredients evenly. Stir in the reserved pasta.

5. When the onions are ready, increase the heat to high and add the remaining 1 tablespoon butter. Heat until the butter is almost smoking, then pour in the egg mixture, stirring just to combine the onion with the egg. Leave the mixture on the heat until it starts to bubble around the edges, about 30 seconds. Remove from the burner and place the skillet in the center of the oven.

6. Bake until the frittata is just set, about 30 minutes. Return the skillet to the stovetop and place over high heat for about 10 seconds, shaking the pan to loosen the frittata; run a spatula around the edges if necessary. Using a spatula, slide the frittata onto a large ovenproof serving dish.

7. Preheat the broiler. Sprinkle the grated cheese on top of the frittata and place it under the broiler 6 to 8 inches away from the heat. Broil until the cheese melts, about 10 seconds.

8. Let the frittata stand at room temperature for at least 5 minutes before cutting into wedges. Serve warm or at room temperature. Garnish each serving with a sprinkling of marjoram leaves.

—*Marcia Kiesel*

• • •

NOSTALGIA SUPPER

Memories of school cafeterias notwithstanding, it's hard to beat the almost sinfully comforting flavors and textures of baked macaroni and cheese. To complement this rich dish, there are two very simple vegetable/salad side dishes, including a fresh pineapple and beet salad tossed with fresh lemon juice but no oil. Serves 4.

Comforting Cafeteria-Style Macaroni and Cheese (p. 106)

Cherry Tomatoes and Cucumber Cubes

Pineapple and Beet Salad (p. 143)

Chocolate Ice Cream Sandwiches (p. 204)

COMFORTING CAFETERIA-STYLE MACARONI AND CHEESE

The buttered crumbs on top are typical of this kind of all-American casserole—and delicious. This recipe couldn't be easier since there is no white sauce to prepare. Try it for a Sunday night supper when you're tucked in at home.

———— **4 Servings** ————
1½ cups milk
1½ teaspoons dry mustard
1 teaspoon Worcestershire sauce
¾ teaspoon salt
Few drops of hot pepper sauce
½ pound elbow macaroni
3½ tablespoons unsalted butter
1 egg, beaten
3½ cups grated sharp Cheddar cheese (about ¾ pound)
½ cup fresh bread crumbs
½ teaspoon paprika

1. Preheat the oven to 350°. Butter a shallow 2-quart baking or gratin dish.

2. In a small heavy saucepan, bring the milk to a simmer over moderate heat. Remove from the heat and stir in the mustard, Worcestershire sauce, salt and hot pepper sauce. Set the seasoned milk aside.

3. In a large pot of boiling salted water, cook the macaroni until tender but still firm, about 8 minutes. Drain well.

4. Transfer the hot macaroni to a medium bowl. Add 1½ tablespoons of the butter and the egg and mix well. Stir in 3 cups of the Cheddar cheese.

5. Spread the macaroni evenly in the buttered baking dish. Pour the reserved seasoned milk over the macaroni and sprinkle with the remaining ½ cup grated cheese.

6. In a small skillet, melt the remaining 2 tablespoons butter over moderate heat. Stir in the bread crumbs until well coated. Scatter the buttered crumbs evenly over the macaroni and sprinkle with the paprika.

7. Bake for 30 minutes, or until the macaroni is bubbling and lightly colored. Transfer to the broiler and broil about 6 inches from the heat until the bread crumbs are golden brown, 1 to 2 minutes.

—*Richard Sax*

• • •

TORTELLI WITH TOMATO SAUCE

Tortelli such as my mother, Theresa Rossi-Ferretti, made entail some effort and were done on a leisurely Sunday.

———— **6 Servings** ————
4 cups all-purpose flour
¼ teaspoon plus a pinch of salt
2 eggs
1 pound whole-milk ricotta cheese
½ cup freshly grated Parmesan cheese

1 tablespoon minced fresh basil
1 tablespoon minced parsley
1 garlic clove, minced
¼ teaspoon pepper
Fresh Plum Tomato Sauce (p. 249)

1. Place the flour and pinch of salt in a large bowl. Beat 1 of the eggs with ½ cup lukewarm water. Mix into the flour. If it is dry, add a bit more water by drops. Let the dough rest in the bowl, covered with plastic wrap, for at least 1 hour.

2. In a medium bowl, beat the remaining egg. Add the ricotta cheese, Parmesan cheese, basil, parsley, garlic, remaining ¼ teaspoon salt and the pepper and beat well. Refrigerate, covered, until ready to use.

3. Divide the dough into 4 pieces. Wrap 3 of the pieces in plastic wrap and set aside. Cut the piece of dough into 2 smaller pieces and roll each piece with a hand-crank pasta machine through the third to last setting, ⅟₁₆ to ⅛ inch thick (or roll the dough by hand to ⅛ inch thick).

4. Drop generous ½-teaspoonfuls of the cheese filling, 1 inch apart in straight rows, on 1 of the sheets of rolled dough. Place the second sheet on top of the filling. Using your finger, press lightly and indent between the filled mounds in both directions.

5. With a fluted pastry wheel or a knife, cut across and down the sheets to create the 2-inch squares of tortelli. Repeat with the remaining dough and filling. *(The recipe can be made to this point up to 2 days ahead, wrapped and refrigerated, or frozen for up to 1 month.)*

6. In a large saucepan, bring 2½ quarts of salted water to a boil over high heat. Add the tortelli and return to a boil. Cook until tender but still firm, about 6 minutes. Drain; then toss in a large bowl with the Fresh Plum Tomato Sauce.

—*Fred Ferretti*

• • •

PEKING NOODLES WITH GROUND PORK AND BEAN SAUCE

These eggless noodles, made only with flour and water, are popular in Beijing, where the staple is wheat rather than rice, and in Shanghai. The preserved beans with which they are cooked also impart a flavor from the north of China.

——— *6 Servings* ———

⅓ cup chicken stock or canned broth
1 tablespoon dark soy sauce*
1½ teaspoons Oriental sesame oil
1 teaspoon Shao-Hsing wine or dry sherry
1 teaspoon distilled white vinegar
2½ teaspoons sugar
⅛ teaspoon salt
Pinch of freshly ground white pepper
¼ pound fresh bean sprouts
½ pound fresh eggless Chinese noodles* or #17 linguine, preferably fresh
1½ tablespoons peanut oil
1 large garlic clove, minced
¼ pound ground pork
1½ tablespoons preserved horse beans with chili*
1 teaspoon Chinese chili sauce
¼ cup thinly sliced scallions
1½ tablespoons minced red bell pepper
*Available at Asian markets

1. In a bowl, combine the chicken stock, soy sauce, sesame oil, wine, vinegar, sugar, salt and white pepper.

2. Bring a large pot of water to a boil. Place the bean sprouts in a mesh strainer and lower them into the boiling water for 10 seconds. Remove and rinse under cold running water. Drain well.

3. Return the pot of water to a boil. Add the noodles, and stir to loosen them. Cook until tender but firm, 1 to 3 minutes for fresh, 10 for dried. Remove from the heat, run cold water into the pot to stop the cooking and drain the noodles immediately. Fill the pot with cold water and rinse the noodles again; drain well.

4. Heat a wok over high heat for 30 seconds. Add the peanut oil and swirl with a spatula to coat the wok. When a wisp of white smoke appears, add the garlic. Stir-fry until lightly browned, 30 to 45 seconds. Add the ground pork and stir well to break up any clumps. Add the horse beans, chili sauce and scallions. Cook, stirring frequently, until the pork is no longer pink, about 2 minutes. Stir in the sauce mixture and boil for 1 minute. Turn off the heat.

5. Arrange the blanched bean sprouts around the edge of a serving dish. Place the noodles in the center of the dish and pour the pork and bean mixture over the noodles. Garnish with the red pepper.

—*Eileen Yin-Fei Lo*

• • •

EGG NOODLES WITH GINGER AND LEEKS

This traditional Cantonese dish can be made with ordinary fresh ginger, but it is best with young ginger, recognizable by its very thin, translucent skin and pinkish shoots.

——— *6 Servings* ———

1½ tablespoons oyster sauce*
1¼ teaspoons light soy sauce
¾ teaspoon sugar
3 tablespoons chicken stock or canned broth
1 teaspoon Oriental sesame oil
Pinch of freshly ground white pepper
½ pound thin Chinese egg noodles* or #18 linguine, preferably fresh

2½ tablespoons peanut oil
¼ cup shredded young ginger or 3
  tablespoons shredded regular
  fresh ginger
1 large leek (white and tender
  green), sliced ¼ inch thick
*Available at Asian markets

1. In a medium bowl, combine the oyster sauce, soy sauce, sugar, chicken stock, sesame oil and white pepper.

2. In a large pot of boiling water, cook the noodles until tender but firm, about 1½ minutes for fresh, 10 for dried. Remove from the heat, run cold water into the pot to stop the cooking and drain the noodles immediately. Return the noodles to the pot and fill with cold water. Toss with your hands to rinse off all the surface starch and drain the noodles again. Rinse once again until the noodles are cool. Let drain for 10 to 15 minutes, loosening with chopsticks to help the draining process.

3. Heat a wok over high heat for 30 seconds. Add the peanut oil and swirl with a spatula to coat the wok. When a wisp of white smoke appears, add the ginger and stir-fry until fragrant, about 30 seconds. Add the sliced leek and stir-fry until wilted, about 1 minute.

4. Add the noodles and mix well. Cook, tossing, until very hot, about 1 minute. Make a well in the center of the noodles and add the oyster sauce mixture. Cook, tossing, until the noodles are well coated with the sauce. Serve at once.
—*Eileen Yin-Fei Lo*

• • •

LONGEVITY NOODLES WITH CLAMS AND TOMATOES

These long noodles are symbolic of the length of life to people in China. They are customarily served on birthdays. To combine them with clams, which symbolize prosperity, makes this a good luck dish indeed.

———— *6 Servings* ————
1 slice of fresh ginger, ¼ inch thick,
  plus 2 teaspoons grated fresh
  ginger
24 littleneck clams, scrubbed well
1 cake of Chinese dried "fried" egg
  noodles* or #8 spaghetti
½ cup chicken stock or canned broth
1 tablespoon oyster sauce*
1½ teaspoons light soy sauce
1½ teaspoons cornstarch
1 teaspoon sugar
¼ teaspoon salt
Pinch of freshly ground white pepper
1 teaspoon Oriental sesame oil
1 teaspoon dry white wine (optional)
3 tablespoons peanut oil
1 medium onion, minced
4 plum tomatoes—peeled, seeded
  and chopped—or 1 can (14
  ounces) Italian peeled tomatoes,
  drained and chopped
1 teaspoon minced fresh hot chile
  pepper or ½ teaspoon crushed hot
  red pepper
½ cup thinly sliced scallion green
*Available at Asian markets

1. Place 8 cups of water and the slice of ginger in a large saucepan and bring to a boil over high heat. Add the clams, cover and return to a boil. Cook until the clams

open, 2 to 3 minutes. Use a pair of tongs to remove the clams as they open and place them in a bowl. Discard the liquid and rinse out the pan.

2. Fill the saucepan with fresh water and bring to a boil. Add the noodles and loosen them with a fork or with chopsticks. Cook until the noodles are tender but firm, about 2 minutes for Chinese noodles or about 10 minutes for spaghetti. Run cold water into the pot and drain. Return the noodles to the pot. Fill with cold water and drain the noodles. Repeat once again.

3. In a small bowl, combine the chicken stock, oyster sauce, soy sauce, cornstarch, sugar, salt, white pepper, sesame oil and white wine. Set the sauce aside.

4. Heat a wok over high heat for 30 seconds. Add the peanut oil and swirl with a spatula to coat the wok. When a wisp of white smoke appears, add the onion. Stir-fry until softened and beginning to brown, about 2 minutes. Add ¾ cup of the tomatoes, the hot pepper and grated ginger. Bring to a boil and cook for 2 minutes.

5. Add the clams and stir until coated. Stir in the reserved sauce and cook until thickened, about 2 minutes. Add the noodles and scallion green. Toss well. Turn off the heat and transfer to a serving dish. Sprinkle the remaining tomatoes over the top and serve hot.
—*Eileen Yin-Fei Lo*

• • •

*Pappardelle with Carrot and
Zucchini Ribbons (p. 105).*

Above, Pasta with Uncooked Puttanesca Sauce (p. 101). Right, Zucchini and Sun-Dried Tomato Pizzas (p. 164).

AMOY RICE NOODLES WITH SHRIMP, ROAST PORK AND SZECHUAN MUSTARD PICKLE

Amoy is a small island off the Chinese mainland near Taiwan. The people there are from Fukien and are famous throughout China for the quality of the rice noodles they manufacture. The Fukienese like their noodles prepared in various ways. Occasionally they add a touch of sweetness by including Chinese ketchup (which is quite similar to American ketchup) in their cooking.

6 Servings

6 ounces very fine dry rice noodles* or capellini
¼ pound shrimp—shelled, deveined and cut lengthwise in half
½ teaspoon grated fresh ginger plus 1 slice of fresh ginger, ¼ inch thick
¼ teaspoon sugar
2 teaspoons dry white wine
1 tablespoon plus ½ teaspoon oyster sauce*
1 tablespoon Oriental sesame oil
1½ teaspoons light soy sauce
¼ teaspoon freshly ground white pepper
1 tablespoon chicken stock or canned broth
2 teaspoons ketchup
3½ tablespoons peanut oil
2 scallions, cut into 2-inch sections (white part quartered lengthwise)
½ cup snow peas (about 2 ounces), cut crosswise on the diagonal into 3 pieces
2 tablespoons Szechuan mustard pickle* (see Note), shredded

Triple-Decker Tostada (p. 157).

PAN-ASIAN BUFFET

The appetizer for this buffet-style dinner is from Vietnam. The main dish is from China. And, although the dessert comes from New York City, its exotic lemon grass flavor comes by way of Southeast Asia. Serves 6.

Vietnamese Stuffed Chicken Wings (p. 19)

Amoy Rice Noodles with Shrimp, Roast Pork and Szechuan Mustard Pickle (p. 113)

Julienned Cucumber and Chinese Cabbage Tossed with Rice Wine Vinegar and Sesame Seeds

🍷 *Variety of Asian Beers*

Union Square Cafe's Lemon Grass Ice Cream (p. 206)

½ medium red bell pepper, cut into thin julienne strips
2 water chestnuts, preferably fresh, cut into thin strips
1 large garlic clove, minced
1 cup shredded Chinese Roast Pork (p. 64)
Pinch of salt
*Available at Asian markets

1. In a large pot of boiling water, cook the noodles, loosening them with a fork or with chopsticks, for 30 seconds; they will still be stiff. If using capellini, cook for 2 minutes. Run cold water into the pot; drain. Return the noodles to the pot and add cold water; drain well. Allow the noodles to drain thoroughly in a strainer set over a bowl, loosening them occasionally. They will soften as they drain.

2. Place the shrimp in a medium bowl. Add the grated ginger, sugar, 1 teaspoon of the wine, 1½ teaspoons of the oyster sauce, ½ teaspoon of the sesame oil, 1 teaspoon of the soy sauce and ⅛ teaspoon of the white pepper. Mix well and set aside.

3. In a small bowl, combine the chicken stock, ketchup and the remaining 1 teaspoon wine, 2 teaspoons oyster sauce, 2 teaspoons sesame oil, 1 teaspoon soy sauce and ⅛ teaspoon white pepper. Set the sauce aside.

4. Heat a wok over high heat for 30 seconds. Add 1 tablespoon of the peanut oil and swirl with a spatula to coat the pan. Add the ginger slice and cook until light brown, about 30 seconds. Add the scallions, snow peas, mustard pickle, red pepper and water chestnuts. Stir-fry until the snow peas and scallions turn bright green, about 30 seconds. Turn off the heat. Remove the vegetables to a bowl.

5. Wipe out the wok with paper towels and place over high heat. Add 1 tablespoon of the peanut oil and heat until a wisp of white smoke appears, about 30 seconds. Add the garlic and cook until it begins to brown, about 30 seconds. Add the shrimp with their marinade, spreading them in a single layer. Cook for 30 seconds. Turn over and mix well.

6. Add the pork and cook, stirring frequently, until the shrimp turn pink, about 2 minutes. Transfer to a bowl and set aside.

7. Rinse the wok and dry over high heat. Add the remaining 1½ tablespoons peanut oil and the salt and heat until a wisp of white smoke appears, about 30 seconds. Add the noodles. Loosen and stir-fry for about 1 minute, until the noodles are hot. Add the shrimp and pork mixture and the reserved vegetables. Toss until well mixed. Stir in the sauce and toss to coat well. Serve at once.

NOTE: Szechuan mustard pickle, also known as Szechuan preserved vegetable, is made with Chinese radishes, turnips or mustard greens cooked with chili powder and salt. It is usually added to soups and stir-fried with vegetables. It can be bought loose in Chinese groceries by weight, but is more often found in cans. Once a can is opened, the pickle should be placed in a sealed glass jar and kept refrigerated. It will keep for at least six months.

—*Eileen Yin-Fei Lo*

• • •

SZECHUAN COOL NOODLES WITH SESAME SAUCE AND PEANUTS

This is a Szechuan dish that is often found in neighboring Hunan as well. It is called cool because the noodles are cooked and allowed to cool before serving.

───── *6 Servings* ─────

8 ounces thin fresh egg noodles (the size of vermicelli), Chinese or Italian
2 tablespoons Oriental sesame oil
2½ tablespoons smooth peanut butter
1 tablespoon Chinese sesame seed paste*
2 tablespoons mushroom soy sauce*
2 teaspoons distilled white vinegar
2 teaspoons hot chili oil
1 tablespoon sugar
Pinch of freshly ground white pepper
⅓ cup hot chicken stock or canned broth
2 tablespoons thinly sliced scallions
3 tablespoons chopped, unsalted dry-roasted peanuts
2 sprigs of fresh coriander, torn into pieces
*Available at Asian markets

1. In a large pot of boiling water, cook the noodles until tender but firm, about 1½ minutes. Run cold water into the pot, then drain the noodles. Return the noo-

dles to the pot. Fill with cold water and drain the noodles. Repeat once again.

2. Place the drained noodles in a large bowl and toss with sesame oil. Refrigerate, uncovered, until cold, about 1 hour.

3. In a medium bowl, combine the peanut butter, sesame paste, soy sauce, vinegar, chili oil, sugar, white pepper and scallions.

4. In a small saucepan, bring the stock to a simmer over low heat. Let cool slightly, then add the hot stock to the sesame mixture and stir to blend well.

5. Pour the sesame sauce over the cool noodles, toss to coat and place in a serving dish. Sprinkle the chopped peanuts on top and garnish with the coriander.

—*Eileen Yin-Fei Lo*

• • •

PAN-FRIED NOODLES WITH CHICKEN AND CHINESE VEGETABLES

This traditional preparation from Shanghai is often referred to as double-fried noodles, because the noodles are fried on both sides.

❢ To balance the soy-flavored sauce and refresh the palate, choose a California Riesling, such as 1987 Jekel, or a German white, such as 1987 Sichel Novum.

───── *6 Servings* ─────

½ pound fine fresh Chinese egg noodles* or fresh or dried capellini
6 ounces skinless, boneless chicken breast, cut into thin strips
2 teaspoons Oriental sesame oil
1¾ teaspoons sugar
1½ teaspoons distilled white vinegar
1½ teaspoons dry white wine
¾ teaspoon cornstarch
¼ teaspoon freshly ground white pepper
½ teaspoon light soy sauce
½ teaspoon salt

2 teaspoons dark soy sauce*
⅔ cup chicken stock or canned broth
6 to 7 tablespoons peanut oil
1 teaspoon grated fresh ginger
1 garlic clove, minced
½ cup snow peas (about 2 ounces), trimmed and cut crosswise on the diagonal into thin strips
3 water chestnuts, preferably fresh, cut into thin strips
¼ cup bamboo shoots, cut into thin strips
2 scallions, cut into ½-inch lengths (white part quartered lengthwise)
*Available at Asian markets

1. In a large pot of boiling water, cook the noodles until tender but firm, about 15 seconds for fresh or about 2 minutes for dried. Run cold water into the pot and drain the noodles. Return to the pot, add cold water and drain again, turning and separating the noodles occasionally until they are quite dry, about 30 minutes. Dry completely on a kitchen towel.

2. In a medium bowl, combine the chicken with 1 teaspoon of the sesame oil, ¾ teaspoon of the sugar, ½ teaspoon of the vinegar, 1 teaspoon of the white wine, ¼ teaspoon of the cornstarch, ⅛ teaspoon of the white pepper, the light soy sauce and the salt. Let marinate for 30 minutes.

3. In a small bowl, combine the remaining 1 teaspoon each of sesame oil, sugar and vinegar, ½ teaspoon wine, ½ teaspoon cornstarch and ⅛ teaspoon white pepper with the dark soy sauce and chicken stock. Set this sauce aside.

4. Pour ¼ cup of the peanut oil into a 9- or 10-inch cast-iron frying pan and set over high heat. When a wisp of white smoke appears, arrange the noodles in the pan in an even layer that covers the entire bottom. Cook, rotating the pan on the burner, until the bottom is evenly browned and crisp, about 4 minutes.

5. Slide the noodle cake onto a dish. Place another dish on top of it and invert so that the cooked side is up. Slide the cake back into the pan and cook, adding another 1 tablespoon oil, if necessary, to prevent sticking, until the second side is browned, about 2 minutes. Turn out the noodle cake onto a large plate or platter and cover loosely with foil to keep warm.

6. Heat a wok over high heat for 30 seconds. Add 2 tablespoons of the peanut oil and swirl with a spatula to coat the pan. Add the ginger and garlic. Cook, stirring, until it begins to brown, about 45 seconds. Add the chicken with its marinade and spread in a thin layer. Cook for 2 minutes, turn over and mix well.

7. Add the snow peas, water chestnuts, bamboo shoots and scallions. Cook, stirring occasionally, until the vegetables soften slightly, about 3 minutes. Make a well in the center and stir in the sauce. Cook until the sauce thickens, about 1 minute. Spoon the chicken, vegetables and sauce on top of the browned noodle cake. Serve by cutting the cake into wedges.

—Eileen Yin-Fei Lo

• • •

YELLOW RICE

Yellow Rice, flavored with coconut milk, turmeric and cumin, is the mainstay of the Indonesian buffet called a rijsttafel.

———— *12 Servings* ————
4 cups rice, rinsed and drained
½ teaspoon ground cumin
⅜ teaspoon turmeric
1 teaspoon salt
1½ cups homemade coconut milk, or
  ¾ cup canned unsweetened*
  mixed with ¾ cup water
***Available at Asian markets**

1. In a large saucepan or flameproof casserole, combine the rice, cumin, turmeric, salt, coconut milk and 5¼ cups of water. Let soak for 30 minutes.

2. Bring to a boil over moderate heat. Reduce the heat to low and cook, covered, for 15 minutes. Remove the pan from the heat, stir the rice once and let stand, still covered, for 10 minutes.

—Copeland Marks

• • •

RICE WITH PEAS

This is a classic Venetian dish that is always served in early spring. This ambrosial combination absolutely requires sweet peas—the younger, the better. If your peas aren't fresh off the vine, you might want to add a pinch of sugar to the pot, or use the best-quality tiny frozen peas. The finished product should be slightly soupy, not as thick as a risotto.

———— *4 Servings* ————
6 cups light chicken stock or 3 cups
  canned broth diluted with 3 cups
  water
4 tablespoons unsalted butter
2 tablespoons olive oil
¼ cup chopped onion
½ cup chopped parsley
2 ounces pancetta, cut into ¼-inch
  dice
2 pounds fresh peas—shelled, rinsed
  and drained—or 1 package (10
  ounces) tiny frozen peas
1 cup arborio rice
3 tablespoons freshly grated
  Parmesan cheese
1 teaspoon salt
¼ teaspoon freshly ground pepper

1. In a medium saucepan, bring the stock to a simmer over moderate heat. Reduce the heat to low to keep it hot.

2. In a large flameproof casserole, melt 2 tablespoons of the butter in the olive oil over moderate heat. Add the onion, parsley and pancetta. Sauté until the fat is rendered from the pancetta and the onion is softened but not browned, about 3 minutes.

3. If you are using fresh peas, add them to the casserole at this point and cook for 1 minute, stirring to coat them with the fat in the pan.

4. Gradually add 1½ cups of the hot stock. Reduce the heat to low and simmer, stirring frequently, until the peas are just tender, 15 to 20 minutes.

5. If using frozen peas, add them at this point. Add the remaining 4½ cups stock and bring to a boil. Stir in the rice. Reduce the heat to moderate to maintain a steady simmer and cook, uncovered, stirring occasionally, until the rice is tender but still firm, about 20 minutes.

6. Stir in the remaining 2 tablespoons butter, the Parmesan cheese, salt and pepper. Simmer for 2 minutes longer, then serve hot.

—Tom Maresca & Diane Darrow

• • •

AMARONE RISOTTO WITH PANCETTA AND PRUNES

The prunes in this risotto underscore the wine used in cooking it, as Amarone can taste somewhat pruny.

❦ In this case, the wine that's in the recipe doesn't go well with the completed dish. The prunes make this sweet-and-sour risotto a little too sweet for a glass of Amarone. Try a California Zinfandel bursting with sweet fruit, such as a 1985 Ridge Howell Mountain or a 1986 Sutter Home California.

———— *6 Servings* ————
2 cups plus 2 tablespoons rich,
  young Amarone
1½ cups chicken stock or low-
  sodium canned broth
2 tablespoons unsalted butter
1 tablespoon olive oil
2 ounces thinly sliced pancetta,
  shredded

2 garlic cloves, minced
¼ pound (1 scant cup) arborio rice
½ cup pitted prunes (about 10),
thickly sliced
¼ cup freshly grated Parmesan
cheese
Salt and freshly ground pepper

1. In a medium nonreactive saucepan, combine 2 cups of the Amarone with the chicken stock and ⅔ cup of water. Bring just to a simmer over moderate heat; do not boil. Reduce the heat to low to keep the mixture at a bare simmer.

2. Meanwhile, in a large, heavy nonreactive saucepan or casserole, melt 1 tablespoon of the butter in the olive oil over moderately high heat. Add the pancetta and cook until it begins to brown, 2 to 3 minutes. Reduce the heat to moderate, add the garlic and cook until soft but not brown, 1 minute.

3. Add the rice and stir well to coat with the fat. Add ½ cup of the simmering liquid and cook, stirring, until completely absorbed by the rice, about 2 minutes. Continue adding more liquid, ½ cup at a time, as it is absorbed by the rice. When you have used about half of the liquid, add the prunes. Add the remaining liquid, in smaller amounts, stirring constantly, until the mixture is creamy but not soupy and the rice is tender but still firm, 25 to 30 minutes (there may be some liquid left over).

4. Stir in the Parmesan cheese and the remaining 1 tablespoon butter. Stir in the remaining 2 tablespoons Amarone. Cook for 1 minute. Season to taste with salt and pepper. Pass extra grated Parmesan cheese on the side if desired.

—David Rosengarten

• • •

RISOTTO WITH FENNEL

This pale, creamy and ethereal dish is soothing to the spirit as well as to the palate. Cooking fresh fennel in this manner transmutes its powerful licorice character into a mild, delicate fragrance.

——— *4 Servings* ———
6 tablespoons unsalted butter
½ cup chopped sweet onion
1 fennel bulb (1 pound)—trimmed,
quartered, cored and cut into ¼-
inch slices
¼ teaspoon salt
Pinch of freshly grated nutmeg
5 cups light chicken stock or 2½ cups
canned broth diluted with 2½ cups
water
1½ cups arborio rice
¼ teaspoon freshly ground pepper
¼ cup freshly grated Parmesan
cheese

1. In a large heavy saucepan or flameproof casserole, melt 3 tablespoons of the butter over low heat. Add the onion and cook until softened but not browned, about 3 minutes. Stir in the sliced fennel. Season with the salt and nutmeg; mix well. Cover and simmer, stirring occasionally, for 10 minutes.

2. Meanwhile, bring the stock to a simmer in another saucepan.

3. After 10 minutes, add the rice to the fennel, stirring to coat each grain with butter. Add 2 cups of the hot stock. Bring to a simmer and cook, uncovered, stirring constantly, until the rice is just tender, adding more stock ½ cup at a time as the rice absorbs the liquid, about 20 minutes. (If you run out of stock before the rice is done, use hot water.) The finished dish should be moist but not soupy.

4. When the rice is tender but still firm, remove from the heat and stir in the pepper, the remaining 3 tablespoons butter and the grated Parmesan cheese. Season with additional salt to taste and serve immediately in warm bowls.

—Tom Maresca & Diane Darrow

• • •

PARSLEY RICE SOUFFLE

This is not a tall, puffy soufflé, but rather a dish that comes out with a modest domed top. It has the advantage of being stable, unlike other soufflés, so it won't fall before you serve it.

——— *4 to 6 Servings* ———
3 tablespoons unsalted butter
1 small onion, minced
¾ cup rice
3 cups chicken stock or canned broth
¼ teaspoon salt
½ cup minced parsley
2 eggs
1 cup milk

1. Preheat the oven to 350°. Grease a 2-quart soufflé dish with 1 tablespoon of the butter.

2. In a medium saucepan, melt the remaining 2 tablespoons butter over moderate heat. Add the onion and cook until it is softened and translucent, about 5 minutes.

3. Add the rice and stir to coat. Add the stock and salt and bring to a boil. Cover, reduce the heat to low and cook until the rice is very tender, about 20 minutes.

4. Stir the parsley into the rice. Let cool for 5 minutes. Beat in the eggs one at a time, then stir in the milk and mix until well blended.

5. Pour the parslied rice into the buttered soufflé dish and bake for about 50 minutes, or until set and lightly browned on top.

—Lee Bailey

• • •

VEGETABLES

VEGETABLES

GREEN AND WAX BEANS WITH PARMESAN CHEESE

If wax beans are unavailable, or simply hard to come by, just double the amount of green beans.

—— *6 Servings* ——
¾ pound green beans
¾ pound wax beans
2 tablespoons unsalted butter
3 tablespoons freshly grated
  Parmesan cheese
Salt and freshly ground pepper

1. Put the green beans and wax beans in a medium saucepan, and cover with cold salted water. Bring to a boil over moderately high heat and continue to cook until the beans are crisp-tender, about 10 minutes; drain well.

2. Transfer the beans to a medium bowl, add the butter and toss well; sprinkle with the Parmesan and toss again to coat. Season with salt and pepper to taste.
—*Lee Bailey*

• • •

GREEN BEAN AND POTATO PUREE

Vegetable purees are not only satisfying and tasty, they are also relatively unfussy. They can be pureed well ahead of time and then reheated in a double boiler, or gratinéed, as here.

—— *6 Servings* ——
1 pound boiling potatoes, peeled and
  cut into ½-inch dice
1 pound green beans, halved
5 tablespoons unsalted butter
¼ teaspoon freshly grated nutmeg
¼ teaspoon salt
¼ teaspoon freshly ground white
  pepper

1. Preheat the oven to 450°. In a large saucepan of boiling salted water, cook the potatoes over moderate heat for 10 min-

utes. Add the beans, cover partially and cook until the beans and potatoes are quite tender, 5 to 10 minutes longer. Drain well.

2. Transfer the potatoes and beans to a food processor and puree, in batches if necessary, until smooth. With the machine on, add 4 tablespoons of the butter, 1 tablespoon at a time, the nutmeg, salt and pepper.

3. Transfer the bean and potato puree to a large buttered baking or gratin dish. Dot the top with the remaining 1 tablespoon butter. Bake for 15 minutes, or until a skin forms on top and the puree is heated through. Serve right from the baking dish.
—*Lee Bailey*

• • •

SHREDDED BRUSSELS SPROUTS

Brussels sprouts have been the most maligned of vegetables—probably because they are usually overcooked. If cooked quickly, they will retain their pleasing yellow-green color and crisp texture.

—— *6 to 8 Servings* ——
2 pints brussels sprouts
1 stick (4 ounces) unsalted butter, at
  room temperature
1 teaspoon fresh lemon juice
½ teaspoon salt
¼ teaspoon freshly ground white
  pepper
⅛ teaspoon cayenne pepper

1. With a small sharp knife, cut each sprout into 3 or 4 slices. *(The sprouts can be sliced, covered and refrigerated 1 day ahead if desired.)*

2. Drop the sprouts into a medium saucepan of boiling salted water. After

the water returns to a boil, cook the sprouts until crisp-tender, about 2 minutes; drain.

3. Toss with the butter, lemon juice, salt, white pepper and cayenne.
—*Camille Glenn*

• • •

RED CABBAGE WITH GRANNY SMITH APPLES

This piquant red cabbage with green apples is a classic combination that has a tart fruitiness.

—— *12 Servings* ——
3 tablespoons unsalted butter
1 onion, thinly sliced
1 garlic clove, crushed through a
  press
1 large head of red cabbage (about 2
  pounds), finely shredded
2 medium Granny Smith or other
  tart green apples—quartered,
  cored and thinly sliced
2 tablespoons tarragon wine
  vinegar
2 teaspoons sugar
½ teaspoon mustard seeds
½ teaspoon salt
½ teaspoon freshly ground pepper

1. In a large nonreactive flameproof casserole, melt the butter over moderately high heat. Add the onion and sauté until softened but not browned, 3 to 4 minutes. Add the garlic and cook for 1 more minute.

2. Add the cabbage and toss. Cover and cook, stirring occasionally, until the cabbage wilts slightly, about 3 minutes.

3. Add the apples, vinegar, sugar, mustard seeds, salt and pepper. Toss well and continue to cook, stirring often, until the apples are tender, about 8 minutes. *(The recipe can be made up to 3 days in advance. Cover and refrigerate. Reheat before serving.)*
—*Bob Chambers*

• • •

SAGE-GLAZED CARROTS

Sage has a natural affinity for root vegetables. Here, fresh sage leaves fried in butter are a crisp and pungent complement to glazed carrots.

——— *12 Servings* ———
*2 pounds carrots, cut crosswise into
   1½- to 2-inch lengths and
   quartered lengthwise*
*2 bunches of fresh sage (about 1 cup
   loosely packed leaves)*
3 tablespoons unsalted butter
1 teaspoon sugar
Freshly ground white pepper

1. In a medium saucepan of salted water, bring the carrots to a boil over moderately high heat. Boil until they are crisp-tender, about 4 minutes. Drain the carrots into a colander immediately.

2. Chop enough of the sage leaves to measure 1 tablespoon; set aside.

3. In a large skillet, melt the butter over low heat. Arrange the remaining whole sage leaves flat in the pan and cook them until crisp and lightly browned, about 2 minutes on each side. Drain on paper towels.

4. Add the carrots and the reserved chopped sage to the skillet. Sprinkle the sugar on top and season with white pepper to taste; toss well. Cook over moderate heat for 3 to 4 minutes. Garnish with the sautéed sage leaves and serve. *(The recipe can be made up to 3 days in advance. Let the carrots cool; cover and refrigerate. Place the sage leaves in a separate bowl, cover tightly with plastic wrap and refrigerate. Before serving, reheat the carrots and garnish with the fried sage leaves.)*

—*Bob Chambers*

• • •

CORN PUDDING WITH CHEESE AND CHILES

To get all of the sweet corn pulp off the cob, after cutting the kernels off with a sharp knife, scrape the cob again with the dull side of the knife blade.

——— *6 Servings* ———
*4 fresh poblano or Anaheim chile
   peppers, preferably a combination
   of green and red chiles*
*2 cups corn kernels with pulp (from
   5 ears of corn)*
3 tablespoons cornstarch
6 ounces sharp Cheddar cheese
1 teaspoon unsalted butter
½ cup thinly sliced scallions
3 eggs
1 cup milk
½ cup chicken stock or canned broth
1 teaspoon salt
1 teaspoon sugar
*¼ teaspoon freshly ground black
   pepper*
⅛ teaspoon freshly grated nutmeg
⅛ teaspoon cayenne pepper
*4 ounces Monterey Jack cheese, cut
   into small dice (about ½ cup)*

1. Roast the poblano or Anaheim chile peppers directly over a gas flame or under the broiler as close to the heat as possible, turning, until charred all over. Seal in a paper bag for 10 minutes; then rub off the blackened skin. Trim off the stems, ribs and seeds. Cut the peppers into ¼-inch dice.

2. Preheat the oven to 375°. In a food processor or blender, puree 1¼ cups of the corn kernels with the cornstarch.

3. Finely dice enough of the Cheddar cheese to measure ½ cup. Grate the remaining Cheddar.

4. In a small skillet, melt the butter over low heat. Add the scallions and cook until softened, 3 to 5 minutes. Remove from the heat and let cool slightly, about 10 minutes.

5. In a large bowl, combine the eggs, milk, chicken stock, salt, sugar, black pepper, nutmeg and cayenne. Add the corn puree and the remaining corn kernels with their pulp. Whisk to blend well. Stir in the sautéed scallions, roasted chiles, Monterey Jack cheese and diced Cheddar cheese.

6. Spoon into a well-buttered 8-inch square baking pan. Sprinkle the grated Cheddar cheese on top.

7. Place the pan in a deep roasting pan and pour in enough warm water to reach halfway up the sides of the baking pan. Bake for 50 to 55 minutes, until the pudding is golden around the edges and just set in the center. Serve hot.

—*Richard Sax*

• • •

SCALLOPED CELERY ROOT AND POTATOES

This dish tastes particularly good with lamb.

——— *6 Servings* ———
*1¼ pounds boiling potatoes, peeled
   and thinly sliced*
*1 large celery root (celeriac), peeled
   and thinly sliced*
2 tablespoons all-purpose flour
*6 tablespoons unsalted butter,
   softened to room temperature*
1 teaspoon Dijon-style mustard
1¼ teaspoons salt
1 cup milk

1. Preheat the oven to 500°. In a large saucepan of lightly salted boiling water, cook the potatoes and celery root until just tender, about 5 minutes. Drain and rinse through a colander.

2. Meanwhile, in a medium bowl, whisk together the flour, butter and mustard until well blended.

3. In a large, buttered baking dish, arrange half the potatoes in a single layer. Spread one-third of the mustard butter on top. Season with ½ teaspoon of the salt. Put all the celery root slices on top, spread with half of the remaining mustard butter and season with ¼ teaspoon of the salt. Cover with the remaining potatoes, mustard butter and ½ teaspoon salt.

4. Pour in the milk and bake, uncovered, for 25 minutes. Reduce the oven temperature to 350° and bake for 5 to 10 minutes, or until golden brown.

—*Lee Bailey*

• • •

GARLIC-BRAISED EGGPLANT AND CHICK-PEA CASSEROLE

Here's a savory Indian meatless main dish. Serve it with a chunk of crusty bread and a nice green salad.

❢ Given the Indian spices in this hearty dish, a light but hop-flavored lager, such as Corona or Steinlager, would harmonize with the flavors better than wine.

——————— *6 to 8 Servings* ———————
¼ cup plus 2 tablespoons vegetable oil
1½ teaspoons cumin seeds
½ teaspoon fennel seeds
½ teaspoon black peppercorns, cracked
2 medium onions, sliced
12 large garlic cloves, thickly sliced
2 teaspoons dry mustard
1 teaspoon crushed hot red pepper
1 teaspoon turmeric or curry powder
1 teaspoon salt
1 small eggplant (about ¾ pound), unpeeled, cut into ½-by-½-by-2-inch sticks
5 plum tomatoes (about ¾ pound), quartered lengthwise
1 can (19 ounces) chick-peas, rinsed and drained

2 tablespoons chopped fresh coriander or mint

1. In a large skillet or flameproof casserole, heat the oil over high heat. Add the cumin seeds and cook until dark brown, about 15 seconds. Add the fennel seeds and black pepper and cook for 5 seconds. Add the onion and garlic and reduce the heat to moderately high. Cook, stirring frequently, until the onion and garlic are lightly browned, about 5 minutes.

2. Stir in the mustard, hot pepper, turmeric and salt. Add the eggplant. Reduce the heat to moderate and cook, stirring gently, until the eggplant is limp, about 5 minutes.

3. Add the tomatoes and cook, stirring constantly, until soft, about 5 minutes.

4. Gently stir in the chick-peas, cover and simmer over low heat until the liquid thickens to a gravy and the flavors have blended, about 5 minutes. Season with additional salt to taste. Sprinkle the coriander over the top and serve.

—*Julie Sahni*

• • •

EGGPLANT-TOMATO COMPOTE

Serve this ratatouille-like compote with Grilled Herb-Stuffed Snapper (p. 40).

——————— *4 Servings* ———————
1 small onion, minced
½ cup extra-virgin olive oil
2 large garlic cloves, thinly sliced
1 large eggplant, cut into ¼-inch dice
6 medium tomatoes—peeled, seeded and chopped—or 1 can (28 ounces) Italian peeled tomatoes, drained and chopped
1 small zucchini—halved lengthwise, seeded and cut into ¼-inch dice

¼ of a medium red bell pepper, cut into ¼-inch dice
¼ cup niçoise olives, chopped
2 tablespoons minced fresh herbs— thyme, basil, oregano and/or Italian flat-leaf parsley
Salt and freshly ground pepper

1. In a large saucepan, cook the onion in the oil over moderately low heat until softened, about 5 minutes. Add the garlic and cook until tender, about 2 minutes.

2. Stir in the eggplant, tomatoes, zucchini and red pepper. Bring to a simmer over moderate heat. Cook uncovered until most of the liquid has evaporated and the vegetables are soft, about 15 minutes.

3. Add the olives and herbs. Season with salt and pepper to taste. Cook for 3 minutes to blend the flavors. Serve warm or at room temperature.

—*Max's Place, Miami*

• • •

BRAISED ENDIVE AND CHERRY TOMATOES

Braising is a traditional method of mellowing the bite of Belgian endive.

——————— *6 Servings* ———————
4 tablespoons unsalted butter
9 medium Belgian endives, halved lengthwise
¼ teaspoon salt
¼ teaspoon freshly ground white pepper
1½ tablespoons fresh lemon juice
½ cup chicken stock or canned broth
1 pint cherry tomatoes
Dash of hot pepper sauce

1. In a large heavy skillet, melt 2 tablespoons of the butter over moderate heat. Add the endives and sauté, turning, until lightly browned, about 8 minutes.

2. Add the remaining 2 tablespoons butter, the salt, white pepper, lemon juice and stock. Reduce the heat to moderately low, partially cover and simmer until the endives are barely tender, another 6 to 8 minutes.

3. Stir in the tomatoes and hot sauce. Increase the heat to moderate and cook until the tomatoes are warmed through, 3 to 4 minutes. Arrange the endives and tomatoes on a warmed platter and pour the pan juices on top.

—*Lee Bailey*

• • •

LIMA BEANS WITH BROWN BUTTER

Lima beans are one of the few vegetables that freeze well, so you can use frozen baby limas—I'll never tell.

—— 6 Servings ——
*4 cups shelled fresh baby limas or 2
  packages (10 ounces each) frozen
4 tablespoons unsalted butter
1 tablespoon minced fresh mint
  (optional)
Salt to taste*

1. Steam the fresh lima beans for a few minutes until tender (the exact amount of time depends on their age), or cook the frozen according to package directions.

2. In a medium skillet, melt the butter over moderate heat until browned, being careful not to let it burn, 3 to 5 minutes. Add the lima beans and toss to coat with the butter. Season with the mint and salt.

—*Lee Bailey*

• • •

FRESH PEAS WITH LETTUCE

Cooking fresh peas with lettuce produces a dish that is about as good as it can get.

—— 6 Servings ——
*4 tablespoons unsalted butter
1/2 large head of iceberg lettuce,
  shredded
3 pounds green peas, shelled (about
  2 cups) or 1 package (10 ounces)
  frozen peas
1 teaspoon salt
1/2 teaspoon sugar (optional)*

In a large heavy saucepan, melt the butter over low heat. Add the lettuce, peas, salt and sugar. Increase the heat to moderate, cover tightly and cook, shaking the pan until the peas start to steam, about 5 minutes. Reduce the heat to moderately low and cook until the peas are just tender, 6 to 8 minutes.

—*Lee Bailey*

• • •

MEXICAN PEPPERS AND ONIONS

I use the long, red, semi-hot chile peppers here. You can use the hotter ones, but if you do, warn your guests. To soak up the juices from the peppers and onions, serve over white rice cooked in chicken stock with half a bay leaf.

—— 6 Servings ——
*3 tablespoons olive oil
3 large red onions, halved
  lengthwise and thinly sliced
3 red chile peppers—halved, seeded
  and cut into 1/4-inch dice
3/4 teaspoon sugar
1/2 teaspoon salt
1 tablespoon plus 2 teaspoons red
  wine vinegar*

1. In a large nonreactive skillet, heat 1 1/2 tablespoons of the olive oil over moderate heat. Add the onions and peppers and toss to coat with the oil. Reduce the

heat to low and cook until the onions are softened but not browned, about 6 minutes.

2. Add the remaining 1 1/2 tablespoons olive oil, the sugar and the salt. Cook, stirring, until the onions begin to brown, about 3 minutes longer. Add the vinegar and cook for 2 minutes more. Serve hot.

—*Lee Bailey*

• • •

GRANDMA'S POTATO, RED PEPPER AND ZUCCHINI GRATIN

This simple vegetable gratin comes from Auberge de la Madone, a small family inn hidden high in the mountains above Nice. One summer's evening, sitting on the terrace beneath an ancient olive tree laden with olives, I was served this gratin as an accompaniment to a deliciously moist sautéed rabbit.

—— 4 Servings ——
*1 garlic clove, halved
1/4 cup extra-virgin olive oil
2 pounds all-purpose or red
  potatoes, peeled and very thinly
  sliced
2 teaspoons salt
2 teaspoons minced fresh thyme or
  1/2 teaspoon dried
2 red bell peppers, cut into thin rings
4 small zucchini (about 4 ounces
  each)*

1. Preheat the oven to 350°. Rub the bottom of a medium gratin dish with the garlic. Grease lightly with 1 teaspoon of the olive oil.

2. Arrange a layer of half the potatoes in the bottom of the dish, overlapping the

121

slices as necessary. Season lightly with salt and thyme and drizzle on 1 tablespoon of the olive oil. Add a layer of half the red peppers and then half the zucchini. Season again with salt and thyme and drizzle 1 tablespoon of the oil over the vegetables. Repeat the layering and seasoning. Drizzle any remaining olive oil over the top.

3. Cover securely with aluminum foil and bake until the vegetables are very soft and tender, about 1 hour.

—*Patricia Wells*

• • •

BUTTERED NEW POTATOES

Removing a small strip of peel from the potatoes creates an attractive contrast between the red skin and the white potato underneath.

——— *6 Servings* ———
2 pounds new or small red potatoes
1 stick (4 ounces) unsalted butter
3 tablespoons club soda
2 teaspoons salt
¼ teaspoon freshly ground pepper

1. Peel away a strip of skin around the center of each potato.

2. In a large skillet, preferably nonstick, melt the butter over moderate heat. Add the club soda, salt and pepper. Add the potatoes in a single layer. Reduce the heat to moderately low, cover tightly and cook, shaking the pan occasionally to prevent sticking, until the potatoes are tender, about 20 minutes. If any liquid remains in the pan, increase the heat to high and cook uncovered for 1 to 2 minutes, shaking the pan, until only a coating of butter remains. Toss the potatoes to coat and serve hot.

—*Lee Bailey*

• • •

DINER HOME FRIES

In diners, cooks fry their potatoes on a well-seasoned griddle. A cast-iron skillet works well, though any heavy pan will do. Nonstick skillets are also fine, providing they are heavy, although you will still need the fat because it is part of the real essence of home fries. Vegetable oil can be substituted for the bacon fat if you prefer. Garlic is untraditional but good; a dusting of paprika for color is up to you.

——— *4 Servings* ———
1¼ pounds all-purpose potatoes (such as Maine), peeled and halved
2 tablespoons bacon fat
2 tablespoons unsalted butter
1 medium onion, chopped
1 garlic clove, minced
1 teaspoon salt
1 teaspoon freshly ground pepper
Paprika (optional)

1. Cook the potatoes in a medium saucepan of boiling salted water until just tender, about 20 minutes. Drain well. Cut the potatoes into 1-inch chunks.

2. In a large heavy skillet, heat 1½ tablespoons each of the bacon fat and butter over moderate heat. Add the potatoes, onion and garlic and toss well to coat with the fat. Fry without stirring, shaking the pan occasionally to prevent sticking. Adjust the heat as necessary to maintain a slow, steady sizzle. From time to time, press the potatoes down with a wide metal spatula. When the bottoms of the potatoes are crusty and golden, after about 8 minutes, you're ready to start turning.

3. Add the remaining ½ tablespoon each bacon fat and butter to the potatoes and season with the salt and pepper. Divide the mixture into 4 wedges with the spatula and flip the wedges, 1 at a time. As you turn, press each wedge down into the fat. Continue to do this cutting, flipping and pressing every 2 minutes or so, until the potatoes become crusty and browned all over, about 10 minutes. Add a little additional fat, if needed, to keep the potatoes lightly coated. If using paprika, add a sprinkling toward the end of the cooking time, combining it with the potatoes as you turn them. Season to taste with additional salt and pepper and serve piping hot.

—*Richard Sax*

• • •

PAN-ROASTED POTATOES WITH LEMON AND MARJORAM

Next time you're in the mood for home fries, try this variation. They're irresistibly good.

——— *4 to 6 Servings* ———
Zest of 1 lemon, cut into thin julienne strips
½ pound thickly sliced smoked bacon, cut crosswise into 1-inch pieces
1½ pounds small red potatoes, cut into 1-inch cubes
1 large onion, chopped
1 teaspoon chopped fresh marjoram
½ teaspoon salt
½ teaspoon freshly ground pepper

1. Preheat the oven to 450°. In a small saucepan of boiling water, blanch the lemon zest for 1 minute. Remove the strips of zest with a slotted spoon and drain well on paper towels. *(The zest can be prepared 1 day ahead. Cover and refrigerate.)*

2. In the same water, blanch the bacon for 1 minute. Drain and dry the bacon well on paper towels.

3. In a large skillet, preferably cast-iron, cook the bacon over moderate heat until crisp and lightly browned, about 3 minutes. Remove all but 3 tablespoons of the bacon fat. Increase the heat to high and when the fat is almost smoking, add the potatoes, onion and lemon zest. Stir to combine and cook for 1 minute.

4. Place the skillet on the bottom rack of the oven and cook for 15 minutes. Stir and then continue cooking until the potatoes and onions are lightly crisped and golden brown, another 10 minutes. Remove from the oven. Season the potatoes with the marjoram, salt and pepper and serve warm.

—*Marcia Kiesel*

• • •

M*A*S*H POTATOES

Wait until your troops get their Hot Lips on these.

———— *8 Servings* ————
4 large Idaho potatoes
3 tablespoons extra-virgin olive oil
10 slices of bacon
½ cup thinly sliced scallions
4 tablespoons unsalted butter
⅓ cup milk
1½ teaspoons caraway seeds
1 teaspoon salt
5 ounces Cheddar cheese, grated (about 1½ cups)

1. Preheat the oven to 400°. Prick the potatoes several times with a fork. Coat each with ½ tablespoon of the olive oil. Bake for about 45 minutes, or until tender when pierced with a fork. Let cool for about 15 minutes.

2. Meanwhile, fry or microwave the bacon until crisp. Drain well. Cut into ½-inch pieces.

3. In a small skillet, heat the remaining 1 tablespoon oil over moderate heat. Add the scallions and sauté until lightly browned, about 2 minutes.

4. Cut the potatoes in half lengthwise and scoop out the insides, leaving a ¼-inch-thick shell. Put the potato pulp into a bowl and add the butter. Mash lightly with a fork. Add the milk, caraway seeds, salt, bacon and scallions. Stir to combine evenly. The potatoes can be left a little lumpy if you prefer.

5. Sprinkle the cheese evenly into the bottoms of the potato skins. Spoon the filling on top. *(The recipe can be prepared to this point up to 1 day ahead and refrigerated or frozen for up to 1 week.)*

6. Preheat the broiler. Arrange the potatoes on a baking sheet and broil 4 inches from the heat for 5 minutes, or until the tops are nicely browned. (Frozen potatoes are best reheated in a 500° oven for 5 to 7 minutes.)

—*F&W*

• • •

PARSLIED POTATO CAKES

The parslied potato cakes can be made well in advance. Once they are baked, let them cool, then cover tightly and freeze. The day you plan to serve them, thaw them, then reheat gently in a covered skillet, with additional oil and butter if needed.

———— *Makes 12 to 14 Small Cakes* ————
3 pounds boiling potatoes, peeled
⅓ cup chopped Italian flat-leaf parsley
1½ teaspoons freshly ground pepper
1 teaspoon salt
1 garlic clove, crushed through a press
2 whole eggs plus 1 egg yolk
About 2 tablespoons unsalted butter
About ¼ cup olive oil

1. Grate the potatoes in a food processor fitted with the grating disk. In a strainer placed over a mixing bowl, squeeze the grated potatoes between your hands to remove any water. Reserve the liquid in the bowl.

2. Place the potatoes in a separate mixing bowl. Stir in the parsley, pepper, salt, garlic, whole eggs and egg yolk. Carefully pour off and discard the water from the reserved potato liquid, saving the potato starch that has settled at the bottom of the bowl. Scrape this starch back into the potato mixture and stir well to combine.

3. In a large skillet, melt 1 tablespoon of the butter in 2 tablespoons of the oil over low heat. When the butter has melted, remove the pan from the heat.

4. Preheat the oven to 400°. Stir the potato mixture to distribute the eggs evenly. Firmly pack the mixture into a round ¼-cup measure, squeezing out any excess liquid. Invert the measuring cup over the skillet and tap the bottom gently until the potato cake slides out. Repeat with the remaining potato mixture, placing the cakes 1½ inches apart in the pan. (Depending on the size of your skillet, it may be necessary to use 2 pans, or do this in 2 batches.)

5. Return the skillet to the stovetop. Cook the potato cakes over moderately high heat until the bottoms are browned, about 2 minutes. Carefully turn over the potato cakes, adding an additional tablespoon butter and 2 tablespoons oil to the pan if needed. Cook the other side until browned, about 2 minutes longer.

6. Transfer the cakes to a baking sheet. Bake for 20 minutes in the middle of the oven.

—*Bob Chambers*

• • •

POTATO PIE A L'ALSACIENNE

Says André Soltner, "My mother, Mimi Soltner, made this potato tart—the favorite of my father, my sister and my brother. It is not nouvelle cuisine."

——— **8 Servings** ———
2 egg yolks
1¾ cups all-purpose flour
1¼ teaspoons salt
1 stick (4 ounces) plus 1 tablespoon unsalted butter, cut into pieces
1¼ pounds boiling potatoes (about 3 medium), peeled and thinly sliced
¼ cup chopped parsley
¼ teaspoon freshly ground pepper
5 ounces sliced mild-smoked bacon, cut crosswise into ¼-inch-wide strips

5 hard-cooked eggs, peeled and thinly sliced
½ cup crème fraîche or heavy cream

1. The day before you make the pie, beat 1 egg yolk with enough ice water to make ¼ cup.

2. Mix the flour and ¾ teaspoon of the salt in a bowl. Rub in the butter with your fingertips until the mixture resembles coarse meal. Pour in the egg yolk beaten with ice water and work with the fingers until just moistened. Gather the dough into a ball. Immediately roll out the dough into a rectangle on a floured work surface. Fold in thirds, wrap in plastic and refrigerate overnight.

3. Preheat the oven to 400°. Divide the dough in half. Roll one half into a 13-inch round. Fit into a 9-inch pie pan or tart pan with a removable bottom. Refrigerate for 10 minutes.

4. Rinse the sliced potatoes in cold water to remove any starch; drain and pat dry on paper towels. Transfer to a medium bowl and toss with the remaining ½ teaspoon salt, the parsley and pepper.

5. In a medium skillet, sauté the bacon over moderately high heat, stirring, until browned on the edges, 1 to 2 minutes. Drain the bacon.

6. Arrange a layer of overlapping slices of potato in the bottom of the prepared pie shell. Cover with the bacon. Arrange the egg slices over the bacon and top with the remaining potato slices. Spoon the crème fraîche over the potatoes and spread smooth with a spatula.

7. Preheat the oven to 400°. Beat the remaining egg yolk with 1 teaspoon water to make an egg glaze. Roll the remaining pastry into a round large enough to cover the pie. Brush the edges of the lower crust

with some of the egg glaze and cover the pie with the top crust. Trim the edges, then crimp to seal.

8. Brush the top crust lightly with more egg glaze. Cut steam vents in the top of the pie with a small sharp knife. Bake in the middle of the oven for 20 minutes.

9. Reduce the oven temperature to 350° and bake for 1 hour. Reduce the oven temperature to 300° and bake for 10 minutes. Let the pie rest for 10 minutes before serving.

—*André Soltner*

• • •

PIPERADE PIE

I like to serve stewed corn made the southern way with this delicious, homey pie. Simply scrape off the kernels, add a pat of butter, salt and white pepper to taste, and just enough milk or cream (a few tablespoons) to make it liquid. Bring to a simmer and cook over moderately low heat for three to four minutes.

——— **6 Servings** ———
¼ cup extra-virgin olive oil
1 small red bell pepper, coarsely chopped
1 sweet onion, coarsely chopped
¼ cup coarsely chopped scallions
2 large garlic cloves, minced
6 fresh Italian plum tomatoes— peeled, seeded and coarsely chopped
1 tablespoon coarsely chopped fresh basil or 1 teaspoon dried
1 teaspoon salt
1 teaspoon freshly ground black pepper
4 dashes of hot pepper sauce
1 tablespoon unsalted butter
5 eggs, lightly beaten
1 prebaked Savory Cheese Crust (at right)

1. Preheat the oven to 350°. In a large skillet, heat the olive oil over moderate heat. Add the red pepper, onion and scallions. Sauté, stirring occasionally, until the vegetables are softened but not browned, about 10 minutes. Add the garlic, tomatoes, basil, salt, pepper and hot sauce. Bring to a boil, reduce the heat and simmer, stirring frequently, until almost all the liquid evaporates, about 10 minutes. Stir in the butter and remove from the heat. Transfer to a bowl and let cool for 15 minutes.

2. Add the eggs to the cooled vegetable mixture and blend well. Spread the filling into the prebaked pie shell and bake for 30 minutes, or until the filling is set but not dry. Let stand for 15 minutes before slicing. Serve warm, at room temperature or slightly chilled.

—*Lee Bailey*

• • •

SAVORY CHEESE CRUST

——Makes a Single 10-Inch Crust——
1 cup all-purpose flour
Pinch of salt
4 tablespoons frozen unsalted
*   butter, cut into small cubes*
2 tablespoons frozen vegetable
*   shortening, cut into small cubes*
1 cup coarsely grated Cheddar
*   cheese*
2 tablespoons ice water

1. In a medium bowl, mix together the flour and salt. Cut in the butter, shortening and cheese until the mixture resembles coarse meal. Stir in the water, gather the dough into a ball and flatten into a 6-inch disk. Cover with plastic wrap and refrigerate for at least 30 minutes.

2. Preheat the oven to 400°. On a lightly floured surface, roll out the pastry

---

PIE FOR DINNER

The main course for this dinner is a combination of a Basque egg, tomato and pepper dish called *pipérade* and a good old-fashioned quiche. Lee Bailey offers this advice for serving this or any other main-course pie at the table: Cut the first piece in the kitchen. Then remove the piece, slip it back in place with the pie server underneath and take the pie to the table for serving. Serves 6.

Pipérade Pie (p. 124)

Stewed Corn

Lima Beans with Brown Butter
(p. 121)

Green Salad

🍷 *White Wine*

Plum Sorbet (p. 210)

Pecan Tiles (p. 240)

Coffee

---

into a 12-inch circle. Fit into a 10-inch pie pan. Trim the dough to ½ inch, turn under and crimp the edges. Prick the pastry all over with a fork. Cover with plastic wrap, refrigerate for 15 minutes.

3. Line the pastry with foil and fill with pie weights or dried beans. Bake for 15 minutes, or until set. Remove the pie weights and continue baking until golden, about 10 minutes. Let cool completely on a rack before filling.

—*Lee Bailey*

• • •

SHERRIED SWEET POTATOES

I do not enjoy overly candied sweet potatoes, but there must be enough butter and sugar to make a beautiful glaze.

——6 to 8 Servings——
8 medium sweet potatoes
⅓ cup sugar
¼ teaspoon salt
4 tablespoons unsalted butter, cut
*   into small pieces*
⅓ cup medium-dry Spanish sherry,
*   such as Amontillado*

1. Preheat the oven to 350°. In a large saucepan, cover the sweet potatoes with hot water. Boil until the potatoes are tender but still firm, about 20 minutes. *(The sweet potatoes can be cooked 1 day ahead; refrigerate.)*

2. Peel the skins off the sweet potatoes and cut them in half. Place in a large baking dish. Sprinkle the sugar and salt over the sweet potatoes. Dot with the butter and drizzle on the sherry.

3. Bake, basting occasionally, until the sweet potatoes are light brown and the glaze is bubbling, about 35 minutes.

—*Camille Glenn*

• • •

BAKED BUTTERY SWEET POTATO CHIPS

Very thin slices of sweet potato are tossed with lemon juice, butter and a touch of sugar and then baked in a skillet.

——8 Servings——
4 medium sweet potatoes (about 2
*   pounds total), peeled*
½ teaspoon salt
½ teaspoon freshly ground pepper
2 teaspoons sugar
1 tablespoon fresh lemon juice

VEGETABLES

**4 tablespoons unsalted butter,
melted**
**Thin strips of lemon zest and a sprig
of fresh mint, for garnish**

1. Preheat the oven to 250°. In a food processor, or with a large sharp knife or mandoline, slice the sweet potatoes very thin, ¹⁄₁₆ to ⅛ inch; rinse in cold water. Drain and dry well with paper towels. Transfer to a large bowl and add the salt, pepper, sugar, lemon juice and butter; toss to coat well.

2. Layer the potatoes in a large oven-proof skillet, mounding them slightly in the center. Pour in any liquid from the bowl. Cover tightly with foil and bake for 50 minutes, or until tender. Serve straight from the skillet, garnished with strips of lemon zest and a sprig of mint.

—*Lee Bailey*

• • •

GRILLED RADICCHIO WITH ANCHOVY-MUSTARD SAUCE

Vivid garnet heads of radicchio are a comparatively new arrival at American vegetable stands. They reveal an intriguingly bitter savor when grilled. The tastiest radicchio is the Treviso variety, with long, narrow heads shaped like loose-leafed Belgian endive. Round-headed Verona radicchio, which resembles baby red cabbage, is less interesting in flavor, but this recipe works well with either variety. We like it as a warm salad after the main course, though it can also be served as an antipasto or as a vegetable.

——————4 to 6 Servings——————
2 anchovy fillets
1 tablespoon Dijon mustard
¼ cup fresh lemon juice

1 garlic clove, lightly crushed
½ teaspoon rosemary, crumbled
1 tablespoon minced parsley
½ cup extra-virgin olive oil
**4 small heads of radicchio (1 to 1¼
pounds), outer leaves removed,
quartered lengthwise, with ends
intact**
Salt and freshly ground pepper

1. In a small bowl, mash the anchovies to a paste. Whisk in the mustard and lemon juice. Add the garlic, rosemary and parsley. Gradually whisk in 6 tablespoons of the olive oil in a thin stream. Set the anchovy-mustard sauce aside.

2. Heat a very large cast-iron skillet or griddle over moderate heat. Brush the radicchio with the remaining 2 tablespoons olive oil and lay them in the pan or on the griddle. Season with salt and pepper to taste. Cook, turning, until the radicchio is lightly browned and fork tender, about 8 minutes.

3. Arrange the grilled radicchio on a serving plate, cut-sides up. Give the sauce a final stir, discard the garlic and spoon the sauce over the radicchio. Serve warm or at room temperature.

—*Tom Maresca & Diane Darrow*

• • •

CANDIED QUINCES

Quinces look like yellowish green apples. They are very tart and need lots of sugar to bring out their wonderful flavor. I prefer candied quinces to candied yams when I serve a roast bird. These are perfect with goose.

——————6 to 8 Servings——————
2 lemons
4 pounds quinces
2 cups sugar
2 tablespoons unsalted butter

1. Half fill a large bowl with cold water. Squeeze the juice from 1 of the lemons into the bowl and add the lemon halves. One at a time, peel, quarter and core the quinces and add to the bowl of acidulated water to prevent discoloring.

2. In a large nonreactive saucepan, combine 6 cups of water with the sugar and the juice of the remaining lemon. Bring to a boil over high heat, stirring to dissolve the sugar. Add the quinces to the syrup. Reduce the heat to moderate and cook, uncovered, until the quinces are soft and the liquid is very syrupy, about 1 hour. Drain the quinces, reserving the syrup (see Note). *(The recipe can be made to this point up to 1 week in advance. Cover and refrigerate the quinces.)*

3. Shortly before serving, melt the butter in a large skillet over moderate heat. Add the candied quinces and cook, stirring, until warmed through.

NOTE: Reserve the syrup in a 1-pint jar. When cold, it has the consistency of jelly. You can refrigerate the jelly for several months. I use it to glaze fruit tarts.

—*Lydie Pinoy Marshall*

• • •

MASHED TURNIPS AND POTATOES

Turnips add a slightly sweet and almost smoky taste to mashed potatoes, made here with buttermilk, shallots and a touch of nutmeg.

———— *6 to 8 Servings* ————
*1 pound white turnips, peeled and
    cut into ½-inch cubes*
*2 pounds all-purpose potatoes,
    peeled and cut into 1-inch cubes*
1 cup buttermilk
3 tablespoons unsalted butter
*1½ tablespoons minced shallot
    (optional)*
¾ teaspoon salt
⅛ teaspoon freshly grated nutmeg

1. Put the turnips and potatoes in separate medium saucepans with cold salted water to cover. Bring both to a boil over high heat, reduce the heat to moderate and simmer until the potatoes are fork tender, about 10 to 12 minutes, and the turnips are very tender, about 14 minutes. Drain the turnips and potatoes and add them to a large mixer bowl.

2. Meanwhile, in a small saucepan, warm the buttermilk, butter, shallot, salt and nutmeg over moderately low heat until the butter melts and the liquid is warm.

3. Pour the buttermilk sauce over the turnips and potatoes and whip with a hand mixer on low speed, increasing it to high, until smooth, 3 to 5 minutes. Serve at once or keep warm in the top of a double boiler.

—*Lee Bailey*

• • •

TURNIPS AND TURNIP GREENS WITH GINGER AND GARLIC

Southern greens are traditionally cooked with pieces of salted or smoked pork. Here soy sauce supplies the saltiness instead, and the meat is omitted entirely.

———— *4 Servings* ————
*½ pound small white turnips, peeled
    and cut into ½-inch dice (or
    substitute whole, unpeeled,
    trimmed baby turnips)*
*2 tablespoons cold-pressed sesame
    oil or safflower oil*
*3 medium-large garlic cloves,
    minced*
1 tablespoon minced fresh ginger
*1½ pounds trimmed turnip greens
    (about 2½ pounds untrimmed),
    chopped into 1-inch pieces*
2½ teaspoons sugar
2 tablespoons soy sauce or tamari

1. In a vegetable steamer over boiling water, steam the turnips, covered, until crisp-tender, 2 to 3 minutes. Do not overcook. Set aside.

2. In a large flameproof casserole, heat the oil over low heat. Add the garlic and ginger and cook, stirring frequently, until the garlic is fragrant but not browned, about 1 minute.

3. Add ¼ cup of water and increase the heat until the mixture simmers. Add the turnip greens by handfuls, letting them wilt slightly before adding the next batch. Cook, uncovered, stirring frequently, until the greens are just wilted and crisp-tender, about 5 minutes.

4. In a small bowl, combine the sugar and soy sauce. Add to the greens and toss to mix. Stir in the turnips and simmer, uncovered, to combine the flavors, about 3 minutes. With a slotted spoon, transfer the greens and turnips to a serving bowl and cover. Boil the liquid over high heat until reduced to a few tablespoons of syrupy glaze, about 5 minutes. Drizzle the glaze over the turnips and greens.

—*Sarah Belk*

• • •

CALAMATA-STUFFED TOMATOES

These Mediterranean-flavored stuffed tomatoes take only five minutes to bake.

———— *6 Servings* ————
1½ cups coarse bread crumbs
*½ cup coarsely chopped
    Calamata olives*
*2 tablespoons freshly grated
    Parmesan cheese*
1 garlic clove, minced
½ teaspoon freshly ground pepper
3 tablespoons extra-virgin olive oil
6 medium tomatoes

1. Preheat the oven to 500°. In a medium bowl, combine the bread crumbs, olives, Parmesan cheese, garlic and pepper. Stir in the olive oil and set aside.

2. Shave a thin slice from the bottom of each tomato to level them. Cut the top third off the tomatoes and create a hollow inside. Reserve the tops for garnish.

3. Spoon ⅓ cup of the olive-bread crumb filling into each tomato and place on a baking sheet. Arrange the tops of the tomatoes, cut-side up, on the baking sheet. Bake on the top rack of the oven until the stuffing is brown and crusty on top, about 5 minutes. Garnish the stuffed tomatoes with the tomato tops.

—*Marcia Kiesel*

• • •

VEGETABLES

(RELATIVELY) QUICK GREENS IN POTLIKKER

Here's an updated version of the traditional boiled greens dish that is so popular throughout the South. Serve with chicken and corn bread or cornsticks for sopping up the potlikker or as a side dish with broiled or grilled pork chops.

———————— 6 Servings ————————
1 tablespoon olive oil
1 pound smoked ham hocks or hog jowls
2 medium onions, chopped
6 large garlic cloves, slivered
12 whole black peppercorns
2 dried hot red peppers
1 teaspoon thyme
1 imported bay leaf
20 sprigs of parsley
3 pounds greens (collards, kale, mustard or turnip), trimmed of tough stems and coarsely chopped
Distilled white or cider vinegar, as accompaniment

1. In a large saucepan, heat the oil over moderate heat. Add the ham hocks, onions and garlic and cook, stirring frequently, until the onions are golden, about 10 minutes.

2. Tie the peppercorns, hot peppers, thyme, bay leaf and parsley in a square of cheesecloth. Add to the saucepan along with 4 quarts of water. Bring to a boil, skim if necessary, reduce the heat and simmer, uncovered, for 1 hour.

3. Add the greens and simmer, uncovered, until tender, about 1 hour more.

4. Remove the greens to a bowl. Increase the heat to high and boil until the liquid is reduced to 2 cups. Return the greens to the pot and heat to warm through, about 3 to 5 minutes.

5. Ladle the greens and some potlikker into small bowls and serve as a side dish. Pass the vinegar in a cruet on the side to sprinkle on the greens.
—*Sarah Belk*

• • •

GRATED ZUCCHINI WITH TOMATOES

To help them retain their texture in this recipe, the grated zucchini are squeezed in a towel to remove excess moisture.

———————— 6 Servings ————————
6 medium zucchini, coarsely shredded
1 tablespoon unsalted butter
1 tablespoon safflower oil
1 medium onion, coarsely chopped
1 large shallot, minced
4 medium Italian plum tomatoes or 1 can (14 ounces) Italian peeled tomatoes, with their juice, chopped
¼ teaspoon freshly ground pepper

1. Put the zucchini in a towel, roll it up and twist it firmly to get out any excess moisture; transfer the zucchini to a bowl.

2. In a large nonstick skillet, melt the butter in the oil over moderately high heat. Add the onion and shallot and sauté until they are softened and translucent, about 4 minutes.

3. Pour any juice from the canned tomatoes into the pan and cook for 2 minutes. Add the tomatoes and pepper and cook, stirring, until almost all the liquid has evaporated, about 4 minutes.

4. Add the zucchini. Cover tightly and cook over low heat, stirring several times, until the zucchini is cooked but still retains its texture, 12 to 15 minutes.
—*Lee Bailey*

• • •

LA MERE POULARD'S ZUCCHINI CREPES

These delightful crêpes from La Mère Poulard, the famous omelet restaurant at Mont-Saint-Michel in Normandy, make an excellent light side dish to accompany chicken or duck. They're also fine on their own with a tossed green salad.

———— *Makes 8 to 10 Small Crêpes* ————
2 medium zucchini (about 1 pound)
2 teaspoons salt
1 egg
2 tablespoons heavy cream
1 tablespoon all-purpose flour
2 garlic cloves, minced
About 2 tablespoons unsalted butter
About 2 tablespoons corn or peanut oil

1. Shred the zucchini in a food processor or with a hand grater. Sprinkle with the salt and drain in a stainless steel strainer for 30 minutes, tossing occasionally. Squeeze out any excess water.

2. In a medium bowl, whisk the egg briefly. Add the heavy cream, flour and minced garlic and whisk to blend. Add the zucchini and, with a fork, toss into the egg mixture until just coated.

3. In a large skillet or on a griddle, melt 1 tablespoon of the butter in 1 tablespoon of the oil over moderately high heat. Spoon 1 heaping tablespoon of the zucchini batter into the pan. Spread with the back of a spoon to form an even 3-inch circle. Repeat to fill the pan. Cook until the underside is deep golden brown, 3 to 4 minutes. Using a wide, flat spatula, turn the crêpes. Press down and cook until the other side is browned, 2 to 3 minutes longer, adjusting the heat as necessary. Repeat in batches with the remaining batter, adding additional butter and oil as necessary.
—*Patricia Wells*

• • •

SWEET AND SOUR VEGETABLE STIR-FRY

Not everything in an Indonesian rijsttafel is chile-hot and spicy. This lightly seasoned vegetarian dish provides a contrast to the more vivid ones found in this multidish meal.

—————— *12 Servings* ——————
2 tablespoons corn oil
3 garlic cloves, chopped
3 small shallots, halved
4 pounds Chinese long beans* (asparagus beans) or standard green beans, cut into 2-inch pieces
2 medium carrots, cut into thin julienne strips
1 large red bell pepper, cut into long slender strips
1 package (10 ounces) frozen baby corn, thawed
1 small head of cauliflower, cut into 1-inch florets
½ teaspoon minced fresh hot chile pepper (green or red) or ¾ teaspoon crushed hot red pepper
2 tablespoons cider vinegar
3 tablespoons ketjap manis*, preferably homemade (p. 256)
2 teaspoons (packed) brown sugar
1 large tomato, cut into ½-inch dice
*Available at Asian markets

1. In a wok or large heavy skillet, heat the oil. Add the garlic and shallots and stir-fry over moderate heat until softened but not browned, about 1 minute. Add the long beans, carrots, bell pepper, baby corn, cauliflower and hot pepper and continue to stir-fry for 5 minutes.

2. Add the vinegar, *ketjap manis* and brown sugar and stir-fry for 3 minutes; the vegetables should still be crunchy. *(The recipe can be prepared to this point up to 3 hours ahead. Set the vegetables aside at room temperature.)*

3. Shortly before serving, reheat the vegetables, if desired. Add the tomato and toss gently to mix. Serve warm or at room temperature.

—Copeland Marks

• • •

MODERN MIXED VEGGIES

Frozen peas and carrots, boiled until soft, slathered with margarine and warmed on a steam table may have been the loathsome accompaniment to many a meat loaf in the past, but that doesn't mean the basic idea is a bad one. Combine firm vegetables (the sort that can be blanched in advance, to shorten the finishing time), toss them in good sweet butter under a shower of fresh herbs, and you have a quick, stylish side dish.

—————— *6 to 8 Servings* ——————
4 carrots, cut into ½-inch pieces
½ head of cauliflower, cut into small florets (about 2 cups)
½ pound green beans, cut diagonally into 1-inch pieces
6 tablespoons unsalted butter
1 medium onion, finely diced
1 garlic clove, minced
1 tablespoon minced fresh thyme or oregano
½ teaspoon salt
½ teaspoon freshly ground pepper
1 tablespoon fresh lemon juice

1. Steam the carrots until almost tender, about 5 minutes. Add the cauliflower on top of the carrots and steam until almost tender but still firm, about 4 minutes. Add the green beans to the other vegetables and continue to steam until the beans are just tender, about 4 minutes longer. *(The cauliflower, carrots and green beans can be cooked up to 1 day in advance. Wrap and refrigerate.)*

2. In a large skillet, melt the butter over low heat. Add the onion and garlic and cook, covered, stirring once or twice, until the onion is softened but not browned, about 7 minutes.

3. Add the steamed vegetables, increase the heat to high and cook, tossing and stirring, until the vegetables are heated through and well coated with butter, about 3 minutes. Stir in the thyme and season with the salt and pepper. Remove from the heat, stir in the lemon juice and serve hot.

—Michael McLaughlin

• • •

FLAGEOLETS WITH GARLIC CLOVES

Flageolets, dried French beans, resemble small navy beans, but they are pale green and have a very subtle flavor. They are the classic accompaniment to a roasted leg of lamb, but are equally good with roasted goose. Substitute white navy beans if flageolets are not available.

—————— *6 to 8 Servings* ——————
1 pound flageolets* (about 2 cups)
6 tablespoons unsalted butter
6 garlic cloves, quartered
1 tablespoon salt (see Note)
¼ teaspoon freshly ground pepper
Several sprigs of fresh thyme or ½ dried
*Available at specialty food shops

1. Put the flageolets in a large saucepan with cold water to cover. Bring to a boil over moderately low heat; drain.

2. Return the beans to the pan and add the butter, garlic, salt, pepper, thyme and 6 cups of water. Bring to a boil, cover and cook over moderate heat until the flageolets are tender, 1 to 2 hours.

3. Drain the flageolets, reserving the broth. *(The beans can be cooked 1 day ahead and refrigerated.)*

4. Before serving, reheat the flageolets in the reserved broth.

NOTE: It is important to salt the beans before they cook to bring out their flavor. Don't worry about the amount of salt that is added here; it sounds like a lot, but most of it is drained off, and you won't taste it in the end.

—*Lydie Pinoy Marshall*

• • •

BLACK-EYED-PEA CAKES WITH TOMATO SALSA

At Carolina's, a popular restaurant in Charleston, these cakes are served as an appetizer (squirted decoratively with a mixture of sour cream thinned with milk). But they're hearty enough for a light lunch or supper.

—————— *6 Servings* ——————
1 cup dried black-eyed peas, rinsed and picked over to remove any grit
1 small smoked ham hock (about ½ pound)
5 cups rich unsalted chicken stock, or 2 cans (13¾ ounces each) chicken broth mixed with 1½ cups water
1 tablespoon unsalted butter
¼ cup minced red onion
2 large garlic cloves, minced
2 tablespoons minced red bell pepper
1 fresh jalapeño pepper, minced
1 egg yolk
About ½ cup fresh bread crumbs
½ teaspoon hot pepper sauce
2 tablespoons chopped fresh coriander
½ teaspoon ground cumin
¼ teaspoon freshly ground black pepper
⅓ cup yellow cornmeal, for dredging
¼ cup vegetable oil, for frying
Tomato Salsa (p. 253)

1. In a large heavy saucepan, combine the black-eyed peas, ham hock and chicken stock. Bring to a boil over moderate heat. Reduce the heat to low, cover and simmer until the peas are very tender, about 1¼ hours.

2. Drain into a large sieve over a heatproof bowl; reserve the ham hock and the cooking liquid for making soup later, if desired. Transfer the peas to a large mixing bowl and let them cool to room temperature.

3. Meanwhile, in a small heavy skillet, melt the butter over moderately low heat. Add the red onion, garlic, red bell pepper and jalapeño pepper; cook until limp and golden, about 5 minutes. Add to the black-eyed peas and let cool.

4. Add the egg yolk, ½ cup bread crumbs, hot sauce, fresh coriander, cumin and black pepper, and mix well with your hands or a potato masher to squash the peas. When the mixture is well blended, test to see if it is stiff enough to shape. If not, add a few more tablespoons of bread crumbs. Refrigerate uncovered for at least 1 hour. *(The recipe can be prepared up to 1 day in advance. Cover and refrigerate until ready to proceed.)*

5. Shape the black-eyed-pea mixture into 12 small cakes about 2½ inches across and ½ inch thick. Dredge in the cornmeal, shaking off any excess.

6. In a large heavy skillet, heat the oil over high heat until it ripples. Add half the black-eyed-pea cakes and fry over high heat, turning once, until brown, 1 to 1½ minutes on each side. Drain on paper towels. Repeat with the remaining cakes.

7. Arrange 2 cakes on each of 6 heated luncheon plates. Spoon about ⅓ cup of the Tomato Salsa onto each plate. Pass the remainder separately.

—*Donald Barickman, Carolina's, Charleston, South Carolina*

• • •

GRILLED POLENTA

The polenta is cooked and molded the night before.

—————— *6 Servings* ——————
1 tablespoon salt
2 cups coarse yellow cornmeal
6 tablespoons unsalted butter

1. Spray a 9-by-5-by-3-inch loaf pan with nonstick cooking spray.

2. In a large saucepan, bring 6½ cups of water and the salt to a boil over high heat. Gradually whisk in the cornmeal until thoroughly incorporated. Reduce the heat to low and cook, stirring constantly, until the cornmeal becomes a smooth porridge, about 20 minutes.

3. Stir in 2 tablespoons of the butter. Scrape the polenta into the prepared pan and smooth the top. Let cool, then cover and refrigerate overnight.

4. Preheat the broiler. Melt the remaining 4 tablespoons butter in a large baking pan with 1-inch sides. Tilt to coat the bottom of the pan.

5. Unmold the polenta from the loaf pan. Cut off and discard about ½ inch of the top to remove the crust. Cut the loaf crosswise into 16 slices ½ inch thick. Arrange the polenta slices close together on the baking pan, turning to coat each one with melted butter.

6. Broil about 6 inches from the heat for 7 minutes, or until the tops are bubbly and beginning to brown. Turn and brown the other side. (The polenta should be crunchy on the outside and soft in the middle.) Serve at once.

—*Lee Bailey*

• • •

SALADS

WARM SOFT-SHELL CRAB SALAD

I can't quite remember when I tasted my first soft-shell crab, but it certainly must have been on one of the crabbing excursions I went on as a child spending summers on Grand Isle, a Gulf island just off the Louisiana coast.

——————— 6 Servings ———————
6 medium soft-shell crabs, cleaned
Milk, for marinade
2 strips of thick bacon, cut crosswise
into 1/4-inch strips
1/4 cup plus 2 tablespoons extra-
virgin olive oil
1 tablespoon balsamic vinegar
1 1/2 tablespoons red wine vinegar
1 teaspoon salt
1/2 teaspoon freshly ground pepper
1/4 teaspoon Worcestershire sauce
6 cups (loosely packed) mixed salad
greens, preferably romaine and
radicchio
1 teaspoon fresh lemon juice
1/3 cup all-purpose flour
1/3 cup cornmeal
4 tablespoons unsalted butter
2 large scallions, chopped
Lemon wedges, for garnish

1. Put the crabs in a medium bowl and cover with milk. Set aside at room temperature for up to 1 hour.

2. In a small nonreactive skillet, fry the bacon over moderately high heat until crisp, about 3 minutes. Remove with a slotted spoon; drain on paper towels and set aside.

3. Pour off all but 1 tablespoon of the bacon fat. Whisk in 3 tablespoons of the olive oil, the balsamic vinegar, the red wine vinegar, 1/4 teaspoon of the salt, 1/4 teaspoon of the pepper and the Worcestershire sauce. Set the skillet of vinaigrette aside.

4. In a large bowl, combine the salad greens. In a small bowl, whisk 1 tablespoon of the olive oil with the lemon juice. Pour over the salad greens and toss

to coat. Season with additional salt and pepper to taste. Arrange the greens on individual salad plates.

5. On a sheet of waxed paper, combine the flour, cornmeal and remaining 3/4 teaspoon salt and 1/4 teaspoon pepper. Drain the crabs and pat dry. Dredge each crab in the flour-cornmeal mixture, shaking off any excess.

6. In a large skillet, melt the butter in the remaining 2 tablespoons olive oil over moderate heat. Add the crabs and sauté until golden brown, about 3 to 4 minutes on each side.

7. Arrange a crab in the center of each bed of greens. Sprinkle the bacon and scallions on top. Quickly warm the vinaigrette and spoon 1 tablespoon over each crab. Garnish with some lemon wedges and serve immediately.

—*Lee Bailey*

• • •

A SOFT-SHELL CRAB SALAD

There's not much in the way of fuss or last-minute preparation for this simple summer menu from Lee Bailey. The ice cream is made ahead of time and the soup can be served cold or at room temperature. Serves 6.

Tomato-Carrot Soup with Chervil
(p. 29)

Warm Soft-Shell Crab Salad
(p. 134)

Melba Toast and Sweet Butter

🍷 *Dry White Wine*

White Chocolate Ice Cream (p. 207)
with Seasonal Berries or Cookies

Iced Tea

CRAB AND AVOCADO SALAD WITH CORIANDER-TOMATILLO VINAIGRETTE

Tart, lemony tomatillos and coriander make a refreshing dressing for this juicy, summery dish.

——————— 4 Servings ———————
1 cup dry white wine
2 large shallots, minced
1/2 pound sole fillet, cut crosswise
into 1/4-inch-thick strips
2 fresh tomatillos, finely chopped
1 garlic clove, minced
1 teaspoon grated lemon zest
1 teaspoon salt
1/2 teaspoon freshly ground pepper
1/2 cup chopped fresh coriander
2 1/2 tablespoons white wine vinegar
1/3 cup extra-virgin olive oil
1 medium cucumber—peeled, seeded
and cut into 1/2-inch dice
1 large tomato, seeded and cut into
1/4-inch dice
4 cups shredded romaine lettuce
1/2 pound lump crabmeat, picked
over to remove any cartilage
2 large ripe avocados, preferably
Hass—cut lengthwise in half and
sliced crosswise 1/4 inch thick
Torn coriander leaves, for garnish

1. In a small saucepan, bring the wine and half of the minced shallots to a boil over high heat. Reduce the heat to low, add the sole and simmer until just opaque throughout, about 3 minutes. Using a slotted spoon, transfer the sole to a plate and set aside at room temperature to cool. Place the sole in the refrigerator to chill.

2. Boil the poaching liquid over high heat until it is reduced to 3 tablespoons, about 5 minutes. Pour the poaching liquid into a shallow bowl and let cool in the refrigerator.

3. In a medium bowl, combine the remaining minced shallots, the tomatillos, garlic, lemon zest, salt, pepper, coriander and vinegar. Whisk in the olive oil and the chilled reduced poaching liquid.

4. In a bowl, combine the cucumber, tomato, lettuce and ½ cup of the vinaigrette and toss. In another bowl, gently combine the chilled sole, crabmeat and the remaining vinaigrette.

5. Arrange the sliced avocado on the outer rim of each of 4 plates. Dividing equally, place the lettuce mixture in the center. Spoon the crab-sole mixture over the lettuce, pouring any excess vinaigrette over the avocado. Garnish with torn coriander leaves.

—*Marcia Kiesel*

• • •

CRAB HOPPIN' JOHN

Though usually featured as a summer meal in itself, this salad can also be served with a number of other dishes in a buffet.

——— **8 to 10 Servings** ———
1 package (10 ounces) frozen black-eyed peas
1 pound lump crabmeat, picked over to remove any cartilage
Juice of 2 lemons
3 cups cooked rice
1 medium red onion, finely chopped
2 celery ribs, finely chopped
¼ cup chopped parsley
½ cup light vegetable oil
½ teaspoon salt
½ teaspoon freshly ground pepper
Hot pepper sauce

1. In a medium saucepan, bring 1 cup of water to a boil over high heat. Add the black-eyed peas and return to a boil. Reduce the heat to moderate and simmer until almost all the water has been absorbed, 20 to 25 minutes. The peas should no longer taste starchy. Set aside

and let cool in the saucepan. Any remaining water will be absorbed during cooling.

2. In a large serving bowl, combine the crabmeat and lemon juice. Add the rice, onion, celery, parsley, oil, salt and pepper.

3. Add the cooled black-eyed peas and toss lightly but thoroughly to combine. Refrigerate, covered, until chilled. Serve with hot sauce on the side.

—*John Martin Taylor*

• • •

WARM MUSSEL SALAD WITH LEMON GRASS AND FRESH CORIANDER

Lemon grass adds a subtle lemon perfume to the mussel cooking liquid.

——— **4 Servings** ———
3 pounds mussels, scrubbed and debearded
⅓ cup dry white wine
2 stalks of lemon grass (bottom third only), finely minced*
2 teaspoons minced fresh ginger
¼ cup fresh lime juice
1½ teaspoons sugar
1 teaspoon salt
⅓ cup plus 1 tablespoon peanut oil
½ teaspoon freshly ground black pepper
½ teaspoon crushed hot red pepper
½ cup finely chopped red onion
1 cup chopped fresh coriander
*Available at Asian markets

1. In a stockpot, place the mussels, wine, lemon grass and ginger. Cover and cook over high heat, shaking the pan once or twice, until the mussels steam open, 3 to 5 minutes. With a slotted spoon, transfer the mussels to a large bowl. Discard any that do not open.

2. In a small jar, combine the lime juice, sugar and salt. Cover tightly and shake to blend well. Add the oil, black pepper, hot pepper and shake until blended.

3. Pour the dressing over the mussels. Add the red onion and coriander and toss. Transfer to a serving bowl and serve warm or at room temperature.

—*Bruce Cost*

• • •

GRILLED SHRIMP AND SCALLOP SALAD WITH LINGUINE AND PARSLEY PESTO

This sunny dish from The Riviera in Dallas combines several tastes and textures, from the sweet bell peppers and scallops to the bitter radicchio and endive. The shellfish and vegetables would be even better cooked on a grill.

❢ The zesty flavors and bitter-sharp accents of this dish call for a dry white with a bit of a bite, such as 1986 Gavi dei Gavi "La Scolca."

——— **4 Servings** ———
1½ pounds large shrimp, shelled and deveined
½ pound jumbo sea scallops
Oregano Vinaigrette (p. 136)
1 medium yellow bell pepper
1 medium red bell pepper
½ cup Italian Parsley Pesto (p. 252)
1½ tablespoons fresh lemon juice
¼ teaspoon crushed hot red pepper
2 medium heads of radicchio, trimmed and quartered lengthwise through the core
4 medium Belgian endives, trimmed and halved lengthwise
⅓ cup extra-virgin olive oil
Salt and freshly ground black pepper
½ pound fresh or imported dry linguine
1 medium bunch of arugula, large stems removed
Flat-leaf parsley leaves, for garnish

1. Preheat the broiler. In a medium bowl, toss the shrimp and scallops with ½ cup of the Oregano Vinaigrette. Cover and marinate in the refrigerator for 2 to 3 hours.

2. Place the bell peppers on a baking sheet and broil as close to the heat as possible, turning, until charred all over. Transfer the peppers to a brown paper bag, fold over the top and set aside to steam for 5 minutes. Peel the peppers. Discard the cores, seeds and ribs. Slice the peppers into thin strips and set aside. Leave the broiler on.

3. Combine the Italian Parsley Pesto with the lemon juice and hot pepper. Set aside at room temperature.

4. Brush the radicchio and endives with the oil and place on a baking sheet. Sprinkle with salt and black pepper to taste. Broil the vegetables for about 2 minutes per side, until lightly charred. Core the radicchio and endives and place on a plate. Drizzle on the remaining vinaigrette.

5. Arrange the shrimp and scallops on a baking sheet and broil, turning once, until lightly browned and just opaque throughout, about 2 minutes per side.

6. In a large pot of boiling salted water, cook the linguine until tender but still firm. Drain and toss with the reserved bell pepper strips and the pesto mixture. While the pasta is still hot, add the arugula and toss until wilted.

7. Arrange 2 pieces each of radicchio and endive on 4 large heated plates. Divide the linguine among the plates and arrange the seafood on top. Garnish with parsley leaves.

—*The Riviera, Dallas*

• • •

OREGANO VINAIGRETTE

——— *Makes About ⅔ Cup* ———
1 small anchovy fillet, minced
2 medium garlic cloves, minced
1 teaspoon minced fresh oregano or ½ teaspoon dried
½ teaspoon Dijon-style mustard
2 tablespoons red wine vinegar
¼ teaspoon salt
¼ teaspoon freshly ground pepper
⅔ cup extra-virgin olive oil

In a small bowl, whisk together the anchovy, garlic, oregano, mustard, vinegar, salt and pepper. Whisk in the oil in a thin stream.

—*The Riviera, Dallas*

• • •

COOL AND SPICY SALAD WITH SHRIMP AND PORK

Here is an example of the classic combination of pork and shrimp that the Vietnamese do so well. Note that the pork is cooked in water to eliminate any fat or strong taste.

——— *6 to 8 Servings* ———
½ pound boneless pork loin, trimmed of excess fat
½ pound medium shrimp, shelled and deveined
1 large cucumber—peeled, seeded and cut into very thin 2-inch-long strips
2 teaspoons salt
6 tablespoons sugar
6 tablespoons distilled white vinegar
3 celery ribs, cut into thin 2-inch strips
2 large carrots, cut into long, thin strips
1 medium onion, thinly sliced
⅓ cup chopped fresh coriander
3 tablespoons chopped fresh mint
½ cup Nuoc Cham Dipping Sauce (p. 251)
3 cups vegetable oil, for deep-frying
*24 dried shrimp chips**
½ cup chopped, unsalted dry-roasted peanuts
*Available at Asian markets

1. Put the pork into a small saucepan with enough cold water to cover. Bring to a simmer over moderate heat and cook until tender, about 25 minutes. Drain, cool slightly and cut into thin 2-inch-long strips. Let cool to room temperature.

2. In a medium saucepan of boiling water, cook the shrimp until just opaque throughout, 2 to 3 minutes. Drain and cool slightly, then cut each shrimp in half lengthwise. Set aside to cool to room temperature. *(The shrimp and pork can be cooked 1 day ahead and refrigerated.)*

3. Place the cucumber strips in a bowl and toss them with 1 teaspoon of the salt. Set aside for 5 minutes, then squeeze to remove any excess moisture.

4. In a measuring cup, combine the remaining 1 teaspoon salt with the sugar and vinegar. Put the celery, carrots and onion in 3 separate bowls. Toss each vegetable with one-third of the vinegar mixture. Let stand for 5 minutes.

5. Remove the vegetables and squeeze dry. Put them in a large bowl. Add the cucumber, pork, shrimp, ¼ cup of the coriander and 2 tablespoons of the mint. Add the Nuoc Cham Dipping Sauce and toss well.

6. In a large saucepan or a wok, heat the oil to 350°. Fry the shrimp chips, 5 or 6 at a time, until they expand fully and float on the surface, about 12 seconds. Try not to let the chips turn brown. Drain on paper towels.

7. Spoon the salad onto a large platter. Sprinkle the top with the remaining coriander, mint and the chopped peanuts. Scatter the shrimp chips around the salad.

—*Marcia Kiesel*

• • •

FRESH TUNA AND WHITE BEAN SALAD

The combination of grilled tuna, tender white beans, fresh herbs and tomatoes makes this a sunny Provençal-style salad. This substantial main-course salad could be served on its own, or as the centerpiece of a multi-dish buffet or picnic.

6 to 8 Servings

2 cups baby lima or other dried white beans, rinsed and picked over to remove any grit
1 pound fresh tuna steak, cut ½ inch thick
¾ cup extra-virgin olive oil
1 tablespoon minced fresh thyme
1 tablespoon minced fresh oregano
1 tablespoon minced parsley
2 tablespoons grainy mustard
1 tablespoon red wine vinegar
¼ cup plus 2 tablespoons fresh lemon juice
½ teaspoon freshly ground pepper
1½ teaspoons salt
4 large tomatoes—peeled, seeded and coarsely chopped

1. Soak the beans overnight in cold water to cover by 2 inches.

2. The next day, drain and rinse the beans. In a medium saucepan, combine the beans with 6 cups of cold water and bring to a boil. Reduce the heat to moderately low and simmer the beans until tender, 20 to 25 minutes.

3. Meanwhile, in a small bowl, whisk together the olive oil, thyme, oregano, parsley, mustard, vinegar, lemon juice, pepper and ½ teaspoon of the salt.

4. Place the tuna in a shallow glass dish. Pour two-thirds of the dressing over the tuna. Cover and let marinate at room temperature for 30 minutes, turning once.

5. Light a grill or preheat the broiler. Drain the beans and place in a bowl. Add the tomatoes, the remaining 1 teaspoon salt and the remaining dressing. Toss well. Set aside to cool.

6. Grill the tuna 4 to 5 inches from the heat, turning once and basting occasionally with the marinade, for 8 to 10 minutes or until just cooked through. Let cool to room temperature.

7. Break the tuna into bite-size chunks and toss with the beans. Cover and refrigerate until serving time.

—Bob Chambers

• • •

CHICKEN SALAD WITH NEW POTATOES AND DILL

I like to cook the chicken the day before I prepare the salad so that I can skim all the fat from the broth.

8 Servings

1 whole chicken (3 to 3½ pounds)
2 medium carrots, chopped
2 celery ribs, chopped
2 large onions, chopped
1 imported bay leaf
10 whole black peppercorns
3 whole cloves
3 cans (10½ ounces each) low-sodium chicken broth
2 pounds small new potatoes
2 tablespoons grainy mustard
1 tablespoon Dijon-style mustard
3 tablespoons fresh lemon juice
2 tablespoons red wine vinegar
¼ cup heavy cream
½ cup extra-virgin olive oil
¾ teaspoon salt
½ teaspoon freshly ground pepper
2 tablespoons chopped fresh dill

1. Place the chicken in a large saucepan, breast-side up. Add the carrots, celery, onions, bay leaf, peppercorns, cloves and chicken broth. Add enough water to cover the chicken and bring to a boil. Reduce the heat to moderately low and

simmer for 40 minutes. Turn the chicken over and simmer for 20 minutes longer.

2. Remove from the heat and let the chicken cool to room temperature in the liquid. Refrigerate for about 5 hours or overnight, until the fat solidifies on the surface of the broth.

3. Skim the fat from the broth. Remove the chicken and set aside. Bring the broth to a boil. Strain through a fine sieve.

4. Return the broth to the pan. Add the potatoes and bring to a boil. Reduce the heat to moderate and simmer until a knife inserted in the largest potato is easily removed, 15 to 20 minutes. Drain the potatoes, reserving the broth for another use. Let cool for 10 minutes, then cut into 1-inch chunks.

5. Meanwhile, in a small bowl, whisk together the grainy mustard, Dijon-style mustard, lemon juice, vinegar, cream, oil, salt, pepper and dill.

6. Remove the skin from the chicken and discard. Remove the meat from the bones and cut it into 1-inch chunks. In a large bowl, toss the chicken with the warm potatoes and the dressing. Cover and refrigerate. Serve the salad at room temperature.

—Bob Chambers

• • •

TUSCAN CHICKEN AND BEAN SALAD

Beans are cooked here without presoaking. It takes a little longer on the stove but less time overall.

4 to 6 Servings

2 cups dried white beans, such as Great Northern
1 bay leaf
1 medium onion, chopped
1 whole free-range chicken breast, bone in
3 garlic cloves, unpeeled
1 red bell pepper

1½ teaspoons salt
2 tablespoons red wine vinegar
½ cup extra-virgin olive oil
2 tablespoons minced fresh thyme or
 1 teaspoon dried
3 tablespoons minced Italian flat-
 leaf parsley
½ teaspoon freshly ground black
 pepper
3 scallions, minced

1. Place the beans, bay leaf and onion in a large heavy pot with 8 cups of cold water. Bring to a simmer over moderate heat and cook until tender, about 1½ hours. Drain the beans and let cool.

2. Preheat the oven to 350°. Place the chicken, garlic cloves and red pepper in a lightly oiled, medium baking pan. Bake for about 35 minutes, turning the garlic and pepper after 15 minutes, until the skin on the chicken is golden brown and the meat is white throughout. Remove from the oven and let stand for about 10 minutes until cool enough to handle.

3. Using a sharp knife, peel the pepper and discard the skin and seeds. Cut the pepper into ½-inch dice.

4. Squeeze the roasted garlic from its skin and place in a large bowl. Using a fork, mash the roasted garlic with 1 teaspoon of the salt. Whisk in the vinegar and then the olive oil. Add the thyme, parsley and black pepper.

5. Skin and shred the roasted chicken, add to the vinaigrette and toss well to coat. Add the beans, minced scallions, diced roasted pepper, the remaining ½ teaspoon salt and additional black pepper to taste. Serve warm or chilled.

—*Molly O'Neill*

• • •

SMOKED CHICKEN AND APPLE SALAD

This salad is a colorful, crunchy combination of chicken, red peppers, tart green apples and toasted pecans all tossed with a savory-mustard vinaigrette.

——————— *3 to 4 Servings* ———————
1 small garlic clove, minced
1 tablespoon Dijon-style mustard
1 tablespoon white wine vinegar or
 rice vinegar
2 tablespoons minced winter savory
¼ teaspoon salt
¼ teaspoon freshly ground black
 pepper
¼ cup plus 2 tablespoons olive oil
1 small red onion, thinly sliced
1 cup pecans
2 large tart green apples, such as
 Granny Smith—peeled,
 quartered, cored and cut into ½-
 inch chunks
1 medium red bell pepper, cut into
 thin julienne strips
¾ pound smoked chicken, turkey or
 pheasant, cut into 1-inch pieces

1. Preheat the oven to 400°. In a small bowl, combine the garlic, mustard, vinegar, savory, salt and black pepper. With a fork, whisk in the oil. Set aside.

2. Put the onion slices in a small bowl. Cover with cold water and soak for 5 to 10 minutes; then drain well.

3. Spread the pecans on a baking sheet and cook in the oven until fragrant and toasted, about 4 minutes. Let cool and crumble into smaller pieces.

4. In a large bowl, combine the onion, apples, red pepper and chicken. Pour the vinaigrette over the salad and toss well. Spoon the salad onto a serving platter, or divide among 6 plates. Sprinkle with the toasted pecans and serve.

—*Marcia Kiesel*

• • •

WATERCRESS SALAD WITH SMOKED CHICKEN AND WALNUT CROUTONS

In the South, wild watercress ("creasy greens") gives this salad an arresting flavor and texture. Elsewhere, the peppery cultivated green still contrasts nicely with the sweet-tangy mustard. The walnut oil and croutons add richness.

❦ The bite of the greens and smoky flavor of the meat dictate a spicy white wine, such as a 1985 Alsace Gewürztraminer from Willm or Trimbach, to stand up to the flavors.

——————— *6 Servings* ———————
¼ cup plus 1 tablespoon walnut oil
1 tablespoon unsalted butter
3 large garlic cloves, slivered
3 slices of stale, firm-textured white
 bread, cut into ½-inch cubes
 (about 1 cup)
½ teaspoon salt
2 teaspoons Honeycup or other
 sweet-spicy mustard
2 teaspoons fresh lemon juice
2 teaspoons red wine vinegar
2 tablespoons olive oil
1 tablespoon vegetable oil
¼ teaspoon freshly ground pepper
2 large bunches of watercress, wild
 if available, tough stems removed
 (about 6 cups)
1 small head of radicchio, torn into
 bite-size pieces
6 ounces smoked chicken, shredded
 into bite-size pieces

1. In a large skillet, heat 2 tablespoons of the walnut oil with the butter over moderately low heat. Add the garlic and cook until fragrant, about 1 minute.

2. Add the bread cubes to the skillet and cook, tossing often, until crisp and golden brown, 5 to 8 minutes. Season with ¼ teaspoon of the salt and set aside.

3. In a small bowl, whisk together the mustard, lemon juice, vinegar and remaining ¼ teaspoon salt. Whisk in the olive oil, vegetable oil, remaining 3 tablespoons walnut oil and the pepper.

4. In a large bowl, toss the watercress, radicchio and smoked chicken with the dressing. Top with the croutons.

—*Sarah Belk*

• • •

CHEF'S SALAD

There are as many versions of chef's salad as there are chefs, and that, at the moment, constitutes quite a multitude. The expected presentation of mounded greens covered with strips of cheese, meat and fowl can be reinterpreted according to whim and availability of ingredients; as long as the overall combination tastes good, the sky's the limit.

8 to 10 Servings
1 cup pine nuts (about 4 ounces)
1 head of romaine lettuce, torn into
*   bite-size pieces*
2 heads of Bibb lettuce, torn into
*   bite-size pieces*
6 Belgian endives, sliced crosswise
*   ¼ inch thick*
4 tender celery ribs, minced
12 radishes, minced
½ cup finely chopped prosciutto
*   (about 3 ounces)*
½ pound smoked ham, cut into thin
*   julienne strips*
½ pound cooked tongue, cut into thin
*   julienne strips*
1 pound boneless cooked chicken
*   breast, cut into ¾-inch dice*
1 pound Jarlsberg cheese, cut into
*   thin julienne strips*
1 large cucumber—peeled, seeded
*   and cut into ½-inch dice*
1 pint cherry tomatoes, quartered
2 cups plain yogurt
¼ cup Dijon-style mustard

CHEF'S SALAD DINNER

Chef's salad is one of the most accommodating and user-friendly dishes. It can be jazzed up or down, depending on your whims and the other components of the menu. If the nacho appetizers put you in a southwestern frame of mind, use some Monterey jack as the cheese and throw in some chopped fresh coriander in place of the dill in the dressing. Serves 8 to 10.

🍷 *Sangritas*

Classic Nachos (p. 14)

―――――――――――

Chef's Salad (p. 139)

Crusty French Bread

🍷 *Dry Savory White, such as 1986*
Hacienda Sauvignon Blanc or 1986
Marquis de Goulaine Muscadet

―――――――――――

Peach Upside-Down Cake (p. 234)
with Sweetened Whipped Cream

Coffee

¼ cup olive oil
1 tablespoon sherry wine vinegar
½ teaspoon salt
1 teaspoon freshly ground pepper
½ cup minced scallions
2 tablespoons minced fresh dill

1. Preheat the oven to 400°. Spread the pine nuts out on a baking sheet and toast in the oven until golden brown, about 4 minutes. Let cool.

2. In a large decorative bowl, toss the romaine and Bibb lettuce with the endives, celery and radishes. Add the pine nuts and prosciutto and toss again.

3. Mound this salad in the center of the bowl. Arrange the smoked ham,

tongue, chicken and cheese in decorative, alternating spokes around the salad.

4. In a medium bowl, toss the cucumber with the tomatoes. Mound in the center of the salad.

5. In a medium bowl, whisk together the yogurt and mustard. Gradually whisk in the olive oil. Add the vinegar, salt and pepper and blend well. Stir in the scallions and dill and mix well. Pass the dressing separately.

—*W. Peter Prestcott*

• • •

HAM AND CHEESE SALAD

Slices of rosy, smoky ham are teamed with Gruyère cheese for a satisfying main-course salad.

8 Servings
1½ pounds baked ham, sliced
*   ¼ inch thick and cut into 3-by-*
*   ¼-inch matchsticks*
1½ pounds Gruyère cheese, sliced
*   ¼ inch thick and cut into 3-by-*
*   ¼-inch matchsticks*
3 scallions, thinly sliced
2 tablespoons chopped Italian flat-
*   leaf parsley*
2 tablespoons white wine vinegar
2 tablespoons Dijon-style mustard
½ teaspoon salt
¼ teaspoon freshly ground black
*   pepper*
Pinch of cayenne pepper
½ cup extra-virgin olive oil

1. In a large bowl, combine the ham and cheese with the scallions and parsley.

2. In a small bowl, whisk the vinegar, mustard, salt, black pepper and cayenne. Gradually whisk in the olive oil in a thin stream.

3. Pour the dressing over the ham and cheese and toss well. Cover and refrigerate. Serve at room temperature.

—*Bob Chambers*

• • •

PORK TENDERLOIN SALAD WITH APPLES AND APRICOTS

Because pork and fruit go very well together, I've included apricots and apples in this salad. Be sure to add the pork pan juices to the dressing for extra flavor.

———————— *8 Servings* ————————
1 tablespoon unsalted butter
½ cup plus 2 tablespoons extra-virgin olive oil
3 pounds pork tenderloin, trimmed
4 ounces dried apricots, cut into thin strips (about ⅔ cup)
2 celery ribs, thinly sliced
3 large shallots, thinly sliced
6 medium Granny Smith apples—peeled, cored and cut into ¾-inch chunks
2 tablespoons fresh lemon juice
2 tablespoons white wine vinegar
1 tablespoon Dijon-style mustard
½ teaspoon salt
¼ teaspoon freshly ground pepper
2 tablespoons chopped parsley

1. Preheat the oven to 450°. In a large skillet, melt the butter in 1 tablespoon of the olive oil over moderately high heat. Add the pork and sauté, turning, until well browned all over, 7 to 10 minutes.

2. Transfer the pork to a baking dish; set the skillet aside. Roast the pork in the oven for 15 to 20 minutes or until a meat thermometer inserted into the thickest part of a tenderloin registers 150°. Let cool for 15 minutes.

3. Meanwhile, in a small heatproof bowl, cover the apricots with 1 cup of very hot water. Let stand for 15 minutes.

4. In the skillet used for the pork, heat 1 tablespoon of the olive oil. Add the celery and shallots and cook over moderately high heat, stirring, until the shallots are softened and translucent, 2 to 3 minutes. Place in a large bowl.

5. Add 1 tablespoon olive oil to the skillet. Add the apples and sauté over moderately high heat, tossing frequently, until just tender, 4 to 5 minutes. Add to the shallots and celery and toss well.

6. Drain the apricots and add to the bowl. Slice the pork ¼ inch thick and then cut each piece into ¼-inch strips. Add to the apple mixture.

7. In a small bowl, whisk the lemon juice with the vinegar and any juices from the baking dish. Whisk in the mustard, salt, pepper and remaining 7 tablespoons olive oil. Pour the dressing over the salad and toss well. Cover and refrigerate. Toss with the parsley before serving.
—*Bob Chambers*

• • •

DANDELION AND BACON SALAD WITH HARD CIDER VINAIGRETTE

Wilted dandelion greens are a southern classic. Served in spring, dandelion greens were a welcome addition to the diet after a long winter of root vegetables and sauerkraut. Here, hard cider and cider vinegar add a fruity note. This salad makes a wonderful lunch served with crusty French bread and sparkling cider.

———————— *6 Servings* ————————
¾ pound small boiling potatoes
½ cup hard cider
½ pound thickly sliced bacon, cut crosswise into ¼-inch strips
¼ cup cider vinegar
¾ pound young dandelion greens, or substitute arugula or chicory (about 5 cups)
¼ teaspoon salt
¼ teaspoon freshly ground pepper
Cider vinegar or hard cider, as accompaniment

1. Place the potatoes in a large saucepan of lightly salted water and bring to a boil. Cook until just tender, about 20 minutes; drain. While still warm but cool enough to handle, peel and quarter. Place the warm potatoes in a large bowl, toss with ¼ cup of the hard cider and cover to keep warm.

2. In a large nonreactive skillet, cook the bacon over moderate heat until crisp and lightly browned, about 7 minutes. Drain on paper towels and set aside. Measure out 7 tablespoons of the drippings into a small bowl and reserve in a warm place; discard the remaining fat.

3. Add the remaining ¼ cup hard cider and the cider vinegar to the skillet and boil over high heat until reduced to ⅓ cup, about 2 minutes. Remove from the heat and set aside.

4. Add the dandelion greens and the reserved bacon and warm bacon drippings to the warm potatoes and toss. Add the hot cider reduction and toss quickly. Season with the salt and pepper. Pass a cruet of cider vinegar or hard cider on the side.
—*Sarah Belk*

• • •

SALAD OF WATERCRESS, ARUGULA AND FENNEL

I like to serve salad after the main course, European style. I also present a choice of cheeses—possibly a Brie, a chèvre and a Roquefort.

❢ It's very hard to serve a great red wine with salad (the vinegar kills the wine), so consider serving a Muscat de Beaumes de Venise. It's a relatively light sweet white wine that will complement the salad, as well as cheese.

———————— *6 to 8 Servings* ————————
1 large bunch of arugula, trimmed
2 bunches of watercress, trimmed
1 small fennel bulb, halved and cut into long thin strips
1 garlic clove, crushed through a press
1½ teaspoons Dijon-style mustard
2 tablespoons red wine vinegar

¾ teaspoon salt
¼ teaspoon freshly ground pepper
⅓ cup light olive oil, such as Bertolli
2 tablespoons minced fresh tarragon
   or 2 tablespoons minced parsley
   combined with ½ teaspoon dried
   tarragon

1. In a salad bowl, combine the arugula, watercress and fennel.
2. In a small bowl, combine the garlic, mustard, vinegar, salt and pepper. Gradually whisk in the olive oil. Whisk in the minced tarragon.
3. Just before serving, pour the dressing over the salad and toss.

—Lydie Pinoy Marshall

• • •

CHARDENOUX'S SALAD OF BLUE CHEESE, NUTS AND BELGIAN ENDIVE

This is one of my favorite wintertime salads: crunchy Belgian endive, freshly cracked walnuts and piquant blue cheese, all tossed in a lemony dressing of fragrant hazelnut oil.

————— 4 to 6 Servings —————
2 tablespoons fresh lemon juice
¼ teaspoon salt
¼ cup hazelnut oil or extra-virgin
   olive oil
2 pounds Belgian endives (about 8
   medium heads)
1 cup walnut pieces, freshly cracked
6 ounces imported French Roquefort
   or Fourme d'Ambert cheese,
   crumbled

1. In a small bowl, combine the lemon juice and salt; stir to dissolve. Gradually whisk in the oil in a thin stream until the dressing is blended.
2. Rinse the endive, pat dry and separate the leaves. Place the whole leaves in

a large salad bowl. Sprinkle the walnuts and crumbled cheese over the endive. Whisk the dressing, drizzle over the salad and toss to coat.

—Patricia Wells

• • •

MIXED GREEN SALAD WITH SOURED CREAM AND BLUE CHEESE DRESSING

The combination of creamy blue cheese and fresh, crisp salad greens is a welcome interlude between the main course and the dessert.

————— 12 Servings —————
⅓ cup heavy cream
1½ tablespoons tarragon wine
   vinegar
6 ounces Saga blue cheese, rind
   removed, at room temperature
¼ cup milk
¼ cup mayonnaise
1 tablespoon grainy mustard
½ teaspoon tarragon
¼ teaspoon salt
Freshly ground pepper
1 medium head of romaine lettuce
1 medium head of curly leaf lettuce
2 bunches of arugula or watercress
2 pints of cherry tomatoes (yellow
   and red if available), halved

1. In a mixing bowl, combine the cream with the vinegar. Stir until the cream thickens, about 1 minute. Break up the blue cheese and blend it into the cream with a fork, leaving some lumps. Whisk in the milk, mayonnaise, mustard, tarragon, salt and pepper and blend well. (The dressing can be made up to 2 days in advance. If it gets too thick, it can be easily thinned again with a small amount of milk.)
2. Thoroughly rinse and drain the various greens. Tear into bite-size pieces. Place in a salad bowl and toss with the tomatoes. (The vegetables can be prepared

up to 1 day ahead. Store the washed greens in airtight plastic bags in the refrigerator. Store the cherry tomatoes uncut.)
3. Divide the salad evenly among 12 salad plates. Drizzle 2 tablespoons of dressing over each portion and serve.

—Bob Chambers

• • •

GREEN SALAD WITH STILTON CHEESE

This salad, which is best served after the entrée, acts as both cheese and salad courses.

————— 6 Servings —————
1 bunch of mâche (lamb's lettuce),
   torn into bite-size pieces
1 head of radicchio, torn into pieces
3 Belgian endives, sliced ½ inch
   thick
1½ tablespoons white wine vinegar
1½ teaspoons Dijon-style mustard
3 tablespoons extra-virgin olive oil
1½ tablespoons safflower oil
¼ teaspoon salt
Freshly ground pepper
Wedge of Stilton cheese

In a large bowl, combine all the greens. In a small bowl, whisk together the vinegar, mustard, olive oil, safflower oil and salt. Pour onto the greens and toss to coat well. Season with pepper to taste. Pass Stilton cheese on the side.

—Lee Bailey

• • •

CABBAGE SALAD WITH GARLIC

Jacques Pépin offers a striking visual presentation by contrasting white against red cabbage.

———— 6 Servings ————
**4½ cups finely shredded green
 cabbage (about ¾ pound)
4½ cups finely shredded red cabbage
 (about ¾ pound)
4 or 5 garlic cloves, crushed through
 a press
1 can (2 ounces) flat anchovy fillets,
 drained
1 tablespoon red or white wine
 vinegar
½ cup olive oil or vegetable oil
½ teaspoon freshly ground pepper
¼ teaspoon salt
¼ cup small sprigs of parsley**

1. Place the green and red cabbage in two separate bowls and set aside.

2. On a work surface, using a sharp heavy knife, chop and mash together the crushed garlic and anchovy fillets into a puree.

3. In a medium bowl, combine the vinegar, oil, pepper and salt. Stir in the garlic-anchovy puree. (Do not make this sauce in a food processor, because it will become too thick.) Divide the sauce between the two bowls of cabbage and toss well to combine.

4. Place the red cabbage in a pretty glass or crystal bowl. Make a well in the center to form a nest. Mound the green cabbage in the center. Garnish with the parsley.

—Jacques Pépin

• • •

RED PEPPER SLAW

I like red peppers so much that I use them two ways—roasted for the flavor and raw for the crunch.

————Makes About 4 Cups————
**3 small red bell peppers—1 whole,
 2 thinly sliced
½ medium head of green cabbage,
 finely shredded
1 small onion, thinly sliced
½ cup thinly sliced sour gherkins or
 other pickles
1 garlic clove, minced
⅓ cup mayonnaise
2 teaspoons white wine vinegar
Salt and freshly ground black pepper**

1. Roast the whole red pepper directly over a gas flame or under the broiler, turning, until charred all over, about 5 minutes. Place the pepper in a paper bag and set aside for 10 minutes to steam. When cool enough to handle, peel the pepper and remove the core, seeds and ribs. Slice into thin strips.

2. In a large bowl, combine the cooked and uncooked red peppers with the cabbage, onion, gherkins, garlic, mayonnaise and vinegar. Season with salt and pepper to taste. Cover and refrigerate until ready to use. *(The recipe can be made up to 1 day ahead.)*

—Marcia Kiesel

• • •

WARM BROCCOLI SALAD

Serve this warm salad right along with the main course, as a piquant side vegetable.

————6 to 8 Servings————
**2 bunches of broccoli
2 tablespoons fresh lemon juice
½ teaspoon dry mustard
¾ teaspoon salt
¼ teaspoon freshly ground white
 pepper
4 dashes of hot pepper sauce
2 tablespoons safflower or corn oil
2 tablespoons extra-virgin olive oil
½ small red onion, minced
¼ cup toasted pine nuts**

1. Using a small sharp knife, cut the florets from the broccoli and separate into 1- to 1½-inch pieces. Trim off the ends of the stalks. Peel the remaining stalks and cut crosswise into ¼-inch-thick slices. Steam the broccoli until just tender, 4 to 5 minutes.

2. Meanwhile, in a small bowl, whisk the lemon juice, mustard, salt, white pepper and hot sauce. Whisk in the safflower oil and olive oil in a thin stream.

3. Transfer the warm broccoli to a medium bowl and toss with the vinaigrette. Add the onion and pine nuts and toss to mix. Serve warm.

—Lee Bailey

• • •

FENNEL AND EGGPLANT SALAD

Thin strips of sun-dried tomatoes would make a nice addition to this salad, as would a garnish of chopped pistachios.

————8 Servings————
**3 eggplants (about 1½ pounds
 each), cut into ½-inch cubes
¾ cup extra-virgin olive oil**

½ teaspoon freshly ground black
    pepper
3 pounds fennel bulbs, trimmed,
    greens reserved
3 yellow bell peppers, cut into thin
    strips
¼ cup fresh lemon juice
2 tablespoons white wine vinegar
1 teaspoon dry mustard
½ teaspoon salt
3 tablespoons minced reserved
    fennel greens or parsley
1 small garlic clove, minced

1. Preheat the oven to 450°. In a large bowl, toss the eggplant with ½ cup of the olive oil and the black pepper.

2. Spread the eggplant cubes out in a single layer on 2 baking sheets. Roast for 45 minutes, stirring every 5 to 7 minutes, until tender and browned.

3. Meanwhile, halve the fennel bulbs lengthwise and cut out the cores. Slice crosswise ⅛ inch thick.

4. In a large skillet, combine the fennel, bell pepper strips and ¼ cup of water. Cook over high heat, stirring constantly, until the water has evaporated and the vegetables are crisp-tender, 3 to 4 minutes. Transfer the vegetables to a large bowl.

5. In a bowl, combine the lemon juice, vinegar, dry mustard, salt, fennel greens, garlic and remaining ¼ cup olive oil.

6. Add the eggplant to the fennel-pepper mixture. Pour on the dressing and toss well. Cover and refrigerate. Serve at room temperature.

—Bob Chambers

• • •

BABY CARROT AND TURNIP SALAD

Sweet, young carrots and turnips join forces in this salad that's dressed with a grainy mustard vinaigrette.

———— 6 to 8 Servings ————

1½ pounds baby turnips, peeled
1½ pounds baby carrots, peeled
1 teaspoon salt
½ teaspoon sugar
2 tablespoons grainy mustard
¼ cup red wine vinegar
¾ cup extra-virgin olive oil
Freshly ground pepper
2 tablespoons minced fresh chives

1. Put the turnips and carrots in a large skillet or flameproof casserole. Add the salt, sugar and cold water to cover. Bring to a boil. Reduce the heat to moderately low and simmer until the vegetables are tender when pierced with a knife, 8 to 10 minutes. Drain well.

2. Meanwhile, in a small bowl, whisk the mustard with the vinegar and oil. Season the dressing with salt and pepper to taste.

3. Toss the warm vegetables with the dressing. Let cool and refrigerate. Before serving, sprinkle with the chives and toss well.

—Bob Chambers

• • •

PINEAPPLE AND BEET SALAD

Beets retain more of their flavor and color when they are baked rather than boiled.

———— 8 Servings ————

2½ pounds medium beets
1 large fresh pineapple (3 to 3½
    pounds)
¼ cup plus 2 tablespoons fresh
    lemon juice

½ teaspoon salt
Freshly ground pepper

1. Preheat the oven to 400°. Wrap the beets in aluminum foil. Bake in the middle of the oven for 1¼ to 1½ hours, or until tender when pierced with a skewer. Remove from the oven and open the foil packet. When the beets are cool enough to handle, peel them under cold water and pat dry. Cut into 1-inch chunks.

2. Cut the rind off the pineapple, removing the "eyes." Quarter the pineapple lengthwise. Cut the core portion from each section and discard. Cut the remaining pineapple into 1-inch chunks. Put the beets and pineapple in separate bowls; cover and refrigerate.

3. Shortly before serving, in a medium bowl, toss the pineapple with the beets, lemon juice, salt and pepper to taste.

—Bob Chambers

• • •

FRESH PEA SALAD WITH PANCETTA

The salty, cured flavor of the pancetta is a fitting complement to the sweet and tender peas. If pancetta is unavailable, use lightly smoked, thick-sliced bacon.

———— 6 Servings ————

2 teaspoons salt
4 pounds of fresh peas, shelled (4
    cups) or 2 packages (10 ounces
    each) frozen baby peas
½ pound pancetta, sliced ¼ inch
    thick
2 large shallots, minced
3 tablespoons red wine vinegar
½ cup heavy cream
2 tablespoons fresh lemon juice
¼ teaspoon freshly ground pepper

1. In a heavy medium saucepan, bring 6 cups of water to a boil with 1½ teaspoons of the salt. Add the peas and cook until tender, 8 to 10 minutes for fresh or 1 minute for frozen. Drain and rinse under cold water to stop the cooking process; drain well. Place the peas in a bowl.

2. Stack the pancetta slices and cut them in thirds. Then slice crosswise ¼ inch wide to make small strips. In the saucepan used for the peas, cover the pancetta with cold water and bring to a boil. Immediately remove from the heat and drain well. Return the pancetta to the pan and cook over moderate heat until some of the fat has been rendered, about 5 minutes.

3. Add the shallots and cook, stirring frequently, until the shallots are translucent and the pancetta begins to brown. Drain off the fat. Add the pancetta and shallots to the peas and toss.

4. Add the vinegar to the same saucepan, and cook over moderate heat for 30 seconds, scraping the bottom of the pan to release the flavorful bits. Pour the vinegar into a small bowl. Whisk in the cream, lemon juice, pepper and remaining ½ teaspoon salt. Add to the peas and pancetta and toss well. Serve at room temperature.

—*Bob Chambers*

• • •

VEGETABLE SALAD A LA GRECQUE

The vegetables in this classic preparation cook separately to keep their flavors distinct. Begin with the mildest vegetable—mushrooms in this case—and finish with cauliflower, the most strongly flavored.

————— *8 Servings* —————
⅔ cup extra-virgin olive oil
2 medium onions, finely chopped
1 bottle dry white wine
1½ cups fresh lemon juice (from about 6 lemons)
3 imported bay leaves
2 teaspoons thyme
2 teaspoons mustard seeds
1 tablespoon salt
¾ teaspoon freshly ground pepper
¾ pound mushrooms, stems trimmed, quartered if large
¾ pound zucchini, trimmed and cut into 3-by-½-inch sticks
¾ pound thin green beans, cut in half
¾ pound small Belgian endives, trimmed and halved lengthwise
¾ pound cauliflower florets
½ cup chopped parsley

1. In a large nonreactive saucepan, heat the olive oil. Add the onions and cook over moderately high heat until translucent, 4 to 5 minutes.

2. Add the wine, lemon juice, bay leaves, thyme, mustard seeds, salt, pepper and 5 cups of water. Bring to a boil. Reduce the heat to moderately low, cover and simmer for 10 minutes.

3. Cook the vegetables one at a time in the broth as follows: Add them to the casserole and return the liquid to a boil; then cook (uncovered except for the mushrooms) until just tender, about 15 minutes for the mushrooms, 1½ minutes for the zucchini, 4 minutes for the beans, 6 minutes for the endives and 4 minutes for the cauliflower. Remove the vegetables to individual bowls with a slotted spoon as they are cooked.

4. Cut the endives into bite-size pieces. Group the vegetables on a platter or in a container and refrigerate. Sprinkle with the parsley before serving.

—*Bob Chambers*

• • •

GREEN BEAN AND BENNE SALAD

In the Low Country, sesame (benne) seeds turn up in biscuits, soups, candies, and in this delightful green salad.

————— *8 Servings* —————
¼ cup sesame seeds
2 pounds green beans, stemmed, but with the tender young green tip left intact
1 teaspoon crushed hot red pepper
¼ cup extra-virgin olive oil
2 tablespoons fresh lemon juice
2 garlic cloves, minced
Salt and freshly ground black pepper

1. Place the sesame seeds in a small dry skillet and roast over moderate heat, stirring frequently, until golden brown, about 5 minutes. Set aside.

2. In a large pot of rapidly boiling water, cook the green beans just until they lose their raw flavor, 3 to 5 minutes. Immediately drain in a colander and rinse under cold running water. Drain well.

3. Place the beans in a bowl and add the roasted sesame seeds, hot red pepper, olive oil, lemon juice and garlic. Toss well. Season with salt and black pepper to taste. Serve at room temperature.

—*John Martin Taylor*

• • •

Strawberry and Fresh Fig Salad (p. 150).

**Above, Potato Pie à l'Alsacienne (p. 124). Right, Grandma's Potato,
Red Pepper and Zucchini Gratin (p. 121).**

CURRIED RICE SALAD

In this salad, the spice of curry powder is tempered by the sweetness of fresh papaya and preserved mango chutney.

8 Servings

2 cups rice
1 tablespoon salt
1 large yellow bell pepper, finely diced
1 large red bell pepper, finely diced
1 large green bell pepper, finely diced
1 ripe papaya—peeled, seeded and finely diced
2 tablespoons finely diced mango pieces from Major Grey chutney
1 tablespoon Dijon-style mustard
4 teaspoons curry powder
Pinch of cayenne pepper
2 tablespoons white wine vinegar
¼ teaspoon freshly ground black pepper
⅓ cup extra-virgin olive oil
½ pint cherry tomatoes, halved

1. In a large saucepan, bring 2 quarts of water to a boil over high heat. Add the rice and 2 teaspoons of the salt. Stir frequently until the water returns to a boil. Cook until the rice is tender, 12 to 15 minutes. Drain the rice in a colander and rinse under cold water; drain well. Let stand for 15 minutes.

2. Meanwhile, in a large bowl, combine the diced bell peppers, the papaya and the mango.

3. In a small bowl, whisk together the mustard, curry powder, cayenne, vinegar, remaining 1 teaspoon salt and black pepper. Gradually whisk in the olive oil in a thin stream; the dressing should be thick.

4. Add the dressing and the rice to the bell peppers and toss well. Cover and refrigerate overnight if you like. Toss with the cherry tomato halves before serving. Serve at room temperature.

—*Bob Chambers*

• • •

FRENCH LENTIL SALAD WITH GLAZED PEARL ONIONS

The secret to this salad is dressing the lentils while they're still warm so that they will absorb all the flavors. Imported French green lentils, which are tiny and hold their shape, are my choice for this salad, but ordinary lentils would work just as well.

6 to 8 Servings

3 medium smoked ham hocks
3 small onions, stuck with 8 whole cloves
6 garlic cloves
1 imported bay leaf
½ cup plus 2 tablespoons extra-virgin olive oil
1 pound pearl onions, peeled
¼ cup tomato paste
3 tablespoons white wine vinegar
1 cup dry white wine
½ cup currants
1¼ teaspoons salt
½ teaspoon freshly ground pepper
1 pound lentils, preferably French green lentils*
2 tablespoons Dijon-style mustard
½ cup chopped Italian flat-leaf parsley
*Available at specialty food shops

1. In a large saucepan, combine the ham hocks, small onions, garlic cloves and bay leaf. Add 2 quarts of cold water and bring to a boil. Reduce the heat to low, cover and simmer for 1 hour.

2. Meanwhile, heat 2 tablespoons of the olive oil in a large nonreactive skillet, preferably nonstick. Add the pearl onions and sauté over moderately high heat, stirring frequently, until lightly browned all over, 5 to 7 minutes.

3. Add the tomato paste, 1 tablespoon of the vinegar, the wine, currants, ½ teaspoon of the salt, ¼ teaspoon of the pepper and enough water just to cover. Bring to a boil, reduce the heat to low and simmer until the onions are tender and glazed and the liquid has reduced to a thick sauce, about 30 minutes. Remove from the heat.

4. Strain the ham hock stock, reserving the garlic cloves and hocks. Return the stock to the pot. Add the lentils and bring to a boil. Reduce the heat to moderately low and simmer, stirring occasionally, until the lentils are tender but still firm, 30 to 35 minutes. Drain off any excess liquid.

5. Meanwhile, remove the meat from the ham hocks and coarsely chop.

6. Crush the reserved garlic cloves into a small bowl. Whisk in the mustard and the remaining 2 tablespoons vinegar, ¾ teaspoon salt, ¼ teaspoon pepper and ½ cup olive oil. Stir in the chopped parsley.

7. In a large bowl, combine the lentils with the onions and their sauce and chopped ham. Add the dressing and toss well. Let cool and refrigerate. Serve at room temperature.

—*Bob Chambers*

• • •

Mixed Green Salad with Soured Cream and Blue Cheese Dressing (p. 141).

RICE SALAD WITH MINT AND TOMATILLOS

Two large green peppers, cut into small dice, can be substituted for the fresh tomatillos. The recipe will be different, but good nonetheless. Canned tomatillos are too soft to be used in this recipe. This salad is best served at room temperature.

——————— 6 to 8 Servings ———————

1¼ cups converted rice
1 teaspoon mild vegetable oil
1¼ teaspoons salt
5 fresh tomatillos
4 medium garlic cloves, unpeeled
1 tablespoon plus 1 teaspoon minced fresh ginger
2 tablespoons sugar
¼ cup fresh lime juice
2 teaspoons Oriental sesame oil
2 teaspoons soy sauce
⅛ teaspoon hot pepper sauce
1 large papaya—peeled, seeded and cut into ¼-inch dice
3 tablespoons finely chopped fresh mint

1. In a medium saucepan, bring 2¾ cups of water to a boil. Add the rice, vegetable oil and 1 teaspoon of the salt and stir well. Cover and simmer over low heat until the water is absorbed and the rice is tender, about 20 minutes. Remove from the heat and let stand, covered, for 10 minutes. Spoon the rice into a large serving bowl and fluff well. Refrigerate, uncovered, until cooled.

2. Remove the husks from the tomatillos. Rinse to remove the sticky coating and dry well. Pierce the tomatillos in 1 or 2 places with a sharp knife.

3. Line a large heavy skillet or a griddle with foil. Add the tomatillos and roast over moderately high heat, turning, until blackened in spots and barely soft, about 10 minutes. Halve and discard the white cores, then dice the tomatillos.

4. Roast the garlic the same way but over moderate heat, turning frequently, until barely soft but not blackened, about 12 minutes. Peel the garlic.

5. In a food processor, puree the garlic. Add the ginger, sugar and the remaining ¼ teaspoon salt. Puree until smooth. Add the lime juice, sesame oil, soy sauce and hot pepper sauce. Process until the dressing is well blended.

6. Add the tomatillos, papaya and mint to the cooked rice and toss to mix. *(The rice and dressing can be prepared to this point up to 1 day ahead and refrigerated separately.)*

7. Two to 4 hours before serving, toss the rice with the dressing. Mix again just before serving.

—Linda Burum & Linda Merinoff

• • •

INDIAN FRUIT AND POTATO SALAD

This spicy fruit and vegetable salad makes a wonderful accompaniment for Indonesian Curried Beef Ribs (p. 57).

——————— 6 Servings ———————

1 medium boiling potato
½ cup fresh lemon or lime juice
1 teaspoon chili powder
½ teaspoon ground cumin
½ teaspoon freshly ground pepper
½ teaspoon garam masala or curry powder
¼ teaspoon ground ginger
Pinch of salt
1 large Granny Smith apple, peeled and cut into ½-inch cubes
2 firm Bosc or Comice pears, peeled and cut into ½-inch cubes
1 cucumber, peeled and cut into ½-inch cubes
1 orange—peeled with a knife to remove the white pith, quartered and thinly sliced

2 cups cantaloupe cubes (¾-inch) or 1 mango, peeled and cut into ¾-inch cubes
2 bananas, thinly sliced

1. In a medium saucepan of boiling water, cook the potato until tender, about 25 minutes. Drain and let cool to room temperature.

2. In a small bowl, mix together the lemon juice, chili powder, cumin, pepper, garam masala, ginger and salt.

3. Pour half of this dressing into a serving bowl. Add the apple and pears to the bowl and toss well. Add the cucumber, orange and cantaloupe to the bowl and toss again.

4. Peel the potato and cut into ½-inch cubes. Add the bananas and potato to the bowl, pour on the remaining dressing and toss gently. Cover and refrigerate until very cold, 1 to 2 hours.

—Linda Burum & Linda Merinoff

• • •

STRAWBERRY AND FRESH FIG SALAD

Strawberries sprinkled with balsamic vinegar have been around for a while. This version, using tender, locally grown berries, sweet juicy figs and a sprinkling of shredded basil, is good as a first-course salad, intermezzo or light refreshing dessert. This recipe can be doubled or tripled.

❦ These soft, but not especially intense fruits are a perfect showcase for a brilliant, rich dessert wine, such as a 1985 Domaine Durban Muscat de Beaumes de Venise from France or a 1985 Heggies Botrytis Riesling from Australia.

——————— 2 Servings ———————

1½ cups halved or quartered strawberries (about 1 pint)
3 fresh ripe figs, quartered
2 teaspoons balsamic vinegar

2 tablespoons shredded fresh basil
leaves

In a small bowl, combine the strawberries, figs, vinegar and basil. Gently toss together. Divide the salad evenly between 2 small plates.

—*Diana Sturgis*

• • •

SPICED FRUIT SALAD

Rujak is a popular fruit salad on several of the Indonesian islands. If you can't find papaya or mango, substitute tart apples, peaches, nectarines or your favorite firm seasonal fruit. Just be sure the fruit, jicama and cucumbers add up to eight cups.

──────── 12 Servings ────────
*½ pound jicama, peeled and cut into
  thin julienne strips*
2 Kirby cucumbers, thinly sliced
*1 cup cubed (½-inch) firm-ripe
  papaya*
*1 cup cubed (½-inch) pineapple or
  canned unsweetened chunks*
*3 kiwis, peeled and cut into ½-inch
  cubes*
*1 firm tart apple, cut into ½-inch
  cubes*
1 mango, peeled and sliced
⅓ cup dry-roasted peanuts
*1 to 2 fresh hot red chile peppers,
  seeded and thinly sliced, or ½ to 1
  teaspoon crushed hot red pepper,
  to taste*
⅓ cup (packed) brown sugar
*2 tablespoons tamarind paste
  dissolved in ⅓ cup water, strained*

1. Put the jicama, cucumbers, papaya, pineapple, kiwis, apple and mango in a serving dish and toss lightly.

2. In a food processor, coarsely chop the peanuts. Add the chile peppers, brown sugar and tamarind liquid. Process to a thick, chunky paste. If it is too thick to act as a dressing, thin with 1 tablespoon hot water.

3. Pour the dressing over the salad and toss well. Refrigerate for at least 1 and up to 3 hours. Serve chilled.

—*Copeland Marks*

• • •

BERRY FRUIT SALAD

Macerating the berries overnight in the refrigerator with sugar and lemon zest yields a lovely syrup and lends a subtle lemon flavor to the berries. Serve them with sweetened whipped cream flavored with fresh lemon juice or with lemon sherbet.

❦ Most berries, while complementary to many dessert wines, are acidic and also pair well with a sweet, crisp white, such as a 1985 Maximin Grünhauser Abtsberg Auslese or a 1985 Chateau St. Jean Russian River Valley Special Select Late Harvest Johannisberg Riesling.

──────── 6 to 8 Servings ────────
*3 cups strawberries (about 1 pint),
  quartered*
3 cups blueberries (about 1 pint)
1½ cups raspberries (about ½ pint)
½ cup sugar, preferably superfine
1½ teaspoons grated lemon zest

In a large glass bowl, toss together the strawberries, blueberries and raspberries with the sugar and lemon zest. Cover the bowl with plastic wrap and refrigerate overnight before serving.

—*Diana Sturgis*

• • •

STRAWBERRY, KIWI AND ORANGE SALAD

The tart, tangy citrus dressing on this salad would work equally well with almost any other combination of fruits.

──────── 8 Servings ────────
*1½ cups fresh orange juice (from
  about 5 oranges)*
⅓ cup fresh lemon juice
¼ cup sugar
2 teaspoons arrowroot
2 tablespoons orange liqueur
4 navel oranges
*4 kiwis, peeled and cut lengthwise
  into eighths*
*5 pints of ripe strawberries, halved
  lengthwise if large*
Fresh mint sprigs, for garnish

1. In a small nonreactive saucepan, combine the orange juice, lemon juice and sugar and bring to a boil. Reduce the heat to low and simmer until reduced to 1⅓ cups, about 10 minutes.

2. Dilute the arrowroot in 1 tablespoon of cold water. Stir into the syrup and return to a boil, stirring. Remove from the heat and let cool to room temperature. Stir in the orange liqueur. Cover and refrigerate for at least 2 hours.

3. Using a sharp knife, peel the oranges, removing all the bitter white pith. Cut in between the membranes to release the sections.

4. Toss the fruit with the dressing up to 2 hours before serving. Garnish with mint sprigs.

—*Bob Chambers*

• • •

SANDWICHES, PIZZAS & BREADS

JALAPENO SCONES WITH TURKEY

These miniature sandwiches are terrific for lunch. Serve them with a bowl of soup or a tossed salad.

——— *Makes 16 Mini Sandwiches* ———
1½ cups cake flour
½ cup yellow cornmeal
1½ cups grated Cheddar cheese (about 6 ounces)
1½ teaspoons baking powder
½ teaspoon baking soda
½ teaspoon salt
2 jalapeño peppers—seeded, deribbed and minced
⅛ teaspoon crushed hot red pepper
4 tablespoons cold unsalted butter, cut into small pieces
½ cup milk
¼ cup mayonnaise
¾ pound thinly sliced smoked turkey or chicken
1 bunch of arugula or watercress

1. Preheat the oven to 350°. Butter a baking sheet.

2. In a food processor, combine the flour, cornmeal, 1 cup of the Cheddar cheese, the baking powder, baking soda, salt, jalapeño peppers and the crushed red pepper; process until blended, about 30 seconds.

3. Add the butter and turn the machine quickly on and off until the mixture resembles coarse meal, about 30 seconds. Sprinkle on the milk and process until the dough just begins to form a ball, 10 to 15 seconds.

4. On a lightly floured work surface, pat the dough into a 6-inch disk and roll to form a circle about ½ inch thick. Using a 2-inch biscuit cutter, cut out 14 rounds. Roll out any dough scraps and cut out 1 or 2 additional scones.

5. Arrange the scones on the prepared baking sheet and sprinkle with the remaining ½ cup Cheddar cheese. Bake the scones for 15 to 20 minutes, or until firm and golden brown. Transfer to a rack to cool.

6. Cut the scones in half and spread each half with the mayonnaise. Place a slice of turkey on the bottom half of each scone and top with a piece of arugula. Cover with the top half of each scone and serve.

—*Mimi Ruth Brodeur*

• • •

BEVERLY HILLS BAGELS

The real star here is the combination of red onion, parsley and capers with the smoked salmon.

——————— *8 Servings* ———————
4 bagels, preferably plain or seeded, 4 inches in diameter
12 ounces cream cheese, at room temperature
¼ cup sour cream
5 ounces sliced smoked salmon, cut into ½-inch squares
3 tablespoons chopped red onion
1 tablespoon chopped Italian flat-leaf parsley
1 tablespoon capers, rinsed and drained
Fresh parsley sprigs, for garnish

1. Slice the bagels in half horizontally. Remove as much bread from the inside of the bagel as possible to form hollow bagel rings. Lightly toast.

2. In a medium bowl, beat the cream cheese and sour cream until smooth and creamy, about 1 minute. Stir in the smoked salmon, red onion, parsley and capers and mix well. (*The spread can be refrigerated, covered, overnight.*)

3. Divide the salmon cream cheese among the 8 bagel halves and spread to fill the hollowed rings. Garnish each with a sprig of parsley. Serve open-faced.

—*F&W*

• • •

WEST BEACH CAFE'S GRILLED AHI TUNA AND SHIITAKE SANDWICHES

Here's a tuna sandwich unlike any you've had before. If ahi tuna is unavailable, any good quality fresh tuna will do just fine.

♥ Both the oiliness of tuna and the earthiness of mushrooms require a deep-flavored but acidic white, such as Sauvignon Blanc, which can act as a foil to the richness of the dish. A 1986 Simi or 1987 Kendall-Jackson is the ideal choice.

——————— *4 Servings* ———————
6 garlic cloves, unpeeled
½ cup mayonnaise
1 tablespoon Dijon-style mustard
1 teaspoon lemon juice
Salt and freshly ground pepper
1 pound fresh ahi or other tuna fillet, sliced ¼ inch thick
½ pound fresh shiitake mushrooms, stems discarded
2 tablespoons olive oil
8 slices of sourdough or whole wheat peasant bread, toasted
2 bunches of arugula, large stems removed

1. Preheat the oven to 275°. Place the garlic cloves on a baking sheet and roast for 30 minutes, or until very soft. Remove from the oven and let cool slightly, then squeeze the garlic cloves from their skins.

2. In a small bowl, mash the garlic with a fork. Add the mayonnaise, mustard and lemon juice. Season with salt and pepper to taste. Refrigerate until ready to use.

3. Brush the tuna and mushrooms with the olive oil and season with salt and pepper to taste.

4. In a dry, medium skillet, cook the tuna slices over moderately high heat for 1 minute on each side. Transfer to a platter.

Add the mushrooms to the pan and sauté until softened, about 2 minutes.

5. Spread the mayonnaise liberally over the toast. Divide the tuna, arugula and mushrooms among 4 pieces of the toast and top with the remaining slices.

—Bruce Marder,
West Beach Café, Los Angeles

• • •

MONTE CRISTO SANDWICHES

These substantial sandwiches are dipped in batter and fried like French toast. They can also be made with sliced cooked chicken or turkey. Serve with potato salad and pickle chips (or French cornichons).

—————— 2 Servings ——————
4 slices of bread, preferably whole
*   wheat or egg bread*
4 teaspoons grainy mustard
6 slices of imported Swiss cheese
*   (about 3 ounces)*
6 slices of best-quality ham (4
*   ounces)*
2 eggs
1 tablespoon milk
¼ teaspoon salt
¼ teaspoon freshly ground black
*   pepper*
Pinch of cayenne pepper
2 tablespoons unsalted butter
1 teaspoon vegetable oil

1. Spread one side of each bread slice with 1 teaspoon of the mustard. Top 2 of the slices with half the cheese, then the ham, then the remaining cheese. Place the remaining bread slices on top, mustard-side down. Trim off any overhanging ham and cheese, but leave the bread crusts on. Press the sandwiches gently so that the layers hold together.

2. In a medium bowl, whisk together the eggs, milk, salt, black pepper and cayenne until well blended.

3. In a large heavy skillet, preferably nonstick, melt the butter in the oil over moderate heat. Dip the sandwiches in the egg mixture, turning to coat the sides and edges. Let any excess egg drip off. Place the sandwiches in the pan and immediately reduce the heat to moderately low.

4. Fry the sandwiches until golden, shaking the pan once or twice to prevent sticking, 4 or 5 minutes. Adjust the heat, if necessary, to maintain a steady but gentle sizzle. Using a spatula, flip the sandwiches and fry until golden and the cheese begins to melt, about 4 minutes longer. Transfer to a plate and serve hot, with a knife and fork.

—Richard Sax

• • •

BOGIE'S HOAGIES

These hoagies will leave your guests saying, "Make it again, Sam."

—————— 4 Servings ——————
½ cup olive oil
3 garlic cloves—2 crushed through a
*   press, 1 halved*
1 pound tomatoes, chopped (about 2
*   cups)*
½ cup shredded fresh basil leaves
½ teaspoon salt
¼ teaspoon freshly ground pepper
2 eggplants (1 pound each), ends
*   trimmed, cut crosswise into*
*   ⅜-inch slices*
1 loaf of Italian bread, halved
*   lengthwise*
½ pound mozzarella cheese,
*   shredded (about 2 cups)*

1. In a large skillet, heat 2 tablespoons of the olive oil over moderately low heat. Add the crushed garlic and cook without browning for 1 minute.

2. Add the tomatoes, increase the heat to moderately high and cook, stirring, until the tomatoes are softened, about 5

minutes. Stir in the basil, salt and pepper. Remove from the heat and set aside.

3. Preheat the broiler. Brush the slices of eggplant on both sides with 4 tablespoons of the olive oil. Arrange the eggplant on a baking sheet in a single layer and broil 4 inches from the heat for about 7 minutes on each side, until browned. Drain on paper towels.

4. Slice each bread half into 4 sections. Brush each cut side of the bread with the remaining olive oil and rub with the halved garlic clove. Broil, cut-side up, 4 inches from the heat, for 2 minutes, or until the bread is toasted. *(The recipe can be prepared to this point up to 4 hours ahead and left at room temperature.)*

5. Preheat the oven to 500°. Spread the tomato mixture onto the toasted bread, cover with a slice of eggplant and sprinkle the mozzarella cheese on top. Arrange on a baking sheet and bake for 5 minutes, or until the cheese melts. Serve warm.

—F&W

• • •

HEROIC ITALIAN

When making a submarine, hoagie, grinder, hero or whatever you call this type of sandwich, it's important to provide a bit of moistening with a little oil and vinegar.

—————— 4 Servings ——————
1 large loaf of semolina bread, sliced
*   horizontally into 3 pieces*
About 3 tablespoons olive oil
About 1 tablespoon balsamic
*   vinegar*
¼ medium head of romaine lettuce
1 jar (6 ounces) marinated
*   artichoke hearts*
1 large tomato, thinly sliced
1 small red bell pepper, thinly sliced

1 small onion, thinly sliced
1/4 pound thinly sliced baked ham
1/4 pound thinly sliced Provolone
  cheese
2 ounces thinly sliced salami or
  pepperoni
1/4 cup olives, preferably Calamata,
  pitted and chopped
1 large kosher garlic pickle, thinly
  sliced lengthwise
Freshly ground black pepper

1. On the bottom slice of bread, drizzle 1 tablespoon of the oil and 1 teaspoon of the vinegar, or more to taste. Layer with half of the lettuce and artichoke hearts, pressing to flatten them. Top with half of the sliced tomato, red pepper, onion, ham, Provolone, salami, olives and pickle slices. Grind lots of black pepper over all.

2. Place the middle slice of bread on the sandwich and repeat the layering procedure. Drizzle the cut side of the top slice of bread with the remaining 1 tablespoon oil and 1 teaspoon vinegar and cap the sandwich.

3. To serve, hold the sandwich firmly. Using a serrated knife, cut with an even, sawing motion to slice the sandwich in quarters.

—*Marcia Kiesel*

• • •

SLOPPY JOES

Depending on where you grew up, "Sloppy Joe" can refer either to a savory ground-beef mixture served on hamburger buns or to multilayered deli sandwiches served at catered parties (usually delivered wrapped in yellow cellophane). This is the ground-beef Sloppy Joe, and I first made this for a friend who missed the ones his mother used to make. Since then, I make this any time I want a deliciously messy, quick supper.

❢ This highly seasoned, directly satisfying dish is tailor-made for a fresh, lively spicy Zinfandel, such as 1986 Nalle or 1985 Burgess.

——————— 4 Servings ———————
1 tablespoon plus 1 teaspoon
  vegetable oil
2 medium red onions, chopped
1 large red or yellow bell pepper,
  chopped
3 large garlic cloves, minced
1 teaspoon salt
1 teaspoon freshly ground black
  pepper
1/2 teaspoon fresh thyme or a pinch of
  dried
1 1/2 pounds ground round or other
  lean ground beef
1 1/2 cups canned tomato sauce
1 cup full-bodied beer, such as Bass
  ale
1 tablespoon Worcestershire sauce
1/4 teaspoon hot pepper sauce
3 tablespoons thinly sliced scallion
  greens
4 pieces of French or Italian bread
  (5 to 6 inches long) or 4 seeded
  rolls, split horizontally

1. In a large skillet, preferably nonstick, heat 1 tablespoon of the oil. Add the onions, bell pepper, garlic, salt, black pepper and thyme. Cook over moderate heat, stirring occasionally, until the vegetables are softened but not browned, about 10 minutes. Transfer the vegetables to a plate.

2. Add the remaining 1 teaspoon oil to the skillet and increase the heat to moderately high. Add the ground beef and cook, breaking up the meat with a wooden spoon, until browned in some spots and still partly rare in others, about 4 minutes.

3. Return the vegetables to the skillet, stir in the tomato sauce, beer, Worcestershire and hot pepper sauce and bring to a simmer. Reduce the heat to low and cook, partially covered, until the mixture has thickened slightly, about 15 minutes. Turn off the heat and stir in the scallions. (*The recipe can be prepared to this point 1 day ahead. Refrigerate, covered; reheat before proceeding.*)

4. Preheat the broiler. Place the bread or rolls, cut-sides up, on a baking sheet and toast under the broiler about 4 inches from the heat until golden brown, about 30 seconds. Place the toast on serving plates and spoon the meat mixture on top.

—*Richard Sax*

• • •

CRUSTY CRAB BURGERS WITH RED PEPPER SLAW

This crab burger has more of what you always wanted from a polite crab cake—and you don't need a fork to eat it.

❢ Both sandwich and slaw are peppery, so a sharp savory California Sauvignon Blanc would be the ideal foil. Try 1987 Beaulieu Vineyard or Rutherford Hill.

——————— 4 Servings ———————
1 pound lump crabmeat, picked over
  to remove any cartilage
2 large scallions, minced
2 teaspoons grainy mustard
1/4 cup mayonnaise
1/4 teaspoon hot pepper sauce
1/4 teaspoon cayenne pepper
Salt and freshly ground black pepper
1 1/2 cups fresh bread crumbs
1 egg
1 tablespoon vegetable oil
4 tablespoons unsalted butter
4 soft sesame seed hamburger buns
  or rolls
Red Pepper Slaw (p. 142)
Lemon wedges, for garnish

1. In a medium bowl, combine the crabmeat, scallions, mustard, mayonnaise, hot pepper sauce, cayenne and salt and black pepper to taste; mix well. Gently fold in 1/2 cup of the bread crumbs. Form the mixture into 4 patties. Refrigerate for about 10 minutes to set.

Here's the Dagwood sandwich for the 1990s. Flour tortillas are layered with guacamole, tomatoes, lettuce and a delicious, smoky black bean chili. For dessert, make a guava "fool" by pureeing canned guava shells and swirling the puree with sour cream for a typically Latin American combination of flavors. Serves 8.

Triple-Decker Tostada (p. 157)

🍷 *Mexican Beer*

Guava-Sour Cream Fool

Sugar Cookies

Coffee

2. In a wide, shallow bowl, lightly beat the egg. Slowly beat in the oil until thoroughly combined. Place the remaining 1 cup bread crumbs on a large plate.

3. One at a time, dip each crab patty into the egg mixture to lightly coat both sides. Then gently press into the bread crumbs to evenly coat.

4. Preheat the oven to 450°. In a large skillet, melt the butter over high heat. When the foam subsides, add the crab patties and cook until the undersides are deep brown, about 4 minutes. Reduce the heat to moderately high. With a spatula, turn the patties and cook until browned on the other side, about 4 minutes. Drain on paper towels.

5. To serve, halve the buns and toast in the oven for about 4 minutes. Place a crab burger on the bottom half of each bun. Top the burgers with about ½ cup each of the Red Pepper Slaw and cover with the top half of the buns. Serve at once with lemon wedges.

—*Marcia Kiesel*

• • •

CHICKEN-PEANUT PITAS

If you have leftover cooked chicken (or shrimp or steak), by all means use it here.

———— *6 Servings* ————
¾ pound thickly sliced smoked bacon
2 whole chicken breasts with bone and skin
1 cup chunky peanut butter
4 garlic cloves, minced
3 tablespoons soy sauce
1 tablespoon honey mustard
1 tablespoon white wine vinegar
1 teaspoon crushed hot red pepper
6 pita breads, 6 inches in diameter
½ medium head of iceberg lettuce, shredded
2 cups alfalfa sprouts
2 large tomatoes, thinly sliced
1 large cucumber—peeled, seeded and thinly sliced
1 small onion, thinly sliced

1. In a large skillet, cook the bacon in 2 batches over moderate heat, turning once, until crisp, about 8 minutes. Drain on paper towels. When the bacon is cool, break it into small pieces. (*The bacon can be prepared up to 1 day ahead; store in an airtight container.*)

2. In a large saucepan, place the chicken breasts and enough cold water to cover. Bring to a boil over high heat. Reduce the heat to low and simmer until cooked through, about 25 minutes. Turn off the heat and let the chicken cool in the poaching liquid, about 1 hour.

3. Drain the chicken. Remove and discard the skin. Pull the meat from the bones. (*The chicken can be prepared to this point up to 2 days ahead; cover and refrigerate.*) Thinly slice the meat.

4. In a medium bowl, combine the peanut butter, garlic, soy sauce, mustard, vinegar and crushed hot pepper. Gradually whisk in 1 cup of warm water until smooth. Set aside.

5. Preheat the oven to 400°. Warm the pita bread in the oven for about 15 seconds until just hot but not crisp.

6. Using a sharp knife, cut off the top quarter of each pita. Stuff the pitas first with the lettuce, alfalfa sprouts, tomatoes, cucumber and onion, then the chicken and bacon. Spoon a generous amount of the peanut sauce into each sandwich.

—*Marcia Kiesel*

• • •

TRIPLE-DECKER TOSTADA

Fried flour tortillas have a lighter, flakier quality than fried corn tortillas. Cook them until just golden and crisp, not dark and brittle, or they'll break easily.

———— *8 Servings* ————
⅓ cup vegetable oil
6 flour tortillas, 10 inches in diameter
½ medium head of iceberg lettuce, separated into leaves
2 large tomatoes, thinly sliced
½ cup chopped fresh coriander
Guacamole (p. 12)
Smoky Black Bean Chili (p. 63)
½ cup sour cream
8 pickled jalapeño peppers, sliced

1. In a large skillet, heat the oil over high heat until almost smoking. One at a time, fry the tortillas in the hot oil until golden brown, about 1 minute per side. Drain on paper towels.

2. Place 1 fried tortilla on a work surface and layer on one-fourth of the lettuce and half of the tomatoes and coriander. Spread half of the Guacamole on top.

3. Layer on another tortilla, another fourth of the lettuce and half of the Smoky Black Bean Chili and sour cream. Sprinkle half of the jalapeño peppers over all. Top with a third tortilla. Repeat the procedure to form a second tostada using all the remaining ingredients.

4. To serve, insert the point of a large, sharp knife into the top of the tostada and cut in half, then cut into quarters.

—*Marcia Kiesel*

• • •

GRILLED MOZZARELLA SANDWICHES WITH SPINACH AND GARLIC

The inspiration for these grilled cheese sandwiches is *tramezzini*, little grilled sandwiches served in bars and cafés in Italy. A minimal filling is placed between two slices of trimmed white bread and toasted without butter or oil on a ridged grill. I finally figured out how to make these at home by using one of those ridged grilling skillets or griddles.

—————— **4 Servings** ——————

1¼ pounds fresh spinach, stemmed and rinsed, or 1 package (10 ounces) frozen spinach—thawed, squeezed dry and chopped
2 tablespoons extra-virgin olive oil
4 garlic cloves, thinly sliced
½ teaspoon salt
¼ teaspoon freshly ground pepper
4 ounces mozzarella cheese, sliced ⅛ inch thick
8 slices of firm-textured white bread, crusts removed

1. In a large pot of boiling salted water, cook the fresh spinach for 1 minute. Drain, rinse under cool water, squeeze dry and coarsely chop.

2. In a medium skillet, heat the olive oil. Add the garlic slices and cook over moderately low heat until lightly browned, about 4 minutes.

3. Add the spinach and 2 tablespoons of water. Increase the heat to moderate.

Stir with a fork to separate the pieces and evenly coat with the oil. Cook until the spinach is tender and the water has evaporated, about 4 minutes. Season with the salt and pepper.

4. Divide the mozzarella among the 8 slices of bread. Top 4 of the slices with the spinach, leaving a ¼-inch margin all around. Close the sandwiches and press lightly. *(The sandwiches can be made ahead to this point, wrapped in plastic wrap, and held at room temperature for up to 3 hours or refrigerated for 2 days. Let return to room temperature before grilling.)*

5. Preheat a cast-iron ridged grill pan or skillet for 10 minutes. Grill the sandwiches over moderate heat until the bread is browned and the cheese has melted, about 4 minutes per side.

—*Anne Disrude*

• • •

SKILLET MELT WITH ANISEED AND GARLIC TOAST

A current favorite "grilled cheese" sandwich uses my mother's skillet-melt approach. Cheese is melted in a skillet, and then peasant bread brushed with olive oil and rubbed with garlic is pressed into the cheese.

—————— **2 Servings** ——————

4 slices of coarse peasant bread, cut ½ inch thick and toasted
2 tablespoons extra-virgin olive oil
1 garlic clove, halved
4 ounces thinly sliced hard sheep cheese, such as Kasseri, Kashkaval or Etorki
1 teaspoon aniseed, crushed
1 teaspoon freshly ground pepper

1. Brush one side of each slice of bread with olive oil, then rub with the cut garlic. Set aside.

2. In a large heavy skillet, preferably cast iron, arrange the cheese slices in a

single layer and cook over moderately low heat until melted, about 3 minutes. Season with the aniseed and pepper. Put the toast slices on top and press into the cheese. Lift the slices out, coated with the melted cheese.

—*Anne Disrude*

• • •

GRILLED BLUE CHEESE AND PEAR SANDWICHES

In these sandwiches, I've tried both the French Bleu de Bresse and a young Italian Gorgonzola and partnered them with a glass of Sauternes or Barsac.

—————— **4 Servings** ——————

⅓ cup creamy blue cheese, preferably Bleu de Bresse, Gorgonzola, Saga Blue or Pipo Crem', at room temperature
⅛ teaspoon freshly ground white pepper
16 slices of French bread, cut on the diagonal ½ inch thick
½ ripe pear, preferably Bartlett or Anjou, cored and cut into 8 thin slices
3 tablespoons unsalted butter, at room temperature

1. In a small bowl, mash the cheese with the white pepper. Spread over one side of each bread slice. Put 1 pear slice on 8 of the bread slices and close up the sandwiches.

2. Preheat a large griddle or heavy skillet, preferably cast iron, over moderate heat.

3. Butter the outside of the sandwiches. Grill in batches on the griddle, turning once, until lightly browned on both sides, 4 to 5 minutes per side.

—*Anne Disrude*

• • •

GRILLED BRIE WITH MUSHROOMS AND TARRAGON

If fresh tarragon sprigs aren't available, soak 1 teaspoon of dried tarragon in cool water for 10 minutes, squeeze dry and add at the beginning of the mushroom sauté in Step 1.

———————— *4 Servings* ————————
2 tablespoons unsalted butter
4 large mushrooms, sliced
2 medium shallots, minced
¼ teaspoon salt
⅛ teaspoon freshly ground pepper
4 ounces cold Brie, cut into ⅛-inch-thick slices
8 slices of firm-textured white bread, crusts removed
4 sprigs of fresh tarragon

1. In a heavy medium skillet, melt the butter over high heat. When the butter begins to brown, add the mushrooms and toss to coat. Sauté, stirring occasionally, until the mushrooms have browned around the edges, 2 to 3 minutes.

2. Add the shallots and cook for 1 minute longer. Transfer the mushrooms to a plate and season with the salt and pepper.

3. Divide the cheese among 4 slices of the bread; top each with the mushrooms, leaving about ¼-inch margin around the edges. Add a tarragon sprig and cover with the remaining 4 slices of bread. *(At this point the sandwiches can be wrapped in plastic wrap and left at room temperature for several hours or refrigerated for several days. Let return to room temperature before grilling.)*

4. Preheat a cast-iron ridged grill pan or skillet for 10 minutes over moderate heat. Grill the sandwiches for 4 minutes per side or until the bread is lightly browned and the cheese has melted. Serve halved as a first course or quartered as an hors d'oeuvre.

—*Anne Disrude*

• • •

SODA FOUNTAIN SOIREE

This is an upscale soup-and-sandwich meal. The soup is made with free-range chicken (although everyday chicken will work as well) and the grilled Brie sandwich lifts grilled cheese to new heights. Instead of the expected pickle chips on the side, serve cornichons to echo the tarragon flavors in the sandwich. Serves 4.

Double Chicken Soup (p. 31)

Grilled Brie with Mushrooms and Tarragon (p. 159)

Cornichons

Homemade Thick-Cut Potato Chips

———————————

Ice Cream Sodas, such as: Cherry Fling (p. 205), Green Goddess (p. 204) or White Lady (p. 205)

CHEESE DREAM REDREAMED

The 1950s gave us a recipe called the Cheese Dream: toasted English muffin halves, each topped with a tomato slice, bacon and American cheese, and then melted under the broiler. It was heaven and still is. This sandwich uses a vinegary coleslaw, instead of the tomato, and rye English muffins to make a sort of Alsatian cheese dream.

———————— *4 Servings* ————————
4 slices of bacon
2 cups shredded green cabbage
½ small red onion, sliced
1 teaspoon caraway seeds
3 tablespoons red wine vinegar
Salt and freshly ground pepper
2 rye English muffins, split and toasted
4 ounces Gruyère cheese, thinly sliced

1. Preheat the broiler. In a large skillet, preferably cast iron, fry the bacon over moderate heat, turning once, until crisp, 3 to 5 minutes. Drain on paper towels. Pour off all but 2 tablespoons of the bacon fat.

2. Add the cabbage, onion and caraway seeds to the skillet. Cook over high heat, stirring, until the cabbage is slightly wilted, about 2 minutes. Add the vinegar and cook, stirring, until all the liquid has evaporated, about 2 minutes longer. Season with salt and pepper to taste.

3. On each muffin half, put 1 slice of cheese, some slaw, then a slice of bacon and top with the remaining cheese. Broil 6 inches from the heat for about 1 minute, until the cheese has melted. Serve hot.

—*Anne Disrude*

• • •

BRUSCHETTA WITH BLUE CHEESE AND CRISP ONION RINGS

These pan-fried onions are less messy and less fattening than deep-fried ones and yet have a more fried-onion flavor.

❢ The cheese and nut flavors here would make a happy match with a flavorsome red, such as 1985 CUNE Rioja Clarete or 1985 Mirassou Petite Sirah.

———————— *4 Servings* ————————
¼ cup walnuts, chopped
½ cup olive oil
4 large, thick slices of peasant bread
4 garlic cloves, peeled
1 large onion, sliced ⅓ inch thick
1 bunch of arugula, large stems removed
¾ pound soft blue cheese, such as Saga blue, trimmed of any rind and sliced ¼ inch thick
2 large tomatoes, thickly sliced

1. Preheat the oven to 400°. Place the walnuts on a baking sheet. Bake until golden brown all over, about 8 minutes.

2. Increase the oven temperature to 450°. Pour ¼ cup of the olive oil onto a large rimmed baking sheet. Press both sides of the bread slices into the oil to coat well. Place on the bottom rack of the oven and bake for 10 minutes or until crisp and golden brown. Remove from the oven and let cool. Rub both sides of the bread with the garlic cloves.

3. In a large skillet, heat the remaining ¼ cup olive oil over moderately high heat until shimmering. Add the onion slices in a single even layer. Cook without stirring until the slices start to brown on the underside, about 4 minutes. Stir and continue to cook, stirring occasionally, until the onion slices are golden brown and crisp, about 10 more minutes. Drain on paper towels.

4. Distribute the arugula evenly over the bread slices and top with the blue cheese. Sprinkle the walnuts over the cheese. Cover each bruschetta with 2 slices of tomato and top the sandwiches with the crisp onion rings.

—*Marcia Kiesel*

• • •

GIANT CALZONE

Draining the ricotta for a few hours prevents the calzone from becoming soggy. Make sure there is someone else around to help you load the calzone onto a pan.

———— **6 Servings** ————
2 cups whole-milk ricotta cheese
3 tablespoons olive oil
1 pound mushrooms, thinly sliced
5 garlic cloves, minced
½ cup chopped parsley
3 ounces thinly sliced prosciutto, cut into thin strips
Freshly ground pepper
1 pound fresh or thawed frozen pizza or bread dough
4½ ounces mozzarella cheese, finely chopped

¼ cup grated Parmesan cheese
1 cup shredded fresh basil
2 eggs, beaten separately
All-purpose flour, for dusting
Cornmeal, for the pan

1. Spoon the ricotta into a fine-mesh sieve set over a bowl. Refrigerate, stirring occasionally, for 4 to 6 hours, until well drained.

2. In a large skillet, heat the olive oil over high heat. When it begins to smoke, add the mushrooms in a single even layer and cook without stirring until the mushrooms start to brown, about 7 minutes. Turn and cook until evenly browned all over, about 5 minutes longer. Remove from the heat and let cool.

3. Add the garlic and parsley to the mushrooms and cook over low heat, stirring occasionally, until the garlic is soft, about 10 minutes.

4. Add the prosciutto and season with pepper to taste. Cook to blend the flavors, about 1 minute. Remove the mixture to a large plate and let cool to room temperature.

5. On a lightly floured surface, roll the pizza dough into a 10-inch circle. Cover with a towel and let rest for 20 minutes.

6. Preheat the oven to 475°. In a medium bowl, combine the drained ricotta with the mozzarella, Parmesan, basil and 1 of the beaten eggs. Season with pepper to taste.

7. On a work surface, roll out the dough to an oval about 18 inches long and 13 inches wide; dust the dough lightly with flour if it sticks. Spread the cooled mushroom mixture lengthwise over the bottom half of the dough, leaving a 1-inch border. Spread the cheese mixture on top of the mushrooms.

8. With your fingers, spread some of the remaining beaten egg all around the edge of the dough. Fold the top half of the dough over the filling, without stretching, and press the edges together to seal. Crimp the edges.

9. Generously sprinkle cornmeal on a large baking sheet. You'll need an extra pair of hands to help lift the calzone onto the pan. If the edges tend to hang over the sides of the pan, curve in the 2 ends to form a crescent. Bake on the bottom rack of the oven for about 15 minutes or until deep golden brown all over.

10. Transfer the calzone to a rack and let cool to room temperature, about 1 hour. Cut crosswise into thick slices and serve.

—*Marcia Kiesel*

• • •

FRESH ARTICHOKE PIZZA

I always use this method with artichokes because it gives them an intense flavor that no other technique can supply. When you select artichokes, choose the biggest ones because they have the most flavorful hearts.

I've used far more garlic than most sane people would, but this cooking method mellows and sweetens the garlic. If it seems too much for your taste, cut it back.

———— *Makes 4 Individual Pizzas* ————
4 large artichokes
½ lemon
2 heads of garlic, cloves separated and peeled (about 24)
8 sprigs of Italian flat-leaf parsley
¼ cup extra-virgin olive oil
1½ teaspoons fresh thyme leaves
¼ teaspoon salt
¼ teaspoon freshly ground pepper
1⅓ cups diced mozzarella cheese (about ½ pound)
Quick Semolina Pizza Dough (recipe follows)

1. With a small sharp knife, cut the leaves from around each artichoke, using a circular motion, until you reach the tender, inner leaves. Cut the tops off the leaves and continue to trim the artichoke heart down to the base, removing all the tough, fibrous outer skin. Cut the heart in half and cut out the choke. Rub the heart all over with the cut lemon.

2. In a large bowl, combine the artichoke hearts, garlic, parsley, olive oil, thyme, salt and pepper; toss to mix.

3. In a large nonreactive saucepan, arrange the artichoke hearts with the garlic-parsley mixture, cut-sides down, in the pan and sprinkle with 3 tablespoons of water. Cover tightly and cook over low heat, turning occasionally, until the artichokes are light brown and very tender, about 30 minutes. Add a few tablespoons of water after 10 minutes, to prevent burning.

4. Remove the pan from the heat. Remove the garlic and parsley from the pan and finely chop. In a small bowl, combine the mozzarella, garlic and parsley. Remove the artichokes from the pan and slice them ¼ inch thick. Reserve the oil remaining in the pan. *(The recipe can be prepared to this point up to 1 day ahead; cover and refrigerate.)*

5. Roll the Quick Semolina Pizza Dough into a log 1½ inches in diameter. Cut into 4 equal pieces. Roll out each piece of dough into a 7-inch round about ⅟₁₆ inch thick. Cover the rounds with plastic wrap. Heat a 9- or 10-inch cast-iron skillet over moderately high heat until hot.

6. Place one of the dough rounds into the hot skillet, reduce the heat to low, cover and cook until the crust is dark brown on the bottom, about 3 minutes. (Check after 2 minutes and adjust the heat, if necessary, to avoid burning the dough.)

7. Remove the pizza crust from the skillet. Layer the crust with ⅓ cup of the mozzarella mixture and the slices of 1 artichoke; season with additional salt and pepper to taste. Brush the top with any remaining oil from the artichoke pan.

8. Return the pizza to the skillet and cook, covered, until the cheese melts, about 2 minutes. Repeat the process with the 3 other rounds.

—*Anne Disrude*

• • •

QUICK SEMOLINA PIZZA DOUGH

This dough takes almost no time at all to assemble, and it can be made ahead of time. You can refrigerate or freeze it, but it must be at room temperature before you cook it. This crust employs baking powder rather than yeast, so there's no rising time involved.

To make sure your skillet is at the right temperature, do a test crust. Cut off a walnut-size piece of dough, roll it into a ⅟₁₆-inch-thick round and put it in the heated skillet. Bubbles should appear on the underside within the first 45 seconds; if they don't, increase the heat a little. If bubbles appear but then burn within the first 3 minutes, reduce the heat. The crust is cooked on only one side; it should be dark brown.

Makes 4 Pizza
——— *Rounds, 7 Inches Each* ———
1 cup semolina flour*
1 teaspoon baking powder
½ teaspoon salt
1 tablespoon extra-virgin olive oil
*Available at specialty food shops

1. In a food processor, combine the semolina flour, ⅓ cup hot water, the baking powder, salt and olive oil. Process until the dough masses together, about 45 seconds.

2. Cover with plastic wrap and let rest for at least 15 minutes or up to 2 hours. *(The recipe can be made up to this point 1 day ahead. Cover with plastic wrap and refrigerate. It can also be frozen. When you are ready to use the dough, roll it out, cover with plastic wrap and let it return to room temperature.)*

—*Anne Disrude*

• • •

SCALLION AND OLIVE PIZZA WITH ROSEMARY

This topping combines elements of several classic Italian vegetable recipes. Here, braised scallions with bay leaves and rosemary are offset by olives and a creamy goat cheese. Don't be afraid to experiment with other varieties of onions; red onions or sweet Vidalia onions, when they are in season, are good alternatives.

——— *Makes 4 Individual Pizzas* ———
¼ cup extra-virgin olive oil
12 bunches of scallions (white and light green), sliced ½ inch thick, plus ¼ cup minced scallion green
3 imported bay leaves
2 sprigs of fresh rosemary plus 1 teaspoon minced
¾ teaspoon salt
¼ teaspoon freshly ground pepper
¼ cup coarsely chopped brine-cured olives, preferably Gaeta or Niçoise
Quick Semolina Pizza Dough (at left)
½ cup goat cheese (about 4 ounces)

1. In a large heavy saucepan, heat the olive oil. Add the sliced scallions, bay leaves, rosemary sprigs and 3 tablespoons of water. Cover and cook over moderately low heat, stirring occasionally, until the scallions are very tender, about 20 minutes. Remove the pan from the heat. Discard the bay leaves and the rosemary sprigs. Stir in the minced rosemary, salt, pepper and olives. *(The recipe can be prepared to this point up to 1 day ahead; cover and refrigerate.)*

2. Roll the Quick Semolina Pizza Dough into a log 1½ inches in diameter. Cut into 4 equal pieces. Roll out each piece of dough into a 7-inch round about ⅟₁₆ inch thick. Cover the rounds with plastic wrap. Heat a 9- or 10-inch cast-iron skillet over moderately high heat, until hot.

3. Place one of the dough rounds into the hot skillet, reduce the heat to low, cover and cook until the crust is dark brown on the bottom, about 3 minutes. (Check after 2 minutes and reduce the heat, if necessary, to avoid scorching.)

4. Remove the pizza crust from the skillet. Spread the crust with 2 tablespoons of goat cheese and top with about ½ cup of the cooked scallion mixture. Return the pizza to the skillet and cook, covered, until the cheese melts, about 2 minutes. Sprinkle with the minced scallion green and serve. Repeat the process with the 3 other rounds.

—*Anne Disrude*

• • •

SPICY SPINACH AND GARLIC PIZZA

I've used spinach in this recipe because it's a favorite of mine, but any green—spring dandelion, baby mustard, beet greens, broccoli rabe or even savoy cabbage—will do.

❦ The mildly spicy, savory toppings of this particular pizza would be best complemented by an equally flavorful medium-bodied red, such as Merlot. Look for 1985 Arbor Crest from Washington or 1984 Louis M. Martini Russian River Valley from California.

——*Makes 4 Individual Pizzas* ——
3 pounds fresh spinach, stemmed
    and washed
¼ cup extra-virgin olive oil
8 garlic cloves, chopped
¼ teaspoon crushed hot red pepper
1 tablespoon plus 1 teaspoon
    anchovy paste
½ teaspoon salt
¼ teaspoon freshly ground black
    pepper
Quick Semolina Pizza Dough
    (p. 161)
1⅓ cups diced mozzarella cheese
    (about ½ pound)

PIZZA PARTY

Here is a get-the-guests-involved party. Make the toppings for the pizza ahead of time (all of those listed below can be made a day ahead) and make a triple recipe of dough. Then, let the guests choose their toppings and make the pizzas to order. Serves 6 to 8.

Spicy Spinach and Garlic Pizza
(p. 162)

Scallion and Olive Pizza with
Rosemary (p. 161)

Zucchini and Sun-Dried Tomato
Pizza (p. 164)

Mixed Green Salad with Fresh Basil

❦ *Crisp Sauvignon Blanc, such as*
1986 Clos du Val or 1987 Kenwood

Lemon Granita with Lemon
Whipped Cream (p. 210)

Cornmeal Crescent Biscotti (p. 243)

---

1. In a large nonreactive saucepan, cook the spinach, covered, with only the water that clings to the leaves, over high heat, stirring occasionally, until tender, about 6 to 10 minutes. Drain, rinse under cold water and squeeze out as much moisture as possible.

2. In a large skillet, heat the olive oil over low heat. Add the garlic and hot pepper and cook until the garlic is lightly browned, about 8 minutes. Stir in the anchovy paste and cook for 1 minute longer.

3. Increase the heat to moderate and add the spinach. Toss the spinach to evenly coat with the oil. Reduce the heat to low and cook for 3 minutes. Season with the salt and pepper and remove the saucepan from the heat. (*The recipe can be*

prepared to this point up to 1 day ahead; cover and refrigerate.)

4. Roll the Quick Semolina Pizza Dough into a log 1½ inches in diameter. Cut into 4 equal pieces. Roll out each piece of dough into a 7-inch round about ¹⁄₁₆ inch thick. Cover the rounds with plastic wrap. Heat a 9- or 10-inch cast-iron skillet over moderately high heat until hot.

5. Place one of the dough rounds into the hot skillet, reduce the heat to low, cover and cook until the crust is dark brown on the bottom, about 3 minutes. (Check after 2 minutes and adjust the heat, if necessary, to avoid burning the dough.)

6. Remove the pizza crust from the skillet. Layer the crust with ⅓ cup mozzarella and top with ½ cup spinach. Return the pizza to the skillet and cook, covered, until the cheese melts, about 2 minutes. Repeat the process with the 3 other rounds.

—*Anne Disrude*

• • •

ASPARAGUS AND PARMESAN CHEESE PIZZA

I've borrowed this topping recipe from Parma, where the great Parmigiano Reggiano is made. Traditionally, the asparagus are served simply with a blanket of Parmesan cheese. Here the asparagus are cut in pieces and cooked until tender, flavored with onion and butter and covered with shavings of the cheese.

❦ Although the bittersweet flavor of asparagus can clash with wine, Parmesan complements it. A crisp, herbaceous California Sauvignon Blanc, such as 1986 Clos du Val or 1987 Kenwood, will bridge the flavors perfectly.

——*Makes 4 Individual Pizzas* ——
1½ pounds asparagus, tough ends
    removed

3 tablespoons unsalted butter
½ cup diced red onion
¼ teaspoon salt
¼ teaspoon freshly ground pepper
Quick Semolina Pizza Dough
  (p. 161)
1⅓ cups diced mozzarella cheese
  (about ½ pound)
½ cup Parmesan cheese shavings,
  about 1 ounce (see Note)

1. Cut the asparagus stalks into 1-inch pieces if skinny, ½-inch pieces if fat. Reserve the tips. Cook the pieces in a large saucepan of boiling salted water until almost tender, about 2 minutes, then add the tips and cook until tender, 2 minutes longer. Drain and pat dry with paper towels.

2. In a large skillet, melt the butter over moderately low heat. Add the red onion and cook until softened, about 5 minutes.

3. Add the asparagus, toss to coat with the butter and cook, tossing frequently, about 2 minutes. Remove from the heat and season with the salt and pepper.

4. Roll the Quick Semolina Pizza Dough into a log 1½ inches in diameter. Cut into 4 equal pieces. Roll out each piece of dough into a 7-inch round about 1⁄16 inch thick. Cover the rounds with plastic wrap. Heat a 9- or 10-inch cast-iron skillet over moderately high heat until hot.

5. Place one of the dough rounds into the hot skillet, reduce the heat to low, cover and cook until the crust is dark brown on the bottom, about 3 minutes. (Check after 2 minutes and reduce the heat, if necessary, to avoid scorching.)

6. Remove the pizza crust from the skillet. Layer the crust with ⅓ cup of the mozzarella mixture and top with ¾ cup asparagus pieces. Return the pizza to the skillet and cook, covered, until the cheese melts, about 2 minutes. Top with one-fourth of the Parmesan shavings (see Note). Repeat the process with the 3 other rounds.

NOTE: Use a vegetable peeler to shave broad but thin pieces from a chunk of Parmesan. If using finely grated cheese, toss with the diced mozzarella instead of putting it on top.

—*Anne Disrude*

• • •

GARLICKY POTATO PIZZA

These pan-roasted diced potatoes are cooked in oil and butter with garlic and rosemary. I left the potato skins on for extra flavor.

—— *Makes 4 Individual Pizzas* ——
1 tablespoon unsalted butter
3 tablespoons extra-virgin olive oil
8 large garlic cloves, thinly sliced
1 sprig of fresh rosemary
1⅓ cups diced mozzarella cheese
  (about ½ pound)
1½ pounds baking potatoes, cut into
  ⅜-inch dice
¾ teaspoon salt
¼ teaspoon freshly ground pepper
3 tablespoons chopped parsley
Quick Semolina Pizza Dough
  (p. 161)

1. In a large heavy skillet, melt the butter in the oil over moderate heat. Add the garlic and rosemary and cook until the garlic is lightly browned, about 3 minutes. Remove the garlic and rosemary with a slotted spoon and chop. In a small bowl, combine the mozzarella, garlic and rosemary; toss to mix.

2. Add the potatoes to the skillet and toss to coat with the oil. Cook, tossing occasionally, until the potatoes are soft and well browned, about 25 minutes.

3. Season with the salt and pepper; add the parsley and toss. Transfer to a large dish or bowl lined with paper towels to absorb the oil.

4. Roll the Quick Semolina Pizza Dough into a log 1½ inches in diameter.

Cut into 4 equal pieces. Roll out each piece of dough into a 7-inch round about 1⁄16 inch thick. Cover the rounds with plastic wrap. Heat a 9- or 10-inch cast-iron skillet over moderately high heat until hot.

5. Place one of the dough rounds into the hot skillet, reduce the heat to low, cover and cook until the crust is dark brown on the bottom, about 3 minutes. (Check after 2 minutes and adjust the heat if necessary, to avoid burning the dough.)

6. Remove the pizza crust from the skillet. Layer the crust with ⅓ cup of the mozzarella mixture and top with about ½ to ¾ cup potatoes. Return the pizza to the skillet and cook, covered, until the cheese melts, about 2 minutes. Repeat the process with the 3 other rounds.

—*Anne Disrude*

• • •

CALABRIAN CAULIFLOWER PIZZA

The versatile cauliflower topping on this pizza is a specialty of Calabria in southern Italy. It's delicious with almost anything; I have it as a salad or toss it with spaghetti, Pecorino Romano cheese and lots of black pepper. In this variation, currants, salty capers and a splash of sharp vinegar give this pizza a salty, savory twist.

—— *Makes 4 Individual Pizzas* ——
1 small head of cauliflower (about 1
  pound), separated into florets and
  cut lengthwise into ⅛-inch slices
¼ cup extra-virgin olive oil
4 garlic cloves, coarsely chopped
Pinch of crushed hot red pepper
½ teaspoon anchovy paste
2 tablespoons currants or raisins
1 tablespoon white wine vinegar
1½ tablespoons capers, drained and
  coarsely chopped
3 tablespoons chopped parsley
½ teaspoon salt
¼ teaspoon freshly ground pepper

Quick Semolina Pizza Dough
(p. 161)
1⅓ cups diced mozzarella cheese
(about ½ pound)

1. In a large pot of boiling salted water, cook the cauliflower until just tender, about 5 minutes; drain well.

2. Meanwhile, in a large nonreactive skillet, heat the olive oil over moderate heat. Add the garlic and hot pepper and cook, stirring, until the garlic is golden brown, about 2 minutes. Add the anchovy paste and currants and cook for 1 minute. Add the vinegar and cook for 1 minute longer.

3. Add the cauliflower and toss to coat. Cook, tossing frequently, for 2 minutes. Remove from the heat and add the capers, parsley, salt and pepper. *(The recipe can be prepared to this point up to 1 day ahead; cover and refrigerate.)*

4. Roll the Quick Semolina Pizza Dough into a log 1½ inches in diameter. Cut into 4 equal pieces. Roll out each piece of dough into a 7-inch round about ¹⁄₁₆ inch thick. Cover the rounds with plastic wrap. Heat a 9- or 10-inch cast-iron skillet over moderately high heat until hot.

5. Place one of the dough rounds into the hot skillet, reduce the heat to low, cover and cook until the crust is dark brown on the bottom, about 3 minutes. (Check after 2 minutes and reduce the heat, if necessary, to avoid scorching.)

6. Remove the pizza crust from the skillet. Layer the crust with ⅓ cup mozzarella and top with about ½ to ¾ cup cauliflower. Return the pizza to the skillet and cook, covered, until the cheese melts, about 2 minutes. Repeat the process with the 3 other rounds.

—*Anne Disrude*

• • •

ZUCCHINI AND SUN-DRIED TOMATO PIZZA

In order to insure the optimum flavor of the zucchini, I have made this recipe yield only two pizzas, but it's easy enough to make two batches. It is essential to cook the zucchini evenly in a large uncrowded pan. When tomatoes are in season, substitute one large fresh beefsteak tomato for the sun-dried tomatoes.

❦ The well-browned zucchini and the sweet piquancy of the sun-dried tomatoes in this mild vegetable pizza are best matched with a flavorful but not overpowering red, such as a young, medium-bodied Rioja. A 1985 Marqués de Cáceres or 1984 Marqués de Riscal would both be ideal choices.

——*Makes 2 Individual Pizzas*——
3 small zucchini (about ¾ pound
total), cut into ⅜-inch pieces
1 teaspoon salt
1 tablespoon oil from oil-packed sun-
dried tomatoes
4 sun-dried tomato halves packed in
oil, minced
3 garlic cloves, lightly smashed
Pinch of crushed hot red pepper
¼ teaspoon freshly ground black
pepper
2 tablespoons minced fresh basil
½ recipe Quick Semolina Pizza
Dough (p. 161)
⅔ cup diced mozzarella cheese
(about ¼ pound)

1. Put the zucchini in a colander and season with ½ teaspoon of the salt; toss and let drain for 5 minutes. Gently press the zucchini with a paper towel to absorb the moisture.

2. Meanwhile, in a large heavy skillet, heat the oil over moderate heat. Add the sun-dried tomatoes, garlic and hot pepper. Cook until the garlic begins to soften, about 2 minutes.

3. Increase the heat to high, add the zucchini and toss to coat with the oil.

Cook, tossing frequently, until the zucchini is evenly browned, about 3 minutes. Remove from the heat, season with the remaining ½ teaspoon salt and all the black pepper. Discard the garlic. *(The recipe can be prepared to this point up to 1 day ahead; cover and refrigerate.)* Add the basil and stir.

4. Roll the Quick Semolina Pizza Dough into a log 1½ inches in diameter. Cut in half. Roll out each piece of dough into a 7-inch round about ¹⁄₁₆ inch thick. Cover the rounds with plastic wrap. Heat a 9- or 10-inch cast-iron skillet over moderately high heat until hot.

5. Place one of the dough rounds into the hot skillet, reduce the heat to low, cover and cook until the crust is dark brown on the bottom, about 3 minutes. (Check after 2 minutes and adjust the heat, if necessary, to avoid burning.)

6. Remove the pizza crust from the skillet. Layer the crust with ⅓ cup mozzarella and top with about ½ cup of the zucchini. Return the pizza to the skillet and cook, covered, until the cheese melts, about 2 minutes. Repeat the process with the remaining round.

—*Anne Disrude*

• • •

CORNMEAL PIZZA WITH GREENS AND FONTINA

In some parts of Italy it is not unusual for broccoli rabe or Swiss chard to find its way onto a pizza. Collards and other southern greens provide the same pleasant bitterness as their Italian counterparts.

❦ This savory dish calls for an equally piquant red, such as Chianti, to point up its rich, cheesy flavor. Try the elegant 1985 Antinori Pèppoli or the straightforward 1986 Frescobaldi.

6 to 8 First-Course or
——*4 Main-Course Servings*——
2 envelopes (¼ ounce each) active
dry yeast
Pinch of sugar

1¼ cups lukewarm water (105° to
    115°)
2¾ cups all-purpose flour
2 teaspoons salt
¾ cup yellow cornmeal
¼ cup plus 2 tablespoons extra-
    virgin olive oil
1 medium onion, finely chopped
2 large garlic cloves, minced
2 pounds watercress or arugula,
    tough stems removed (see Note)
Pinch of crushed hot red pepper
2 ounces very thinly sliced
    Smithfield ham or prosciutto
½ pound Italian Fontina cheese,
    shredded
¼ pound mozzarella cheese,
    shredded or cut into thin slices

1. In a medium bowl, combine the yeast, sugar and warm water. Stir gently to mix, then let stand until bubbly, about 5 minutes.

2. Add 1 cup of the flour and the salt and mix thoroughly. Add the cornmeal and another cup of the flour and mix well.

3. Sprinkle the remaining flour on a work surface. Turn out the dough and knead, incorporating the flour a little at a time, until smooth and elastic, 5 to 10 minutes. Place the dough in a lightly oiled bowl and turn to coat. Cover the bowl with plastic wrap and let rise in a warm place until doubled in bulk, about 1 hour.

4. Punch the dough down, cover and let rise until doubled in bulk, about 1 hour longer.

5. Meanwhile, in a large skillet, heat 2 tablespoons of the olive oil over moderately low heat. Add the onion and cook until it begins to soften, about 5 minutes. Add the garlic and cook until fragrant, about 30 seconds.

6. Increase the heat to moderate. Add the watercress and cook, partially covered, tossing frequently, until the water-

cress is wilted and the liquid it exudes has evaporated, about 5 minutes.

7. Stir in the hot red pepper. Drain the greens in a colander and press with a wooden spoon to force out any excess liquid. When cool enough to handle, chop coarsely and set aside.

8. Preheat the oven to 500°. Working quickly, divide the dough into 4 equal pieces. Form each piece of dough into a ball and roll it out on a floured surface to form a pizza round ¼ inch thick and 7 to 8 inches in diameter.

9. Place a large heavy ungreased baking sheet in the oven for 5 minutes. Place two dough rounds on the hot baking sheet, brush each lightly with 1½ teaspoons of the oil and return to the oven. Bake until pale golden brown, 8 to 12 minutes. Repeat with the other 2 rounds.

10. Spread the ham on the pizza crusts, leaving a ½-to-1-inch border. Divide the greens equally among the pizzas, covering the ham. Top with the cheeses, distributing them evenly and covering the greens completely. Drizzle on the remaining 2 tablespoons oil. Bake the pizzas, two at a time, until the cheese is melted and bubbly and the crust is golden brown, 5 to 8 minutes.

NOTE: To substitute kale for the watercress, wash and trim 1 pound of kale. Stack the leaves and cut into ¼-inch-wide strips. Blanch for 1 minute in boiling salted water. Drain thoroughly, then squeeze out any excess water. Cook the onion and garlic as the recipe directs. Add the kale and the crushed hot red pepper and toss over moderate heat for 1 minute. Proceed as directed in Step 8.

—*Sarah Belk*

• • •

CUSTARD-FILLED CORN BREAD WITH FRESH CORN KERNELS

This recipe is adapted from *Cross Creek Cookery* by Marjorie Kinnan Rawlings, who called her somewhat different version "Aunt Effie's Custard Johnny Cake." It's one of those "put-it-in-the-oven-and-watch-what-happens" recipes. As it bakes, the batter forms a wonderfully crusty top and bottom with a creamy center.

——————6 to 8 Servings——————
1 cup yellow cornmeal
½ cup unbleached all-purpose flour
1 tablespoon sugar
1 teaspoon baking soda
1 teaspoon salt
1 cup buttermilk
2 eggs, well beaten
1½ cups milk
¾ cup corn kernels (from 1 large ear
    of corn)
2 tablespoons unsalted butter, cut
    into small pieces

1. Preheat the oven to 400°. In a large bowl, sift together the cornmeal, flour, sugar, baking soda and salt. Make a well in the center of the dry ingredients and pour in the buttermilk and eggs; stir until almost blended. Stir in 1 cup of the milk and the corn kernels until just combined; do not overmix.

2. Put the butter in a 10-inch cast-iron skillet and heat in the oven until the butter melts, 2 to 3 minutes. Remove from the oven and swirl to coat the bottom and sides of the pan.

3. Scrape the batter into the hot pan and sprinkle the remaining ½ cup milk over the surface. Bake for 30 to 35 minutes, or until the corn bread is golden brown and crusty on the outside but still quivers slightly when the pan is shaken. Cut into thick wedges and serve hot with sweet butter.

—*Richard Sax*

• • •

CORN LIGHT BREAD

Loaf corn bread is one more creation that proves the versatility of cornmeal—as if more proof were needed. This version is not commonly found in southern restaurants or even in private kitchens—perhaps because it contains sugar and flour, two ingredients seldom used in southern corn bread. It deserves appreciation!

Makes One 9-Inch Loaf
2 cups white cornmeal
½ cup sugar
1 teaspoon salt
½ cup all-purpose flour
2 teaspoons baking powder
1 teaspoon baking soda
2 tablespoons vegetable shortening or bacon fat
2 cups buttermilk

1. Preheat the oven to 350°. In a medium bowl, sift the cornmeal, sugar, salt, flour, baking powder and baking soda.

2. Put the shortening in a 9-by-5-by-3-inch loaf pan and set it in the oven until melted, about 2 minutes. Spread to evenly coat the bottom and sides of the pan.

3. Add the buttermilk and 1 tablespoon of the melted shortening from the loaf pan to the dry ingredients. Stir just until blended. Return the pan to the oven to heat again.

4. When the remaining shortening in the pan is smoking hot, pour in the batter. Bake for 1 hour, or until the loaf is firm, browned and crusty. Turn the loaf out onto a rack to cool slightly before slicing (it crumbles badly when sliced oven-hot, but holds together well when warm).

—*John Egerton*

• • •

KENTUCKY SPOONBREAD

When basic corn pone—meal and water—is enriched with milk, butter and eggs, the result is an elegant soufflé-like corn bread. Serve spoonbread straight from the dish as an accompaniment to virtually any meat-and-vegetables meal.

4 Servings
1 cup white cornmeal
¾ teaspoon salt
1 cup cold milk
2 eggs, well beaten
2 tablespoons unsalted butter, melted and cooled

1. Preheat the oven to 400°. Butter a 1-quart soufflé dish or an 8-inch-square baking pan.

2. In a large saucepan, combine the cornmeal and salt with 2 cups of cold water. Bring to a boil over high heat. Reduce the heat to moderately low and cook for 5 minutes, stirring constantly. (The mixture will be very stiff at first.)

3. Set the baking dish in the oven until it is hot. Remove the saucepan from the heat and very gradually stir in the cold milk, the eggs and the melted butter, in that order, until thoroughly blended.

4. Pour the batter into the hot baking dish and bake for 40 minutes, or until the spoonbread is firm in the center and well browned on top. Serve hot.

—*John Egerton*

• • •

CORNMEAL YEAST BREAD

"Why not," I asked myself one day, "create a bread with a light cornmeal flavor and the crackling, crisp crust of a French baguette?" So I did. These loaves have a lighter crumb than standard southern corn breads so that they are somewhat more refined. You can slice the bread on the diagonal as you would French bread and serve it with lunch or dinner or with butter and damson plum preserves for breakfast or afternoon tea. Or slice it very thin, toast and serve with southern liver pudding, pork rillettes, foie gras or chicken liver mousse to accompany aperitifs.

Makes 4 Loaves
2 envelopes (¼ ounce each) active dry yeast
Pinch of sugar
1½ cups lukewarm water (105° to 115°)
3 to 3¾ cups all-purpose flour
1 cup yellow cornmeal
1 tablespoon salt
1 egg yolk
1 tablespoon milk

1. In a small bowl, mix the yeast and sugar with 1 cup of the warm water and let stand until bubbly, about 5 minutes.

2. In a large bowl, mix 3 cups of the flour with the cornmeal and salt. Add the remaining ½ cup warm water and the dissolved yeast mixture and stir until well combined.

3. Turn the dough out onto a lightly floured work surface and knead, adding additional flour as needed to avoid stickiness, until smooth and elastic, about 10 minutes. Place the dough in a lightly oiled bowl and turn to coat the dough with oil. Cover with plastic wrap and let rise in a warm place until the dough is doubled in bulk, about 2 hours.

4. Punch down the dough, cover and let rise again in a warm place until doubled, about 1½ hours.

5. Preheat the oven to 425°. Divide the dough into 4 equal portions and roll each portion with the palms of your hands into a narrow, 12-inch-long loaf. Place the loaves on a baking sheet lightly sprinkled with cornmeal.

6. In a small bowl, beat the egg yolk and milk together. Brush the top of each loaf with the egg glaze (see Note). Using a sharp knife, cut diagonal slashes 2 inches apart along the length of the loaves. Let the dough rest 5 minutes. Brush again with the egg glaze. Bake in the center of the oven for 20 to 25 minutes, or until the loaves sound hollow when tapped on the bottom.

NOTE: The egg glaze results in a shiny golden crust. For a crackly-crisp crust, omit the glaze and sprinkle the uncooked loaves with water just before baking.

—*Sarah Belk*

• • •

SHAKER FRESH HERB BREAD

This is a lovely bread, one that makes great toast and savory sandwiches. The pronounced herb flavor goes especially well with fresh vegetable sandwich fillings, chicken salad and cold cuts, too. The dough itself is easy to handle and has enough body to hold a well-rounded shape in the oven. These loaves can be baked directly on a baking sheet, as described, or slid onto baking tiles. Dried herbs can be substituted, halving the quantities.

——— *Makes 2 Free-Form Loaves* ———

1 envelope (¼ ounce) active dry yeast
¼ cup lukewarm water (105° to 115°)
½ cup old-fashioned rolled oats
½ cup buttermilk
1½ cups milk
1 tablespoon sugar
3 tablespoons minced fresh dill
2 teaspoons minced fresh thyme
2 teaspoons minced fresh sage
1 teaspoon caraway seeds
1 cup whole wheat flour
About 4 cups unbleached all-purpose flour
1 egg, lightly beaten
3 tablespoons unsalted butter, melted
2 teaspoons salt
Cornmeal or semolina, for the baking sheet
Egg wash: 1 egg beaten with 1 tablespoon milk

1. In a small bowl, sprinkle the yeast over the water and set aside to dissolve. Put the oats into another bowl. Warm the buttermilk to about body temperature and pour it over the oats. Stir and set aside until softened, about 10 minutes.

2. In a small saucepan, scald the milk. Transfer the hot milk to a large mixing bowl and stir in the sugar, dill, thyme, sage and caraway seeds. Let cool to lukewarm (105° to 115°) then blend in the softened oats and the yeast.

3. Add the whole wheat flour and 1 cup of the unbleached flour and beat vigorously with a wooden spoon for 1 minute. Cover this sponge with plastic wrap and set aside in a warm draft-free spot for about 30 minutes.

4. With a wooden spoon, beat the egg, melted butter and salt into the sponge. Beat in 3 cups of unbleached flour, 1 cup at a time, until the dough is too stiff to stir, then turn the dough out onto a floured surface. With floured hands, knead the dough, using just enough additional flour to prevent sticking, until it is smooth, soft and moderately elastic, about 10 minutes.

5. Place the dough in a lightly oiled bowl, turn to coat the entire surface. Cover and set aside in a warm spot, until doubled in bulk, about 45 minutes.

6. While the dough rises, very lightly oil a large baking sheet and dust it heavily with cornmeal or semolina.

7. Punch the dough down and turn it out onto a floured surface. Divide the dough in half, knead each half briefly and form them into tight balls. Place the balls on the prepared baking sheet, leaving plenty of room between them for expansion. Cover loosely with plastic and set aside in a warm spot until almost doubled in bulk, about 45 minutes.

8. Preheat the oven to 375°. Brush each loaf sparingly with the egg wash; try not to let it run down the sides and onto the sheet. Using a sharp, serrated knife, make 4 or 5 shallow slashes, 3 to 4 inches long, on the surface. Bake for 45 minutes, until the crust is nicely browned and the bottom sounds hollow when tapped with a finger. (For uniform browning, it is often a good idea to turn the baking sheet 180 degrees about midway through the baking.) Transfer the loaves to a rack. To store, cool thoroughly before placing in plastic bags.

—*Ken Haedrich*

• • •

HONEY OAT BREAD

This eggy yeast bread combines elements of Jewish challah and Italian semolina bread. It is a perfect international candidate for French toast.

——————— *Makes 1 Loaf* ———————

1 envelope (¼ ounce) active dry yeast
⅔ cup lukewarm water (105° to 115°)
¼ teaspoon sugar
2½ cups old-fashioned rolled oats
About 1½ cups durum wheat flour*
1½ teaspoons salt
4 eggs, at room temperature
⅓ cup honey
2 tablespoons unsalted butter, melted, or corn oil
1 to 2 tablespoons poppy seeds or sesame seeds (optional)
*Available at Italian or specialty food markets

1. In a small bowl, sprinkle the yeast over the warm water. Add the sugar and let stand until bubbly, 5 to 10 minutes.

2. Meanwhile, in a food processor, process the rolled oats until finely ground. On a work surface, toss together the ground oats, 1 cup of the flour and the salt and form into a mound. Make a wide well in the center.

3. In a small bowl, lightly beat 3 of the eggs with a fork. Stir in the honey and butter. Pour the egg mixture into the well and add the yeast mixture.

4. Stirring with the fingers of one hand, begin incorporating the dry ingredients into the liquid in the well. With a pastry scraper in the other hand, combine the ingredients, forming the dough into a ball. Scrape the work surface clean and dust lightly with flour. Knead the dough, adding the remaining ½ cup flour as necessary, 2 tablespoons at a time, until the dough is smooth and elastic, 7 to 10 minutes (you may have some flour left over).

5. Rinse out a large bowl with warm water, transfer the dough to the bowl and cover with plastic wrap. Let rise in a warm place until doubled in bulk, about 1 hour.

6. Punch down the dough. Turn out onto a work surface and shape into a thick loaf, about 15 inches long. Transfer to a large ungreased baking sheet. Cover with a towel and let rise until doubled in bulk, about 45 minutes.

7. Preheat the oven to 375°. In a small bowl, beat the remaining egg with 1 tablespoon of water. Gently brush the egg glaze on the risen loaf. Sprinkle the poppy seeds on top, if desired, and bake for 35 minutes or until the bread is deep golden brown. Transfer the loaf to a wire rack to cool completely before slicing.

—*Tracey Seaman*

• • •

GOLDEN SQUASH AND SESAME LOAF

I have been making variations of this bread every fall for many years (it makes great French toast). To get a well-rounded top, be sure to shape the dough as described here, rolling it out and then up again. This keeps tension in the dough, which, because it contains both cornmeal and squash, isn't as elastic as some.

I've been known to sieve two or three tablespoons of brown sugar over the rolled dough to give the bread a sweet swirl.

——————*Makes 2 Loaves*——————
2 cups cubed, peeled butternut squash (from a 1-pound squash)
1½ cups milk
⅓ cup sugar
1 envelope (¼ ounce) active dry yeast
¼ cup lukewarm water (105° to 115°)
1 teaspoon finely grated lemon zest
1 cup yellow cornmeal, preferably stone-ground
2 cups whole wheat flour
1 egg, lightly beaten
4 tablespoons unsalted butter, at room temperature
1 tablespoon salt
3½ to 4¼ cups unbleached all-purpose flour
¼ cup toasted sesame seeds
1 cup raisins
Egg wash: 1 egg beaten with 2 tablespoons milk

1. In a medium saucepan, cover the squash with 4 cups of water. Bring to a boil, cover and reduce the heat to moderately low. Cook the squash until very tender, about 15 minutes; drain.

2. In a blender or food processor, puree the squash until smooth. Scrape the puree into a large mixing bowl and set aside.

3. In a small saucepan, scald the milk over moderate heat. Remove from the heat and mix in the sugar, stirring until dissolved. Whisk the milk into the pureed squash. Let cool to lukewarm (105° to 115°).

4. In a small bowl, sprinkle the yeast over the lukewarm water. Let dissolve for 10 minutes, then stir into the squash mixture along with the lemon zest. Add the cornmeal and whole wheat flour and beat vigorously with a wooden spoon for 1 minute. Cover this sponge with plastic wrap and set aside in a warm, draft-free place for about 30 minutes.

5. With a wooden spoon, beat the egg, butter and salt into the sponge. Beat in about 3 cups of the unbleached flour, 1 cup at a time, until the dough becomes too stiff to work. Turn the dough out onto a floured surface and knead with floured hands for 12 minutes, incorporating enough of the remaining flour to keep the dough from sticking. The dough should be smooth and able to hold its shape fairly well, though it won't be very elastic.

6. Place the dough in a lightly oiled bowl, cover with plastic wrap and let rise in a warm, draft-free spot until doubled in bulk, about 45 minutes.

7. Butter two 8½-by-4½-inch loaf pans. Sprinkle the sides and bottom of each pan with 1 tablespoon of the toasted sesame seeds.

8. Spread half of the raisins over the top of the dough and punch down. Add the remaining raisins, punching and kneading them into the dough. Divide the dough in half.

9. Keeping one half covered in the bowl, knead the other half briefly on a lightly floured surface, then roll into an oblong about ½ inch thick and 8 inches wide at the widest point. Starting at a long edge, roll the dough up like a carpet, keeping a little tension on it. Pinch the seam together, tucking the ends under. Lift the dough roll into one of the prepared pans, seam-side down, and cover loosely with plastic wrap.

10. Repeat for the other half of the dough, then set aside in a warm, draft-free spot until doubled in bulk, about 30 minutes.

11. When the breads are nearly doubled, preheat the oven to 375°. Very lightly brush each loaf with a little of the egg wash. Using a serrated knife, make 3 or 4 shallow, diagonal slits in the tops of the loaves. Sprinkle the top of each loaf evenly with 1 tablespoon of the sesame seeds.

12. When fully doubled, brush the loaves again with the egg wash and bake in the lower third of the oven for 45 to 50 minutes, or until they are well browned and have a soft, hollow sound when gently tapped with a finger. Check the loaves halfway through to be sure they're browning evenly; turn the pans if necessary. Unmold the loaves and let cool on a rack for at least 30 minutes before slicing. To store, cool thoroughly before placing in plastic bags.

—Ken Haedrich

• • •

EASTER BREAD

My grandmother, Lucille Rossi, made this as an Easter treat, but it kept so well that we would eat it for many days after.

——————*Makes 1 Loaf*——————
2 envelopes (¼ ounce each) active dry yeast
¼ cup lukewarm water (105° to 115°)
⅛ teaspoon salt
¾ cup plus 1 teaspoon sugar
About 4½ cups all-purpose flour
8 eggs at room temperature—3 lightly beaten, 5 in the shell, dyed Easter colors if desired

¼ cup warm milk
1 stick (4 ounces) unsalted butter, melted
1 egg yolk

1. In a small bowl, combine the yeast, water, salt and 1 teaspoon of the sugar. Set aside until bubbly, about 5 minutes.

2. In a large bowl, stir 4½ cups of the flour and the remaining ¾ cup sugar with a whisk to combine. Make a well in the center of the dry ingredients.

3. In a small bowl, mix the 3 beaten eggs with the warm milk and pour into the well with the yeast mixture and melted butter. With a wooden spoon, incorporate the liquids into the dry ingredients until the dough comes together. Turn out onto a lightly floured work surface. Knead the dough until smooth, about 5 minutes.

4. Rinse the large bowl with warm water. Return the dough to the bowl and turn to coat. Cover the bowl with plastic wrap and let rise in a warm place until doubled in bulk, 1½ to 2 hours.

5. Punch down the dough and turn it out onto a work surface, dusted with additional flour if necessary. Roll it into an 18-inch log. Transfer the dough to a large, ungreased baking sheet and curve the ends around to form a wreath. Set aside, lightly cover with a towel and let rise until doubled, 45 to 60 minutes. Preheat the oven to 350°.

6. Press the whole eggs into the top of the wreath. In a small bowl, mix the egg yolk with 1 teaspoon of water and glaze the bread around the eggs. Bake for 45 to 50 minutes, or until well browned and a tester comes out clean.

—Fred Ferretti

• • •

TOASTING BREAD

The bread I make for toasting is very simple and quick. It has only one rising and can be baked two to three weeks ahead of time. Slice it and freeze it to simplify last-minute preparations.

——————*Makes 2 Loaves*——————
1 tablespoon active dry yeast (I use Red Star)
2¼ cups lukewarm water (105° to 115°)
1 teaspoon sugar
5 to 5½ cups unbleached all-purpose flour
½ cup whole wheat flour
1 tablespoon salt

1. In a large bowl, sprinkle the yeast over ¼ cup of the warm water; stir in the sugar. Let stand until foamy, about 5 minutes.

2. Add the remaining 2 cups warm water, then gradually stir in 2½ cups of the all-purpose flour, about ¼ cup at a time. Mix in the whole wheat flour and the salt. Gradually mix in 2 more cups of the unbleached flour.

3. Turn the dough out onto a floured surface and knead, adding more of the remaining flour to prevent sticking, until the dough is smooth and silky to the touch, about 5 minutes.

4. Cut the dough into 2 equal pieces; shape each piece into a sausage. Put the dough into two well-buttered 6-cup loaf pans, preferably black tin. Cover the pans with plastic wrap, set in a warm place and let stand until the dough has risen three-fourths of the way up the sides of the pans, about 1 hour.

5. Preheat the oven to 400°. Bake the loaves until they are golden and sound hollow when turned out and tapped, about 30 minutes if using black pans or about 40 minutes for shiny metal or glass. Unmold onto a rack and let cool for about

1 hour before slicing. *(Or wrap the cool bread in aluminum foil and freeze until needed. To thaw, put in a 300° oven, still wrapped in the foil, for 15 minutes.)*

—*Lydie Pinoy Marshall*

• • •

ANGEL BISCUITS

Yeast biscuits and rolls are the slow but sure standards that gave the South its sterling reputation as a hot-bread heaven. These biscuits can be baked all at once, or portions of the dough can be pulled off for baking and the rest kept refrigerated in a tightly covered bowl. Dough kept for two or three days is at least as good as freshly made, if not better.

—— **Makes About 3 Dozen Biscuits** ——
5½ cups all-purpose flour
¼ cup sugar
1 tablespoon baking powder
1 teaspoon baking soda
1 teaspoon salt
1 cup solid vegetable shortening
1 envelope (¼ ounce) active dry yeast
2 tablespoons lukewarm water (105° to 115°)
2 cups buttermilk

1. In a large bowl, sift together the flour, sugar, baking powder, baking soda and salt. Cut in the shortening until the mixture resembles coarse meal.

2. In a medium bowl, combine the yeast with the lukewarm water. Let stand until foamy, 5 to 10 minutes. Add the buttermilk and stir until completely blended. Stir this liquid into the dry ingredients with a fork. Gather the dough into a ball.

3. On a floured surface, knead the dough until soft and smooth, adding more flour as necessary to reduce stickiness, about 5 minutes.

4. Roll out the dough to a thickness of about ½ inch. Using a 2-inch-round cut-ter, stamp out the biscuits and place them close together on a baking sheet. Cover with a kitchen towel and let rise in a warm place for 30 minutes.

5. Preheat the oven to 400°. Bake the biscuits for 10 to 15 minutes, or until nicely browned.

—*John Egerton*

• • •

CRUSTY GARLIC ROLLS

These rolls go especially well with hearty, stick-to-the-ribs soups, such as Veal Shank Soup (p. 31).

———— **Makes 18** ————
2 envelopes (¼ ounce each) active dry yeast
1 tablespoon sugar
1¼ cups lukewarm water (105° to 115°)
3 tablespoons extra-virgin olive oil
2 tablespoons unsalted butter
4 garlic cloves, crushed through a press
⅛ teaspoon freshly ground pepper
3½ cups all-purpose flour
2 teaspoons salt

1. In a small bowl, combine the yeast, sugar and the lukewarm water. Stir and let stand until the sugar has completely dissolved, about 15 minutes. Add 1 table-spoon of the olive oil.

2. Meanwhile, in a small skillet, melt the butter in the remaining 2 tablespoons oil over low heat. Add the garlic and pepper and cook until the garlic is soft-ened and fragrant, about 2 minutes. Re-move from the heat and let cool slightly.

3. In a bowl, combine the flour and salt. Add the garlic and yeast; mix well. On a floured surface, knead the dough until stiff. Transfer to an oiled bowl, turn the dough over to oil the surface. Cover with a kitchen towel and let rise until doubled in bulk, about 1 hour.

4. Preheat the oven to 425°. On a well-floured surface, knead the dough slightly. Roll out to ¼ inch thick. Using a 3-inch biscuit cutter, cut into rounds. Transfer to a large greased baking sheet. Gather up the scraps of dough and reroll and cut to make more rounds, until all the dough is used. Bake for 15 minutes, or until gold-en. Serve warm.

—*Lee Bailey*

• • •

CAROLINA POTATO ROLLS

Adding potatoes will make almost any dough moist, flavorful and nutritious.

To freeze the rolls, cool, then wrap in aluminum foil. They will keep for up to two weeks. When ready to use, place the frozen or thawed rolls in a 325° oven. They will crisp up beautifully.

———— **Makes 30 Rolls** ————
1 envelope (¼ ounce) active dry yeast
¼ cup lukewarm water (105° to 115°)
½ cup hot mashed potatoes
1 stick (4 ounces) plus 1 teaspoon unsalted butter
3 tablespoons sugar
1¼ teaspoons salt
1 egg
½ cup lukewarm milk (105° to 115°)
3 cups all-purpose flour
2 to 3 tablespoons poppy seeds, for garnish

1. In a small bowl, combine the yeast with the warm water.

2. Put the hot mashed potatoes in a large mixer bowl, add 5 tablespoons plus 1 teaspoon of the butter, the sugar, salt and egg. Beat well.

3. Beat in the yeast. Add the milk alternately with the flour. Beat well.

4. Turn out the dough onto a lightly floured surface. Knead thoroughly by hand for 5 minutes, adding just enough flour if needed to prevent the dough from being overly sticky.

5. Put the dough into a greased bowl and turn to coat the top. Cover with plastic wrap and set aside in a warm place to rise until doubled, about 1½ hours.

6. Punch down the dough. Place on a lightly floured surface and divide into two pieces. Roll out one piece of dough ¼ inch thick. Cut into disks with a 2½-inch round cutter.

7. Melt the remaining 3 tablespoons butter and pour into a shallow bowl. Dip one side of each disk in the melted butter. Fold over, buttered-side in, like a pocketbook. In an 8- or 9-inch square baking pan, place the rolls, seam-side up, touching each other lightly. Sprinkle half of the poppy seeds over the potato rolls. Repeat with the remaining dough and poppy seeds in a second pan.

8. Cover the rolls with plastic wrap and let stand until doubled in bulk, about 1 hour. Preheat the oven to 375°.

9. When the rolls have risen, place them in the middle of the oven and bake for 18 minutes, or until golden brown. Serve warm.

—*Camille Glenn*

• • •

POTATO-ONION PINWHEELS

This is a very nice soft dough to handle. As with most potato-based doughs, it will seem a little sticky, especially at first. After 10 minutes of kneading, however, the tackiness will be minimal. Don't try to knead in enough flour to totally eliminate the stickiness, or the rolls will be somewhat dry. I much prefer to bake these in glass or ceramic dishes because the sides and bottoms brown much better than in metal pans.

———— *Makes 18 Rolls* ————

1 large all-purpose potato, peeled and cut into 1-inch dice
1 envelope (¼ ounce) active dry yeast
½ cup cold milk
¾ cup rye flour
½ cup cornmeal
⅓ cup vegetable oil
1 tablespoon salt
About 4 cups unbleached all-purpose flour
4 tablespoons unsalted butter
1½ cups minced onions (2 to 3 medium)
Egg wash: 1 egg beaten with 1 teaspoon milk

1. In a medium saucepan, cover the potato with 4 cups of water. Bring to a boil over moderately high heat and cook, uncovered, until tender, 10 to 15 minutes.

2. Drain the potato, reserving ¾ cup of the potato water. Pour ¼ cup of the reserved potato water into a small bowl. Let cool to lukewarm (105° to 115°), then sprinkle on the yeast and set aside to proof.

3. Combine the cold milk and the remaining ½ cup potato water. Pour about ¼ cup of this liquid into a mixing bowl, add the cooked potatoes and beat with an electric mixer until smooth. Beat in the remaining ¾ cup liquid. Let cool to lukewarm, then stir in the yeast, the rye flour and the cornmeal. Beat vigorously with a wooden spoon for 1 minute, cover and set aside for 30 minutes.

4. Beat in the vegetable oil and salt. With a wooden spoon, beat in 4 cups of unbleached flour, 1 cup at a time, until the dough is too stiff to stir. Turn out onto a floured surface and knead with floured hands for about 10 minutes, using only as much additional flour as necessary to prevent sticking, until the dough is fairly elastic and quite smooth; it may still be a little tacky, but that's okay. Put the dough into a large, lightly oiled bowl and

turn to coat the entire surface. Cover and let rise in a warm spot until doubled in bulk, 1 to 1½ hours.

5. While the dough rises, melt the butter in a large skillet. Add the onions and cook over moderately low heat until softened and lightly browned, about 15 minutes. Scrape the onions onto a plate. Butter two 10-inch glass pie pans or two square 8- or 9-inch square glass baking pans.

6. Punch down the dough and knead briefly. Let the dough sit for several minutes. On a lightly floured surface, roll the dough into an 18-by-12-inch rectangle. Cover the entire surface evenly with the cooked onions. Cut the dough in half to form two 9-by-12-inch rectangles.

7. Starting at a short edge, roll up one of the rectangles. Pinch the dough at the seam to secure. Slice the log into 1-inch-thick rounds. Arrange the slices, spiral-side up, in one of the pans. Repeat with the remaining rectangle of dough. Cover the pans loosely with plastic wrap and set aside in a warm spot until the rolls are touching and have doubled in bulk, about 40 minutes.

8. Preheat the oven to 375°. Brush the rolls lightly with the egg-milk glaze. Bake the rolls in the middle of the oven for 25 to 30 minutes, until lightly browned. Remove the rolls from the pans and let cool slightly on a rack before serving.

—*Ken Haedrich*

• • •

SANDWICHES, PIZZAS & BREADS

SOFT PRETZELS WITH MUSTARD

I must thank master baker Carlo Bussetti for valuable advice in developing this recipe. These pretzels are made like bagels—boiled briefly in a water bath (with a little liquid malt for shine) before baking. They're glazed outside, chewy within and have a rich, well-developed flavor. Like most breads, these pretzels are best on the day they are baked.

—————— *Makes 10 Large Pretzels* ——————
1 cup plus 2 tablespoons lukewarm
water (105° to 115°)
1 envelope (¼ ounce) active dry
yeast
⅓ cup plus 1 teaspoon liquid malt*
(malted barley)
1 tablespoon sugar
1½ tablespoons solid vegetable
shortening, melted and cooled
slightly
½ of a beaten egg (about 1 fluid
ounce)
3⅓ cups bread flour (about 1
pound), plus more as needed
1 tablespoon coarse (kosher) salt
Mustard, as accompaniment
*Available at health food stores

1. In a liquid measuring cup, stir together the water, yeast, 1 teaspoon of the malt and the sugar. Set aside until foamy, about 10 minutes.

2. Pour the yeast mixture into a food processor and add the shortening, egg and 1⅔ cups of the flour. Turn the machine on and off briefly to combine the ingredients. Add the remaining 1⅔ cups flour and process until the dough cleans the bowl. It shouldn't feel sticky, dry or stiff. (Add more flour if necessary. If the dough is dry, add a few drops of lukewarm water.) Finally add 1 teaspoon of the salt and knead the dough in the processor for 1 minute. (If using an electric mixer, knead the dough for about 10 minutes.)

3. Place the dough on a lightly floured surface and knead by hand until smooth. Transfer to a lightly greased bowl, turn to coat and cover the bowl with a kitchen towel or plastic wrap. Place in a warm, draft-free place and let rise until the dough has doubled, about 1 hour.

4. Punch down the dough. On a lightly floured surface, roll the dough gently with both palms into an evenly shaped log about 20 inches long. Cut the log into 10 even pieces. Roll each piece into a "rope" about 18 inches long, tapering the ends slightly. Form the ropes into pretzels and set them aside, covered with a kitchen towel. Let rise again until slightly puffy, about 15 minutes.

5. Preheat the oven to 400°. Grease 2 large baking sheets. Fill a large, wide casserole two-thirds full of water. Add the remaining ⅓ cup malt, partially cover and bring to a simmer over high heat. Spread a kitchen towel on a work surface next to the pot of water.

6. Working in batches, gently add 3 or 4 of the pretzels to the water and simmer, uncovered, for 1 minute, turning the pretzels with a skimmer halfway through; they will puff up slightly from the heat. Lift out each pretzel with the skimmer and let drain, then set it down on the towel for a moment to drain further. Immediately transfer the pretzels to a greased baking sheet. Repeat with the remaining pretzels. Sprinkle the remaining 2 teaspoons coarse salt over the pretzels. Cover with a kitchen towel and let the pretzels rest for 5 minutes.

7. Bake the pretzels until golden, about 20 minutes. Exchange the position of the baking sheets to ensure even browning. Transfer the pretzels to a wire rack and let cool. Serve warm or at room temperature, with mustard.

—*Richard Sax*

• • •

DOUBLE-OAT FLATBREAD CRACKERS

Serve a piquant bean dip with this crunchy cracker. For a different-flavored cracker, just throw in a tablespoon of dried rosemary, marjoram or basil when you combine the dry ingredients.

—————— *Makes 4 Dozen* ——————
1 cup lukewarm water (105° to 115°)
¼ teaspoon sugar
1 envelope (¼ ounce) active dry
yeast
1¼ cups old-fashioned rolled oats
1½ cups durum wheat flour*
½ cup oat bran
½ teaspoon salt
2 tablespoons extra-virgin olive oil
1 tablespoon honey
¼ cup poppy or sesame seeds
*Available at Italian or specialty
food markets

1. In a small heatproof bowl, combine the warm water and sugar; sprinkle the yeast on top. Set aside until foamy, 5 to 7 minutes.

2. In a food processor, process the rolled oats until finely ground. Add the flour, oat bran and salt; process to mix.

3. Add the olive oil, honey and yeast mixture to the processor. Blend well. Scrape down the sides of the bowl and process again to knead the dough until smooth and elastic, about 20 seconds longer.

4. Rinse a medium bowl in hot water. Shape the dough into a disk, transfer to the warmed bowl and cover tightly with plastic wrap. Set aside in a warm place until doubled in bulk, about 1½ hours.

5. Transfer the dough to a lightly floured surface. Punch down and knead briefly, about 1 minute. Reshape the dough into a disk. Return it to the bowl, cover tightly and let rise until increased in bulk by about half, about 1 hour longer.

6. Preheat the oven to 450°. Sprinkle the poppy seeds on a lightly floured surface. Remove the dough from the bowl and cut into 4 pieces. Work with 1 piece at a time; wrap the other pieces in plastic wrap. Place the pieces of dough on the poppy seeds and roll it out to a 6-by-12-inch rectangle. Using a serrated pastry wheel or small knife and a ruler as a guide, cut the dough crosswise into 12 strips, 1 inch wide. Transfer the strips to a large ungreased baking sheet. Repeat with the remaining dough.

7. Bake the crackers for 12 to 15 minutes, or until crisp and brown. Carefully transfer to a rack and let cool completely.

—Tracey Seaman

• • •

THYME CROUTONS

Serve these little croutons as a crunchy addition to soup, stew or salad.

———— Makes About 3 Cups ————
3 tablespoons olive oil
3 cups diced (⅜ inch) French or other firm-textured white bread
½ teaspoon freshly ground pepper
½ teaspoon thyme

1. Preheat the oven to 375°. In a large ovenproof skillet, heat the olive oil over low heat. Add the bread and season with the pepper and thyme. Toss to mix.

2. Place the skillet in the oven and bake until the croutons are crisp and nicely browned, 10 to 12 minutes. Drain on paper towels. *(The croutons can be made up to 2 days in advance. Store in an airtight container at room temperature.)*

—Bob Chambers

• • •

PARMESAN CROUTONS

These croutons may be made in a variety of shapes and sizes. Cubed, they are perfect for soup, but when they are cut into larger triangles, these cheese-sprinkled toasts become a wonderful crisp base for canapés or a savory accompaniment to salads.

———— Makes About 2 Cups ————
4 tablespoons unsalted butter
1 tablespoon vegetable oil
4 thin slices of firm-textured white bread, crusts removed
1 tablespoon plus 1 teaspoon freshly grated Parmesan cheese

1. In a large heavy skillet, preferably nonstick, melt the butter in the oil over moderately high heat. When the foam subsides, add the bread slices and fry until lightly browned, about 2 minutes. Turn the bread and fry the other side for 2 minutes.

2. Sprinkle on the cheese, turn the bread one more time and cook until the cheese is lightly browned, about 1 minute. Drain on paper towels. Let cool for 5 minutes, then cut into ½-inch cubes.

—W. Peter Prestcott

• • •

BREAKFAST & BRUNCH

BLOODY MARYS

Breathes there a host who does not in his heart believe that he possesses the best possible formula for a Bloody Mary? There are dozens of ways to tinker with the recipe. Some add a pinch of celery salt, some prefer to use spicy vegetable juice and others—gasp—go so far as to eliminate the vodka. There is no accounting for some people's taste. The recipe will not be harmed by multiplying the quantities. It is wise to make up a pitcherful before the arrival of the guests.

Ancient saying: Two swallows may not make a summer, but three will certainly signify a fall. . .

——————— *4 Servings* ———————
3 cups tomato juice
1 cup vodka
2 tablespoons fresh lemon juice
1 tablespoon fresh lime juice
1 teaspoon Worcestershire sauce
3 drops of hot pepper sauce
Freshly ground pepper
4 lime wedges and 4 small celery ribs with leaves, for garnish

Combine the tomato juice, vodka, lemon juice, lime juice, Worcestershire sauce and hot sauce. Mix thoroughly. Pour into 4 glasses filled with ice. Dust with a small pinch of pepper. Garnish each glass with a wedge of lime and a celery rib.
—*Irena Chalmers*

• • •

RED AND BLACK FRUIT-FILLED GRAPEFRUIT CUPS

The contrasting colors of the fruit make a dramatic presentation on the table. Choose red cherries, strawberries, raspberries, red currants, pomegranates, watermelon or red-skinned apples. For the black fruit, select from blueberries, blackberries, black raspberries, black cherries and black plums. You could also fill some of the halves with all white or yellow fruit or all green fruit, though green is difficult because after green grapes, you find yourself stumped. Maybe this is why kiwis were invented.

——————— *12 Servings* ———————
6 grapefruit
Approximately 12 cups pitted/sliced/ diced (as necessary) assorted red and black seasonal fruits (see above)
1 cup crème de cassis
Fresh violet or nasturtium blossoms, for garnish

1. Cut each grapefruit in half crosswise; squeeze the juice and reserve it (or use it for the Fresh Grapefruit Juice with Mango and Mint at right). Using a grapefruit spoon or knife, scoop out and discard the remaining pulp and membranes.
2. Fill each grapefruit half with part red fruit and part black fruit or, alternatively, fill 6 of the halves with all red fruit and 6 with all black fruit. Drizzle 1 tablespoon plus 1 teaspoon of the cassis over the fruit in each grapefruit cup. Decorate with the fresh blossoms.
—*Irena Chalmers*

• • •

FRESH GRAPEFRUIT JUICE WITH MANGO AND MINT

Mango nectar softens and perfumes the grapefruit juice, and the sparkling water adds a refreshing fizz. If mint leaves are not to be found, add a thin slice of cucumber and, with it, another dimension.

——————— *12 Servings* ———————
4 cups fresh grapefruit juice (from about 6 grapefruits)
1 can (12 ounces) mango nectar
1 bottle (1 liter) seltzer or club soda
12 sprigs of fresh mint or 12 thin slices of unpeeled cucumber, for garnish

In a large punch bowl, combine the grapefruit juice, mango nectar and seltzer. Stir well. Place a mint sprig or cucumber slice on the edge of each of 12 tall glasses filled with ice, and let guests help themselves.
—*Irena Chalmers*

• • •

CARROT-CURRANT OATMEAL

Flecks of grated carrot add vitamin A and a bright touch of color to this satisfying hot cereal. Serve with your favorite topping: warm milk, butter or margarine, honey, maple syrup, brown sugar.

——————— *4 Servings* ———————
2 medium carrots, shredded
½ teaspoon salt
½ cup currants or raisins
⅔ cup oat bran
1⅓ cups old-fashioned rolled oats
½ teaspoon cinnamon

1. In a medium saucepan, combine the carrots and salt with 4 cups of water. Bring to a boil over moderately high heat. Reduce the heat to moderately low, add

BRUNCH IS BACK

Irena Chalmers claims that, along with other values and styles from the past, the brunch is back. Here is her proposed menu for celebrating the revival. Serves 12.

🍸 *Champagne*

🍸 *Bloody Marys (p. 176)*

🍸 *Fresh Grapefruit Juice with Mango and Mint (p. 176)*

Red and Black Fruit-Filled Grapefruit Cups (p. 176)

Pipérade (p. 194) or Kedgeree (p. 194)

Popovers Filled with Mushrooms and Bacon (p. 195)

Assorted Fresh Breads

Marmalades and Preserves

Sour Cream Coffee Cake with Chocolate and Walnuts (p. 191)

Cheese and Fruit Platter

Coffee and Tea

the currants and simmer until the carrots are soft and the currants have plumped, about 3 minutes.

2. Stir in the oat bran, rolled oats and cinnamon. Cook, stirring constantly, until thickened, about 5 minutes. Serve at once with the accompaniment of your choice.

—*Tracey Seaman*

• • •

OAT BRAN BANANA PANCAKES

These light and airy pancakes with a subtly sweet hint of banana are low in fat.

—— *Makes About 18 Pancakes* ——
1 cup oat bran
1 cup all-purpose flour
2 teaspoons baking soda
1 tablespoon sugar
1 extremely ripe medium banana, mashed (about ½ cup)
2 teaspoons vanilla extract
1½ cups plain yogurt
4 egg whites
2 tablespoons unsalted butter or margarine, melted
Warm maple syrup, for serving
½ cup coarsely chopped pecans, for garnish

1. In a medium bowl, toss together the oat bran, flour, baking soda and sugar. Using a wooden spoon, stir in the banana and vanilla until well distributed. Add the yogurt, stirring until incorporated.

2. Heat a large skillet, preferably cast iron, over moderate heat until hot. Meanwhile, in a separate medium bowl, beat the egg whites with an electric hand mixer until soft peaks form. Beat one-third of the egg whites into the batter to lighten it. Fold in the remaining egg whites with a rubber spatula. Fold in the melted butter until just incorporated.

3. Ladle a few ¼-cup scoops of batter into the heated skillet, spreading the batter into 3½- to 4-inch circles. Cook

until bubbles appear on the surface, about 1 minute. Flip and cook until the bottoms are well browned, about 1 minute longer. Repeat with the remaining batter. Serve hot, with warm maple syrup and a sprinkling of pecans if desired.

—*Tracey Seaman*

• • •

CORNMEAL BREAKFAST PANCAKES WITH FRESH CORN KERNELS

Tender corn kernels pair nicely with crunchy cornmeal in this recipe. Serve these pancakes with butter, warm maple syrup and crisp, thickly sliced bacon.

—— *Makes About 18 Pancakes* ——
1½ cups yellow cornmeal
¼ cup unbleached all-purpose flour
2 tablespoons sugar
1 teaspoon baking soda
½ teaspoon salt
2 cups buttermilk
2 tablespoons unsalted butter, melted
1 egg, separated
1¼ cups fresh corn kernels (from 3 to 4 ears of corn)
1 teaspoon vegetable oil

1. In a medium bowl, combine the cornmeal, flour, sugar, baking soda and salt. Make a well in the center and pour in the buttermilk, butter and egg yolk. Working quickly, stir just until the ingredients are moistened. Add the corn kernels and stir until just combined (the batter should not be perfectly smooth).

2. Beat the egg white until stiff but not dry. Fold the beaten white into the cornmeal batter.

3. On a griddle or in a large heavy skillet, heat the oil over moderate heat. Working in batches, spoon about 3 tablespoons of the batter for each pancake onto the griddle; space the pancakes about 1 inch apart to allow for spreading. Cook until bubbles form on the surface of the pancakes, about 2 minutes. Turn with a spatula and cook until golden brown on the second side, about 2 minutes longer. Transfer the pancakes to a platter; cover to keep warm while cooking the remaining batches.

—Richard Sax

• • •

GINGERBREAD CORN CAKES

These soft, spicy hotcakes were made to be eaten with apples in any form: baked, as skillet-fried rings or as applesauce. If you can track down some boiled cider to drizzle on them, all the better. For a special breakfast or brunch, finish them off with a mound of sweetened whipped cream and a dusting of nutmeg.

——Makes About 18 Pancakes——
1 cup whole wheat flour
¼ cup unbleached all-purpose flour
¼ cup yellow cornmeal
2½ teaspoons baking powder
1 teaspoon ground ginger
½ teaspoon cinnamon
½ teaspoon ground cloves
½ teaspoon freshly grated nutmeg
½ teaspoon salt
2 eggs
¼ cup unsulphured molasses
1¾ cups milk
¼ cup vegetable oil

1. In a large bowl, combine the whole wheat flour, all-purpose flour, cornmeal, baking powder, ginger, cinnamon, cloves, nutmeg and salt. Toss to mix well. In a separate bowl, beat the eggs lightly. Whisk in the molasses, milk and oil.

2. Make a well in the center of the dry ingredients and pour in the liquid mixture. Whisk several times, just until

smooth. Do not overmix. The batter will be thin at this point; it will thicken as it stands. Let rest for 5 minutes.

3. Preheat a griddle or a large skillet (preferably cast iron) over moderate heat until a drop of water skitters on the surface. Lightly oil the griddle. Ladle a few ¼-cup scoops of batter onto the griddle, allowing them room to spread. Cook over moderate heat until the bubbles burst on the surface, about 1 minute. Flip the pancakes and cook until golden underneath, about 1 minute longer. Continue with the remaining batter, serving the pancakes hot off the griddle.

—Ken Haedrich

• • •

BLUEBERRY BUCKWHEAT PANCAKES

After many attempts, I've finally created a pillowy soft and delicate pancake with just the right buckwheat flavor. For the most even distribution of the blueberries, it's best to drop them individually onto the pancakes once they're on the griddle, before you flip them. If using frozen berries, thaw first by spreading them on several layers of paper towels on a baking sheet. Otherwise, the excess moisture tends to make the pancakes soggy. Serve these pancakes with fresh blueberry sauce or a 3-to-1 mix of yogurt and dark maple syrup as accompaniment.

——Makes About 16 Pancakes——
1 cup whole wheat flour
½ cup buckwheat flour
2 teaspoons baking powder
½ teaspoon baking soda
¼ cup (packed) dark brown sugar
½ teaspoon salt
2 eggs
1½ cups buttermilk
1 cup milk
4 tablespoons unsalted butter,
*   melted, or ¼ cup vegetable oil*
1 teaspoon finely grated lemon zest
1 cup blueberries, fresh or frozen

1. In a large bowl, toss together the whole wheat flour, buckwheat flour, baking powder, baking soda, brown sugar and salt. In a separate bowl, beat the eggs lightly. Whisk in the buttermilk, milk, butter and lemon zest.

2. Make a well in the center of the dry ingredients and pour in the liquid mixture. Stir with a few easy strokes, just until blended. Do not overmix. Let the batter rest for 10 minutes.

3. Preheat a griddle or a large heavy skillet (preferably cast iron) over moderate heat until a drop of water skitters on the surface. Lightly oil the griddle. Stir the batter 3 or 4 times, then ladle a few ¼-cup scoops of batter onto the griddle, allowing them room to spread. Cook over moderate heat for about 30 seconds. Distribute 1 scant tablespoon of the blueberries evenly on top of each pancake. When bubbles burst on the surface of each pancake, flip them and cook until golden underneath, about 1 minute longer. Continue with the remaining batter, serving the pancakes hot off the griddle.

—Ken Haedrich

• • •

LEMON-PECAN FEATHER CAKES

This is the only pancake in my entire repertoire that I can still eat eight of in one sitting. They're not called feather cakes for nothing! As well as being extremely light, they're intensely flavored from the toasted pecans and the lemon zest. A free-standing electric mixer can make the critical egg beating a snap. It's very important that these pancakes be cooked as soon as they are ready because the batter quickly deflates.

——Makes About 16 Pancakes——
½ cup pecan halves
2 tablespoons sugar
¾ cup whole wheat flour

1/4 cup unbleached all-purpose flour
1 teaspoon baking soda
1/2 teaspoon salt
1 tablespoon fresh lemon juice
1 cup light cream or half-and-half
4 eggs—2 whole, 2 separated
1/2 teaspoon vanilla extract
1 teaspoon finely grated lemon zest

1. Preheat the oven to 350°. Spread the pecan halves on an ungreased baking sheet and toast until fragrant, 10 to 12 minutes. Transfer to a plate and let cool.

2. In a blender or food processor, pulverize the pecans with 2 teaspoons of the sugar to the consistency of fine meal. In a large bowl, combine the whole wheat flour and all-purpose flour, baking soda, salt and pecan meal. Toss to mix well.

3. In a small bowl, mix together the lemon juice and the cream. Set aside.

4. In a medium mixer bowl, combine the 2 whole eggs, 2 egg yolks and the remaining 4 teaspoons sugar. Beat with an electric mixer on high speed for 8 to 10 minutes, until the eggs are at least quadrupled in volume and thick enough to hold a crease made by a rubber spatula for 5 to 10 seconds.

5. Stir in the reserved lemon-cream, the vanilla and the lemon zest until just blended. Do not overmix. Make a well in the center of the dry ingredients and pour in the liquid mixture. Stir just until no dry streaks are visible.

6. In a small mixer bowl, beat the egg whites until they form soft peaks. Carefully fold them into the batter.

7. Preheat a griddle or large heavy skillet (preferably cast iron) over moderate heat until a drop of water skitters on the surface. Lightly oil the griddle. Stir the batter 3 or 4 times, then ladle a few 1/4-cup scoops of batter onto the griddle, allowing them room to spread. Cook over

moderate heat until the bubbles burst on the surface, about 1 minute. Flip the pancakes and cook until golden underneath, about 1 minute longer. Continue with the remaining batter, serving the pancakes hot off the griddle.

—Ken Haedrich

• • •

THREE-GRAIN FLAPJACKS

These have to be my favorite mixed-grain pancakes. They are fortified by rolled oats and are surprisingly soft in texture.

——*Makes About 18 Pancakes*——
3/4 cup old-fashioned rolled oats
1 cup lukewarm milk
1/2 cup stone-ground cornmeal
1/2 cup buttermilk
1/4 cup unsulphured molasses
1/4 cup vegetable oil
2 eggs
1 1/4 cups whole wheat flour
2 teaspoons baking powder
1/2 teaspoon baking soda
1/2 teaspoon salt

1. In a small bowl, combine the oats and milk; let stand for 10 minutes.

2. Put 1 cup of cold water into a small heavy saucepan. Whisk in the cornmeal and bring to a boil over high heat, whisking constantly. When the mixture starts to thicken, reduce the heat slightly. Cook, stirring, until quite thick, 2 to 3 minutes. Scrape the cornmeal mixture into a medium bowl and let cool for 5 minutes.

3. Whisk in the buttermilk, molasses and oil. Whisk in the eggs, one at a time. Stir in the reserved softened oats.

4. In a large bowl, toss together the whole wheat flour, baking powder, baking soda and salt. Make a well in the center and pour in the wet mixture. With a wooden spoon, beat just until a few dry streaks remain. Let the batter stand for 10 minutes.

5. Preheat a griddle or large heavy skillet (preferably cast iron) over moderate heat until a drop of water skitters on the surface. Lightly oil the griddle. Stir the batter 3 or 4 times, then ladle a few 1/4-cup scoops of batter onto the griddle, allowing them room to spread. Cook over moderate heat until the bubbles burst on the surface, about 1 minute. Flip the pancakes and cook until golden underneath, about 1 minute longer. Continue with the remaining batter, serving the pancakes hot off the griddle.

—Ken Haedrich

• • •

ORANGE, RYE, FENNEL SEED CAKES

In these light and cakey pancakes, the coarsely ground rye flour lends a wholesome flavor and a nubby texture. But the real surprise here is how the flavors of the orange and fennel perfectly complement one another. The taste of these cakes is even further enhanced when you serve them with honey-orange sauce.

——*Makes About 18 Pancakes*——
1 cup whole wheat flour
1/2 cup rye flour
2 1/2 teaspoons baking powder
1/2 teaspoon salt
1/2 teaspoon fennel seeds, crushed
3 eggs
1 3/4 cups milk
1/4 cup vegetable oil
Finely grated zest of 1 large orange
1 tablespoon sugar
Slices of orange, for garnish

1. In a large bowl, combine the whole wheat flour, rye flour, baking powder, salt and crushed fennel seeds. Mix well. In a separate bowl, beat the eggs well with a whisk. Add the milk, oil, orange zest and sugar; whisk until well blended.

2. Make a well in the dry ingredients, pour in the liquid mixture and stir just until blended. Do not overmix. Let rest for 5 minutes.

3. Preheat a griddle or a large heavy skillet (preferably cast iron) over moderate heat until a drop of water skitters on the surface. Lightly oil the griddle. Stir the batter 3 or 4 times, then ladle a few ¼-cup scoops of batter onto the griddle, allowing them room to spread. Cook over moderate heat until the bubbles burst on the surface, about 1 minute. Flip the pancakes and cook until golden underneath, about 1 minute longer. Continue with the remaining batter, serving the pancakes hot off the griddle, garnished with half-moon slices of orange.

—*Ken Haedrich*

• • •

WHOLE WHEAT BANANA NUT PANCAKES

These are a favorite of my wife, Karen. She eats them with sliced bananas, a lot of maple syrup, a dollop of sour cream and a sprinkle of nutmeg.

—— *Makes 12 to 16 Pancakes* ——
1 very large ripe banana, thickly sliced
¾ cup milk
½ cup sour cream
2 eggs
2 tablespoons sugar
4 tablespoons unsalted butter, melted, or ¼ cup vegetable oil
1 cup whole wheat flour
1 teaspoon baking powder
½ teaspoon baking soda
½ teaspoon salt
¼ teaspoon freshly grated nutmeg
½ cup finely chopped walnuts, pecans or other nuts

1. In a blender, combine the banana, milk and sour cream and blend until smooth, about 1 minute.

2. In a medium bowl, beat the eggs until frothy. Whisk in the banana mixture, sugar and melted butter.

3. In a separate bowl, toss together the whole wheat flour, baking powder, baking soda, salt and nutmeg. Make a well in the center of the dry ingredients and pour in the liquid mixture. With a wooden spoon, beat just until a few dry streaks remain. Do not overmix. Let stand for at least 5 minutes, then fold in the nuts.

4. Preheat a griddle or heavy skillet (preferably cast iron) over moderate heat until a drop of water skitters on the surface. Lightly oil the griddle. Stir the batter 3 or 4 times, then ladle a few ¼-cup scoops of batter onto the griddle, allowing them room to spread. Cook over moderate heat until the bubbles burst on the suface, about 1 minute. Flip the pancakes and cook until golden underneath, about 1 minute longer. Continue with the remaining batter, serving the pancakes hot off the griddle.

—*Ken Haedrich*

• • •

BLUEBERRY CORNMEAL MUFFINS

These are tender, light muffins, with just a slight crunch of cornmeal. I recommend using a nonstick muffin pan—an excellent kitchen investment.

—— *Makes 12 Muffins* ——
1½ cups sifted unbleached all-purpose flour
½ cup yellow cornmeal
⅓ cup sugar
1 tablespoon baking powder
1 teaspoon baking soda
¼ teaspoon salt
1 cup buttermilk
3 eggs
4 tablespoons unsalted butter, melted
1½ cups (½ pint) blueberries

1. Preheat the oven to 425°. Generously butter 12 muffin cups, 2½ inches in diameter. (If you prefer, butter only the upper rims of the muffin cups and line with paper liners.)

2. In a medium bowl, sift together the flour, cornmeal, sugar, baking powder, baking soda and salt.

3. In a medium bowl, whisk together the buttermilk, eggs and melted butter until smooth. Make a well in the center of the dry ingredients and pour in the buttermilk mixture. Stir to combine, using no more than 15 to 20 strokes; streaks of flour may remain.

4. Add the berries and stir quickly until the mixture is just blended but still lumpy. Do not overmix.

5. Fill each muffin cup about half full with batter. Place in the middle of the oven and reduce the heat to 400°. Bake for 20 to 25 minutes, until the muffins are light golden on top.

6. Place the muffin pan on a wire rack to cool slightly, 1 to 2 minutes. Remove the muffins from the pan and serve warm with sweet butter.

—*Richard Sax*

• • •

Marie-Claude Gracia's Chocolate Cake (p. 238).

Below, Peach Upside-Down Cake (p. 234). Near right, Baked Nebraska (p. 203). Far right, Fudge Pie (p. 226).

**Left, Montrachet's Banana Tartlets with Caramel Sauce
(p. 230). Above, Blueberry Pie (p. 225).**

RASPBERRY MUFFINS

If you have a few berries left in the basket, beat them into softened sweet butter and serve it alongside the warm muffins for an extra treat.

─────── *Makes 12 Muffins* ───────
1¾ cups all-purpose flour
¾ cup yellow cornmeal
⅔ cup sugar
1 tablespoon baking powder
2 eggs
½ cup milk
5 tablespoons unsalted butter, melted
1 to 1¼ cups small raspberries (about ½ pint)

1. Preheat the oven to 400°. Generously butter 12 muffin cups, 2½ inches in diameter.

2. In a bowl, mix together the flour, cornmeal, sugar and baking powder.

3. In a medium bowl, whisk together the eggs, milk and melted butter. Pour over the dry ingredients and fold lightly with a spatula until just blended; there may be some dry streaks in the batter.

4. Spoon half of the batter into the muffin cups and, with a dampened finger, make a slight depression in each one. Place 5 or 6 raspberries in each depression, avoiding the cup sides. Spoon the remaining batter on top, dividing it evenly among the 12 cups. Do not spread the batter; it will even out as it bakes.

5. Bake the muffins for 20 minutes, until golden and well risen. Remove from the pan while still hot and serve warm or at room temperature.

—Diana Sturgis

• • •

DOUBLE-CORN AND CHEDDAR MUFFINS

Like all muffins, these are best eaten hot from the oven. They are *the* thing to serve with a bowl of spicy chili or a hearty soup and salad. If your corn kernels are tender, you can fold them into the batter uncooked. But if they happen to be a bit tough, better cook them briefly in a little water, drain and cool before proceeding. You can substitute frozen, thawed corn kernels. Just be sure to pat them dry.

─────── *Makes 12 Muffins* ───────
1½ cups unbleached all-purpose flour
⅔ cup yellow cornmeal, preferably stone-ground
2 tablespoons sugar
1 tablespoon baking powder
1 teaspoon salt
2 eggs
1 cup milk
5 tablespoons unsalted butter, melted
1 cup corn kernels
1 cup grated Cheddar cheese (about 4 ounces)

1. Preheat the oven to 400°. Butter 12 muffin cups, 2½ inches in diameter.

2. In a large mixing bowl, combine the flour, cornmeal, sugar, baking powder and salt.

3. In a separate bowl, beat the eggs lightly. Then whisk in the milk and melted butter. Make a well in the dry ingredients, pour in the liquids and stir gently, just until combined.

4. Fold in the corn and cheese. Divide the batter among the 12 cups, filling each about three-quarters full.

5. Bake the muffins in the middle of the oven for about 25 minutes, until lightly browned. Transfer the muffin pan to a rack and let cool for several minutes before removing the muffins.

—Ken Haedrich

• • •

BLUEBERRY OAT BRAN SCONES

These muffinlike scones are a welcome snack anytime. Serve with homemade jam or honey butter.

─────── *Makes 12 Scones* ───────
1½ cups oat bran
1½ cups all-purpose flour
⅓ cup (packed) light brown sugar
2 teaspoons baking powder
1 teaspoon cream of tartar
1 stick (4 ounces) cold unsalted butter, cut into tablespoons
2 eggs
⅓ cup plain yogurt
1 teaspoon vanilla extract
1½ cups (½ pint) blueberries

1. Preheat the oven to 400°. In a medium bowl, toss together the oat bran, flour, brown sugar, baking powder and cream of tartar. Cut in the butter until crumbly.

2. In a small bowl, lightly beat the eggs with a fork. Blend in the yogurt and vanilla. Stir into the dry ingredients with a fork until the dough just holds together. Stir in the blueberries.

3. Transfer the dough to a large ungreased baking sheet and pat lightly into a 10-inch circle. Using a large knife, cut through the dough to divide into 12 equal wedges, wiping the knife in between cuts.

Custard-Filled Phyllo (p. 202).

4. Bake for 20 to 25 minutes, until the scones are firm and golden brown and a tester inserted in the center comes out clean.

—Tracey Seaman

• • •

OATMEAL SCONES WITH BLUEBERRIES AND CREAM

These oatmeal scones are also delicious served warm with jam or sweet butter in place of the blueberries and whipped cream.

——— *Makes 10 to 12 Scones* ———
1 cup old-fashioned rolled oats
¾ cup all-purpose flour
3 tablespoons plus 2 teaspoons granulated sugar
1 teaspoon baking powder
6 tablespoons cold unsalted butter, cut into pieces
¾ cup plus 1 tablespoon heavy cream
1½ teaspoons milk
1 cup fresh blueberries or 1 package (9 ounces) frozen
1 tablespoon Grand Marnier or other orange liqueur
2 teaspoons cornstarch
1 tablespoon confectioners' sugar

1. Preheat the oven to 350°. In a food processor, combine the oatmeal, flour, 3 tablespoons of the granulated sugar and the baking powder; process until blended, about 30 seconds.

2. Add the butter and turn the machine quickly on and off until the mixture resembles coarse meal, about 30 seconds. Sprinkle 5 tablespoons of the heavy cream over the mixture and turn the machine on and off until the dough just begins to cohere and form a ball, 10 to 15 seconds.

3. Remove the dough to a work surface and pat into a 6-inch disk. Roll out the dough into a circle about ½ inch thick. Using a 2½-inch biscuit cutter, stamp out 10 rounds. Roll out any scraps of dough and stamp out 1 to 2 additional scones.

4. Arrange the scones on a lightly greased baking sheet. Brush the tops with the milk and sprinkle with the remaining 2 teaspoons granulated sugar. Bake the scones for 15 to 20 minutes or until golden brown. Transfer to a rack to cool.

5. Meanwhile, in a small nonreactive saucepan, combine the blueberries, Grand Marnier and cornstarch and bring to a boil, stirring frequently. Simmer until slightly thickened, about 1 minute. Remove from the heat and let cool.

6. In a bowl, beat the remaining ½ cup cream with the confectioners' sugar until stiff peaks form, about 1 minute.

7. Cut the scones in half. Spoon the blueberries over the bottom half of each scone. Top with 1½ tablespoons of the whipped cream and the top half of each scone. Serve immediately.

—Mimi Ruth Brodeur

• • •

BUCKWHEAT SCONES WITH SMOKED SALMON

These flavorful scones are also good served plain with butter.

——— *Makes 10 to 12 Scones* ———
1⅓ cups all-purpose flour
⅔ cup buckwheat flour
1½ teaspoons dill seed
1 teaspoon baking powder
1 teaspoon baking soda
¼ teaspoon salt
6 tablespoons cold unsalted butter, cut into small pieces
⅔ cup milk
4 ounces cream cheese, at room temperature
1½ teaspoons chopped capers
1½ teaspoons fresh lime juice
1 small shallot, minced
¼ teaspoon freshly ground pepper
¾ pound thinly sliced smoked salmon
Dill sprigs and drained capers, for garnish
Lemon wedges, as accompaniment

1. Preheat the oven to 350°. In a food processor, combine the all-purpose flour, buckwheat flour, dill seed, baking powder, baking soda and salt; process until blended, about 30 seconds. Add the butter and turn the machine quickly on and off until the mixture resembles coarse meal, about 45 seconds. Pour in the milk and process until the dough just begins to form a ball, about 30 seconds.

2. On a lightly floured work surface, pat the dough into a 6-inch disk and roll out to form a circle about ½ inch thick. Using a 2½-inch biscuit cutter, cut out 10 rounds. Roll out any scraps of dough and cut out 1 or 2 more scones.

3. Arrange the scones on a greased baking sheet and bake for 15 to 20 minutes, until firm and golden brown. Transfer to a rack to cool.

4. Trim the tops of the scones to form a level surface. In a small bowl, beat the cream cheese until smooth. Add the capers, lime juice, shallot and pepper and beat until well blended.

5. Spread about 1 tablespoon of the cream cheese mixture over each scone. Top with a slice of smoked salmon and garnish with dill and capers. Serve with lemon wedges.

—Mimi Ruth Brodeur

• • •

BRAN SCONES

Serve these high-fiber scones with strawberry jam for breakfast or afternoon tea.

——— *Makes 16 Scones* ———
1³⁄₄ cups all-purpose flour
1¹⁄₂ teaspoons baking powder
¹⁄₂ teaspoon baking soda
¹⁄₄ cup plus 1 tablespoon sugar
6 tablespoons cold unsalted butter,
*   cut into small pieces*
¹⁄₂ cup buttermilk
2 tablespoons plus 2 teaspoons
*   heavy cream*
¹⁄₃ cup All-Bran cereal
Strawberry or raspberry jam, as
*   accompaniment*

1. Preheat the oven to 350°. In a medium bowl, combine the flour, baking powder, baking soda and ¼ cup of the sugar. Cut in the butter until the mixture resembles coarse meal.

2. In a small bowl, stir together the buttermilk, 2 tablespoons of the cream and the cereal. Pour over the flour mixture and mix with a fork until the dough masses together.

3. On a lightly floured work surface, pat the dough into a small disk and roll into a circle about 1 inch thick. Using a 2-inch biscuit cutter, cut the dough into 14 rounds. Roll out any scraps and cut out 1 or 2 additional scones.

4. Arrange the scones on a lightly greased baking sheet. Brush the tops with the remaining 2 teaspoons cream and sprinkle with the remaining 1 tablespoon sugar.

5. Bake for 15 to 20 minutes, or until firm and golden brown. Transfer to a rack to cool. Serve with strawberry jam.

—*Mimi Ruth Brodeur*

• • •

HERREN'S SWEET ROLLS

A great, old, family-run Atlanta café called Herren's closed in 1987 after 53 years of operation. One of its daily specialties was yeast rolls, served at dinner and supper as a Parker House-type of hot bread and at breakfast as a cinnamon sweet roll. Here is the sweet version.

——— *Makes About 18 Rolls* ———
¹⁄₂ cup milk
1 stick (4 ounces) plus 2 tablespoons
*   unsalted butter, melted*
¹⁄₂ cup plus 2 tablespoons sugar
1 envelope (¹⁄₄ ounce) active dry
*   yeast*
¹⁄₂ cup lukewarm water (105° to
*   115°)*
2 to 2¹⁄₄ cups all-purpose flour, sifted
¹⁄₂ teaspoon salt
2 tablespoons cinnamon

1. In a small heavy saucepan, bring the milk to a boil over moderately high heat. Add 2 tablespoons of the butter and 2 tablespoons of the sugar and remove from the heat. Stir until the sugar dissolves. Pour into a large mixing bowl and set aside until lukewarm (105° to 115°).

2. In a small bowl, sprinkle the yeast over the lukewarm water. Stir to mix, then add to the warm milk mixture.

3. Sift 2 cups of the flour with the salt, then add to the yeast mixture, ½ cup at a time. Beat with a wooden spoon until the dough forms a ball, about 5 minutes. Turn the dough out onto a floured surface and let rest for 15 minutes. Then knead the dough until soft and smooth, adding a little more flour if the dough is sticky, about 5 minutes.

4. Transfer the dough to a greased bowl and turn to coat. Cover with a cloth and set in a warm place to rise until doubled in bulk, about 1 hour.

5. On a lightly floured surface, roll out the dough to a rectangle ¼ inch thick

(about 12 by 8 inches). Brush the surface generously with some of the remaining melted butter.

6. Combine the remaining ½ cup sugar with the cinnamon. Sprinkle ⅓ cup of the cinnamon sugar evenly over the buttered dough. Beginning with a long edge, roll up the dough. Slice the roll into ¾-inch-thick rounds.

7. Brush a baking sheet with some of the melted butter and sprinkle on 2 tablespoons of the cinnamon sugar. Lay the cinnamon rolls in the prepared pan, cut-sides up, without crowding. Brush the tops with the remaining melted butter and sprinkle on the remaining cinnamon sugar. Set aside in a warm place until doubled in bulk, about 30 minutes.

8. Preheat the oven to 350°. Bake the cinnamon rolls in the middle of the oven until nicely browned, about 20 minutes. Transfer to a rack to cool.

—*John Egerton*

• • •

SOUR CREAM COFFEE CAKE WITH CHOCOLATE AND WALNUTS

There are few things you can do for your fellow man that will give as much satisfaction as baking a cake and serving it fresh from the oven.

——— *12 Servings* ———
2 cups plus 2 tablespoons all-
*   purpose flour*
³⁄₄ cup plus 2 tablespoons sugar
2 sticks (8 ounces) unsalted butter,
*   at room temperature*
2 teaspoons baking powder
1 teaspoon baking soda

¼ *teaspoon salt*
3 eggs
1 cup sour cream
2 teaspoons vanilla extract
1 cup chopped walnuts (about 4
  ounces)
4 ounces bittersweet chocolate,
  broken into small pieces

1. Preheat the oven to 350°. Butter a 9-inch springform pan. Dust the pan with 2 tablespoons each of the flour and sugar and tap out the excess.

2. In a medium mixer bowl, beat the butter with the remaining ¾ cup sugar at high speed until light and creamy, about 7 minutes.

3. In another bowl, combine the remaining 2 cups flour with the baking powder, baking soda and salt. Sift twice.

4. Add ½ cup of the flour mixture to the mixer bowl and blend in on low speed. Beat in 1 of the eggs. Continue to blend in another cup of the flour mixture, ½ cup at a time, alternately with the remaining 2 eggs. Beat in the remaining flour mixture along with the sour cream and vanilla.

5. Using a spatula, thoroughly fold in the chopped walnuts and chocolate pieces. Pour the batter into the prepared baking pan, spread with the spatula and smooth the surface.

6. Bake for 45 to 55 minutes, until the cake begins to shrink from the sides of the pan, the surface cracks slightly and a cake tester inserted into the center comes out clean.

7. Let the cake cool in the pan for 10 minutes, then unmold and transfer to a wire rack. Let stand for at least 2 hours—until completely cool—before serving. *(The coffee cake can be made up to 1 week ahead; wrap well and freeze. Defrost in the wrapping overnight.)*

—*Irena Chalmers*

• • •

BANANA BREAD

Fruit and nut loaves have always been a common offering in southern kitchens where bread making is practiced. Cranberries, dates, figs and pumpkins are among the most popular flavorings, and even zucchini makes a fine loaf. But the all-time favorite, in my book, is this soft, moist banana bread. Use bananas that are so overripe that the skin is black and the fruit is very mushy.

——— *Makes One 9-Inch Loaf* ———
1 stick (4 ounces) unsalted butter, at
  room temperature
1 cup sugar
2 eggs, lightly beaten
3 large, very ripe bananas, mashed
2 cups all-purpose flour
1 teaspoon baking soda
1 cup coarsely chopped pecans
  (about 4 ounces)

1. Preheat the oven to 325°. Grease a 9-by-5-by-3-inch loaf pan and line the bottom with waxed paper.

2. In a large bowl, beat the butter and sugar until light and fluffy. Blend in the eggs and the mashed bananas. Sift in the flour with the baking soda. Add the pecans and mix lightly until blended.

3. Pour the batter into the prepared loaf pan and bake for 1 hour and 10 minutes, or until a cake tester inserted in the center of the loaf comes out clean. (It may need to bake an additional few minutes, but avoid overbaking. Test the loaf every 5 minutes after the first hour.) Let cool on a rack for 5 minutes, then unmold and let cool completely.

—*John Egerton*

• • •

STEAMED WINTER SQUASH AND DATE-NUT BREAD

This bread reminds me of the harvest moon: big and round, colored a radiant shade of orange. I love it with cream cheese and honey for breakfast or with a brothy soup and green salad for lunch or supper. I like to add dates and walnuts to the batter, but there's plenty of room here for substitutions. Raisins and pecans are nice. So are chopped, dried apricots. Wrapped tightly in plastic, this bread has good keeping qualities. You will need a one-pound coffee can for steaming it.

——— *Makes 1 Loaf* ———
2 cups cubed, peeled butternut
  squash (from a 1-pound squash)
2 tablespoons unsalted butter, at
  room temperature
⅓ *cup honey*
Grated zest of 1 orange
½ *cup yellow cornmeal, preferably*
  stone-ground
½ *cup whole wheat flour*
½ *cup unbleached all-purpose flour*
1½ teaspoons baking powder
¾ *teaspoon salt*
½ *teaspoon cinnamon*
½ *cup chopped pitted dates*
½ *cup chopped walnuts*

1. In a medium saucepan, cover the squash with 4 cups of water. Bring to a boil, cover and reduce the heat to moderately low. Cook until very tender, about 15 minutes; drain.

2. In a blender or food processor, combine the squash with the butter and puree until smooth. Scrape the puree into a mixing bowl and whisk in the honey and orange zest; set aside.

3. Butter the insides of a 1-pound coffee can, including the plastic lid. Pour about 3½ inches of water into a saucepan or stockpot (the pot should be tall enough to accommodate the coffee can standing

DO-AHEAD BRUNCH

With the exception of the mimosas, which should be served chilled and not mixed until just before drinking, everything on this brunch menu is served at room temperature and can be made ahead of time. Serves 10 to 12.

🍸 *Tangerine Mimosas*

Gravlax with Mustard Sauce (p. 13) and Dark Bread

Asparagus Tart à la Bicyclette (p. 193)

Smoked Chicken and Apple Salad (p. 138)

Fresh Pea Salad with Pancetta (p. 143)

Steamed Winter Squash and Date-Nut Bread (p. 192)

Gingerbread Tea Cake (p. 232)

Bran Scones (p. 191)

Fruit Preserves

Cream Cheese

Sweet Butter

Coffee

on a trivet or steaming rack). Put a trivet or rack in the center of the pot, cover and bring to a boil.

4. In a medium bowl, combine the cornmeal, whole wheat flour, unbleached flour, baking powder, salt and cinnamon. Toss well to mix. Toss in the dates.

5. Make a well in the dry ingredients and add the squash puree. Stir just until blended, then fold in the walnuts. Spoon the batter into the prepared coffee can, then put on the lid. Press a double layer of foil over the top and secure it with twine.

6. When the water comes to a boil, reduce the heat to an active simmer. Place the can on the trivet; the water should come about halfway up the sides of the can. Cover the pot and steam the bread until the top is springy to the touch and a cake tester emerges clean, about 1 hour and 40 minutes.

7. Remove the foil and lid and let cool on a rack for 5 minutes. Invert the can and let the bread slide out. Let cool on a rack for at least 15 minutes before slicing with a serrated knife. To store, cool thoroughly, then wrap in plastic.

—*Ken Haedrich*

• • •

GRILLED TORTILLA PACKETS WITH MOZZARELLA AND JAM

These are perfect breakfast sandwiches.

——————— **1 Serving** ———————
2 flour tortillas, 6 inches in diameter
4 slices mozzarella cheese, cut into ¼-inch-thick slices (2 ounces total)
2 teaspoons favorite jam or fruit butter

1. Heat a large griddle or heavy skillet, preferably cast iron, over moderate heat. Heat the tortillas, one at a time, in the skillet until they become soft and pliable, about 30 seconds.

2. On each tortilla, arrange 1 slice of mozzarella in the middle. Spread 1 teaspoon of jam on top of the cheese and top with the remaining cheese. Fold the bottom flap over the cheese, fold in the sides, then roll the tortilla over snugly to secure the top flap. Press lightly to make a slightly flattened packet. *(The packets can be made ahead to this point, wrapped in plastic and kept several hours at room temperature or refrigerated overnight.)*

3. Arrange the packets, seam-side down, in the skillet and grill over moderate heat, turning once, until the tortillas are browned and the cheese is completely melted, about 4 minutes per side.

—*Anne Disrude*

• • •

ASPARAGUS TART A LA BICYCLETTE

Asparagus, nature's deluxe harbinger of spring, is glorious in all its forms. This rich custard tart is delicious warm or at room temperature.

——————— **6 to 8 Servings** ———————
1½ pounds thin asparagus
Caraway Pie Dough (p. 194)
4 ounces cream cheese, cut into small pieces, at room temperature
1 egg yolk
1 cup heavy cream
3 whole eggs
¾ teaspoon salt
½ teaspoon freshly ground white pepper
¼ pound thinly sliced boiled ham, cut into 2-by-⅛-inch strips
⅓ cup freshly grated Parmesan cheese

1. Peel the asparagus stems. Cut the tips to 2½ inches; thinly slice 2½ inches of the stalks. Discard the remainder.

2. In a medium saucepan of boiling water, blanch the asparagus until just tender, about 3 minutes. Drain and rinse under cold water; drain well.

3. Roll out the Caraway Pie Dough to a 12-inch round. Fit into a flour-dusted 10-inch tart pan with a removable bottom. Trim off the excess dough. Prick lightly with a fork and freeze for 10 minutes.

4. Meanwhile, preheat the oven to 425°. In a bowl, blend the cream cheese with the egg yolk. Gradually mix in the cream; the texture will be slightly lumpy. Beat in the whole eggs, one at a time. Blend in the salt and white pepper.

5. Evenly distribute the sliced asparagus stalks and ham over the pastry. Pour in half of the custard mixture. Bake on the lowest shelf of the oven for 15 minutes.

6. Remove the tart from the oven and pour in the remaining custard. Arrange the asparagus tips around the pie like the spokes of a wheel. Sprinkle the Parmesan cheese over the top.

7. Reduce the oven temperature to 375°. Bake the tart on the bottom shelf of the oven for 40 minutes, or until a skewer inserted in the center comes out clean. Let the tart rest for 15 minutes before serving.

— *W. Peter Prestcott*

• • •

CARAWAY PIE DOUGH

Makes a
Single 10-Inch Tart Shell
1 1/2 cups all-purpose flour
1/8 teaspoon salt
1/2 teaspoon caraway seeds
5 tablespoons cold unsalted butter, cut into tablespoons
2 tablespoons cold vegetable shortening, cut into tablespoons
2 to 3 tablespoons ice water

1. In a food processor, combine the flour, salt and caraway seeds. Process for 3 seconds. Add the butter and shortening and process, turning the machine quickly on and off, until the mixture resembles oatmeal.

2. With the machine on, pour in 2 tablespoons of the ice water and process just until the dough begins to mass together; do not overprocess. Add more water if the pastry does not mass together. Gather the dough into a ball and pat into a 6-inch disk. Cover with waxed paper and refrigerate until firm.

—*W. Peter Prestcott*

• • •

PIPERADE

If you have mastered the skill of making scrambled eggs, you will be able to toss off a piperade with no difficulty at all.

12 Servings
3 tablespoons vegetable oil or light olive oil
2 large Bermuda onions, halved and thinly sliced
2 medium green bell peppers, cut into 1/4-inch strips
2 medium red bell peppers, cut into 1/4-inch strips
2 medium yellow bell peppers, cut into 1/4-inch strips
1 pint cherry tomatoes, halved
1 pound baked ham, cut into 1/2-inch dice
Fluffy Scrambled Eggs (p. 195)

1. In a large skillet, heat the oil over moderate heat. Add the onions and cook until softened but not browned, about 5 minutes. Stir in the green, red and yellow bell peppers and cook until crisp-tender but still brightly colored, about 8 minutes. *(The recipe can be made to this point up to 2 hours before serving; set aside at room temperature.)*

2. Add the tomatoes and ham to the skillet and cook over moderately low heat until just warm. Do not overcook (the tomatoes should retain their shape).

3. Arrange the Fluffy Scrambled Eggs on a warmed serving dish. Form a trough in the middle of the eggs and fill with the warm vegetables and ham.

—*Irena Chalmers*

• • •

KEDGEREE

This is one of those ancient dishes that over the course of time have achieved a certain mystique. It is customarily found within one of the covered silver dishes arrayed on the English hunt table. After the horsey crowd and their hounds have been chasing around the countryside in search of an elusive fox, a dish of kedgeree can turn out to be the real prize.

Though the fish of choice is traditionally finnan haddie, or smoked haddock, any firm-fleshed smoked fish—such as whitefish or sturgeon—works well. Look for these in specialty food stores.

12 Servings
1 cup rice
1 teaspoon salt
1/2 pound smoked haddock (see headnote)
1 cup cold milk
2 tablespoons unsalted butter
2 medium onions, finely chopped
2 teaspoons curry powder
1/4 cup heavy cream
2 tablespoons fresh lemon juice
2 cups freshly shelled peas or 1 package (10 ounces) frozen peas, cooked and drained
3 hard-cooked eggs, chopped
Freshly ground pepper

1. In a medium saucepan, combine the rice, salt and 2 cups of cold water. Bring to a boil over moderately high heat. Reduce the heat to low, cover and simmer for 20 minutes. Transfer the rice to a large saucepan and fluff with a fork.

2. Meanwhile, place the smoked haddock in a small skillet just large enough to accommodate it. Add the milk and simmer, uncovered, for 5 minutes. Remove the fish with a slotted spatula and drain on paper towels. Strain the milk through a sieve and reserve. Break the fish into 1-inch pieces and add to the rice.

3. In a medium saucepan, melt the butter. Add the onions and cook over low heat until softened but not browned, about 10 minutes.

4. Stir in the curry powder until blended. Add the reserved milk and the cream. Simmer over moderately low heat, uncovered, until the liquid is reduced to ½ cup, about 15 minutes.

5. Stir into the rice. Stir the lemon juice and peas into the rice. The mixture will appear rather moist at this point, but the rice will absorb the liquid as it stands. *(The recipe can be made to this point up to 2 hours before serving; let stand, covered, at room temperature.)*

6. Cover and cook the kedgeree over moderately low heat, stirring often, until heated through, about 10 minutes, or reheat in a microwave. Stir in the chopped eggs and season with pepper to taste. Transfer to a warm platter and serve at once.

—Irena Chalmers

• • •

POPOVERS FILLED WITH MUSHROOMS AND BACON

The response to fresh-out-of-the-oven popovers is similar to that brought on by being served a soufflé. This may be because, at their peak, both are like castles in the air, and there is no time to hang around admiring their architecture. They must be eaten at once while they are still hot properties.

———— *12 Servings* ————
1½ cups milk
3 eggs
1½ tablespoons unsalted butter, melted
1½ cups sifted all-purpose flour
½ teaspoon salt
Mushrooms and Bacon (at right)

1. Preheat the oven to 450°. Oil 12 three-ounce muffin cups, preferably cast iron, and place in the oven for 10 minutes until very hot.

2. In a medium bowl, combine the milk, eggs and melted butter. Whisk in the flour and salt until combined. Divide the batter among the muffin cups, filling each three-quarters full.

3. Bake for 15 minutes. Without opening the oven door, lower the temperature to 400°. Continue baking for 15 minutes longer, until the popovers have puffed and doubled in size. They will be firm and nicely browned.

4. Make a well in the center of each popover and fill with the hot Mushrooms and Bacon. Transfer the filled popovers to a warmed serving platter or serve them in their muffin cups.

—Irena Chalmers

• • •

FLUFFY SCRAMBLED EGGS

This may appear mad on the surface, when nowadays two eggs are considered more than enough for one person for a month. I have added a few extra not only because they will most certainly be eaten but also because a generous quantity of eggs in a beautiful dish is one of the most comforting sights at the start of the day.

———— *12 Servings* ————
1½ sticks (6 ounces) unsalted butter
30 eggs
¾ cup milk
Salt and freshly ground pepper
⅓ cup minced fresh chives (optional)

1. In a large flameproof casserole (or in 2 batches, using 2 skillets), melt the butter over moderate heat.

2. Meanwhile, in a large bowl, whisk together the eggs, milk, salt and pepper to taste and ¼ cup of the minced chives until the egg whites are thoroughly incorporated.

3. Add the eggs to the casserole. Using a spatula or large spoon to stir, slowly scramble the eggs over moderate heat for 8 to 10 minutes, or until they are cooked to your liking. Garnish with the remaining 4 teaspoons minced chives.

—Irena Chalmers

• • •

MUSHROOMS AND BACON

This delicious combination works just as well topping toasted English muffin halves as it does filling popovers.

———— *12 Servings* ————
1 pound thick-sliced bacon, cut into 1- inch pieces
4 tablespoons unsalted butter
3 small onions, finely chopped
1 pound white button mushrooms, thinly sliced
½ pound fresh shiitake mushrooms, stems removed, caps thinly sliced

1. In a large heavy skillet, cook the bacon over moderately high heat until crisp, about 5 minutes. Remove with a slotted spoon and drain on paper towels. Pour off the bacon fat.

2. Add the butter and onions to the skillet and cook over moderately high heat, stirring, until softened but not browned, about 5 minutes.

3. Add the button and shiitake mushrooms and cook until tender and the juices in the pan have completely evaporated, about 8 minutes. *(The recipe can be made to this point up to 1 hour before serving. Set aside at room temperature.)*

4. When ready to serve, toss the reserved bacon with the mushrooms and onions in the skillet. Cook, stirring over moderately low heat until heated through, about 8 minutes.

—Irena Chalmers

• • •

DESSERTS

PEAR FLOATING ISLAND

Islands of molded pear puree float in raspberry sauce for a light and refreshing dessert with pure fruit flavor.

──────── *8 Servings* ────────
1½ pounds pears, such as Comice
Juice of 1 large lemon
⅔ cup sugar
1 envelope unflavored gelatin
2 packages (10 ounces each) frozen
*   raspberries in light syrup, thawed*

1. Peel the pears, reserving the skins. Halve the pears lengthwise. In a medium saucepan, place the pear halves, peelings, lemon juice, ⅓ cup of the sugar and 4 cups of cold water. Bring to a boil over high heat. Reduce the heat to moderate and cook until the pears are very tender, about 15 minutes. Remove from the heat and let cool to room temperature. Refrigerate in the poaching liquid until chilled, about 2 hours.

2. Drain the pears, reserving ⅓ cup of the poaching liquid. Discard the peelings. Quarter and core the pears, then coarsely chop. In a blender, combine the pears with the reserved poaching liquid and the remaining ⅓ cup sugar. Blend to a smooth puree and transfer to a bowl.

3. In a small saucepan, warm ⅔ cup of the pear puree over moderate heat until hot but not boiling, 1 to 2 minutes. Remove from the heat, sprinkle the gelatin over the puree and stir until the gelatin is completely dissolved. Stir this mixture into the remaining pear puree in the bowl until blended.

4. Set the bowl of puree in a larger bowl half-filled with ice and water. With an electric mixer, whip the puree at high speed until thick, about 5 minutes.

5. Line a 4-cup bowl with enough plastic wrap to leave 3 inches overhanging. Pour the puree into the lined bowl

and smooth the surface with a spatula. Fold the overhanging plastic wrap over the puree and refrigerate until set, at least 2 hours or overnight.

6. Drain the raspberries, reserving ½ cup of the syrup. Place the raspberries and the reserved syrup in a blender and puree until smooth. Strain the puree through a fine-mesh sieve to remove the seeds. Refrigerate until cold.

7. At serving time, fold back the plastic wrap from the pear mold and center a plate over the bowl. Turn out the mold and peel off the plastic wrap. Cut the pear mold into 8 wedges and serve on individual plates in a pool of the raspberry sauce.

—*Michel Richard, Citrus,*
Los Angeles

• • •

MERINGUE TART

This very simple dessert is meringue baked in a springform to create a tart shell, which is then filled with whipped cream flavored with toasted pecans.

──────── *6 Servings* ────────
1 cup chopped pecans or walnuts
½ cup granulated sugar
½ cup confectioners' sugar
3 egg whites
1 cup heavy cream, chilled
1 teaspoon vanilla extract
Grated semisweet chocolate, for
*   garnish*

1. Preheat the oven to 300°. Coat a 9-inch springform pan with nonstick cooking spray.

2. Spread the nuts on a baking sheet and bake for about 15 minutes, until lightly toasted. Set aside to let cool.

3. In a small bowl, combine the granulated and confectioners' sugar. In a large bowl, beat the egg whites until soft peaks form. Gradually beat in the combined sugars until stiff peaks form. Scrape the meringue into the prepared pan and smooth the top level. Bake for 1 hour, or until light golden. Let cool on a rack, about 20 minutes.

4. In a large bowl, whip the cream until stiff. Fold in the vanilla and toasted nuts. With the back of a spoon, crush the center of the meringue to form a circular nest (if it has not already settled by itself). Fill with the whipped cream. Smooth the top so it's level with the sides and decorate with the grated chocolate.

5. Refrigerate for 1 hour, or until chilled. Remove the pan sides shortly before serving.

—*Lee Bailey*

• • •

CAFE ANNIE'S BANANA AND TAMARIND SOUFFLE

Robert Del Grande, chef-owner of Houston's Cafe Annie, is a big fan of bananas. This soufflé is his newest banana creation. For a variation, I like to serve a dollop of this soufflé on top of a slice of flourless chocolate cake, topping it off with fresh banana slices and Del Grande's chocolate sauce.

──────── *12 Servings* ────────
4 tablespoons unsalted butter, cut
*   into pieces*
1 cup granulated sugar
2 whole eggs
¼ cup all-purpose flour
1 cup milk
Pinch of coarse (kosher) salt
3 egg yolks plus 9 egg whites
½ teaspoon vanilla extract
3 medium bananas, unpeeled
2½ tablespoons hazelnut liqueur,
*   such as Frangelico*
Grated zest and juice of 1 lime

1½ tablespoons tamarind paste,*
 dissolved in 1 tablespoon water
 and strained
6 tablespoons confectioners' sugar
*Available at Asian markets

1. Preheat the oven to 350°. With 2 tablespoons of the butter, butter 1 dozen 6-ounce custard cups, 3 inches in diameter. Dust with 3 tablespoons of the granulated sugar. Set aside on a baking sheet.

2. In a medium saucepan off the heat, beat the whole eggs, ¾ cup of the granulated sugar and the flour until smooth. In a separate saucepan, bring the milk and salt just to a boil; immediately remove from the heat.

3. Gradually whisk the hot milk into the egg mixture. Place the saucepan over moderate heat and cook, stirring, until the mixture begins to sputter and thicken. It will look, smell and taste like very sweet cream of wheat.

4. Remove from the heat and beat in the egg yolks, one at a time, until smooth. Beat in the remaining 2 tablespoons butter, then the vanilla. Pour into a bowl and press a piece of plastic wrap onto the surface to prevent a skin from forming. Let the soufflé base cool to room temperature. *(The recipe can be made to this point up to 5 days in advance; keep refrigerated.)*

5. Place the unpeeled bananas on a baking sheet in a 350° oven. Bake for 15 to 20 minutes, until the skins split (if it's not visible on top, check the underside of the banana) and there is a sweet caramelized aroma. Scoop out the pulp, discarding the skins, and mash the bananas coarsely in a large bowl.

6. Beat the cooled soufflé base, the hazelnut liqueur, lime zest and juice and tamarind paste into the bananas.

7. In a separate bowl, beat the egg whites until they hold soft peaks. Add the remaining 1 tablespoon granulated sugar to the egg whites and beat until stiff.

8. Using a rubber spatula, fold about one-third of the egg whites into the bananas to lighten them. Fold in the remaining egg whites just until no streaks remain.

9. Spoon the mixture into the prepared dishes and bake for 20 to 25 minutes, until fully risen and golden brown on top. Dust with the confectioners' sugar and serve immediately.

—*Linda Merinoff*

• • •

FRESH PINEAPPLE MOUSSE

Although fresh pineapple will prevent gelatin from gelling, cooking the pineapple beforehand eliminates the problem.

——— *6 to 8 Servings* ———

1 small pineapple—peeled, cored
 and chopped
¼ cup fresh lemon juice
½ cup superfine sugar
1½ envelopes unflavored gelatin
Grated zest of 1 large lemon
4 egg whites
1 cup heavy cream

1. In a food processor, puree the pineapple until smooth. Measure out 2 cups of the puree and reserve the rest for another use.

2. In a small nonreactive saucepan, combine the 2 cups of pineapple puree with the lemon juice, sugar and ½ cup of water. Bring to a boil over moderately high heat. Reduce the heat to low and simmer until the sugar is dissolved, about 5 minutes. Remove from the heat.

3. In a small bowl, sprinkle the gelatin over ½ cup of water and set aside for 5 minutes. Scrape into the hot pineapple syrup. Stir in the lemon zest. Pour into a large bowl and let cool completely.

4. In a medium bowl, beat the egg whites until stiff but not dry. Fold the beaten egg whites into the cooled pineapple syrup.

5. In a separate bowl, beat the cream until soft peaks form. Fold the cream into the pineapple mixture. Transfer the mousse to a 2-quart soufflé dish, cover and refrigerate until set, about 4 hours.

—*Lee Bailey*

• • •

DOUBLE CRANBERRY MOUSSE IN CHOCOLATE-PAINTED TULIP CUPS

Fresh cranberries are cooked with cranberry juice concentrate—a double dose of flavor—folded with whipped cream and served in an edible cup.

——— *12 Servings* ———

¾ cup (6 ounces) frozen cranberry
 juice concentrate
1 package (12 ounces) fresh or
 frozen cranberries
¼ teaspoon cinnamon
⅛ teaspoon allspice
Pinch of ground cloves
1½ cups heavy cream
¼ cup confectioners' sugar
Chocolate-Painted Tulip Cups
 (recipe follows)
Candied orange zest, for garnish

1. In a medium nonreactive saucepan, bring the cranberry juice concentrate to a boil. Add the cranberries, cinnamon, allspice and cloves. Return to a boil, reduce the heat to moderate and simmer, stirring frequently, until the mixture thickens slightly, about 5 minutes. Remove from the heat and let cool. Transfer to a covered container and refrigerate overnight. *(The recipe can be made to this point up to 1 week in advance.)*

2. In a large bowl, beat the heavy cream with the confectioners' sugar until soft peaks form. Fold in 1 cup of the cranberry mixture. *(The recipe can be made to this point up to 1 day ahead. Cover and refrigerate.)*

3. Spoon the cranberry mousse into the Chocolate-Painted Tulip Cups. Place a dollop of the remaining cranberry mixture on top of the mousse. Garnish with a few strips of candied orange zest.

—Bob Chambers

• • •

CHOCOLATE-PAINTED TULIP CUPS

Diana Sturgis, test kitchen director at *Food & Wine*, developed this extremely reliable recipe for tulip cups. Here, the bottoms of the cookie cups are painted with chocolate to keep them from turning soggy after they are filled.

——— *Makes 12 to 14 Cups* ———
⅔ cup sugar
½ cup all-purpose flour
1 to 1½ teaspoons grated orange zest, to taste
1 whole egg plus 2 egg whites
½ teaspoon vanilla extract
4 tablespoons unsalted butter, melted
3 ounces semisweet chocolate

1. In a medium bowl, combine the sugar, flour, orange zest, whole egg, egg whites and vanilla. Beat with a wooden spoon until well mixed. Stir in the butter and 1 tablespoon of water; the batter will be thin. *(The recipe can be made to this point up to 1 day before baking the tulip cups. Refrigerate, tightly covered. Stir before using and add up to 1 tablespoon additional water, if necessary, to restore the consistency.)*

2. Preheat the oven to 425°. Butter a large cookie sheet. Drop 4 separate tablespoons of the batter onto the sheet. Using the back of a spoon, spread into 4-inch circles, spaced about 1 inch apart.

3. Bake in the bottom third of the oven until the cookies have a golden-brown border about 1 inch wide, 6 to 8 minutes. Meanwhile, cut 4 pieces of aluminum foil, each 4 inches square, and set 4 narrow glasses or jars (such as 2-inch-diameter spice jars) bottom-side up on the work surface.

4. Remove the cookies from the oven. Working quickly, scrape a cookie from the sheet with a wide metal spatula and invert it over the spice jar. Cover with a square of foil to protect your hands and mold the soft hot cookie into a tulip shape. Repeat with the remaining cookies. If they harden on the cookie sheet, return to the oven for about 30 seconds to restore pliability. As soon as they are set, remove the shaped tulip cups from their molds and set aside carefully.

5. Scrape the cookie sheet clean and repeat Steps 2 through 4 until all the batter is used.

6. Melt the chocolate in a double boiler over hot—but not boiling—water. With a dry pastry brush, lightly paint the inner bottom and one-third up the inside of each tulip cup with the chocolate. Let cool until the chocolate has hardened. *(The tulips can be made up to 2 days in advance and stored at room temperature in an airtight tin.)*

—Diana Sturgis

• • •

HOMEMADE BUTTERSCOTCH PUDDING

I've tried variations on this pudding, including the use of caramelized white sugar instead of the classic brown. That version was delicious, but it was caramel pudding—not butterscotch. This one has that real butterscotch flavor.

——— *4 to 6 Servings* ———
2½ cups milk
4 egg yolks
¾ cup (firmly packed) dark brown sugar
3 tablespoons cornstarch
2 tablespoons cold unsalted butter, cut into teaspoons
2½ teaspoons vanilla extract
Whipped cream, as accompaniment

1. Rinse a heavy medium saucepan with cold water and shake out the excess (this helps prevent the milk from sticking). Add 2 cups of the milk and bring nearly to a boil over moderate heat.

2. Meanwhile, in a medium bowl, whisk together the egg yolks, brown sugar, cornstarch and remaining ½ cup milk until well blended.

3. Gradually pour ¾ cup of the hot milk into the egg yolk mixture, ¼ cup at a time, whisking vigorously after each addition. Return this mixture to the remaining hot milk in the pan and cook over moderate heat, whisking constantly, until the custard begins to simmer and thickens slightly, about 2 minutes. Remove from the heat and whisk in the butter and vanilla.

4. Strain the pudding into a bowl, scraping it from the bottom of the sieve. Spoon the pudding into individual serving bowls or glass sundae dishes. To avoid pudding "skin," lay a piece of waxed paper or plastic wrap directly on the surface. Let cool on a wire rack for 10 minutes, then refrigerate for at least 30 minutes. *(The pudding can be made up to 2 days in advance.)*

5. Serve with a dollop of whipped cream (lightly flavored with sugar and vanilla if you like).

—*Richard Sax*

• • •

LEMON CUSTARD

This light lemony custard can be served on its own—with fresh raspberries or crisp sugar cookies—or as part of Peach and Ginger Trifle (p. 202), for which it was designed.

———— *Makes About 2½ Cups* ————
Juice and grated zest of 2 large
*   lemons*
1 stick (4 ounces) unsalted butter,
*   cut into tablespoons*
1 cup sugar
4 eggs
1 cup heavy cream

1. In a double boiler, combine the lemon juice, lemon zest, butter and sugar. Stir occasionally over simmering water until the butter melts and the sugar dissolves, about 5 minutes.

2. In a medium bowl, beat the eggs lightly until blended. Gradually whisk about one-third of the hot lemon mixture into the eggs. Stir into the remaining lemon mixture in the double boiler. Continue to cook over the simmering water, stirring constantly, until the curd is thick and steaming, about 3 minutes. Remove from the heat, strain and let cool. Cover with plastic wrap touching the surface. Refrigerate until chilled. *(The recipe can be made to this point up to 1 day ahead.)*

3. Whip the cream until stiff. Fold the whipped cream into the cold lemon curd until completely blended. Refrigerate the custard until serving time.

—*Marion Cunningham*

• • •

CAPPUCCINO CREME CARAMEL

This rich but light dessert forms its own sauce as it cooks. Its creamy texture is ensured by slow, gentle cooking in a water bath.

———— *8 Servings* ————
½ teaspoon lemon juice or cider
*   vinegar*
1 cup sugar
1½ cups heavy cream
1 cup milk
1 tablespoon plus 1 teaspoon instant
*   coffee granules*
6 egg yolks plus 3 egg whites

1. Preheat the oven to 325°. Lightly oil a baking sheet.

2. In a medium saucepan, combine the lemon juice, ½ cup of the sugar and ½ cup of water. Stir over low heat until the sugar has dissolved and the liquid is clear, about 2 minutes. Increase the heat to moderate and bring to a boil. With a wet pastry brush, wash down any splashes of syrup from the sides of the pan to prevent crystallization of the bubbling sugar syrup. Boil without stirring until the syrup is golden, 10 to 15 minutes.

3. Quickly pour half of the caramel into a 9-inch metal pie pan and drizzle the remaining caramel onto the oiled baking sheet. Working quickly, tilt the pan and the baking sheet to spread the caramel as thin as possible.

4. Without rinsing the saucepan, add the cream, milk, coffee granules and ¼ cup of the sugar. Bring the mixture almost to a boil over moderate heat, stirring occasionally.

5. Meanwhile, in a large heatproof bowl, whisk together the egg yolks, egg whites and the remaining ¼ cup sugar until blended. Gradually whisk in the hot cream mixture.

6. Place the prepared pie pan in a larger pan and set near the oven. Pour the custard into the pie pan (it will fill the pan). Place both pans in the middle of the oven and pour about 1 inch of lukewarm water into the larger pan. Bake for 40 minutes, or until the custard is set but still wobbly in the middle.

7. Remove the custard from the oven and set aside until cool to the touch, about 20 minutes. Transfer the pie pan to a rack and let cool to room temperature. Refrigerate until chilled, about 1 hour. *(The recipe can be prepared to this point up to 1 day ahead and refrigerated, covered.)*

8. Loosen the custard from the sides of the pie pan with a knife. Place a large round serving platter on top of the pan and invert to unmold the custard.

9. With a rolling pin, crush the caramel that was drizzled on the baking sheet. Sprinkle it over the center of the custard. Serve chilled. *(The finished dessert can be refrigerated for up to 4 hours before serving.)*

—*Diana Sturgis*

• • •

COLD MARMALADE CUSTARD

This can be made up to two days ahead; keep refrigerated. You can serve it either cold or at room temperature.

———— *6 Servings* ————
1 tablespoon unsalted butter
4 cups milk
1 cup heavy cream
½ cup sugar
2 whole eggs plus 4 egg yolks
1 teaspoon grated lemon zest
½ cup orange marmalade

1. Preheat the oven to 325°. Grease a 2-quart soufflé dish with the butter and set aside.

2. In a small heavy saucepan, combine the milk, cream and sugar. Cook over moderately low heat, until the liquid is heated through, 5 to 10 minutes.

3. Meanwhile, in a medium bowl, beat together the whole eggs and egg yolks until blended. Add the lemon zest to the beaten eggs. Gradually whisk the hot milk into the eggs. Pour the mixture into the buttered soufflé dish.

4. Fill a large roasting pan with water halfway up. Transfer the soufflé dish to the pan and place in the oven. Bake for 50 to 60 minutes, or until the custard is set but still slightly wobbly.

5. In a small saucepan, melt the marmalade. Pour over the top of the warm custard and let cool. Serve at room temperature or chilled.

—*Lee Bailey*

• • •

CUSTARD-FILLED PHYLLO

The foods—such as this *galaktaboureko*—that my mother, Christine Cotsibos, cooked were very, very Mediterranean.

——— *Makes About 25 Pieces* ———
2¹⁄₃ cups sugar
1 cinnamon stick
2 teaspoons fresh lemon juice
3 cups milk
¹⁄₄ cup plus 3 tablespoons Cream of Wheat
5 eggs, separated
1¹⁄₄ teaspoons vanilla extract
³⁄₄ teaspoon baking powder
1 pound phyllo dough
2 sticks (8 ounces) unsalted butter, melted

1. In a small saucepan, combine 2 cups of the sugar, the cinnamon stick, lemon juice and 1½ cups of water. Bring to a boil over moderate heat. Simmer for 10 minutes. Remove from the heat and let cool; then refrigerate, covered, until cold. (*The syrup can be made up to 1 week in advance; keep refrigerated.*)

2. Meanwhile, in a medium saucepan, bring the milk and the remaining ⅓ cup

sugar to a boil over moderately low heat. Gradually add the Cream of Wheat. Cook, stirring constantly, until slightly thickened, about 2 minutes. Transfer to a large bowl and let cool in an ice bath; the mixture will thicken as it cools.

3. In a medium bowl, beat the egg yolks with the vanilla until thick and lemon colored. Fold the egg yolks into the Cream of Wheat.

4. Beat the egg whites with the baking powder until stiff but not dry. Fold the egg whites into the Cream of Wheat mixture until no streaks of white remain. Set the filling aside.

5. Preheat the oven to 350°. Lightly butter a 16-by-12-by-2-inch roasting pan.

6. Lay the stack of phyllo sheets on a work surface and cover with a damp kitchen towel to prevent drying out. Place the melted butter over a pan of warm water to keep it liquid. Lay 1 sheet of phyllo dough in front of you and brush generously with melted butter, covering the entire sheet. Lay the dough in the bottom of the roasting pan, buttered-side up. Continue to layer the pan with the buttered sheets of dough until you have used half the dough.

7. Pour the reserved filling into the phyllo-lined pan and smooth the top. Generously brush another sheet of phyllo with melted butter and place it on the filling. Repeat with the remaining sheets of phyllo dough. Brush the top with the remaining melted butter.

8. Using a sharp knife, cut the dessert crosswise into 2-inch-wide strips, slicing through the top layer of dough and about halfway through the filling. Bake in the middle of the oven for 35 to 40 minutes, or until the crust is golden brown and a toothpick inserted in the center of the filling comes out clean.

9. Transfer the pan to a rack and immediately pour the reserved cold syrup evenly over the top. Let cool. Cut into diamond shapes.

—*Jim Nassikas*

• • •

LIME SPONGE PUDDING

Here's a variation on the old lemon sponge pudding. As this bakes, the top half magically becomes a light cake and the bottom half a creamy custard.

——— *8 Servings* ———
3 eggs, separated
1¹⁄₂ cups milk, scalded
1 cup sugar
¹⁄₂ cup all-purpose flour
2 tablespoons unsalted butter, melted
¹⁄₃ cup lime juice (from about 5 limes)
1 tablespoon grated lime zest

1. Preheat the oven to 325°. In a medium bowl, beat the egg yolks with a whisk. Slowly whisk in the scalded milk. Whisk in the sugar, flour, butter, lime juice and lime zest.

2. In another medium bowl, beat the egg whites until stiff but not dry. Fold the egg whites into the lime mixture. Spoon into eight 6-ounce custard cups.

3. Arrange the cups in a baking pan. Add 1 inch of hot water to the pan and bake for about 15 minutes, until the tops are dry and lightly golden. Serve at room temperature or chilled.

—*Marion Cunningham*

• • •

PEACH AND GINGER TRIFLE

This trifle has an angel food cake flavored with fresh ginger as its base. The fresh, snappy ginger taste goes well with almost any fruit you might choose to use.

——— *12 to 14 Servings* ———
Ginger Angel Food Cake (p. 235)
Lemon Custard (p. 201)
8 peaches, peeled and sliced or 2 packages (1 pound each) frozen unsweetened peach slices, thawed
1 cup heavy cream

1. Using a large serrated knife, slice the Ginger Angel Food Cake horizontally into 3 rings. Cut each ring into 8 wedges. Line the bottom of a 3½- to 4-quart glass serving bowl with 8 of the cake wedges. Spoon about half of the Lemon Custard over the cake.

2. Reserve 1½ cups of the prettiest peach slices for garnish. Arrange the remaining peach slices over the custard.

3. Line the sides of the bowl with 8 more wedges of cake, overlapping if necessary. Place the remaining cake wedges over the peaches and press gently. Spoon the rest of the Lemon Custard over the top and smooth the surface with the back of the spoon. Arrange the reserved peach slices decoratively on top.

4. Refrigerate for at least 6 hours before serving so that the cake softens and the flavors mellow. (*The recipe can be made to this point up to 1 day ahead.*)

5. Whip the cream until stiff. Spoon or pipe over the top of the trifle.

—*Marion Cunningham*

• • •

BAKED NEBRASKAS

This showstopping dessert makes a glamorous ending to any meal. And it is perfect for entertaining since most of the preparation can be done in advance.

6 Servings

2 pints raspberry, lemon or
pineapple sherbet
1 pound cake (10 ounces), sliced
horizontally into thirds
2 tablespoons unsalted butter,
melted
⅓ cup apricot preserves
2 tablespoons dark rum
4 egg whites, at room temperature
½ cup superfine sugar

1. Scoop the sherbet into 6 balls and freeze on a baking sheet.

2. Preheat the broiler. Using a 2¾-inch round cookie cutter, cut the pound cake into 6 rounds.

3. Brush both sides of each round with the melted butter and arrange in a single layer on a baking sheet. Broil the pound cake about 4 inches from the heat, turning once, until lightly browned, about 1 minute on each side. Let cool slightly.

4. In a small heavy saucepan, combine the apricot preserves and rum. Cook over moderate heat, stirring, until melted, about 3 minutes. Strain through a fine sieve and let cool.

5. Spread the apricot glaze on 1 side of the pound cake rounds. Top each with a frozen scoop of sherbet, return to the baking sheet and freeze for 15 minutes.

6. In a large bowl, beat the egg whites until stiff peaks form. Add the sugar, 1 tablespoon at a time, and beat until firm, glossy peaks form. Mound the meringue over the sherbet, making sure that both the sherbet and cake are completely covered. (*The Nebraskas can be prepared to this point up to 2 hours ahead. Return to the freezer. Let soften at room temperature for 5 minutes before proceeding.*)

7. Broil until the tops are browned, about 45 seconds. Serve immediately.

—*W. Peter Prestcott*

• • •

TROPICAL JAVA DESSERT

Frankly, this is an invented dessert inspired by the sweet tooth that most Javanese cultivate. It is easy to assemble and fulfills the requirement for a sweet, cooling dessert after a well-seasoned Indonesian meal. In America, we sometimes refer to coffee as Java, a coincidence that is appropriate here.

12 Servings

2 cups shelled walnuts (about ½
pound)
½ gallon coffee ice cream
¾ cup honey, at room temperature
2 cans lychees (20 ounces each),
drained
Dark rum (optional)

1. Preheat the oven to 350°. Spread out the walnuts on a baking sheet and toast for 10 minutes, or until lightly browned. (*The nuts can be toasted up to 2 days in advance.*)

2. To serve, scoop out a generous portion of the coffee ice cream into 12 individual bowls. Top each serving with about 1 tablespoon honey, 3 or 4 lychees, a generous sprinkling of toasted walnuts and a splash of rum if desired. Serve immediately.

—*Copeland Marks*

• • •

ICE CREAM SANDWICHES

These look pretty close to the ones we all remember from childhood, but if you use excellent cocoa and premium ice cream, they'll taste even better.

Makes 6
Large Sandwiches

2 cups unbleached all-purpose flour
¼ cup plus 3 tablespoons
unsweetened cocoa powder
¼ teaspoon baking powder
¼ teaspoon salt
1 stick (4 ounces) plus 3 tablespoons
unsalted butter, at room
temperature
¾ cup sugar
1 egg
1 teaspoon vanilla extract
2 to 2½ pints vanilla or coffee ice
cream

1. Preheat the oven to 350°. Line a 10½-by-15½-inch jelly-roll pan with parchment paper or aluminum foil with the dull side up, pressing it along the edge and leaving an overhang on all sides. Butter the paper.

2. Sift together the flour, cocoa, baking powder and salt.

3. In an electric mixer, beat the butter at moderately high speed until light and creamy. Scrape down the sides of the bowl. With the mixer on, gradually add the sugar; scrape down the sides of the bowl. Add the egg and vanilla and beat until well blended. Reduce the speed to very low and add the flour mixture. Mix until just barely blended; do not overmix.

4. Turn off the machine and finish mixing by hand with a large rubber spatula. (The dough should have the consistency of modeling clay; if too dry, add a few drops of cold water.)

5. Transfer the dough to the prepared pan. Using your fingers, press the dough over the bottom of the pan to an even thickness. With a toothpick, make holes in the dough at ½-inch intervals.

6. Bake until the cookie is set and the surface looks slightly dry, 8 to 9 minutes. Do not overbake, or it will be brittle. Transfer the pan to a wire rack. Cut the cookie in half crosswise while it is still hot, then let cool completely.

7. Meanwhile, place the ice cream in the refrigerator to soften until spreadable, about 10 minutes.

8. Holding the edges of the parchment paper, lift off the cookie and place it on a work surface. Place a clean sheet of foil in the baking pan. With two spatulas, carefully transfer one of the cookie halves to the foil. Gently spread the ice cream over this half of the cookie in an even layer ¾ inch thick, leaving a narrow border on all sides. With two spatulas, carefully set the second cookie on top and press very gently into place. Smooth the sides. Cover the sandwich with plastic wrap and freeze until the ice cream is hard, about 2 hours.

9. Remove the sandwich from the freezer and let stand for about 5 minutes to make it easier to cut. Dip a large chef's knife in hot water, wipe dry and cut the sandwich into 6 even rectangles. If you are not serving them immediately, wrap each sandwich individually in plastic wrap and store in the freezer for up to a week.

—*Richard Sax*

• • •

CHOCOLATE ICE CREAM SANDWICHES

Slices of good, pure, egg-leavened pound cake are sandwiched with chocolate ice cream and topped with whipped cream and shaved chocolate.

—————*Makes 8 Sandwiches* —————
½-gallon block of chocolate ice cream
2 cups all-purpose flour
½ teaspoon salt
2 sticks (8 ounces) unsalted butter, at room temperature
1⅔ cups sugar
5 eggs, at room temperature
2 teaspoons vanilla extract
Sweetened whipped cream and shaved chocolate, for garnish

1. Cut the block of ice cream in half lengthwise. Reserve one half for another use. Cut the remaining half into 8 slices, about ¾ inch thick. Place the slices of ice cream on a cookie sheet lined with waxed paper and freeze until serving time. *(This can be done up to 2 days ahead; cover with plastic wrap.)*

2. Preheat the oven to 325°. Grease and flour a 9-by-5-by-3-inch loaf pan.

3. Sift together the flour and salt onto a large piece of waxed paper. In a large mixer bowl, beat the butter on high speed until creamy, about 1 minute. Gradually beat in the sugar. Beat until the mixture is light and fluffy, about 3 minutes. Add the eggs 1 at a time, beating well after each addition. Stir in the vanilla.

4. Gradually beat in the sifted flour on medium speed. Increase to high and beat until all the flour is incorporated and the batter is smooth, about 2 minutes.

5. Turn the batter into the prepared loaf pan and smooth the top with a rubber spatula. Bake for 1½ hours, or until a cake tester inserted into the center of the cake comes out clean.

6. Remove from the oven and set on a rack to cool for 5 minutes. Then turn out onto the rack to cool completely. Cut the cake into 16 even slices. *(The cake can be cut several hours in advance; wrap well in plastic wrap.)*

7. To assemble each sandwich, place a slice of ice cream between 2 slices of cake. Garnish with a dollop of whipped cream and some shaved chocolate.

—*Marion Cunningham*

• • •

GREEN GODDESS

Midori is a sweet, melon-based liqueur.

—————*Makes 1 Ice Cream Soda* —————
3 tablespoons Midori liqueur
1 can of gingerale
2 large scoops of pistachio ice cream
Seltzer or club soda (optional)
Whipped cream
Honeydew melon balls on toothpicks

1. In a tall glass, combine the liqueur with enough gingerale to half fill the glass. Stir with a long spoon and leave the spoon in the glass. Add 1 scoop of the ice cream and wait for the fizzing to subside. Pour in a splash of seltzer to cut the sweetness. Add the second scoop of ice cream and drizzle in enough gingerale to fill the glass.

2. Top with a squirt of whipped cream and garnish with the melon balls. Slide in a straw and serve at once.

—*Diana Sturgis*

• • •

CHERRY FLING

Be sure to use a sweet cherry liqueur, such as Cherry Heering, and not kirsch, which is a cherry brandy.

——— *Makes 1 Ice Cream Soda* ———
1 tablespoon cherry liqueur
1 can of black cherry soda
2 large scoops of cherry-vanilla ice cream
Whipped cream
1 fresh cherry on the stem

1. In a tall glass, combine the liqueur with enough cherry soda to half fill the glass. Stir with a long spoon and leave the spoon in the glass. Add 1 scoop of the ice cream and wait for the fizzing to subside. Add the second scoop of ice cream and drizzle in enough cherry soda to fill the glass.

2. Top with a squirt of whipped cream and garnish with the cherry. Slide in a straw and serve at once.

—Diana Sturgis

• • •

ORANGE GRAND SLAM

This soda is made with one of the vanilla ice-cream-and-fruit-sorbet combinations now available. If you can't find it, use 1½ scoops of vanilla ice cream and ½ scoop of orange sorbet per serving.

——— *Makes 1 Ice Cream Soda* ———
1 tablespoon orange liqueur
1 can of orange soda
2 large scoops of vanilla ice cream/orange sorbet
Seltzer or club soda (optional)
Whipped cream
1 orange slice

1. In a tall glass, combine the orange liqueur with enough orange soda to half fill the glass. Stir with a long spoon and leave the spoon in the glass. Add 1 scoop of the ice cream and wait for the fizzing to subside. Pour in a splash of seltzer to cut the sweetness. Add the second scoop of ice cream and drizzle in enough orange soda to fill the glass.

2. Top with a squirt of whipped cream and garnish with the orange slice. Slide in a straw and serve at once.

—Diana Sturgis

• • •

BLACK AND WHITE ICE CREAM SODA

For a slight variation on this soda, use a coffee liqueur, such as Kahlúa, in place of the chocolate liqueur.

——— *Makes 1 Ice Cream Soda* ———
1 tablespoon chocolate liqueur, such as Vandermint
¼ cup Chocolate Syrup (recipe follows)
1 tablespoon milk
1 can of seltzer or club soda
1 large scoop each of vanilla and chocolate ice cream
Whipped cream
A mint sprig or peppermint stick

1. In a tall glass, combine the chocolate liqueur, Chocolate Syrup and milk. Stir in enough seltzer to half fill the glass. Stir with a long spoon and leave the spoon in the glass. Add the vanilla ice cream and wait for the fizzing to subside. Add the chocolate ice cream and drizzle in enough seltzer to fill the glass.

2. Top with a squirt of whipped cream and garnish with a mint sprig. Slide in a straw and serve at once.

—Diana Sturgis

• • •

CHOCOLATE SYRUP

——— *Makes About 1 Cup* ———
½ cup unsweetened cocoa powder
⅔ cup light corn syrup
1 teaspoon vanilla extract

In a saucepan, whisk the cocoa powder and corn syrup with ⅓ cup water. Bring to a boil, stirring constantly, and boil for 30 seconds. Remove from the heat and add the vanilla. Let cool and refrigerate in a covered jar for up to 1 month.

—Diana Sturgis

• • •

WHITE LADY

Amaretto is an Italian liqueur made with bitter almonds. And amaretti are hard Italian macaroons also made with bitter almonds.

——— *Makes 1 Ice Cream Soda* ———
1 tablespoon amaretto liqueur
1 can of cream soda
2 large scoops of vanilla ice cream
Seltzer or club soda (optional)
Whipped cream
1 teaspoon crushed amaretti cookies

1. In a tall glass, combine the amaretto with enough cream soda to half fill the glass. Stir with a long spoon and leave the spoon in the glass. Add 1 scoop of the ice cream and wait for the fizzing to subside. Pour in a splash of seltzer to cut the sweetness. Add the second scoop of ice cream and drizzle in enough cream soda to fill the glass.

2. Top with a squirt of whipped cream and garnish with the amaretti. Slide in a straw and serve at once.

—Diana Sturgis

• • •

MERRY BERRY ICE CREAM SODA

Garnish this soda with either fresh strawberries or raspberries.

——— Makes 1 Ice Cream Soda ———
¼ cup Berry Syrup (recipe follows)
1 can of seltzer or soda water
2 large scoops of strawberry ice cream
Whipped cream
2 fresh berries

1. In a tall glass, combine the Berry Syrup with enough seltzer to half fill the glass. Stir with a long spoon and leave the spoon in the glass. Add 1 scoop of the ice cream and wait for the fizzing to subside. Add the second scoop of ice cream and drizzle in enough seltzer to fill the glass.

2. Top with a squirt of whipped cream and garnish with the fresh berries. Slide in a straw and serve at once.

—Diana Sturgis

• • •

BERRY SYRUP

——— Makes About 1 Cup ———
1 package (10 ounces) frozen raspberries or strawberries in light syrup, thawed
¼ cup light corn syrup

In a food processor or blender, puree the fruit with its syrup. Strain the puree through a fine-mesh sieve and stir in the corn syrup. Refrigerate in a covered jar for 5 days or freeze for up to 1 month.

—Diana Sturgis

• • •

FRESH PEACH ICE CREAM

For best results, prepare the peaches and make the custard the night before and use a hand-cranked churn. When the ice cream is softly frozen, remove the dasher. Stir the ice cream once and pack it in four parts ice to one part coarse salt, or freeze for two hours before eating.

——— 8 Servings ———
8 to 10 very ripe, large freestone peaches
10 almonds, finely chopped (optional)
2 tablespoons fresh lemon juice
1 cup sugar
2 cups milk
6 egg yolks
1 cup heavy cream, well chilled

1. In a large pot of boiling water, blanch the peaches for a few seconds. Transfer the peaches to a colander to drain. Peel and halve the peaches. Remove and reserve the pits.

2. Place the peaches in a bowl and crush with your hands until no large clumps remain; do not puree.

3. One at a time, place the reserved peach pits in a kitchen towel and tap with a hammer to open them. Remove the almond-like kernels from the center of the pits. Finely chop the kernels. (The almonds listed above can be substituted for the peach pit kernels.)

4. Add the kernels to the peach pulp, along with the lemon juice and ¼ cup of the sugar. Cover the bowl with plastic wrap and refrigerate until very cold, preferably overnight.

5. In a medium saucepan, scald the milk over moderate heat; do not let it boil.

6. Set a wide stainless steel bowl over a pot of gently simmering water. Add the egg yolks and the remaining ¾ cup sugar to the bowl and whisk together until light in color. Gradually stir in the scalded milk. Cook, stirring constantly with a wooden spoon, until the custard coats the back of the spoon, about 12 minutes.

7. Strain the custard into a bowl through a fine-mesh sieve. Let cool slightly, then cover and refrigerate until very cold, preferably overnight.

8. When the peach mixture and the custard are cold, combine them. Add the heavy cream and stir until blended. Pour the mixture into an ice cream maker and freeze according to the manufacturer's instructions.

—John Martin Taylor

• • •

UNION SQUARE CAFE'S LEMON GRASS ICE CREAM

The delicate, balmy flavors of lemon grass add a special exotic charm to this ice cream from New York's Union Square Café.

——— Makes About 1 Quart ———
2 cups milk
2 cups heavy cream
1 cup sugar
½ pound lemon grass* (bottom third only), thinly sliced
6 egg yolks
*Available at Asian markets

1. In a saucepan, combine the milk, cream, sugar and lemon grass. Bring just to a boil over moderate heat, stirring to dissolve the sugar. Remove from the heat, cover and let steep for 20 minutes.

2. In a medium bowl, beat the egg yolks lightly. Gradually whisk in 1 cup of the hot liquid to warm the egg yolks. Whisk the egg yolks into the remaining liquid in the saucepan. Cook, stirring, over low heat until thick enough to coat a spoon, about 8 minutes; do not let boil.

3. Strain the liquid into a medium bowl and let cool. Pour into an ice cream maker and freeze according to the manufacturer's instructions.

—Bruce Cost

• • •

PEANUT BUTTER ICE CREAM WITH CHOCOLATE SAUCE

This dessert, as presented at Morton's restaurant in Charleston, is stunning. You can try your hand at "painting" this dish with the Chocolate Sauce, Crème Anglaise and Raspberry Coulis using plastic squirt bottles—it's far easier than it sounds. Or simply spoon the sauces on top.

——————6 to 8 Servings ——————
1 cup (firmly packed) creamy
*   peanut butter*
4 cups milk
8 egg yolks
¾ cup sugar
Chocolate Sauce (p. 255)
Crème Anglaise (p. 255)
Raspberry Coulis (p. 254)

1. In a medium saucepan, heat the peanut butter and milk over moderately low heat, whisking constantly, until the peanut butter dissolves completely, 3 to 5 minutes. Remove from the heat and cover to keep warm.

2. In a mixer bowl, beat the egg yolks and sugar until thick and pale, about 8 minutes. Gradually beat in the hot peanut butter and milk in a slow stream. Strain into a bowl and let cool to room temperature, stirring every 10 minutes. Or, if you prefer, quick-chill in an ice bath.

3. Pour the mixture into an ice cream maker and freeze according to the manufacturer's instructions. (Or pour into a large baking dish, set it in the freezer and freeze for 30 to 40 minutes until mushy. Transfer to a mixer bowl, beat at high speed until fluffy and return to the freezer for about 45 minutes, until soft-firm. If the ice cream should become brick-hard, let it soften a bit before serving.)

4. To serve, coat the bottom of 6 to 8 dinner plates with about ¼ cup Chocolate Sauce. Decoratively drizzle the Crème Anglaise and Raspberry Coulis over the chocolate. Arrange 3 small scoops of ice cream on each plate. Drizzle a spiral of Raspberry Coulis onto each scoop and garnish with a sprig of mint. Pass any remaining Chocolate Sauce separately.
—Marcelo Vasquez, Morton's,
Charleston, South Carolina

• • •

AUBERGE DU SOLEIL'S BANANA ICE CREAM

A good banana ice cream, like this one, should be delicate, to let the taste of the bananas come through. You can serve the ice cream plain, in a tulip cookie cup (see Almond Tuile Cookie Cups, p. 242, or Chocolate-Painted Tulip Cups, p. 200) or in an almond cookie cornucopia as I had it at the Auberge in Rutherford, California. Unfortunately, this isn't currently on the Auberge's menu, though other scrumptious desserts are.

——————Makes About 1 Quart ——————
2 cups milk
1 vanilla bean, split
8 egg yolks
1¼ cups sugar
3 medium bananas, pureed (about
*   1½ cups)*
2 tablespoons dark rum
2 tablespoons fresh lemon juice
Generous pinch of freshly grated
*   nutmeg*

1. Place the milk in a large saucepan. Scrape the seeds of the vanilla bean into the milk and bring to a boil over high heat. Immediately remove from the heat, cover the pan and let the mixture steep for 10 minutes.

2. Meanwhile, in a medium bowl, beat together the egg yolks and sugar until the mixture forms a ribbon on the surface when the beater is lifted, about 5 minutes. Gradually whisk 1 to 2 ladles of the hot milk into the eggs. Then stir the egg yolk mixture into the remaining milk.

3. Cook the custard over moderately low heat, stirring constantly, until it thickens enough to lightly coat the back of a wooden spoon and a clear trail remains when a finger is drawn across the spoon, 6 to 8 minutes. Do not let the custard boil. Remove from the heat and let cool completely.

4. Beat the banana puree, rum, lemon juice and nutmeg into the cooled custard. Transfer the mixture into an ice cream maker and freeze according to the manufacturer's instructions.

5. Transfer to a covered container and freeze for at least 6 and up to 24 hours. Transfer the ice cream to the refrigerator to soften for about 20 minutes before serving.

—Linda Merinoff

• • •

WHITE CHOCOLATE ICE CREAM

This delicious dessert recipe is from my friend Lee Klein.

——————Makes About 1½ Pints ——————
1 cup heavy cream
1 cup milk
⅓ cup sugar
Pinch of salt
4 egg yolks
1½ teaspoons vanilla extract
4 ounces white chocolate, coarsely
*   chopped*
⅓ cup buttermilk
2 teaspoons fresh lemon juice

1. In the top of the double boiler or in a medium nonreactive bowl, combine the heavy cream, milk, sugar, salt and egg yolks. Whisk gently over simmering water until the custard becomes hot and thickens enough to lightly coat the back of a wooden spoon and a clear trail remains when a finger is drawn across the spoon, about 6 minutes.

2. Remove from the heat. Add the vanilla and white chocolate; stir until smooth. Let cool to room temperature, stirring occasionally. Refrigerate, covered, until cold, about 1 hour. *(The recipe can be prepared to this point up to 2 days ahead.)*

3. Stir the buttermilk and lemon juice into the cold white chocolate mixture. Transfer the mixture to an ice cream maker and freeze according to the manufacturer's instructions. *(The ice cream can be stored, covered, in the freezer for several hours, but for best results, serve as soon as possible.)*

—*Lee Bailey*

• • •

ROSE CHAMPAGNE SORBET

The better the quality of Champagne, the better the flavor of this sorbet. If you like, serve this sorbet as a palate cleanser between courses.

——— *12 Servings* ———
1 cup sugar
¼ cup fresh lemon juice
1 bottle (750 ml) of good-quality rosé
  Champagne or sparkling rosé
  wine

1. In a small saucepan, combine the sugar with 1 cup of water. Bring to a boil, stirring constantly until the sugar dissolves. Add the lemon juice. Remove the syrup from the heat and let cool, then refrigerate until chilled.

2. Combine the Champagne with the chilled syrup. Pour the mixture into an ice cream maker and freeze according to the manufacturer's instructions.

3. Transfer to a covered container and freeze at least overnight and for up to 3 days before serving. Serve in chilled glasses or bowls.

—*Bob Chambers*

• • •

FROZEN LEMON-ANISE CREAM

This creamy dessert is as smooth and silky as ice cream, but requires no machinery. The refreshing combination of lemon and anise is very Italian.

——— *6 Servings* ———
½ cup sugar
1 tablespoon lemon zest
3½ tablespoons fresh lemon juice
¾ teaspoon anise seed, crushed
1 cup heavy cream
4 egg whites
Pinch of salt
Mint sprigs, for garnish

1. Tape a double fold of foil 3 inches wide around the lip of six ½-cup ramekins to form a collar.

2. In a small saucepan, combine the sugar, lemon zest, lemon juice and ½ cup of water. Boil over high heat until reduced to ½ cup, about 8 minutes. Remove from the heat, add the anise seed and let cool slightly.

3. Meanwhile, in a medium metal bowl, whip the cream until soft peaks form. Cover and refrigerate.

4. In a large bowl, beat the egg whites and salt with an electric mixer on high speed until firm peaks form, about 3 minutes. Drizzle the sugar syrup into the egg whites in a slow steady stream while beating. Be sure to scrape in all the syrup that clings to the pan. Continue to beat until the syrup is fully incorporated and soft, glossy peaks form. Fold one-third of the egg whites into the whipped cream and then fold in the remaining egg whites until just blended.

5. Divide the cream among the prepared ramekins, filling them about ⅜ inch up the sides of the foil collars. Cover with plastic wrap and freeze until firm, about 2 hours. *(The recipe can be made up to 2 days ahead.)*

6. To serve, remove the foil from the ramekins and garnish with a sprig of mint. If the cream is too hard, let stand at room temperature for about 5 minutes.

—*Marcia Kiesel*

• • •

SEMIFREDDO RAPIDO

This is a very quickly assembled version of a classic Italian dessert. Serve with sugar cookies.

——— *12 Servings* ———
3 packages (10 ounces each) frozen
  raspberries in light syrup
2 packages (20 ounces each) frozen
  peach slices
1½ cups heavy cream, well chilled
¼ cup raspberry or peach liqueur
  (optional)

1. Working in 2 or 3 batches, puree the frozen fruit in a food processor until smooth but not liquefied, about 4 minutes. With the machine on, gradually add one-third to half of the heavy cream to each batch and process until the mixture is frosty, smooth and thick.

2. Immediately spoon the semifreddo into chilled bowls or stemmed wineglasses and refrigerate. Just before serving, spoon 1 teaspoon of the liqueur over each dessert.

—*W. Peter Prestcott*

• • •

ESPRESSO GRANITA WITH HAZELNUT-CINNAMON WHIPPED CREAM

This frozen dessert, which is very Italian in spirit, is for coffee lovers. It can be habit forming; no matter how much you've eaten, you'll always find room for a scoop.

———Makes About 3 Cups———
3 cups strongly brewed hot espresso
½ cup plus 1½ tablespoons sugar
¾ cup heavy cream, chilled
1½ tablespoons Frangelico liqueur
1 teaspoon cinnamon

1. In a medium stainless steel bowl, combine the espresso and ½ cup of the sugar. Stir until the sugar dissolves, about 1 minute. Let cool to room temperature, then freeze for 2 to 3 hours. Break up any ice crystals that have formed with a fork. Return to the freezer and whisk every hour until all the liquid is frozen and the granita has a crunchy, slushy consistency, about 6 hours.

2. In a medium bowl, beat the cream with the Frangelico, cinnamon and remaining 1½ tablespoons sugar until stiff peaks form, about 2 minutes. Cover and refrigerate the hazelnut-cinnamon whipped cream for up to 2 hours before serving.

3. Scoop the granita into chilled glasses and serve at once with a dollop of the whipped cream on top.

—Joyce Goldstein

• • •

SANGRIA SORBET

In this dessert I combine all the ingredients of a sangria into one sprightly sorbet. This pairs wonderfully with the Pine Nut Wafers (p. 241).

———Makes About 1 Quart———
1¼ cups sugar
2 teaspoons grated lemon zest
1¼ cups fresh lemon juice (from about 6 lemons)
½ cup dry red wine
½ cup dry white wine
Pinch of salt

1. In a medium nonreactive saucepan, dissolve the sugar in 1½ cups of water over moderate heat, stirring occasionally, about 5 minutes. Let the syrup cool to room temperature.

2. Add the lemon zest, lemon juice, red and white wine and salt to the sugar syrup. Stir well. Refrigerate until chilled, about 30 minutes.

3. Transfer to an ice cream maker and freeze according to the manufacturer's instructions.

—Joyce Goldstein

• • •

MINT GRANITA

This granita is especially refreshing after a fish dinner. Either spearmint or peppermint can be used.

———Makes About 1½ Quarts———
¾ cup sugar
Leaves from 2 bunches of fresh peppermint or spearmint, coarsely chopped (about 2 cups packed)
¼ cup fresh lemon juice

1. In a medium saucepan, bring 4 cups of water and the sugar to a simmer over moderate heat. Cook until the sugar is completely dissolved, about 2 minutes. Stir in the chopped mint and let cool. Refrigerate until chilled.

2. Strain the mint syrup through a fine sieve and discard the mint. Stir in the lemon juice.

3. Pour into a 9-by-13-inch metal pan. Freeze until ice crystals begin to form around the edges, about 30 minutes. Stir well and return to the freezer. Continue freezing, stirring every 30 minutes, until the granita is frozen through, about 2 to 2½ hours. *(The recipe can be made up to 1 hour before serving; transfer to a covered container to store.)*

—Michele Scicolone

• • •

COFFEE GRANITA

If you are sensitive to caffeine, use decaffeinated espresso coffee.

———Makes About 1½ Quarts———
¾ cup finely ground Italian espresso coffee
⅓ cup sugar
1 cup heavy cream

1. In an espresso maker or drip coffeepot, brew the coffee with 4 cups of water according to the manufacturer's directions. Add the sugar and stir until dissolved. Let cool slightly, then cover and refrigerate until cold.

2. Pour the coffee into a 9-by-13-inch metal pan. Freeze until ice crystals begin to form around the edges, about 30 minutes. Stir well and return the pan to the freezer. Continue freezing, stirring every 30 minutes, until the granita is frozen through, about 2 to 2½ hours. *(The recipe can be made to this point up to 1 hour before serving; transfer to a covered container to store.)*

3. To serve, whip the cream until soft peaks form. Scoop the granita into serving bowls and top with the whipped cream.

—Michele Scicolone

• • •

 DESSERTS

LEMON GRANITA WITH LEMON WHIPPED CREAM

Even if you don't like lemons, you'll love this granita. Tangy, sweet and sour, this is one of the most heavenly ices you'll ever have. Granita is a relative of sorbet, but it is technically an ice and therefore has a crunchier texture.

—— *Makes About 1½ Quarts* ——
1 cup granulated sugar
Pinch of salt
2 cups plus 2 teaspoons fresh lemon juice (from about 10 lemons)
2 tablespoons plus 1 teaspoon grated lemon zest
1 cup heavy cream, chilled
2 tablespoons confectioners' sugar

1. In a medium stainless steel bowl, combine the granulated sugar, salt and 3¾ cups of hot water. Stir until the sugar dissolves, about 1 minute. Add 2 cups of the lemon juice and 2 tablespoons of the lemon zest.

2. Let the syrup cool to room temperature, then freeze for 2 to 3 hours. Break up any ice crystals that have formed with a fork. Return to the freezer and whisk every hour until all the liquid is frozen and the granita has a crunchy, slightly slushy consistency, about 6 hours.

3. In a medium bowl, beat the cream with the confectioners' sugar and remaining 2 teaspoons lemon juice and 1 teaspoon lemon zest until stiff peaks form, 1 to 2 minutes.

4. Scoop the granita into chilled glasses and serve at once with a scoop of whipped cream.

—*Joyce Goldstein*

• • •

POMEGRANATE-TANGERINE ICE

This deep-red and distinctively flavored ice would go well with some fresh fruit or delicate, crisp sweet wafers.

—————— *6 Servings* ——————
6 tablespoons sugar
4 cups pomegranate juice*
1½ cups tangerine juice
1 tablespoon grated lemon zest
*Available at health food stores and Middle Eastern groceries

1. In a medium nonreactive saucepan, combine the sugar and 2 tablespoons of water. Cook over moderate heat just long enough to dissolve the sugar. Let cool slightly.

2. Pour the pomegranate and tangerine juices into a large bowl. Add the syrup and the lemon zest; stir well.

3. Freeze in an ice cream maker according to the manufacturer's instructions. (Or pour into a shallow dish and place in the freezer, stirring occasionally as ice crystals form. If it freezes solid, break it up with a fork and transfer to a food processor for a few seconds.)

—*Lee Bailey*

• • •

LEMON GRANITA

Granita can be frozen in an ice cream maker, but for the authentic grainy texture, it is best to still-freeze it.

—————— *Makes About 1½ Quarts* ——————
1 cup sugar
Finely grated zest of 1 lemon
¾ cup fresh lemon juice

1. In a medium saucepan, bring 4 cups of water and the sugar to a simmer over moderate heat. Cook, uncovered, until the sugar is completely dissolved, about 3

minutes. Let cool slightly, then refrigerate until cold.

2. In a bowl, combine the sugar syrup, lemon zest and lemon juice. Pour into a 9-by-13-inch metal pan. Freeze until ice crystals begin to form around the edges, about 30 minutes. Stir well and return to the freezer. Continue freezing, stirring every 30 minutes, until frozen through, about 2 to 2½ hours. (*The recipe can be made up to 1 hour before serving; transfer to a covered container to store.*)

—*Michele Scicolone*

• • •

PLUM SORBET

Serve this plummy sorbet with Pecan Tiles (p. 240).

—————— *6 to 8 Servings* ——————
⅔ cup sugar
1 tablespoon fresh lemon juice
2 pounds Black Friar plums, pitted

1. In a large nonreactive saucepan, combine the sugar, lemon juice and 2 cups of water. Bring to a boil over moderate heat. Add the plums, return to a simmer and cook, skimming occasionally, until the fruit is soft, about 10 minutes.

2. Working in batches, pour the plums and syrup into a food processor and puree until smooth. Transfer to a bowl and let cool to room temperature. Cover with plastic wrap and refrigerate until chilled.

3. Transfer the plum puree to an ice cream maker and freeze according to the manufacturer's instructions.

—*Lee Bailey*

• • •

STRAWBERRY GRANITA

Raspberries or blackberries can be substituted for the strawberries. Adjust the amount of sugar to the sweetness of the fruit.

———— *Makes About 1½ Quarts* ————
1 cup sugar
1 pint strawberries
½ cup fresh orange juice
¼ cup fresh lemon juice

1. In a small saucepan, combine 3 cups of water with the sugar. Bring to a simmer over moderate heat. Cook until the sugar is completely dissolved, about 5 minutes. Let cool slightly, then cover and refrigerate until cold.

2. In a food processor, puree the strawberries until smooth. Add the chilled sugar syrup, the orange juice and the lemon juice. Puree until thoroughly blended.

3. Pour the mixture into a 9-by-13-inch metal pan. Freeze until ice crystals form around the edges, about 30 minutes. Stir well and return to the freezer. Continue freezing, stirring every 30 minutes, until the granita is frozen through, about 2 to 2½ hours. (*The recipe can be made up to 1 hour before serving; transfer to a covered container to store.*)

—*Michele Scicolone*

• • •

CANTALOUPE SORBET

To complement the taste and appearance of this dish, top with Blueberry Compote (p. 214).

———— *Makes About 1 Quart* ————
2 cantaloupes (1½ pounds each)—
  peeled, seeded and cut into 1-inch
  dice
¾ cup plus 1 tablespoon sugar
Pinch of salt
1 tablespoon kirsch

1. Puree the cantaloupe in a food processor in batches until smooth, about 30 seconds.

2. In a medium saucepan, combine the sugar and salt with 1 cup of the melon puree. Cook over moderately high heat, stirring frequently, until all the sugar dissolves, about 4 minutes.

3. Transfer to a large bowl and stir in the remaining puree. Refrigerate to chill well. Stir in the kirsch.

4. Transfer to an ice cream maker and freeze according to the manufacturer's instructions.

—*Joyce Goldstein*

• • •

BLACKBERRY SORBET

The Almond Tuile Cookie Cups (p. 242) make wonderful edible "dishes" for this sorbet. Top with a dollop of whipped cream and crown with some berries.

———— *Makes About 1¾ Quarts* ————
4 pints blackberries (about 14 cups)
1 cup sugar
Pinch of salt
1 tablespoon fresh lemon juice
1 tablespoon crème de cassis

1. In a food processor, puree the blackberries in batches. Pass through a strainer to remove the seeds.

2. In a medium saucepan, combine the sugar, salt and 1 cup of water. Cook over moderately high heat until the sugar dissolves, about 3 minutes.

3. Stir the lemon juice, cassis and sugar syrup into the berry puree. Refrigerate until chilled.

4. Transfer to an ice cream maker and freeze according to the manufacturer's instructions.

—*Joyce Goldstein*

• • •

PEACH AND CHAMPAGNE SORBET

A splash of Champagne and the addition of sliced peaches turn this into an extravagant dessert.

———— *Makes About 1 Quart* ————
1½ pounds peaches
½ cup plus 1 tablespoon sugar
1 tablespoon grated lemon zest
¾ cup Champagne
2 tablespoons fresh lemon juice

1. Put the peaches in a large saucepan and cover them with boiling water. Cook for 2 minutes. Drain and rinse in cold water. Peel the peaches; halve them and remove the pits. Transfer the peaches to a food processor and coarsely puree. Pour into a medium bowl.

2. In a medium nonreactive saucepan, bring the sugar and ½ cup of water to a boil over moderately high heat. Add 2 teaspoons of the lemon zest and let simmer about 3 minutes. Remove from the heat and set the syrup aside for about 10 minutes.

3. Strain the syrup into the peach puree and blend well. Add the Champagne, the lemon juice and the remaining 1 teaspoon lemon zest. Stir well. Refrigerate until chilled.

4. Transfer to an ice cream maker and freeze according to the manufacturer's instructions.

—Joyce Goldstein

• • •

SANTA ROSA PLUM SORBET

Garnish this luscious sorbet with sliced plums and serve with the Pecan Cookies (p. 241).

———— *Makes About 1 Quart* ————
1½ pounds very ripe Santa Rosa plums (or, if unavailable, Black Friar), halved and pitted
1 cup sugar
Pinch of salt
1 tablespoon kirsch or Grand Marnier

1. Put the plums in a large saucepan with ½ cup of water, or enough to cover the bottom of the pan. Cook the plums over moderate heat until tender, about 5 minutes.

2. Puree the plums and cooking liquid in a food processor. Add the sugar and salt and blend well. Pass the plum puree through a large strainer to remove any particles of skin.

3. Pour the puree into a large bowl, and refrigerate to chill well. Stir in the kirsch.

4. Transfer to an ice cream maker and freeze according to the manufacturer's instructions.

—Joyce Goldstein

• • •

STRAWBERRIES WITH LEMON AND SUGAR

Dressing strawberries with lemon juice is an old Italian trick. The acidity brightens the fruit's own flavor without adding a lemony taste to the dish.

———— *4 Servings* ————
1 teaspoon grated lemon zest
¼ cup fresh lemon juice
2 tablespoons sugar
1 quart strawberries

In a medium bowl, combine the lemon zest, lemon juice and sugar. Halve or quarter the strawberries, if they are large, and add to the bowl. Toss well. Serve at once or let stand for up to 2 hours.

—Tom Maresca & Diane Darrow

• • •

PRUNES IN RED WINE

As long as you think a bit ahead, it takes mere seconds to prepare this simple bistro dessert. In the wintertime, it's delicious without berries. In the summer months, it can be transformed into a sunny dessert by adding fresh, sliced strawberries just before serving.

———— *6 to 8 Servings* ————
2 cups dried prunes (about 1 pound)
1 cup full-bodied red wine, such as Gigondas
¼ cup sugar
2 thin slices of lemon, seeds removed
4 thin slices of orange, seeds removed
2 cups sliced fresh strawberries (optional)

1. The day before serving, place the prunes in a medium bowl with 2 cups of water, cover and let sit at room temperature to plump for 24 hours.

2. Drain the prunes; discard the soaking liquid. In a medium nonreactive saucepan, combine the prunes with the wine, sugar, lemon slices and orange slices. Bring to a boil over high heat, remove from the heat and let cool. The prunes can be served at room temperature or slightly chilled. Stir in the sliced fresh strawberries just before serving.

—Patricia Wells

• • •

HONEY-PEPPER GRAPEFRUIT WITH CINNAMON STRIPS

The tartness of the grapefruit is a bold but perfect partner to the Cinnamon Strips that follow. But if grapefruit is too sharp for you, try this recipe with orange slices instead. If you have trouble removing the pith, dip the grapefruit into boiling water for a few seconds.

———— *6 Servings* ————
3 small pink grapefruits, peeled with all the white pith removed
1 cup honey
1 tablespoon coriander seeds, slightly crushed
¾ teaspoon whole black peppercorns
Cinnamon Strips (at right)

1. Cut the grapefruits crosswise into ¼-inch slices. Cut each of these in half and remove any seeds and the white center membrane. Transfer to a heat-proof glass bowl.

2. In a small saucepan, combine the honey and ¼ cup plus 2 tablespoons of water. Tie the coriander seeds and peppercorns in a small piece of cheesecloth and add to the saucepan. Bring slowly to a boil over moderate heat to make a light syrup.

3. Pour the honey sauce over the grapefruit. Let stand until cool, then cover and refrigerate overnight, stirring once or twice. Serve chilled, with the Cinnamon Strips as accompaniment.

—Lee Bailey

• • •

CINNAMON STRIPS

I often make these strips when I have leftover pie dough. They make a nice mid-morning or late-evening nibble all by themselves, and they are especially appealing because they're a throwback to my childhood.

Makes About 3 Dozen

1 cup all-purpose flour
½ cup plus ½ tablespoon sugar
½ teaspoon baking powder
Pinch of salt
6 tablespoons unsalted butter—4
  tablespoons cold and cut into
  pieces, 2 tablespoons at room
  temperature
1 egg, lightly beaten
2¼ teaspoons cinnamon
2 tablespoons milk

1. In a medium bowl, combine the flour, ¼ cup of the sugar, the baking powder and salt; mix well. Cut in the 4 tablespoons cold butter until the mixture resembles coarse meal. Stir in the egg with a fork, tossing the dough to moisten evenly.

2. On a floured surface, gather the dough together and knead for a minute or two until smooth. Pat the dough into a 6-inch disk. Cover with plastic wrap and refrigerate for at least 1 hour before rolling out.

3. Preheat the oven to 425°. On a sheet of lightly floured waxed paper, roll out the dough into a 12-inch circle. Spread the 2 tablespoons soft butter over half the circle.

4. In a small bowl, combine 3 tablespoons of the sugar with the cinnamon. Sprinkle the cinnamon-sugar generously over the buttered area.

5. With the waxed paper still attached, fold the unbuttered dough over the buttered half to form a semicircle. Press down slightly and carefully peel the waxed paper off the top.

6. Brush with the milk, and sprinkle with the remaining 1½ tablespoons sugar. Cut into ½-inch strips about 4 inches long.

7. Bake on an ungreased cookie sheet for 15 minutes, or until golden brown. Let the strips cool, then remove the waxed paper from the bottom.

—Lee Bailey

• • •

CINNAMON-MINT PEACHES WITH STRAWBERRY SAUCE

You can also make this summery dessert with nectarines.

6 Servings

1 cup granulated sugar
1 cinnamon stick, about 2½ inches
  long
1 sprig of mint, plus a few leaves for
  garnish
6 firm medium peaches
2 cups whole strawberries, plus
  sliced strawberries, for garnish
½ cup superfine sugar
1 teaspoon fresh lemon juice
1 tablespoon framboise (optional)

1. In a large saucepan, combine 3 cups of water with the granulated sugar, cinnamon and mint sprig. Bring to a boil over high heat, stirring to dissolve the sugar.

2. Add the peaches and reduce the heat to low. Cook, turning the peaches occasionally, until tender, about 8 minutes. Remove from the heat and let cool to room temperature. Cover and refrigerate until chilled. *(This recipe can be prepared to this point up to 1 day ahead.)*

3. In a food processor, puree the whole strawberries, superfine sugar, lemon juice and framboise until smooth. Transfer the sauce to a bowl and refrigerate, covered.

4. To serve, peel, halve and pit the peaches. Place 2 halves on each plate. Spoon the strawberry sauce over the peaches. Garnish with the strawberry slices and mint leaves. Serve chilled or at room temperature.

—Lee Bailey

• • •

GINGERED PEACHES

Any extra syrup is delectable drizzled over pound cake or ice cream. Serve the peaches with Brown Sugar Shortbread (p. 240).

6 Servings

2 cups sugar
3 tablespoons finely chopped fresh
  ginger
6 peaches, halved and pitted

1. In a medium saucepan, combine the sugar, ginger and 2½ cups of water. Bring to a boil over moderate heat. Reduce the heat and simmer for 10 minutes; set aside.

2. Place the peaches in a large saucepan. Cover them with boiling water and cook for 30 seconds. Drain the peaches and slip off their skins.

3. Transfer the peaches to the syrup and bring to a boil over high heat. Reduce the heat and simmer, turning once or twice, until tender, about 10 minutes.

4. Let the peaches cool in the syrup, about 1 hour. Transfer the peaches and their syrup to a bowl and refrigerate until chilled.

—*Lee Bailey*

• • •

WARM BLACKBERRY COMPOTE

Blackberries, marionberries or a mixture of the two are wonderful when served over vanilla ice cream or as a filling for crêpes. Whidbeys, a loganberry liqueur from Washington State, provides the syrup, or you can substitute crème de cassis.
❦ Blackberries, particularly when warm, are not especially tart and can be paired successfully with a soft, sweet, rich dessert wine, such as a 1983 Château Doisy-Védrines Sauternes or a 1986 Villa Mt. Eden Late Harvest Sauvignon Blanc.

——— *Makes About 2 Cups* ———
½ cup Whidbeys liqueur or crème de cassis
1 tablespoon quick-cooking tapioca
3½ cups (about 1 pint) blackberries
2 tablespoons sugar

1. In a medium nonreactive saucepan, combine the liqueur and tapioca; set aside to soften for 10 minutes.

2. Bring the mixture to a boil over moderate heat. Stir in the blackberries, cover and cook over low heat until the fruit is tender, about 5 minutes.

3. Gently stir in the sugar until dissolved. Remove from the heat, cover and let stand until the tapioca is dissolved, about 10 minutes. Serve at room temperature or chilled.

—*Diana Sturgis*

• • •

STAR GLAZED APPLES

Warm baked apples have always been a favorite of mine, more so lately since they take little preparation and are lower in calories than most desserts. Of course, I usually sabotage the calorie count by serving them with vanilla ice cream or a little whipped cream. Allow about five minutes extra cooking time if your apples are larger than those called for below.
❦ The flavor of baked apples finds a delicious echo in late-harvest Rieslings, such as 1983 Robert Mondavi Johannisberg Riesling Botrytis.

——— *6 Servings* ———
6 large baking apples, preferably Cortland (about ½ pound each)
1 tablespoon unsalted butter, at room temperature
½ cup damson plum jam
6 tablespoons chopped pitted prunes (about 3 ounces)
½ cup apple cider
Vanilla ice cream or lightly sweetened whipped cream, as accompaniment

1. Preheat the oven to 350°. Using an apple corer, completely remove the cores from the apples. Using a sharp paring knife, score the skin on top of each apple into a 5-pointed star that covers the top third of the apple.

2. Smear the butter over the apples and place them, star-sides up, in a medium baking dish. Drop 2 teaspoons of the plum jam into the center of each apple, followed by 1 tablespoon of the chopped dried prunes. Pack down gently and add 2 more teaspoons of the jam to each apple to fill the core cavities to the top.

3. Drizzle the apple cider over the apples and add ¼ cup of water to the baking dish. Bake the apples in the middle of the oven until they are tender when pierced deeply with a skewer, about 40 minutes.

4. Let the apples cool for a minute or so; then, with the tip of a knife, lift the points of apple skin at the top and peel back slightly to reveal the star design. Spoon some of the hot cooking juices over each apple.

5. With a spatula, transfer the apples to a serving plate or individual plates or bowls. Spoon the pan juices over them. Serve the baked apples warm or at room temperature, with ice cream or whipped cream if desired.

—*Diana Sturgis*

• • •

BLUEBERRY COMPOTE

Serve this simple berry compote by itself or as a topping for Cantaloupe Sorbet (p. 211).

——— *Makes About 2 Cups* ———
3 cups blueberries
1 tablespoon fresh lemon juice
½ teaspoon grated lemon zest
½ teaspoon cinnamon
⅓ cup port

1. In a large nonreactive saucepan, combine 2 cups of the blueberries with the lemon juice, lemon zest, cinnamon and port. Simmer over low heat until the blueberries are soft and tender, about 5 minutes.

2. Strain half the cooked blueberries so that they won't be too thick and pulpy; discard the pulp and pour the liquid back into the pan. Stir in the remaining 1 cup uncooked blueberries and serve warm.

—*Joyce Goldstein*

• • •

BANANA FRITTERS

Chef John Makin adapted these from northern Filipino banana *lumpia* (spring rolls). They are just bananas wrapped in thin pasta and fried. Makin remembers buying bags of them to take to the movies when he lived in the Philippines. Use *lumpia* wrappers or spring roll skins, available at Asian markets. Don't use won ton skins, since they aren't delicate enough. When he was at Duckworth restaurant, in St. Helena, California, Makin served them with a passion fruit sauce flavored with late-harvest Riesling, but they're just as delicious dusted with confectioners' sugar.

Makes 16 Fritters

4 large bananas—peeled, split lengthwise and halved crosswise
16 spring roll wrappers* (see Note)
2 tablespoons plus 2 teaspoons dark brown sugar
2 egg whites, lightly beaten
1 quart vegetable oil, for deep-frying
Confectioners' sugar and sprigs of fresh mint, for garnish
*Available at Asian markets

1. Place one piece of banana about 2 inches from the edge of a spring roll wrapper and sprinkle with ½ teaspoon of the brown sugar. Fold the edge of the wrapper up over the banana, then bring the sides in and fold up like an envelope. Seal the last fold with some egg white and set aside fold-side down. Repeat with the remaining bananas, wrappers, brown sugar and egg white.

2. In a large saucepan, heat the oil over moderate heat until it reaches 375°.

Deep-fry the fritters, 4 at a time, until golden brown and crisp, about 3 minutes. Drain well on paper towels. Dust lightly with confectioners' sugar and garnish with mint sprigs.

NOTE: Look for very thin Thai or Vietnamese spring roll wrappers made with wheat flour.

—*Linda Merinoff*

• • •

COMMANDER'S PALACE BANANAS FOSTER

Try the classic version from Commander's Palace in New Orleans (below), or for a less rich but still delicious variation of Bananas Foster, use tropical coconut sherbet rather than ice cream, as is offered at Bayamo, a Cuban-inspired restaurant in New York City. Select thick and relatively straight bananas when you make this dessert, since the very thin, more curved ones are difficult to turn without breaking.

2 Servings

2 tablespoons banana liqueur
6 tablespoons light or dark rum
4 tablespoons unsalted butter
¼ cup (packed) light brown sugar
2 ripe bananas, split lengthwise and halved crosswise
¼ teaspoon cinnamon
½ pint French vanilla ice cream

1. Mix together the banana liqueur and rum; set aside.

2. In a medium skillet, melt the butter over moderate heat. Stir in the brown sugar. Add the bananas and immediately turn to coat. Sprinkle the cinnamon on top.

3. Pour in the liqueur and rum and swirl around the pan to mix. Carefully ignite the alcohol in the pan. Spoon the liquid over the bananas to baste, until the

flame subsides. Remove the pan from the heat.

4. Place a scoop of the ice cream in the center of each serving plate and arrange the bananas around it. Spoon the sauce on top and serve immediately.

—*Linda Merinoff*

• • •

RHUBARB AND STRAWBERRY CROUSTADE

Rhubarb's flavor and tang marry well with strawberries in this light, crisp croustade. The pastry base is made with phyllo dough, which I love to use for pie shells. Keep the sheets you are not working with covered, because they dry out in minutes. The crust can be baked and the filling prepared several hours ahead.

6 to 8 Servings

⅔ cup granulated sugar
1 pound fresh rhubarb, cut into ½-inch dice
6 sheets of phyllo dough
1½ tablespoons unsalted butter, melted
1 teaspoon confectioners' sugar
1 cup heavy cream, chilled
1 pint strawberries, sliced

1. In a heavy medium saucepan, combine the granulated sugar and 1 cup of water. Bring to a boil over high heat, stirring to dissolve the sugar.

2. Set a strainer over a heatproof bowl. Add the rhubarb to the saucepan and return to a boil. Reduce the heat to moderate and cook until the rhubarb is slightly tender, 1 to 2 minutes; do not overcook. Strain at once over a bowl to catch the syrup and let the rhubarb drain well. Chill the rhubarb.

3. Return the syrup to the saucepan and boil over moderate heat until reduced to a scant ½ cup, 10 to 12 minutes. Let cool to room temperature.

4. Preheat the oven to 375°. Lay one sheet of phyllo over an ungreased 9-inch metal pie pan. Fit the phyllo into the pan, allowing the ends to hang over. Lightly brush the pastry lining the pan bottom with melted butter; do not brush the sides or the overhang. Fit a second sheet of phyllo in the pan perpendicular to the first and lightly brush the bottom with melted butter. Repeat the layering and buttering to cover the pan with the remaining phyllo.

5. Working with one sheet at a time and from the top, gently crumple each overhanging piece of phyllo to form a high rim around the edge of the pie pan. Tuck the edges of the bottom sheet inside the pan to facilitate unmolding. Lightly brush the top of the shell with the remaining melted butter.

6. Bake the pastry shell in the middle of the oven for 15 minutes, or until golden brown. Let cool in the pan for 5 minutes, then carefully lift the shell out of the pan and transfer it to a serving platter. Sift the confectioners' sugar over the edges and set aside at room temperature.

7. In a large bowl, whip the cream until soft peaks form. Gradually beat in ⅓ cup of the rhubarb syrup and beat until stiff. Fold in the rhubarb and refrigerate for up to 2 hours, if desired.

8. In a bowl, drizzle the remaining rhubarb syrup over the sliced strawberries. Toss to coat and refrigerate.

9. Just before serving, scoop the rhubarb cream into the shell and spoon the strawberries on top.

—Diana Sturgis

• • •

GOOSEBERRY FOOL

A fool is a sweetened berry puree folded into whipped cream. I like to serve this tart-sweet dessert with plain thin, crisp sugar cookies.

——— *6 to 8 Servings* ———
4 cups (about 1½ pints) green gooseberries, ends trimmed with scissors
½ cup granulated sugar
1½ cups heavy cream, chilled
⅓ cup confectioners' sugar

1. In a heavy, medium, nonreactive saucepan, combine the gooseberries with 2 tablespoons of water. Cook, covered, over moderate heat until the berries are soft, about 10 minutes.

2. Stir in the granulated sugar, reduce the heat to low and simmer, uncovered, until the sugar dissolves, about 5 minutes.

3. Puree in a food processor or blender and press through a sieve. Pour the puree into a bowl, cover and refrigerate until chilled, about 1 hour, or overnight.

4. In a large bowl, beat the heavy cream and confectioners' sugar until stiff peaks form. Fold the chilled gooseberry puree into the whipped cream, leaving some streaks of puree visible. Spoon the fool into stemmed glasses. Refrigerate for up to 6 hours before serving.

—Diana Sturgis

• • •

CHILLED BEAUJOLAIS AND STRAWBERRY SOUP WITH BANANA CREAM

The frothy banana and strawberry flavors of a young Beaujolais are matched by actual bananas and strawberries in this red wine-based dessert soup.

——— *4 Servings* ———
12 ounces (about 3 cups) strawberries
¼ cup plus 3 tablespoons sugar
1½ cups Beaujolais nouveau
1 medium banana, cut into pieces
1 teaspoon lemon juice
2 tablespoons heavy cream

1. Halve one-third of the strawberries and place them in a nonreactive bowl. Add 2 tablespoons of the sugar and ¼ cup of the Beaujolais *nouveau*. Stir well, cover and refrigerate for at least 2 hours.

2. Place the remaining strawberries in a food processor. Add ¼ cup of the sugar and the remaining 1¼ cups Beaujolais *nouveau*. Puree until smooth, about 10 seconds. Transfer to a bowl, cover and refrigerate until chilled, 2 to 3 hours.

3. Place the banana in a food processor. Add the remaining 1 tablespoon sugar, the lemon juice and the heavy cream. Puree until smooth, about 10 seconds. Transfer to a bowl and refrigerate until chilled, 2 to 3 hours.

4. When ready to serve, divide the strawberry puree among 4 chilled soup plates. Spoon the marinated strawberry halves into the soup and pour the Beaujolais marinade on top. Divide the banana cream among the plates, swirling it decoratively into the soup with a spoon.

—David Rosengarten

• • •

ALMOND CREAM SUNDAE WITH FRESH FRUIT AND HOT CHOCOLATE

This gorgeous sundae uses fruit as the base instead of ice cream.

——————— *6 Servings* ———————
2 tablespoons unsalted butter
2 tablespoons plus 2 teaspoons sugar
Pinch of salt
½ cup sliced almonds (about 2 ounces)
4 medium Bartlett pears, peeled and cut into ½-inch dice
2 large peaches, peeled and cut into ½-inch dice
1 teaspoon fresh lemon juice
1½ cups mascarpone* (see Note)
1½ tablespoons confectioners' sugar
8 drops of almond extract
½ pound semisweet chocolate
½ cup raspberries or strawberries
*Available at Italian markets and specialty food shops

1. In a large skillet, melt the butter with 2 tablespoons of the sugar and the salt over high heat. Add the almonds and stir to coat evenly. Cook, tossing occasionally, until golden brown, about 3 minutes. Spread the candied almonds on a large plate to cool; set aside. *(The almonds can be prepared up to 1 day in advance. Let cool; store in an airtight container or plastic bag.)*

2. In a large bowl, combine the pears, peaches, lemon juice and remaining 2 teaspoons sugar. Cover and refrigerate for up to 4 hours.

3. In a medium bowl, combine the mascarpone, confectioners' sugar and almond extract. Whisk to blend well, cover and refrigerate. *(The almond cream can be prepared up to 4 hours in advance. Remove from the refrigerator about 30 minutes before serving.)*

4. In a small stainless steel bowl set over a pot of simmering water, melt the chocolate, stirring occasionally. Remove from the heat and cover to keep warm.

5. Place the pears and peaches in 6 tall parfait glasses. Divide the raspberries among the sundaes. Place equal amounts of the almond cream over the fruit and pour the hot chocolate over the top. Garnish each sundae with candied almonds and serve immediately.

NOTE: If mascarpone is unavailable, substitute crème fraîche, but in Step 3, whisk until the cream mounds softly.

—*Marcia Kiesel*

• • •

SUMMER PUDDING

The vibrant flavor and color of this cool English pudding make it a light, bright finale for any warm-weather meal. The six cups of fresh berries are tossed with just enough sugar to balance their tartness and heated to get their juices flowing before being spooned into a bread-lined mold.

——————— *4 to 6 Servings* ———————
1 pint raspberries
½ pint red currants, black currants or blackberries
½ pint blueberries
½ cup sugar
11 slices of firm-textured white bread, such as Pepperidge Farm
Assorted fresh berries, for garnish
Sweetened whipped cream

1. In a medium nonreactive saucepan, combine the raspberries, red currants and blueberries with the sugar. toss well to completely coat the berries. Set the pan over moderate heat, cover and cook for 5 minutes. Uncover and stir gently. If the berries are still quite firm, continue to cook until they are soft but not broken down, about 1 minute longer. (The berry juices and sugar will have formed a syrup.) Remove from the heat.

2. Using a long sharp knife, trim the crusts sparingly from the bread. Arrange 4 of the slices close together on a work surface to form a square. Cover with 4 more slices to form a second layer. Using the base of a 3-cup soufflé dish as a template, trim the double-decker bread square into a circle to make 8 fan-shaped pieces. Discard the bread trimmings. Halve the 3 remaining bread slices crosswise and set all the prepared bread aside.

3. Line the soufflé dish with plastic wrap, allowing a generous overhang. Smooth the plastic wrap to remove as many wrinkles as possible. Line the base of the dish with 4 of the fan-shaped pieces of bread. Line the sides of the dish with 5 of the rectangles; they will fit snugly.

4. With a slotted spoon, transfer the berries to the bread-lined dish; pack them in so that they are level with the top of the bread. Cover the fruit with the remaining 4 fan-shaped pieces of bread. Strain the berry syrup evenly over the bread.

5. Set the soufflé dish on a large plate to catch any juices that might overflow. Place a small place on top of the pudding and weigh it down with about 2 pounds of canned goods. Refrigerate overnight.

6. To unmold the pudding, remove the small plate and weights. Invert the soufflé dish onto a serving platter and lift off the dish. Carefully peel off the plastic wrap. Garnish the top of the pudding with fresh berries.

7. To serve, use a sharp knife to cut the pudding in wedges. Pass the sweetened whipped cream separately.

—*Diana Sturgis*

• • •

PIES, CAKES & COOKIES

SWEET POTATO PIE

Sweet potatoes, thanks in large measure to George Washington Carver of the Tuskegee Institute in Alabama, who diversified the crop in the United States, have been closely identified with southern black cookery and soul food since early in this century. This is one of many variations on this smooth and spicy pie.

——————— **8 Servings** ———————
3 medium sweet potatoes (1¾ pounds)
4 tablespoons unsalted butter, at room temperature
½ cup (packed) brown sugar
2 eggs, beaten
½ teaspoon vanilla extract
½ teaspoon cinnamon
⅛ teaspoon ground cloves
⅛ teaspoon ground ginger
⅛ teaspoon freshly grated nutmeg
⅛ teaspoon allspice
⅛ teaspoon ground mace
Pinch of salt
½ cup evaporated milk
Pie Shell (p. 226)
Whipped cream, for garnish

1. In a medium saucepan of boiling water, cook the sweet potatoes until tender, about 30 minutes. Drain, let cool, then peel and mash. Measure out 3 cups.

2. Preheat the oven to 350°. In a medium bowl, beat together the butter and brown sugar until creamy. Add the eggs, vanilla, cinnamon, cloves, ginger, nutmeg, allspice, mace and salt. Stir in the 3 cups mashed sweet potatoes. Add the evaporated milk and beat with an electric mixer until smooth.

3. Pour the filling into the Pie Shell and bake on the bottom rack of the oven for 50 to 60 minutes, until the center is firm. Serve warm or cool, with a dollop of whipped cream if desired.

—*John Egerton*

• • •

OLD-FASHIONED BRANDIED PUMPKIN PIE

Otto Seelbach, a member of the Louisville Seelbach Hotel family, who knew good food, told me years ago that a pumpkin pie should "cry"—that is, small teardrops of moisture should rise to the top after the pie rests for a while. In other words, a delicious pumpkin pie must be moist and luscious. This is *the* pumpkin pie that cries.

——————— **Makes One 9-Inch Pie** ———————
Old-Fashioned Pie Dough (at right)
1 cup canned unsweetened pumpkin
1 cup heavy cream or evaporated milk
3 eggs
1 cup (packed) light brown sugar
1 teaspoon cinnamon
½ teaspoon ground ginger
¼ teaspoon freshly grated nutmeg
¼ cup brandy
Chilled Bourbon Custard (p. 254) or sweetened whipped cream, as accompaniment

1. Preheat the oven to 400°. Line the pie shell with aluminum foil and weigh down with dried beans or pie weights. Place the pie pan on the bottom rack of the oven and bake for 15 minutes, or until the crust is almost dry and lightly colored. Remove the beans and the foil and set the partially baked crust aside to cool for 15 minutes.

2. Meanwhile, place the pumpkin in a large bowl. Gradually whisk in the cream. Add the eggs one by one, whisking until well blended.

3. Combine the sugar with the spices and beat them into the pumpkin mixture. Add the brandy and mix well. Spoon the filling into the partially baked crust.

4. Place the pie on the lowest shelf of the oven and bake for 8 minutes. Reduce the oven temperature to 350° and continue to bake until a knife inserted in the middle of the pie comes out clean, 40 to 45 minutes longer. Serve warm or cold, with Chilled Bourbon Custard or whipped cream.

—*Camille Glenn*

• • •

OLD-FASHIONED PIE DOUGH

——————— **Makes a Single 9-Inch Crust** ———————
1 cup plus 2 tablespoons all-purpose flour
¼ teaspoon baking powder
¼ teaspoon salt
6 tablespoons cold unsalted butter, cut into small pieces
1 tablespoon sugar
1 egg yolk
1 tablespoon ice water

1. In a large bowl, combine the flour, baking powder and salt; mix well. Cut in the butter until the mixture resembles coarse meal. Mix in the sugar. Add the egg yolk and ice water and stir to form a dough. Pat the dough into a 6-inch disk; wrap and refrigerate until chilled, about 20 minutes.

2. On a lightly floured sheet of waxed paper, roll out the dough into an 11-inch circle. Invert the pastry into a buttered 9-inch metal pie plate and peel off the paper. Fit the pastry evenly into the dish without stretching. Trim the dough to ½ inch beyond the rim of the pan. Fold the edge under and crimp decoratively. Refrigerate the pie shell while you make the filling. *(The unbaked crust can be formed 1 day ahead.)*

—*Camille Glenn*

• • •

Sour Cream Coffee Cake with Chocolate and Walnuts (p. 191).

Left, Cornmeal Breakfast Pancakes with Fresh Corn Kernels (p. 177). Above, Red and Black Fruit-Filled Grapefruit Cups (p. 176).

BLUEBERRY PIE

My friend Jenny from Maryland always adds spice to her berry pies. Combined with orange zest, the allspice really brings out the blueberry flavor without overpowering the fruit.

6 to 8 Servings

4 cups blueberries (about 1½ pints)
1 tablespoon grated orange zest
½ cup plus 1 teaspoon sugar
3 tablespoons quick-cooking tapioca
½ teaspoon ground allspice
Pie Crust Pastry (at right)
Egg glaze: 1 egg yolk beaten with 1 teaspoon of water

1. Preheat the oven to 400°. In a medium bowl, toss together the blueberries and orange zest. In a small bowl, mix together ½ cup of the sugar, the tapioca and the allspice.

2. On a lightly floured surface, roll out one of the Pie Crust Pastry disks to an 11-inch round and fit it into a 9½- to 10-inch pie dish without stretching. With a scissors, trim the pastry to within ½-inch of the edge of the pie dish.

3. Pour the blueberries evenly into the dish and sprinkle the sugar-tapioca mixture over the top.

4. Roll the remaining pastry disk into an 11-inch round. Drape the pastry over the berries and trim to within 1 inch of the edge of the dish. Tuck the edge of the pastry rim neatly under the bottom crust. Crimp the edge decoratively to seal. Cut a 5-inch cross in the center of the crust.

5. Brush the pie crust with the egg glaze and fold open the cross to form a square. Brush the turned-up pastry corners with glaze. Sprinkle the crust with the remaining 1 teaspoon sugar.

6. Set the pie on a baking sheet in the middle of the oven and bake for 50 minutes, or until the pastry is golden and the sugar and tapioca are absorbed by the berries. If the pastry is browning too quickly, loosely cover the pie with a sheet of aluminum foil for the last 10 minutes.

—*Diana Sturgis*

• • •

PIE CRUST PASTRY

This tender pastry holds up well to a very moist filling, and you can freeze it for up to a month.

Makes a Double 9-Inch Crust

1 egg
4 to 6 tablespoons ice water
2½ cups all-purpose flour
½ teaspoon salt
½ cup solid vegetable shortening
4 tablespoons cold unsalted butter, cut into pieces

1. In a measuring cup, lightly beat the egg. Add enough of the ice water to measure ½ cup.

2. In a large bowl, combine the flour, salt, shortening and butter. Rub or cut the fat into the flour until the mixture resembles coarse meal.

3. Pour the liquid into the dry ingredients and stir the mixture into a dough.

4. Turn the dough onto a sheet of waxed paper and knead briefly into a smooth ball. Divide the dough in half, pat each piece into a smooth 6-inch disk, wrap separately in plastic wrap and refrigerate for 1 hour. (If the pastry is made a day ahead, let it sit at room temperature for 10 minutes or so to prevent it from cracking when you roll it out.)

—*Diana Sturgis*

• • •

Three-Berry Preserves (p. 258).

MOCHA PECAN PIE

Thanks to the persistence of an inspired but unknown (to me, anyway) southern cook, efforts to improve on perfection have resulted in this confection: a dynamite pecan pie with the addition of chocolate and coffee.

8 Servings

6 ounces semisweet chocolate, chopped
¼ cup plus 1½ tablespoons coffee liqueur, such as Kahlúa or Tia Maria
3 eggs, lightly beaten
½ cup (packed) dark brown sugar
1 cup light corn syrup
2 teaspoons vanilla extract
¼ teaspoon salt
1 stick (4 ounces) unsalted butter, melted
1 cup coarsely chopped pecans (about 4 ounces)
Pie Shell (p. 226)
1 cup heavy cream, chilled

1. Preheat the oven to 350°. In a heavy medium saucepan, combine the chocolate and ¼ cup of the coffee liqueur. Melt over low heat, stirring until smooth.

2. In a large bowl, combine the eggs, sugar, corn syrup, vanilla and salt. Beat until blended. Add the melted chocolate mixture and blend well. Stir in the melted butter and the pecans.

3. Pour the filling into the Pie Shell and bake for 45 to 50 minutes, or until the pie is barely set in the center. Transfer to a rack to cool.

4. Before serving, whip the cream with the remaining 1½ tablespoons coffee liqueur until soft peaks form. Serve a generous amount of whipped cream with each slice.

—*John Egerton*

• • •

PIE SHELL

For a standard pie with a bottom crust, whether prebaked or not, this familiar recipe will do nicely. It will also make about six tartlet shells.

——Makes a Single 9-Inch Crust ——
1½ cups all-purpose flour
¼ teaspoon salt
½ cup solid vegetable shortening or lard
3 tablespoons ice water

1. In a medium bowl, sift the flour with the salt, then sift again. Cut in the shortening until the mixture is thoroughly blended. Add the ice water, 1 tablespoon at a time, stirring with a fork. As soon as the dough forms a cohesive ball, flatten into a 6-inch disk, wrap in waxed paper and refrigerate for 30 minutes.

2. On a lightly floured surface, roll out the dough to a round about ⅛ inch thick. Fold the rolled dough in half and ease it gently into a 9-inch pie pan. Open it out and carefully press it into place. Trim the edges to ½ inch from the rim. Fold the extra dough under and crimp decoratively. Refrigerate for at least 20 minutes before filling and baking.

—John Egerton

• • •

CHOCOLATE PEANUT BUTTER PIE

Chocolate and peanut butter freaks—I'm afraid I qualify—will really love this rich and gooey pie. The recipe comes from my friend Lee Klein.

——— 10 to 12 Servings ———
1 stick (4 ounces) plus 1 tablespoon unsalted butter
⅓ cup all-purpose flour
⅓ cup (packed) light brown sugar
1 cup salted peanuts
6 ounces semisweet chocolate, broken into pieces
2 eggs, separated
3 tablespoons granulated sugar
⅔ cup creamy peanut butter
2 teaspoons vanilla extract
1 cup ricotta cheese
¼ cup confectioners' sugar
1 cup heavy cream

1. Preheat the oven to 350°. Melt 3 tablespoons of the butter.

2. In a food processor, combine the flour, brown sugar and ¾ cup of the peanuts. Turn the machine quickly on and off until the nuts are coarsely ground. Transfer to a mixing bowl and stir in the melted butter.

3. Transfer to a 9-inch pie pan and press with your fingers to evenly cover the bottom and sides. Bake for 10 minutes. Turn off the heat and let stand in the oven for 30 minutes. Remove from the oven and let cool to room temperature. (*The crust can be prepared to this point up to 1 day ahead and refrigerated.*)

4. In a food processor, finely grind the chocolate. Add the egg yolks and process briefly to blend.

5. In a small saucepan, combine the granulated sugar, 2 tablespoons of water and the remaining 6 tablespoons butter. Bring to a boil over high heat.

6. With the machine on, gradually add the butter syrup to the chocolate mixture. Scrape down the sides of the bowl and process until the chocolate mixture is smooth. Transfer to a bowl.

7. Beat the egg whites until stiff but not dry. Stir about one-third of the egg whites into the chocolate. Fold in the remaining egg whites until just blended. Pour into the pie shell, smooth the top and refrigerate for 1 hour.

8. In a medium bowl, combine the peanut butter and vanilla. Add the ricotta and blend well. Add the confectioners' sugar and blend again.

9. In another bowl, whip the cream until stiff. Fold the whipped cream into the ricotta mixture. Evenly spread the peanut cream over the chocolate layer. Coarsely chop the remaining ¼ cup peanuts and sprinkle over the top. Refrigerate until chilled, about 2 hours. Serve in very thin slices.

—Lee Bailey

• • •

FUDGE PIE

Creamy, thick and chocolatey says it all. For a luxurious touch, serve with unsweetened whipped cream.

——— 10 Servings ———
1 stick (4 ounces) unsalted butter
2 ounces unsweetened chocolate
2 eggs, lightly beaten
1 cup sugar
¼ cup all-purpose flour
¼ teaspoon salt

2 teaspoons vanilla extract
Prebaked Pie Crust (recipe follows)

1. Preheat the oven to 350°. In a small heavy saucepan, combine the butter and chocolate. Cook over low heat, stirring occasionally, until the chocolate is melted. Remove from the heat and let cool.

2. In a medium bowl, whisk together the eggs, sugar, flour, salt and vanilla. Beat until smooth. Stir in the melted chocolate and blend well.

3. Pour into the Prebaked Pie Crust and bake for 30 to 35 minutes, or until the center is just set (it should give a little when you touch it, but it shouldn't be liquid). Let cool on a rack.

—Marion Cunningham

• • •

PREBAKED PIE CRUST

—— *Makes a Single 9-Inch Crust* ——
1½ cups all-purpose flour
¼ teaspoon salt
½ cup solid vegetable shortening
3 to 4 tablespoons ice water

1. Preheat the oven to 425°. In a medium bowl, mix the flour and salt together. Cut in the shortening until the mixture resembles coarse meal. Add 3 tablespoons of the ice water, 1 tablespoon at a time, stirring lightly with a fork after each addition. Add 1 more tablespoon of water if needed so that the dough holds together. Gather and flatten into a disk.

2. On a lightly floured surface, roll out the dough until it is about ⅛ inch thick. Transfer the dough to a 9-inch pie pan and fit it against the bottom and sides without stretching. Trim to ½ inch of the edge, fold the extra dough under and crimp decoratively.

3. With a fork, prick the bottom and sides of the shell all over at ½-inch intervals. Press a 12-inch square piece of heavy-duty aluminum foil snugly against the bottom and sides of the shell to prevent the dough from shrinking.

4. Place the pie shell in the upper third of the oven and bake for 6 minutes. Remove the foil and continue baking for 8 to 10 minutes longer, until light brown, dry and crisp. Remove from the oven and let cool completely on a rack.

LARD CRUST:
Substitute 1¼ cups all-purpose flour, ⅛ teaspoon salt and ½ cup lard for the quantities listed above. The amount of water is the same.

—Marion Cunningham

• • •

SKILLET APPLE TART

An oat bran and cream cheese pastry adds a nutty flavor to this simple rustic apple and caramel tart.

❣ Apple-based desserts have an affinity with certain fruity white wines, such as the off-dry, perfumed 1987 Kendall-Jackson Muscat Canelli or the honey-sweet Jekel Late Harvest Riesling.

—————— *8 Servings* ——————
4 tablespoons unsalted butter
½ cup (packed) light brown sugar
½ teaspoon cinnamon
4 medium, tart green apples, such as Granny Smith—peeled, quartered and cored
⅓ cup oat bran
1 cup plus 1 tablespoon all-purpose flour
¼ teaspoon salt
4 ounces cream cheese, chilled
⅓ cup vegetable shortening, chilled
1 to 2 tablespoons ice water

1. Preheat the oven to 425°. In a 9-inch cast-iron skillet, melt the butter over moderate heat. Add the brown sugar and cinnamon and stir briefly to distribute over the bottom of the pan. Cook until the sugar melts, about 3 minutes.

2. Add the apples and 1 tablespoon of water. Increase the heat to moderately high and simmer, turning the apples occasionally to coat with the sugar syrup, for 20 minutes. Reserve in the pan.

3. Meanwhile, make the pastry. In a food processor, combine the oat bran, 1 cup of the flour and the salt. Process briefly to mix.

4. Add the cream cheese and shortening and process, scraping the bowl down once, until the dough is crumbly, about 10 seconds. Add the ice water and process until the dough begins to mass together, about 10 seconds. Do not overprocess.

5. On a lightly floured surface, roll out the dough to a 10-inch circle.

6. Arrange all but 2 of the apple quarters rounded-sides down, in a circle in the skillet. Place the remaining 2 pieces in the center. Sprinkle the remaining 1 tablespoon flour on top. Lay the crust on top of the apples and trim off the excess.

7. Bake the tart for 20 minutes, or until the pastry is golden. Let cool for 5 minutes, then invert onto a cake plate. Serve warm.

—Tracey Seaman

• • •

MELON TART WITH MUSCAT DE BEAUMES DE VENISE

❦ The tart calls out for the rich, sweet minty flavors of Muscat de Beaumes de Venise. The Muscat should be as young as possible; look for the 1986 Jaboulet or the 1986 Domaine Durban.

─────── *8 to 10 Servings* ───────
1 ripe melon (about 2½ pounds), such as cantaloupe
1 cup plus 1 tablespoon Muscat de Beaumes de Venise
½ cup sugar
4 egg yolks
½ cup heavy cream
¼ cup milk
3 tablespoons all-purpose flour
½ cup apricot jam
Prebaked Tart Shell (recipe follows)
Mint leaves, for garnish

1. Quarter the melon lengthwise, discarding the seeds. Remove and discard the rind. Slice the melon lengthwise into very thin wedges.

2. In a small bowl, combine ⅔ cup of the Beaumes de Venise with 5 tablespoons of the sugar. Stir to dissolve the sugar.

3. Pour one-third of the wine syrup into a large, shallow nonreactive dish. Add a layer of melon wedges. Pour another third of the wine syrup over the melon. Add the remaining melon slices and top with the remaining wine syrup. Refrigerate for 12 to 24 hours.

4. In a bowl, whisk the egg yolks with 2 tablespoons of the sugar until pale.

5. In a small heavy saucepan, whisk the cream, milk and flour until smooth. Bring to a boil, whisking constantly, over moderate heat. Gradually whisk the hot liquid into the egg yolks. Return the mixture to the saucepan and cook, whisk-

ing constantly, until the pastry cream is thick and shiny and has lost its raw taste, about 4 minutes.

6. Remove from the heat and whisk in ⅓ cup of the Beaumes de Venise. Let cool. Cover with plastic wrap touching the surface and refrigerate for 2 hours or overnight. *(The recipe can be prepared to this point up to 1 day ahead.)*

7. In a small heavy saucepan, combine the apricot jam with the remaining 1 tablespoon each sugar and Beaumes de Venise. Bring to a boil over high heat and cook for 1 minute; strain.

8. Brush a thin layer of the glaze over the bottom of the cooled Prebaked Tart Shell. Spread the pastry cream evenly in the shell. Remove the melon slices from the wine syrup and pat dry with paper towels. Arrange the melon slices over the pastry cream, placing the tip of each wedge at the center of the tart and overlapping them to form a pinwheel design. Reheat the remaining glaze and brush it over the melon. Let the tart stand at room temperature for at least 15 minutes before serving. Garnish with the mint.

—David Rosengarten

• • •

PREBAKED TART SHELL

─────── *Makes a 9-Inch Tart Shell* ───────
1⅓ cups all-purpose flour
1 tablespoon sugar
¼ teaspoon salt
1 stick (4 ounces) unsalted butter, cut into small pieces and chilled
1 egg, lightly beaten

1. In a food processor, combine the flour, sugar and salt. Process for 1 to 2 seconds to mix.

2. Add the butter and process just until the butter is the size of peas, 5 to 7 seconds. With the machine on, add the egg and process just until a smooth dough forms, about 8 to 10 seconds.

3. Transfer to a floured work surface and form into a ball. Flatten the dough into a 6-inch disk. Cover with plastic wrap and refrigerate for at least 2 hours and for up to 3 days.

4. Preheat the oven to 375°. On a lightly floured surface, roll out the dough into a 12-inch circle, turning constantly to prevent sticking. Place the dough in a 9- to 9½-inch tart pan with a removable bottom. Fit the dough evenly into the pan without stretching and run the rolling pin over the rim to trim away the extra dough. Prick the pastry shell all over with a fork. Refrigerate for 30 minutes to prevent shrinking.

5. Line the pastry with aluminum foil or parchment paper and weigh down with pastry weights or dried beans. Bake for 10 minutes. Remove the foil and weights and prick the pastry again with a fork. Return to the oven and bake 15 minutes longer or until the sides and bottom are lightly browned. Let cool completely.

—David Rosengarten

• • •

BLACKBERRY JAM TART

The pastry dough recipe here comes directly from pastry chef and cooking teacher Nicholas Malgieri.

─────── *6 Servings* ───────
1 cup all-purpose flour
½ cup plus 1 tablespoon sugar
½ teaspoon baking powder
Pinch of salt
1 stick (4 ounces) plus 2 tablespoons cold unsalted butter
4 eggs—1 beaten, 3 separated
¼ cup plus 2½ tablespoons blackberry jam

**¼ cup plus 2 tablespoons fresh
    bread crumbs**
**¼ cup plus 2 tablespoons ground
    pecans**
Whipped cream, as accompaniment

1. In a medium mixer bowl, combine the flour, ¼ cup of the sugar, the baking powder and salt. Cut in 4 tablespoons of the butter until the mixture resembles coarse meal. Stir in the beaten egg to moisten evenly. On a floured surface, gather the dough and knead for a minute or two until smooth. Pat the dough into a 6-inch disk, cover with plastic wrap and refrigerate for at least 1 hour.

2. Preheat the oven to 425°. Roll out the pastry to a 12-inch circle. Without stretching the pastry, line the bottom and halfway up the sides of a 9-inch spring-form pan. Spread the jam evenly over the bottom and refrigerate.

3. Melt the remaining 6 tablespoons butter. In a medium bowl, beat together the 3 egg yolks with ¼ cup of the sugar until thickened and pale. Stir in the butter, bread crumbs and pecans; mix well.

4. In another medium bowl, beat the 3 egg whites until they form soft peaks. Add the remaining 1 tablespoon sugar and beat until stiff peaks form. Fold one-fourth of the egg whites into the egg-nut mixture to lighten it. Fold in the remaining egg whites. Spread this evenly over the jam.

5. Bake for 25 to 30 minutes, or until it has risen and turned golden brown. Let cool. Serve at room temperature plain or with whipped cream.

—Lee Bailey

• • •

ELIZABETH'S PECAN-ALMOND TART

This ambrosial tart is Elizabeth Terry's reinvention of the classic pecan pie. It's also one of the most popular desserts at Elizabeth on 37th in Savannah.

——— **12 to 16 Servings** ———
1¼ cups light corn syrup
1 cup sugar
**5 tablespoons unsalted butter, cut
    into small pieces**
4 eggs
1½ teaspoons vanilla extract
Pastry Tart Shell (at right)
**1½ cups coarsely chopped pecans
    (about 6 ounces)**
**⅓ cup sliced blanched almonds,
    lightly toasted**
1 quart vanilla ice cream
**Butterscotch-Bourbon Sauce
    (p. 255)**

1. Preheat the oven to 350°. In a small heavy saucepan, combine the corn syrup and sugar. Bring to a boil over moderate heat, stirring frequently. Boil, uncovered, until the sugar dissolves, about 2 minutes. Remove from the heat, add the butter and stir until melted.

2. In a large heatproof bowl, lightly beat the eggs. Gradually whisk in the hot syrup; mix in the vanilla.

3. Set the Pastry Tart Shell on a heavy baking sheet and pour in the filling. Scatter the pecans evenly over the top, then sprinkle on the almonds.

4. Bake the tart, uncovered, in the middle of the oven for 30 minutes, or until the filling is brown and set to the touch in the center. Remove from the oven, transfer the tart to a rack and let cool to room temperature.

5. To serve, cut the tart into thin wedges, top each with a scoop of vanilla ice cream and a generous ladling of the Butterscotch-Bourbon Sauce.

*—Elizabeth Terry, Elizabeth
on 37th, Savannah*

• • •

PASTRY TART SHELL

——— **Makes an 11-Inch Tart Shell** ———
1½ cups all-purpose flour
⅛ teaspoon salt
**1 stick (4 ounces) cold unsalted
    butter, cut into ½-inch cubes**

1. In a large bowl, combine the flour and salt. Cut the butter cubes into the flour until the mixture resembles coarse meal. Add ¼ cup of very cold water in a thin stream, tossing until the dough begins to mass together. Add a few more drops of water if necessary. Gather the dough into a ball and press into a 6-inch disk. Wrap tightly and refrigerate until cold but still malleable, 30 to 60 minutes.

2. On a lightly floured surface, roll out the dough ⅛ inch thick. Fit into an 11-inch tart pan with a removable bottom. Trim the pastry so it overhangs the rim 1 inch all around, then fold back the overhanging pastry inside the pan to reinforce the pastry walls. Press the pastry firmly against the bottom and sides of the pan without stretching it. Refrigerate the tart shell for 30 minutes before filling.

*—Elizabeth Terry, Elizabeth
on 37th, Savannah*

• • •

MONTRACHET'S BANANA TARTLETS WITH CARAMEL SAUCE

I like the fact that this pastry dough will keep in the refrigerator, tightly wrapped for about a week. A small scoop of vanilla, banana or—the choice at Manhattan's Montrachet restaurant—praline ice cream is a most fitting accompaniment.

——————— *Makes 10 Tartlets* ———————
¼ cup (packed) light brown sugar
6 tablespoons unsalted butter, at room temperature
3 tablespoons granulated sugar
½ egg, lightly beaten
1 cup all-purpose flour
Pinch of baking powder
Pinch of salt
Pinch of freshly grated nutmeg
¼ teaspoon vanilla extract
5 large bananas
Caramel Sauce (at right)

1. Pass the brown sugar through a sieve onto a baking sheet lined with parchment. Cover and leave in a dry place overnight; or dry in a preheated 250° oven for 15 minutes. Sieve again and reserve.

2. In a large bowl, beat together the butter and granulated sugar until smooth. Beat in the egg, flour, baking powder, salt, nutmeg and vanilla and mix until just incorporated. Do not overmix. Divide the dough evenly and pat into 2 disks. Wrap in plastic wrap and refrigerate for 30 minutes.

3. Roll 1 disk of dough out ⅛ inch thick. Cut out five 4-inch pastry circles and place on an ungreased baking sheet. Prick all over with a fork. Refrigerate for at least 10 minutes. Repeat with the remaining disk of dough.

4. Preheat the oven to 350°. Bake the pastry for 10 to 15 minutes, until dry and lightly colored. Do not overbake, or the pastry will become too brittle. Let cool on a rack.

5. Thinly slice the bananas on a slant. Arrange in a layer to cover the pastry.

6. Preheat the broiler. Sprinkle about 1 teaspoon of the dried brown sugar over each tartlet. Broil 6 to 7 inches from the heat until the tops are browned and glazed, about 1 minute. Serve each tartlet with 1½ tablespoons of the Caramel Sauce.

—Linda Merinoff

• • •

CARAMEL SAUCE

——————— *Makes About 1 Cup* ———————
1 cup sugar
½ cup heavy cream

1. Place the sugar and ½ cup of water in a small heavy saucepan. Stir to dissolve the sugar. Bring the syrup to a boil over high heat, swirling occasionally but not stirring. Boil until the syrup turns a deep golden brown, about 7 to 8 minutes.

2. Remove the pan from the heat and slowly whisk in the cream, continually scraping up from the bottom of the pan, until smooth. Return to low heat and cook until thickened slightly, 3 to 4 minutes. Let the sauce cool to lukewarm before serving.

—Linda Merinoff

• • •

SAND TART

This delicious, delicate cake has a pleasantly grainy texture that results from the combination of cornmeal and potato starch. It's related to a rich shortcake, but the baking powder and the beaten egg whites keep it light, and the flavor is subtle. Have a slice with a glass of dessert wine for a serene conclusion to your meal.

——————— *6 to 8 Servings* ———————
2 sticks (8 ounces) plus 2 tablespoons unsalted butter, at room temperature
1 cup fine white cornmeal
1 cup potato starch
1 tablespoon baking powder
½ teaspoon salt
1 cup plus 2 tablespoons granulated sugar
2 eggs, separated
1 tablespoon anisette liqueur
½ teaspoon vanilla extract
2 tablespoons confectioners' sugar

1. Preheat the oven to 350°. Butter a 10-inch cake pan with 2 tablespoons of the butter.

2. In a medium bowl, sift together the cornmeal, potato starch, baking powder and salt.

3. In a separate medium bowl, cream the granulated sugar and the remaining 2 sticks butter with an electric hand mixer until light and fluffy, 2 to 3 minutes. Beat in the egg yolks, anisette and vanilla. Gradually beat in the cornmeal mixture to make a dense batter.

4. In another medium bowl, beat the egg whites until they stand in soft peaks. Fold the beaten egg whites into the batter in 2 batches. Transfer the batter to the buttered cake pan.

5. Bake the cake for 35 minutes, or until a toothpick inserted into the center comes out clean. Remove from the oven and let cool completely.

6. Sprinkle the top with the confectioners' sugar. Because this is such a delicate cake, it's best to serve it directly from the pan. Cut with a very sharp knife and remove the pieces carefully with a cake server.

—*Tom Maresca & Diane Darrow*

• • •

FRESH CORN BUTTER CAKE

This rich, buttery cake, made with pureed corn kernels and a touch of cornmeal, has the texture of moist pound cake. Use only the freshest, sweetest ears of corn for this recipe. The best time to make it, in fact, is when you have leftover cooked corn on the cob.

———— *12 Servings* ————
5 large ears of fresh corn
2 cups sifted cake flour
3 tablespoons yellow cornmeal
1¼ teaspoons baking powder
¾ teaspoon baking soda
¼ teaspoon salt
1½ sticks (6 ounces) unsalted
  butter, at room temperature
1 cup granulated sugar
3 eggs, at room temperature
½ teaspoon vanilla extract
⅔ cup sifted confectioners' sugar
1 tablespoon fresh orange juice
1½ teaspoons orange marmalade

1. In a large saucepan, boil or steam the corn until tender, 5 to 7 minutes. Set aside until cool.

2. Working over a bowl, cut the corn kernels from the cobs and scrape the cobs with the dull side of the knife to extract all pulp and liquid. Transfer the kernels, pulp and liquid to a food processor or blender and puree until smooth.

3. Strain the puree through a medium-mesh sieve. Measure out 1 generous cup of strained corn puree and set aside. (Reserve any remaining corn puree for another use.)

4. Preheat the oven to 350°. Butter and flour an 8-cup fluted ring mold, such as a kugelhopf pan. Sift together the flour, cornmeal, baking powder, baking soda and salt.

5. In a medium bowl, beat the butter with an electric mixer on high speed until creamy, about 1 minute. Gradually beat in the granulated sugar until light and fluffy, about 5 minutes.

6. Add the eggs, one at a time, beating well after each addition. Beat in the vanilla extract.

7. Beat one-third of the dry ingredients into the butter mixture on low speed until just combined. Beat in one-third of the corn puree. Repeat 2 more times alternately adding the remaining dry ingredients and the corn mixture. Do not overmix. Using a rubber spatula, fold the batter until just smooth. Scrape into the prepared pan; smooth the surface.

8. Bake the cake in the lower third of the oven for 45 to 50 minutes, until it is golden brown on the outside and a toothpick inserted into the center comes out clean. Set aside and let cool slightly, about 10 minutes. Unmold the cake onto a rack.

9. Meanwhile, in a small bowl, stir together the confectioners' sugar, orange juice and marmalade. (Add additional orange juice if the mixture is too thick to spread.) Brush the glaze evenly over the warm cake. Let cool to room temperature. Cut into wedges and serve. *(The cake can be made up to 2 days in advance. Cover with plastic wrap and refrigerate.)*

—*Richard Sax*

• • •

BUTTER PECAN LOAF

A scoop of homemade bourbon ice cream would jazz up this rich cake.

———— *Makes 1 Loaf Cake* ————
1 stick (4 ounces) unsalted butter
¾ cup pecans
2 cups all-purpose flour
1½ teaspoons baking powder
¼ teaspoon salt
4 eggs
1¼ cups sugar
⅔ cup heavy cream
6 tablespoons Cognac or other
  brandy

1. Preheat the oven to 325°. Butter a 9-by-5-by-3-inch loaf pan. Line the bottom of the pan with waxed paper. Butter the paper, then dust the sides and the bottom of the pan with flour; tap out any excess.

2. In a large skillet, melt the butter over moderately low heat. Add the pecans and cook, stirring, until the nuts are a rich brown, about 5 minutes.

3. Drain the nuts in a strainer placed over a measuring cup, tossing to remove as much butter as possible. (There should be ½ cup of melted butter in the cup; if there isn't, add enough melted butter to measure ½ cup.) Let the butter cool to room temperature and reserve. Coarsely chop the toasted pecans and reserve.

4. In a medium bowl, sift together the flour, baking powder and salt.

5. In a large mixer bowl, beat the eggs on medium speed to break them up. Gradually add the sugar on medium-high speed and beat until light and fluffy, about 6 minutes. Add the cream and beat to blend.

6. Reduce the speed to low, add the flour mixture and beat until just blended; do not overmix. Scrape down the sides of the bowl. Add the Cognac and the chopped pecans and stir to blend. Fold in the reserved melted butter until there are no streaks.

7. Pour the batter into the prepared pan. Bake for 1½ hours, or until a cake tester inserted into the center comes out clean. Let the cake cool in the pan for 10 minutes, then unmold and finish cooling on a wire rack.

8. When completely cooled, wrap in plastic wrap and overwrap with aluminum foil. Let the cake stand in a cool place for at least 1 day before slicing. The cake will keep, tightly wrapped, for up to 1 week.

—Janet Fletcher

• • •

LEMON-LIME POUND CAKE

Serve a sliver of this cake surrounded by sugared blackberries.

——— *Makes 1 Loaf Cake* ———
2 sticks (8 ounces) unsalted butter,
    at room temperature
2 cups sugar
5 eggs, at room temperature
1 tablespoon grated lemon zest
1 tablespoon grated lime zest
2 cups sifted all-purpose flour
½ teaspoon salt
¼ teaspoon baking powder
1½ tablespoons fresh lemon juice
1½ tablespoons fresh lime juice

1. Preheat the oven to 325°. Butter and flour a 9-by-5-by-3-inch loaf pan.

2. In a large mixer bowl, cream the butter until smooth, about 1 minute. Gradually add 1½ cups of the sugar and beat until light and fluffy, 4 to 5 minutes. Add the eggs, one at a time, beating well after each addition; beat in the grated lemon and lime zest.

3. Sift together the flour, salt and baking powder onto a sheet of waxed paper. Gradually add the dry ingredients to the butter mixture in 4 to 5 additions, beating on low speed until just blended after each addition.

4. Spoon the batter into the prepared pan. Bake the cake for 1 hour and 15 minutes, or until a cake tester inserted into the center comes out clean and the edges of the cake begin to pull away from the sides of the pan. Leave the cake in the pan and allow it to cool on a rack for 5 minutes.

5. Meanwhile, in a small nonreactive saucepan, combine the remaining ½ cup of sugar, the lemon juice and the lime juice. Cook over moderate heat, stirring until the sugar dissolves, 1 to 2 minutes. Do not boil. Remove the citrus glaze from the heat.

6. Invert the pan to unmold the cake. Set it on a rack over a sheet of waxed paper. While the cake is still warm, brush all over with the hot citrus glaze. Let cool completely. Wrap in plastic wrap and then overwrap with aluminum foil. Let the cake stand in a cool place for at least 1 day before slicing. The cake will improve overnight and will keep, tightly wrapped, for up to 1 week.

—Janet Fletcher

• • •

GINGERBREAD TEA CAKE

Slice this tea cake and serve it on a platter with spiced poached pears.

——— *Makes 1 Loaf Cake* ———
4 tablespoons unsalted butter, at
    room temperature
¼ cup solid vegetable shortening
¼ cup (packed) brown sugar
¼ cup granulated sugar
1 egg, at room temperature
1½ cups sifted all-purpose flour
1 teaspoon ground ginger
½ teaspoon cinnamon
¼ teaspoon ground cloves
¼ teaspoon ground mace
¼ teaspoon salt
1 teaspoon baking powder
½ teaspoon baking soda
½ cup unsulphured molasses
½ cup boiling water
½ cup dried currants
Confectioners' sugar, for dusting

1. Preheat the oven to 350°. Butter and flour a 9-by-5-by-3-inch loaf pan.

2. In a large mixer bowl, beat the butter and shortening until creamy, about 3 minutes. Add the brown sugar and granulated sugar and beat until light, scraping the sides of the bowl occasionally with a rubber spatula, about 3 minutes. Add the egg and beat until just blended.

3. Sift together the flour, ginger, cinnamon, cloves, mace, salt, baking powder and baking soda onto a sheet of waxed paper. Combine the molasses with the boiling water and stir until the molasses dissolves. Add the dry ingredients to the butter mixture alternately with the molasses. Beat until just blended; do not overmix. Stir in the currants.

4. Pour the batter into the prepared pan. Bake for 50 to 55 minutes, or until a cake tester inserted into the center comes out clean and the edges of the cake begin to pull away from the sides of the pan.

5. Leave the cake in the pan and allow it to cool on a rack for 5 minutes. Invert the pan to unmold the cake; finish cooling on the rack. Wrap first in plastic wrap and then in aluminum foil. Let the cake stand in a cool place for at least 1 day before slicing. The cake improves upon standing and will keep for up to 10 days. Shortly before serving, sift confectioners' sugar over the top.

—Janet Fletcher

• • •

PRUNE CAKE

This large, moist cake is made with chopped prunes and a brown sugar and walnut filling. It keeps, well-wrapped, for several days and serves many.

─── *12 to 14 Servings* ───
²/₃ cup (packed) brown sugar
1 teaspoon cinnamon
¹/₂ cup chopped walnuts
¹/₂ cup plus 2 teaspoons granulated sugar
3 eggs
1 cup milk
1 stick (4 ounces) unsalted butter, melted
2¹/₂ cups all-purpose flour
1 tablespoon baking powder
¹/₂ teaspoon salt
1 box (12 ounces) pitted prunes, chopped

1. Preheat the oven to 350°. Butter and flour a 10-inch tube or Bundt pan. In a small bowl, mix together the brown sugar and cinnamon, stirring with a fork until the cinnamon is well distributed. Stir in the walnuts and set aside.

2. In a large bowl, combine ¹/₂ cup of the granulated sugar, the eggs, milk and melted butter. Whisk to blend well.

3. In a medium bowl, stir together the flour, baking powder and salt. Add the dry ingredients to the liquid ingredients. Beat with a wooden spoon until smooth. Fold in the prunes.

4. With a rubber spatula, spread no more than one-third of the batter over the bottom of the prepared pan. Sprinkle half of the brown sugar filling over the batter. Spread another third of the batter on top. Cover with the remaining brown sugar and spread the remaining batter over all.

5. Bake for 1 hour, or until a cake tester inserted into the center comes out clean. Remove from the oven and let cool for 10 minutes in the pan. Then remove from the pan and let cool completely on a rack. Sprinkle the remaining 2 teaspoons granulated sugar over the top.

—Marion Cunningham

• • •

RUM RAISIN BANANA CAKE

This moist and flavorful cake comes from the repertoire of Tracey Seaman, the newest member of *Food & Wine*'s test kitchen.

♟ The raisiny, spicy notes in this banana-flavored cake require a sweet, powerful dessert wine of equal intensity, such as Beaulieu Vineyard Muscat de Frontignan or 1986 Domaine de Durban Muscat Beaumes de Venise.

─── *8 to 10 Servings* ───
¹/₂ cup dark rum
¹/₂ cup raisins
1¹/₂ cups all-purpose flour
¹/₂ teaspoon salt
¹/₂ teaspoon baking powder
¹/₂ teaspoon baking soda
¹/₂ teaspoon ground ginger
1 teaspoon cinnamon
1 stick (4 ounces) unsalted butter, at room temperature
1 cup (packed) dark brown sugar
3 eggs, separated, at room temperature
¹/₂ teaspoon vanilla extract
2 very ripe, medium bananas, mashed or pureed (about 1 cup)
¹/₃ cup plain yogurt
¹/₂ cup (packed) ground walnuts
²/₃ cup confectioners' sugar
1 tablespoon light rum
1 tablespoon milk or cream
2 tablespoons minced crystallized ginger, for garnish

1. Preheat the oven to 350°. Grease and flour a 9-inch springform pan.

2. In a small saucepan, set the dark rum over moderate heat until warm, about 3 minutes. Remove from the heat and add the raisins. Set aside to cool, about 20 minutes.

3. In a medium bowl, combine the flour, salt, baking powder, baking soda, ginger and cinnamon. Whisk to blend thoroughly.

4. In a medium mixer bowl, beat together the butter and brown sugar on high speed for 2 minutes, until fluffy. Add the egg yolks and vanilla and beat on medium speed for 1 minute. Add the banana puree and the yogurt and mix on medium speed until smooth, about 1 minute.

5. In a medium bowl, beat the egg whites until stiff but not dry.

6. Add the flour mixture to the banana mixture and beat on low speed, until just blended. Drain the raisins and stir into the batter. Gently stir one-third of the egg whites into the batter to lighten the mixture. Fold in the remaining egg whites. Then fold in the ground nuts.

7. Transfer the batter to the prepared pan and bake for 45 minutes, or until a cake tester inserted in the center comes out clean. Let cool for 10 minutes in the pan on a rack, then remove the sides and let cool completely.

8. In a small bowl, combine the confectioners' sugar, light rum and milk; stir to blend well. Pour this glaze over the cooled cake, allowing it to drip down the sides. Garnish the top of the cake with the minced crystallized ginger.

—Tracey Seaman

• • •

PIES, CAKES & COOKIES

GRACE STUCK'S APPLESAUCE FRUITCAKE

The grandmother of a dear friend made this recipe each year for her family's Minnesota Christmas celebration. Dark and moist, the applesauce-and-molasses-based fruitcake is filled with a tangy assortment of dried—not candied—fruit. The recipe yields 10 small loaves (5 by 3 inches), which will keep up to three months, making these a perfect do-ahead gift for the holidays. If you make them in advance, brush the cake periodically with more brandy. Chilling them will make slicing easier.

—— Makes 10 Mini Loaves ——

3 cups unsweetened applesauce, preferably homemade
2 sticks (8 ounces) unsalted butter, cut into chunks
1¼ cups sugar
½ cup dark molasses
⅓ cup honey
1 box (15 ounces) golden raisins
1 box (15 ounces) dark raisins
1 cup dried currants
1 cup dried tart cherries, coarsely chopped, or substitute more currants*
1 cup dried apricots, coarsely chopped
2 cups walnuts, coarsely chopped (about ½ pound)
2 cups pecans, coarsely chopped (about ½ pound)
4½ cups all-purpose flour
1 tablespoon plus 1 teaspoon baking soda
2 teaspoons cinnamon
1 teaspoon freshly grated nutmeg
1 teaspoon allspice
1 teaspoon salt
½ teaspoon ground cloves
Walnut and pecan halves, for garnish
½ cup brandy
**Available at specialty food shops*

1. In a medium nonreactive saucepan, heat the applesauce over moderate heat. Add the butter, a few pieces at a time, and stir until the butter is melted and the applesauce is hot and bubbling, 4 to 5 minutes.

2. Add the sugar, molasses and honey and cook, stirring, until the sugar dissolves, about 1 minute longer. Let the applesauce cool to room temperature.

3. Preheat the oven to 275°. Butter and flour ten 5-by-3-by-2-inch loaf pans (available in disposable foil). In a large bowl, combine the golden and dark raisins, the currants, cherries, apricots, walnuts and pecans with the applesauce.

4. In a medium bowl, sift together the flour, baking soda, cinnamon, nutmeg, allspice, salt and cloves. Fold into the applesauce-fruit mixture until just blended. Quickly divide the batter among the pans and smooth the tops with a rubber spatula dipped in water. Press walnut and pecan halves into the tops to decorate.

5. Bake the fruitcakes for 60 to 70 minutes, or until a knife inserted in the center comes out clean. Let the cakes cool in the pans for 1 hour. Unmold them onto a rack and let cool to room temperature. Brush the brandy all over the fruitcakes. Wrap tightly first in plastic wrap, then in aluminum foil. Store in a cool, dry place for at least 1 week and up to 3 months before serving.

—*Bob Chambers*

• • •

PEACH UPSIDE-DOWN CAKE

In the Sixties, pineapple upside-down cake was a real favorite in my house. Since then, I've eaten wonderful *tarte Tatins* and luscious desserts with warm glazed peaches on top. This upside-down cake ties them all together. I like to serve it with vanilla ice cream or lightly sweetened whipped cream.

—— 8 Servings ——

1 cup all-purpose flour
1 teaspoon baking powder
1 stick (4 ounces) plus 3 tablespoons unsalted butter, at room temperature
½ cup granulated sugar
2 eggs, at room temperature
2 tablespoons peach schnapps or brandy
⅔ cup (lightly packed) dark brown sugar
6 small peaches (about 1½ pounds), quartered and pitted

1. Preheat the oven to 375°. In a small bowl, thoroughly mix together the flour and baking powder.

2. In a medium bowl, beat 1 stick of the butter until pale and creamy, about 2 minutes. Add the granulated sugar and beat until light and fluffy, about 3 minutes. Add the eggs, one at time, beating well after each addition. Fold the flour mixture into the batter until no white streaks remain. Stir in the schnapps.

3. In a heavy 9-inch ovenproof skillet (preferably cast iron), melt the remaining 3 tablespoons butter. Add the brown sugar and cook over moderate heat, stirring occasionally, until melted and bubbly, 3 to 5 minutes. Remove from the heat.

4. Arrange the peach quarters in the skillet in 2 tight concentric circles, beginning with the outer ring. Cook over moderately high heat until the peach juices bubble, about 3 minutes. Remove from the heat and with 2 small spoons, quickly turn over each peach quarter. Return to the heat and cook for 3 minutes longer. Remove from the heat.

5. Using a large spoon, evenly distribute the cake batter over the hot peaches. Quickly spread the batter smooth. Don't worry if the fruit is not completely covered; the batter swells as it cooks. Bake in the middle of the oven for 20 minutes, or until a cake tester inserted in the center comes out clean.

6. Let the cake cool for 5 minutes, then turn out onto a large platter. Serve warm or at room temperature.

—Diana Sturgis

• • •

GINGER ANGEL FOOD CAKE

Serve this cake by itself (perhaps topped with fresh fruit) or as part of Peach and Ginger Trifle (p. 202), for which it was designed.

—Makes One 10-Inch Tube Cake—
4 ounces fresh ginger (about a 4-inch piece), peeled and quartered
1½ cups sugar
1 cup cake flour
2 cups egg whites (about 12)
1½ teaspoons cream of tartar
½ teaspoon salt

1. Preheat the oven to 350°. In a food processor, combine the ginger and ¼ cup of the sugar. Process until blended into a thick paste. Set aside.

2. In a medium bowl, sift the cake flour and ¾ cup of the sugar together 3 times.

3. In a large mixer bowl, beat the egg whites on high speed until foamy, about 1 minute. Beat in the cream of tartar and salt. Add the remaining ½ cup sugar, 1 tablespoon at a time, beating continuously. Continue to beat until the egg whites form soft peaks that hold their shape, 8 to 10 minutes longer.

4. Sift the flour mixture evenly over the whites in 2 batches and mix on the lowest speed until barely incorporated, about 5 seconds. Do not overmix. Add the reserved ginger paste and blend in on the lowest speed for a few seconds. With a rubber spatula, gently fold a few more times to insure blending.

5. Turn the batter into an ungreased 10-inch tube pan. Cut through the center of the batter with the rubber spatula to eliminate air pockets.

6. Bake for 35 minutes, or until a cake tester inserted into the center comes out clean. Remove from the oven and invert the pan until cool. Free the cake from the sides of the pan with a long narrow knife.

—Marion Cunningham

• • •

CRANBERRY JELLY ROLL

This is the best cake roll recipe I know. It is also the simplest, eliminating the usual time-consuming separate handling of egg yolks and whites. Tart and sweet, this dessert is good after a rich meal.

——— 10 Servings ———
½ cup cake flour
½ teaspoon baking powder
¼ teaspoon salt
5 eggs
½ cup granulated sugar
1 teaspoon vanilla extract
2 to 3 tablespoons confectioners' sugar, for dusting
Cranberry Jelly (recipe follows), at room temperature
Sweetened whipped cream, for garnish

1. Preheat the oven to 350°. Grease a 15½-by-10½-by-1-inch jelly-roll pan and line with waxed paper. Grease and lightly flour the waxed paper. Mix the flour, baking powder and salt in a bowl, stirring with a fork to blend well.

2. In a medium mixer bowl, beat the eggs and granulated sugar at high speed until pale, fluffy and light, about 4 minutes. Gradually add the flour mixture and the vanilla and beat on low speed for just a few seconds. Finish folding the flour into the egg mixture with a rubber spatula until no white streaks show.

3. Spread the batter evenly in the jelly-roll pan. Bake for 12 minutes, or until the top of the cake is golden.

4. Spread a kitchen towel (larger than the cake) on the counter, with the long side nearest you, and sift some of the confectioners' sugar on top. Invert the warm cake onto the towel.

5. Remove the waxed paper and discard. Roll the cake in the towel from the long side. Transfer to a rack to cool. Leave the cake rolled up until you are ready to fill it.

6. To assemble, gently unroll the cake and spread the Cranberry Jelly right to the edges. Reroll the cake and place on a serving dish, seam-side down. Dust the top with the remaining confectioners' sugar. Slice the jelly roll and serve with sweetened whipped cream.

—Marion Cunningham

• • •

CRANBERRY JELLY

——— Makes About 1¼ Cups ———
½ pound (2 cups) fresh cranberries, rinsed and picked over
1 cup sugar
⅛ teaspoon salt

1. In a medium saucepan, bring 1½ cups of water to a boil. Add the cranberries and boil over moderately high heat for 20 minutes, stirring occasionally.

2. Puree the cranberries in a food processor and strain. Return the puree to the pan and cook over low heat, stirring frequently, for 3 minutes.

3. Add the sugar and salt and cook until the sugar is dissolved, about 2 minutes. Pour into a bowl, let cool and refrigerate until gelled. *(The recipe can be made up to 1 week ahead; keep refrigerated.)*

—*Marion Cunningham*

• • •

COCONUT CAKE

In several widely separated parts of the South, coconut cake and boiled custard have become traditional desserts offered as the climax of holiday feasts. Because this cake is so rich, only small servings are called for—but larger ones are hard to resist. This recipe is among the finest in a crowded field of superlative confections. When selecting a coconut, choose one that feels heavy and sounds as if it has a lot of liquid inside. If you prefer to save time, you can substitute three cups of unsweetened grated coconut, which is available in health food stores.

──────── *12 Servings* ────────
1 large fresh coconut (about 2
  pounds)
2½ cups sugar
2 sticks (8 ounces) unsalted butter,
  at room temperature
3 whole eggs plus 2 egg yolks
3 cups all-purpose flour
1 tablespoon baking powder
¼ teaspoon salt
1 cup milk
2 teaspoons vanilla extract
Seven-Minute Frosting (recipe
  follows)

1. Punch holes in the "eyes" of the coconut, drain the "milk" and reserve it. Crack the hard shell with a hammer. Cut

the meat away from the shell and peel off the dark outer skin with a vegetable peeler. Grate the coconut by hand with a metal grater or in a food processor fitted with a grating disk.

2. Measure the reserved coconut milk and add enough water to make 1 cup. Place it in a small saucepan with ½ cup of the sugar and bring to a boil over low heat, stirring to dissolve the sugar. Stir in ½ cup of the grated coconut, cook for 3 or 4 minutes longer and set the coconut drizzle aside.

3. Preheat the oven to 350°. Butter two 9-inch round cake pans. Line the bottoms with wax paper and butter the paper.

4. In a large mixer bowl, beat the butter with the remaining 2 cups sugar until light and fluffy, 5 to 8 minutes. Gradually beat in the whole eggs and the egg yolks one at a time. In another bowl, sift together the flour, baking powder and salt. Sift again 2 more times.

5. In a small bowl, combine the milk and the vanilla. Stir one-third of the sifted dry ingredients into the butter and egg mixture, then stir in one-third of the milk. Repeat twice more with the remaining dry ingredients and milk.

6. Divide the batter evenly between the 2 cake pans. Bake for 25 to 30 minutes, or until the cake is light golden on top and a toothpick inserted in the center comes out clean; take care not to overbake. (The cake should be moist, not dry and crumbly.) Let the cakes cool on a rack for 5 minutes. Invert the pans, remove and peel off the waxed paper. Set the cakes right-side up to cool completely.

7. Set the first cake layer on a large platter. Poke holes in the top with a fork and spoon half of the coconut drizzle evenly over the surface. Top with ½ cup of the grated coconut. Set the second

cake layer in place, and repeat the poking, drizzling and sprinkling of grated coconut.

8. Spread the Seven-Minute Frosting over the top and sides of the cake. Sprinkle the remaining grated coconut over the entire surface.

—*John Egerton*

• • •

SEVEN-MINUTE FROSTING

──────── *Makes About 4 Cups* ────────
2 egg whites
1½ cups sugar
⅛ teaspoon cream of tartar
2 teaspoons vanilla extract

1. In the top of a double boiler, combine the egg whites, sugar, cream of tartar and ⅓ cup of water. Set over rapidly boiling water and beat with an electric hand mixer on high speed for 7 minutes.

2. Remove from the heat but leave the pan over the hot water. Add the vanilla and beat until the frosting is thick and forms soft peaks, 4 to 5 minutes longer.

—*John Egerton*

• • •

NATCHEZ LEMON CAKE

This butter cake is filled and frosted with a rich lemon curd.

──────── *12 to 14 Servings* ────────
1 stick (4 ounces) plus 3 tablespoons
  unsalted butter, at room
  temperature
1½ cups sugar
2 tablespoons grated lemon zest
2½ teaspoons fresh lemon juice
4 eggs
2 cups all-purpose flour
2½ teaspoons baking powder
¼ teaspoon salt

¾ cup milk
Lemon Filling (recipe follows)

1. Preheat the oven to 375°. Grease three 8-inch cake pans. Line the bottom of the pans with waxed paper; grease the paper.

2. In a medium mixer bowl, beat the butter and sugar together at high speed until light and fluffy, about 2 minutes. Beat in the lemon zest and lemon juice. Add the eggs, 1 at a time, beating thoroughly after each addition.

3. In another medium bowl, sift the flour, baking powder and salt. Sift again. Fold one-third of the dry ingredients into the butter mixture and then fold in half of the milk. Repeat with the remaining flour and milk, ending with the flour. Turn the batter into the prepared pans.

4. Bake for 20 to 25 minutes, or until a toothpick inserted into the center of the cakes comes out dry. Let cool for 5 minutes, loosen the edges and invert onto a cooling rack.

5. To assemble the cake, put one layer on a cake plate, bottom-side up. Poke the cake with a toothpick or skewer at 2-inch intervals. Spoon the Lemon Filling over the cake a little at a time until it's absorbed; continue until it starts to run off. Put the second layer on top of the first layer and poke more holes. Spoon more filling on top of the second layer. Arrange the third layer on top, right-side up. Spoon the remaining lemon filling all over the cake and allow it to run down the sides. This filling is very liquid and may take a while to set.

—Lee Bailey

• • •

LEMON FILLING

————*Makes About 2 Cups*————
1⅓ cups sugar
3 tablespoons cornstarch
Pinch of salt
⅓ cup fresh lemon juice
4 teaspoons grated lemon zest
2 tablespoons butter, at room temperature
6 egg yolks, lightly beaten

1. In the top of a double boiler, combine the sugar, cornstarch and salt. Stir in 1 cup of water, the lemon juice and zest. Add the butter and cook, stirring, for 6 minutes.

2. Remove from the heat and gradually whisk in the egg yolks in a thin stream. Return to the heat and cook until the mixture begins to coat the back of a spoon, about 6 minutes. (If any egg white solidifies, remove it.) Let cool for about 45 minutes, stirring occasionally, before spreading on the cake.

—Lee Bailey

• • •

ALI BABA

In France, the classic desserts for Christmas and New Year's festivities are *gâteau St. Honoré, bûche de Noël* and *savarin*, which is the least well known in the States but is my favorite dessert. It is a light yeast cake soaked in a syrup made of sugar, water and a liqueur. The *Ali Baba* is a *savarin* soaked with Grand Marnier, decorated with mixed glacéed fruits and served with lightly whipped cream. It is very important to use good glacéed fruits.

————*6 to 8 Servings*————
2 teaspoons active dry yeast
¼ cup lukewarm milk (105° to 115°), plus 1 tablespoon cold milk
1¾ cups plus 4 teaspoons sugar
2 eggs, at room temperature, lightly beaten
7 tablespoons unsalted butter, at room temperature
1½ cups all-purpose flour
½ teaspoon salt
⅓ cup Grand Marnier
½ cup chopped mixed glacéed fruits
Grand Marnier-flavored whipped cream, as accompaniment

1. In a large bowl, combine the yeast with the ¼ cup lukewarm milk and 1 teaspoon of the sugar. Let stand until foamy, about 5 minutes. Add the eggs and the butter and mix to blend well.

2. In a separate bowl, combine the flour, 2 tablespoons of the sugar and the salt. With a wooden spoon, gradually incorporate the flour into the egg and butter mixture 2 to 3 tablespoons at a time.

3. When all the flour is added, beat the soft dough against the side of the bowl with a wooden spoon or with your hand until the dough is very smooth and satiny, about 5 minutes. Cover the bowl with plastic wrap or a kitchen towel and let the dough rise in a warm place until doubled in size, about 1½ hours.

4. Butter a 4-cup ring mold and dust it with 1 tablespoon of the sugar. Punch down the dough, divide it into small pieces and arrange them evenly inside the ring mold. Cover the mold with plastic wrap and let stand in a warm place until the dough rises to the top of the mold, about 45 minutes. Meanwhile, preheat the oven to 400°.

5. Sprinkle 1 tablespoon of the sugar over the top of the dough. Bake for 20 to 25 minutes, or until golden brown. Let the cake rest on a wire rack for 5 minutes.

6. Meanwhile, in a small saucepan combine 1½ cups of the sugar with 1½ cups of water. Bring to a boil over high heat, stirring to dissolve the sugar. Remove from the heat and add ¼ cup of the Grand Marnier.

7. Unmold the cake; you may need to pry the edges loose with the blade of a blunt knife. Return the hot cake to the mold. Prick the top of the cake all over with a fork and gradually drizzle ½ cup of the syrup over the cake. Invert the cake onto a platter, remove the mold and prick the top with a fork and drizzle with another ½ cup of the syrup. Add the remaining Grand Marnier to the syrup left in the pan and set aside.

8. In a small saucepan, combine the remaining 1 tablespoon milk and 1 tablespoon sugar. Bring to a boil over moderate heat, stirring to dissolve the sugar. Brush this glaze all over the cake. Decorate the top with the glacéed fruits. *(The cake can be made a day ahead. Wrap in plastic and set aside at room temperature.)*

9. Shortly before serving, fill the center of the cake with the whipped cream. Serve with the remaining Grand Marnier syrup in a sauceboat on the side.

—*Lydie Pinoy Marshall*

• • •

OPERA'S CHOCOLATE SOUFFLE TORTE

This rich and deceptively light chocolate cake is moist in the center.

——————*8 to 12 Servings*——————
½ pound semisweet chocolate, broken into small pieces
1 stick (4 ounces) plus 1 tablespoon unsalted butter, cut into small pieces
5 eggs, separated
¾ cup granulated sugar
Confectioners' sugar or chocolate shavings, for garnish

1. Preheat the oven to 350°. Butter and flour an 8-by-2-inch round cake pan. In a double boiler over barely simmering water, melt the chocolate with the butter, stirring occasionally. Remove from the heat and let cool.

2. In a medium bowl, beat the egg yolks with ½ cup of the granulated sugar until light and fluffy. Whisk in the cooled chocolate mixture until evenly combined.

3. In a large bowl, beat the egg whites until foamy. Gradually beat in the remaining ¼ cup granulated sugar until soft peaks form. Gently fold the chocolate mixture into the beaten egg whites in 3 or 4 batches.

4. Pour the batter into the prepared pan. Bake for 50 minutes, or until the cake is firm to the touch. The top of the cake will be covered with cracks. Cool on a rack in the pan for 20 minutes; the cake will deflate.

5. Invert the cake onto a serving plate and let cool completely, about 1 hour. Serve at room temperature, dusted with confectioners' sugar or sprinkled with chocolate shavings.

—*Opera, Los Angeles*

• • •

MARIE-CLAUDE GRACIA'S CHOCOLATE CAKE

I firmly believe that one can never have too many chocolate cakes in one's repertoire. Marie-Claude Gracia, chef of La Belle Gasconne in the southwestern village of Poudenas, is one of my favorite French cooks. I love the pureness and simplicity of her recipe. The cake is moist, rich, but not cloying; and it's one you can make with your eyes closed.

❢ Serve with a glass of sherry, a sweet Sauternes or a Banyuls.

——————*8 to 10 Servings*——————
1 stick (4 ounces) plus 3 tablespoons unsalted butter, at room temperature
12 ounces bittersweet chocolate, preferably Lindt or Tobler, broken into pieces
¾ cup granulated sugar
5 eggs, separated
⅓ cup unbleached all-purpose flour
Confectioners' sugar, for garnish

1. Preheat the oven to 350°. Using 1 tablespoon of the butter, generously grease a 9-inch springform pan.

2. In a double boiler, combine the chocolate, the remaining 10 tablespoons butter and the granulated sugar. Cook over barely simmering water, stirring occasionally, until melted and smooth, about 8 minutes. Remove from the heat.

3. Let the chocolate mixture cool for 10 minutes; then whisk in the egg yolks. Stir in the flour just until blended.

4. In a large bowl, beat the egg whites just until they form firm peaks; do not overbeat. Stir one-third of the egg whites into the chocolate batter until blended. Fold in the remaining egg whites until the mixture is well blended and no streaks of white remain. Spoon the batter into the springform pan.

5. Bake the cake in the middle of the oven for 35 to 40 minutes, until firm and springy and a tester inserted near the center comes out clean.

6. Let the cake cool on a rack for 2 hours, then remove the sides of the springform. Let the cake cool completely, about 1 hour longer. Invert the cake onto a platter and carefully remove the springform bottom. This cake is traditionally served without icing. To garnish, dust the top with a sprinkling of confectioners' sugar.

—Patricia Wells

• • •

CHOCOLATE BROWNIE LOAF

This fudgy cake is studded with walnuts and subtly flavored with coffee. For best results, use Dutch-process cocoa; it is darker and more mellow than other cocoa powders.

———— Makes 1 Loaf Cake ————
1¼ cups all-purpose flour
1¼ cups sugar
6 tablespoons Dutch-process cocoa
*   powder*
1 tablespoon instant coffee granules
1 teaspoon baking soda
¾ teaspoon salt
1 cup toasted walnuts, coarsely
*   chopped*
1½ cups sour cream
1 egg
1½ teaspoons vanilla extract
4 tablespoons unsalted butter,
*   melted and cooled*

1. Preheat the oven to 350°. Butter a 9-by-5-by-3-inch loaf pan. Line the bottom of the pan with waxed paper. Butter the paper, then dust the bottom and sides of the pan with flour; tap out any excess.

2. In a medium bowl, stir together the flour, sugar, cocoa, coffee, baking soda and salt until well blended. Stir in the nuts.

3. In a large bowl, whisk together the sour cream, egg, vanilla and melted butter. Add the dry ingredients to the liquid ingredients and stir with a rubber spatula until just blended. Pour the batter into the prepared pan and spread evenly.

4. Bake the cake for 1 hour and 10 minutes, or until a cake tester inserted into the center comes out clean. Leave the cake in the pan and allow it to cool on a rack for 10 minutes, then unmold and finish cooling on the rack. Wrap carefully in plastic wrap, then overwrap with aluminum foil. Let the cake stand in a cool place for at least 1 day before slicing. The cake will keep, tightly wrapped, for up to 10 days.

—Janet Fletcher

• • •

THE BIG EASY COOKIE

These cookies truly live up to their name.

Makes About
———— 20 Large Cookies ————
2⅓ cups all-purpose flour
1 teaspoon baking soda
½ teaspoon salt
2 sticks (8 ounces) unsalted butter,
*   at room temperature*
1 cup (packed) dark brown sugar
½ cup granulated sugar
2 eggs, at room temperature

9 ounces bittersweet chocolate, cut
*   into ½-inch pieces*
1½ cups coarsely chopped pecans
*   (about 6 ounces)*

1. Preheat the oven to 375°. In a medium bowl, toss together the flour, baking soda and salt.

2. In a large bowl, beat the butter with an electric mixer, until soft and creamy, about 3 minutes. Gradually beat in the brown sugar and granulated sugar. Add the eggs 1 at a time. On low speed, gradually add the flour mixture, ½ cup at a time. Stir in the chocolate and the nuts.

3. Fill a ¼-cup measuring cup with cookie dough. Drop the entire ¼ cup of dough onto a cookie sheet for each cookie, allowing 3 inches in between for spreading. Flatten each cookie slightly with a fork. Bake for 15 to 17 minutes, or until lightly golden.

—Diana Sturgis

• • •

HAZELNUT CHUNK COOKIES

Diana Sturgis, test kitchen director at *Food & Wine*, combines high-quality chocolate with her favorite nuts.

Makes About
———— 20 Large Cookies ————
1½ cups hazelnuts or filberts (about
*   6 ounces)*
2⅓ cups all-purpose flour
1 teaspoon baking soda
½ teaspoon salt
2 sticks (8 ounces) unsalted butter,
*   at room temperature*
1 cup (packed) dark brown sugar
½ cup granulated sugar
2 eggs, at room temperature
1 teaspoon vanilla extract
9 ounces bittersweet chocolate, cut
*   into ½-inch chunks*

1. Preheat the oven to 375°. Spread the nuts on a cookie sheet and bake until fragrant, 6 to 8 minutes. Place the nuts in a dish towel and rub to remove some of the skin. Coarsely chop and set aside.

2. In a medium bowl, toss together the flour, baking soda and salt.

3. In a large bowl, beat the butter with an electric mixer until soft and creamy, about 3 minutes. Gradually beat in the brown sugar and the granulated sugar. Beat in the eggs, one at a time, and then the vanilla. Gradually add the flour mixture. Stir in the chocolate and the hazelnuts.

4. Fill a ¼-cup measuring cup with the cookie dough. Drop the entire ¼ cup of dough onto a cookie sheet, allowing 3 inches between each cookie for spreading. Flatten each cookie slightly with a fork. Bake for about 15 minutes, or until light golden. Let cool before serving.

—*Diana Sturgis*

• • •

TRIPLE-FIBER OAT COOKIES

These crunchy, chewy, grainy cookies are satisfying, but one is never enough.

————*Makes About 3 Dozen*————
2 sticks (8 ounces) unsalted butter, at room temperature
½ cup (packed) light brown sugar
½ cup granulated sugar
1 egg
½ teaspoon vanilla extract
1 cup oat bran
½ cup all-purpose flour
½ teaspoon baking soda
3 cups old-fashioned rolled oats

1 cup (packed) pitted prunes, chopped
½ cup whole almonds (about 4 ounces), chopped

1. Preheat the oven to 375°. Lightly grease 2 large cookie sheets.

2. In a medium bowl, beat the butter and brown sugar with an electric hand mixer at high speed until light and fluffy, about 2 minutes. Add the granulated sugar and beat for 2 minutes longer. Add the egg and vanilla; beat until well mixed.

3. In another bowl, toss together the oat bran, flour and baking soda. Add to the butter mixture and beat at medium-low speed until blended, about 1 minute.

4. Stir in the rolled oats with a wooden spoon (the dough will be coarse and a bit crumbly). Stir in the prunes and almonds.

5. Scoop up the dough by generous tablespoons, form into 1-inch balls and flatten slightly into disks. Place about 1 inch apart on the prepared baking sheets. Bake in the middle of the oven for 12 to 15 minutes, or until golden brown. Transfer to a rack and let cool completely.

—*Tracey Seaman*

• • •

BROWN SUGAR SHORTBREAD

Shortbread is one of the easiest cookies you can make—and it even improves with time.

————*8 Servings*————
1 stick (4 ounces) unsalted butter, at room temperature
⅓ cup (packed) light brown sugar
½ teaspoon vanilla extract
1¼ cups all-purpose flour

1. Preheat the oven to 325°. Butter an 8-inch round cake pan.

2. In a medium mixing bowl, combine the butter, brown sugar and vanilla. Beat with an electric mixer until fluffy. Gradually add the flour, ¼ cup at a time. When the dough becomes too stiff to beat, mix by hand. Transfer to the cake pan, pat the dough into an even layer and prick the surface all over with a fork.

3. Bake for about 50 minutes, until lightly browned. Remove to a wire rack to cool. Cut into 8 wedges and serve.

—*Lee Bailey*

• • •

PECAN TILES

Serve these crisp, curved cookies with Plum Sorbet (p. 210).

————*Makes About 16 Cookies*————
2 egg whites
Pinch of salt
½ teaspoon vanilla extract
½ cup superfine sugar
¼ cup plus 2 tablespoons all-purpose flour
¾ cup finely chopped pecans
3 tablespoons unsalted butter, melted

1. Preheat the oven to 425°. Grease 2 large cookie sheets.

2. In a large bowl, beat the egg whites with the salt until foamy, about 30 seconds. Stir in the vanilla and sugar.

3. In a small bowl, toss the flour and pecans together. Sprinkle the nut mixture over the egg whites and stir in the melted butter; mix well.

4. Drop a level tablespoon of batter onto one of the cookie sheets. With the back of a spoon, spread it into a 3-inch round. Spread 3 more cookies onto the sheet, allowing 2 inches between each cookie. Bake until the cookies are golden around the edges, about 6 minutes.

5. With a metal spatula, quickly scrape each cookie off the sheet and drape over a horizontal rolling pin or wine bottle. Let it remain there long enough to harden into a curved tile shape, about 5 minutes. Meanwhile, bake another batch of cookies on the second cookie sheet. Wipe the used cookie sheets with a paper towel and butter again for the next two batches.

—*Lee Bailey*

• • •

PECAN COOKIES

These rich cookies made with ground toasted pecans and a hint of bourbon are delicious alongside Santa Rosa Plum Sorbet (p. 212).

———*Makes About 6 Dozen*———
½ pound shelled pecans
2 cups plus 1 tablespoon all-purpose flour
2 sticks (8 ounces) unsalted butter, at room temperature
1⅓ cups sugar
1 egg yolk
1 teaspoon salt
1½ teaspoons vanilla extract
2 tablespoons bourbon

1. Preheat the oven to 350°. Put the pecans on a cookie sheet and toast in the oven for about 10 minutes, until golden brown. Set aside to cool. Line 2 cookie sheets with baker's parchment or waxed paper.

2. Finely grind the cooled pecans with the flour in a food processor, about 1 minute. Remove and set aside.

3. In the food processor, combine the butter and sugar. Add the egg yolk, salt, vanilla and bourbon; process until smooth, about 30 seconds. Add the pecan flour and process until just blended, about 20 seconds.

4. Transfer to a lightly floured surface and shape the dough into 2 logs about 1½ inches in diameter. Wrap them in plastic wrap and refrigerate until firm. *(The recipe can be prepared to this point up to 2 days in advance.)*

5. Cut the dough logs into ¼-inch-thick slices. Put the slices on the cookie sheets, leaving 1 inch between them, and bake for about 20 minutes, until the cookies are light golden. Remove to a rack to cool.

—*Joyce Goldstein*

• • •

PINE NUT WAFERS

These crisp wafers will stay fresh in an airtight tin for two to three days.

———*Makes About 2 Dozen*———
1 cup pine nuts
⅔ cup sugar
¼ cup plus 2 tablespoons all-purpose flour
1 tablespoon cornstarch
¼ teaspoon salt
1 teaspoon vanilla extract
2 egg whites
1 stick (4 ounces) unsalted butter, melted and cooled slightly

1. Preheat the oven to 425°. Butter 2 large cookie sheets.

2. In a large bowl, mix together the pine nuts, sugar, flour, cornstarch and

salt. Stir in the vanilla and egg whites. Add the butter and stir until blended and smooth.

3. Drop level tablespoonfuls of the batter at 5-inch intervals onto one of the cookie sheets. With the back of a spoon, spread each one into a 2½-inch round. Allow 2 inches between each wafer for spreading.

4. Bake about 6 minutes, until the wafers are golden brown around the edges. Working quickly, with a wide metal spatula, scrape the wafers from the cookie sheet and cool them on a rack. Repeat with the remaining dough, using the second cookie sheet. Bake only one sheet at a time.

—*Joyce Goldstein*

• • •

FRENCH MACAROONS WITH CHOCOLATE CREAM FILLING

In France macaroons are not made with coconut, but with an almond meringue. The young pastry chef at Taillevent, Gilles Bajolles, taught me how to make macaroons that are crisp outside and moist inside. The secret is not to beat the egg whites too stiffly before the sugar is added. These freeze well.

———*Makes About 3 Dozen*———
4 egg whites
3 tablespoons granulated sugar
2 cups sifted confectioners' sugar
1 scant cup of almond powder* (see Note)
¼ cup heavy cream
2 ounces bittersweet chocolate, broken into small pieces
1 tablespoon praline paste* or hazelnut butter*
*Available at specialty food shops and health food stores

1. Preheat the oven to 425°. In a large bowl, beat the egg whites until soft peaks form. Add the granulated sugar and beat until stiff and shiny. Fold in the confectioners' sugar and the almond powder until blended.

2. Line 2 large cookie sheets with parchment paper. Fit a pastry bag with a plain ¼-inch tip and pipe out 1-inch meringues, or form with 2 teaspoons.

3. Put an empty cookie sheet or jelly-roll pan on the top rack of the oven to absorb some of the heat and prevent the tops of the meringues from burning. Set the meringues in the middle of the oven and bake for 10 minutes, or until they are light golden in color. Set the cookie sheets on a rack and let cool. Then carefully scrape the meringues from the parchment with a wide metal spatula.

4. In a small saucepan, bring the cream to a boil over low heat. Add the chocolate and stir until melted. Remove from the heat and stir in the praline paste. Refrigerate until stiff enough to spread, about 15 minutes.

5. Spread a small dab of the chocolate filling onto the flat side of one meringue and sandwich with another. Repeat to fill all the meringues. Wrap well and freeze until ready to serve.

NOTE: To make your own almond powder, finely grind 5 ounces blanched almonds with 1 tablespoon granulated sugar in a food processor.

—*Lydie Pinoy Marshall*

• • •

ALMOND TUILE COOKIE CUPS

These cookie cups make wonderful containers for ice cream, mousse and sorbets, such as Blackberry Sorbet (p. 211).

——— *Makes 20 to 24 Cups* ———
1½ sticks (6 ounces) unsalted
  butter, at room temperature
1 cup sugar
¼ teaspoon almond extract
6 egg whites
1 cup all-purpose flour

1. In a medium mixer bowl, beat the butter on high speed until soft. Gradually add the sugar and beat until light and fluffy, about 4 minutes.

2. Add the almond extract and 1 tablespoon of water. Beat in the egg whites, one at a time. Add the flour and mix until just smooth. Allow the batter to rest at room temperature for at least 2 hours.

3. Preheat the oven to 425°. Butter a large cookie sheet. Drop a heaping tablespoon of batter onto the sheet. With the back of a spoon, spread it into a 4-inch round. Form three more cookie rounds on the sheet, leaving a 2-inch space between each. Bake for about 8 minutes until light golden brown.

4. Working quickly, scrape each cookie from the tray with a wide metal spatula and press into a custard cup. The cookie will quickly harden into a cup shape. Repeat with the remaining cookies. If they become too crisp to shape, rewarm them in the oven for about 15 seconds until they soften again. Repeat with the next sheet of cookies, but bake only one sheet at a time. When your first cookie sheet cools, wipe it with a paper towel and butter it for the next batch. Let the cookies cool completely before storing in an airtight container to maintain their freshness. They will keep for up to 3 days.

—*Joyce Goldstein*

• • •

CHOCOLATE-WALNUT BISCOTTI

Biscotti di cioccolata are sometimes called *mostaccioli* because of their mustache shape.

——— *Makes About 4 Dozen* ———
2 cups walnut halves (about 8
  ounces)
3 ounces unsweetened chocolate
5 tablespoons plus 1 teaspoon
  unsalted butter
2 cups all-purpose flour
2 teaspoons baking powder
3 eggs
1 cup sugar
1 teaspoon grated orange zest

1. Preheat the oven to 350°. Place the walnuts on a cookie sheet and toast until golden brown, about 10 minutes. Let cool and then chop coarsely.

2. In a double boiler over simmering water, melt the chocolate and butter together. Remove from the heat and stir until smooth. Let cool for 10 minutes.

3. Sift together the flour and baking powder. In a large bowl, beat the eggs lightly. Gradually beat in the sugar. Add the orange zest. Stir in the cooled chocolate until blended. Stir in the flour and baking powder until incorporated. Fold in the chopped walnuts. Divide the dough in half, wrap in plastic wrap and refrigerate at least 1 hour or overnight.

4. Butter a large cookie sheet and preheat the oven to 350°. Shape each half of the dough into a 14-by-2½-inch log. Place about 4 inches apart on the prepared pan. Smooth the tops and sides with a rubber spatula. Bake for 40 to 45 minutes, or until the logs are firm when pressed in the center. Remove the baking sheet from the oven. Do not turn off the oven.

5. Slide the logs onto a cutting board. With a large knife, cut each log diagonally into ½-inch slices. Stand the slices upright on edge on the prepared cookie sheet. Return to the oven and bake for 15 minutes longer, or until crisp. Transfer to wire racks to cool completely.

—*Michele Scicolone*

• • •

CORNMEAL CRESCENT BISCOTTI

These cookies, *crumiri*, come from Piedmont where cornmeal is often eaten in the form of polenta. These delicate biscotti are well suited to being served with light sparkling wines. If anything, they require only a quick dip as opposed to a heavy dunking.

———*Makes About 4 Dozen* ———
1¾ cups all-purpose flour
¾ cup fine yellow cornmeal

1 teaspoon salt
2 sticks (8 ounces) unsalted butter, at room temperature
¾ cup sugar
1 egg
1 teaspoon vanilla extract

1. Preheat the oven to 375°. Butter and flour 2 large cookie sheets.

2. On a piece of waxed paper, combine the flour, cornmeal and salt. In a large bowl, beat the butter and sugar with a hand-held electric mixer until light and fluffy. Beat in the egg and vanilla. Stir in the dry ingredients with a wooden spoon until well blended. Cover and refrigerate the dough until firm enough to handle, at least 1 hour.

3. Scoop up 1 heaping tablespoon of the dough and roll into a log about 2 inches long. Bend to form a crescent shape. Repeat with the remaining dough. As they are shaped, place the biscotti about 2 inches apart on the prepared cookie sheets. With your hands or the back of a wooden spoon, lightly flatten the biscotti.

4. Bake for 15 to 20 minutes, or until golden brown. Transfer to racks to cool.

—*Michele Scicolone*

• • •

TOASTED SESAME SEED BISCOTTI

Biscotti regina reign in Sicily, where sesame seeds were introduced by the Arabs who ruled there for hundreds of years. Unhulled sesame seeds, available in health food stores, will give the cookies an authentic flavor.

———*Makes About 2 Dozen* ———
1 cup (about 4 ounces) unhulled sesame seeds
2 cups all-purpose flour
⅔ cup sugar
1 teaspoon baking powder
½ teaspoon salt
½ cup solid vegetable shortening
2 eggs
1 teaspoon vanilla extract
1 teaspoon grated lemon zest

1. Preheat the oven to 350°. Spread the sesame seeds on a baking sheet or in a roasting pan and toast, shaking the pan occasionally, until golden brown, about 15 minutes. Set aside to cool.

2. Lightly grease a cookie sheet. In a bowl, combine the flour, sugar, baking powder and salt. Cut in the shortening until the mixture resembles coarse meal.

3. In a small bowl, beat together the eggs, vanilla and lemon zest. Pour into the dry ingredients and stir until thoroughly incorporated.

4. Shape the dough into 2-by-¾-inch logs. Roll the logs in the sesame seeds, patting the seeds into the dough. With your hands or the back of a spoon, lightly flatten the biscotti and place 1 inch apart on the prepared cookie sheet. Bake for 30 to 35 minutes, or until golden brown. Transfer to wire racks to cool.

—*Michele Scicolone*

• • •

STOCKS, SAUCES & CONDIMENTS

BROWN STOCK

Deep amber, flavorful brown stock forms the basis for many sauces.

——— *Makes 4 to 5 Quarts* ———
6 pounds beef shin with bones
6 pounds veal bones
6 carrots, cut into 2-inch lengths
3 onions—unpeeled, halved and each half stuck with 1 whole clove
3 leeks (white part only), split lengthwise, plus 1 leek (including green top), quartered
2 celery ribs with leaves, cut into 2-inch lengths
1 small white turnip
2 cups coarsely chopped tomatoes, canned or fresh
Bouquet garni: 6 sprigs of parsley, 1 teaspoon thyme, 1 large bay leaf, 7 peppercorns and 2 unpeeled garlic cloves tied in a double thickness of cheesecloth

1. Preheat the oven to 450°. Place the meat and bones in a large roasting pan in 1 or 2 layers, or in 2 roasting pans if necessary. Bake, uncovered, for 30 minutes. Add the carrots and onions and bake, turning occasionally, until the bones are deep brown but not charred, 30 to 60 minutes longer.

2. Transfer the bones and vegetables to a large stockpot. Pour off and discard any fat from the roasting pan. Add 2 to 3 cups of cold water to the pan and deglaze over medium heat, scraping up any browned particles that cling to the bottom. Pour the liquid into the stockpot, add enough additional cold water to cover the bones—about 4 quarts—and bring the water slowly to a simmer over low heat: to insure a clear stock, this slow heating should take about 1 hour. Skim off all the scum that rises to the surface.

3. Add the leeks, celery, turnip, tomatoes, bouquet garni and enough additional water to cover. Simmer, partially covered, over low heat for 5 to 8 hours, skimming the surface occasionally. Add additional water to cover as necessary.

4. Carefully ladle the stock into a large bowl through a colander lined with several thicknesses of dampened cheesecloth. Do not press on the bones and vegetables, or the resulting stock will be cloudy. Refrigerate, uncovered, overnight; then remove any fat from the surface. The stock may be refrigerated for 3 to 4 days, then reboiled, or frozen for several months.

—F&W

• • •

RICH CHICKEN STOCK

Although this deliciously rich stock calls for two whole chickens in addition to chicken parts, the whole birds are removed as soon as they are cooked, so you can eat them as is or use the meat for other dishes, salads or sandwiches. You may substitute additional chicken parts for the whole chickens. Use this stock as a base for soups or sauces.

——— *Makes About 3 Quarts* ———
4 pounds chicken backs, necks and/ or wings
2 whole chickens (about 3 pounds each), including necks and gizzards
3 large carrots, sliced
2 large onions, sliced
4 medium leeks—split lengthwise, rinsed and sliced crosswise (or substitute 1 extra onion)
2 celery ribs with leaves, sliced
Bouquet garni: 8 sprigs of parsley, 1 teaspoon thyme, 1 bay leaf, ½ teaspoon peppercorns and 3 whole cloves tied in a double thickness of cheesecloth

1. Place the chicken parts in a large, heavy stockpot: place the whole chickens on top. Add 6 quarts of cold water and place over low heat. Heat to simmering without stirring; for a clear stock, this should take about 1 hour. While the water is heating, skim off any scum that rises to the surface.

2. Add the carrots, onions, leeks, celery and bouquet garni. Simmer, partially covered, without stirring, for about 45 minutes. Remove both chickens. Continue simmering the stock, without stirring, for about 4 hours, skimming occasionally. (The meat can be removed from the two chickens as soon as they are cool enough to handle and the bones returned to the pot.)

3. Ladle the stock carefully through a colander lined with several layers of dampened cheesecloth. Strain a second time, if desired, for an even clearer stock. Let cool to room temperature; then cover and refrigerate. Remove the congealed fat from the top. If using the hot stock immediately, remove the fat by first skimming and then blotting the surface with paper towels, or use a degreasing utensil designed for that purpose.

—F&W

• • •

BROWN CHICKEN STOCK

—— Makes 3 Cups ——
3 to 4 pounds chicken backs, wings
  and/or necks
1 medium onion, unpeeled and
  quartered
1 celery rib, thickly sliced
1½ cups dry white wine
2 medium tomatoes, quartered
1 sprig of fresh thyme or ¼ teaspoon
  dried
½ imported bay leaf
½ teaspoon black peppercorns

1. Preheat the oven to 500°. Place the chicken, onion and celery in a roasting pan and roast, turning the bones once or twice, until they are a dark golden brown, about 30 minutes.

2. Transfer the chicken and vegetables to a stockpot. Pour off any fat from the roasting pan and place it on top of the stove. Add the wine to the pan and bring to a boil, scraping up any browned bits from the pan. Pour into the stockpot.

3. Add the tomatoes, thyme, bay leaf, peppercorns and 2½ quarts of water. Bring to a boil over high heat, reduce the heat to moderately low and simmer, uncovered, for 3 hours, skimming off the foam and fat occasionally.

4. Strain the stock into a large saucepan. Skim off any fat. Boil over high heat until the stock is reduced to 3 cups.

—*F&W*

• • •

RICH FREE-RANGE CHICKEN STOCK

Free-range chickens make the best-flavored stock. Save the carcasses from roast chickens for this purpose.

—— Makes 2 Quarts ——
4 to 5 pounds free-range chicken
  backs, wings and/or legs and
  thighs
1 onion, halved
1 carrot, quartered
1 imported bay leaf
½ teaspoon salt
¼ teaspoon thyme

1. In a large stockpot, place the chicken parts, onion, carrot, bay leaf, salt and thyme. Add 4 quarts of cold water and bring to a boil over high heat. Reduce the heat to moderately low and simmer, uncovered, for 4½ hours, skimming off the foam and fat occasionally.

2. Strain into a large saucepan and skim once more. Boil over high heat until the stock is reduced to 2 quarts. Let cool, cover and refrigerate for up to 3 days or freeze for up to 3 months.

—*Molly O'Neill*

• • •

GOOSE STOCK

This recipe will yield enough stock to make the Cream of Carrot and Lemon Soup (p. 29) and to use as basting liquid for the Roasted Goose with Chicken Liver Stuffing (p. 97).

—— Makes 2 Quarts ——
Reserved wing tips, second wing
  joints, wishbone and neck of a
  goose, or 1 more pound of chicken
  parts
2 pounds chicken necks, backs and/
  or wings
1 pound carrots
1 celery rib
2 medium onions, each stuck with
  2 cloves
Bouquet garni: 3 sprigs of parsley, 1
  teaspoon thyme and 1 bay leaf tied
  in cheesecloth
1½ teaspoons salt

1. Using a cleaver, cut up the goose and chicken parts into small pieces.

2. Put the goose and chicken parts in a stockpot. Add at least 4 quarts of cold water to cover. Bring to a boil over moderately low heat, skimming the surface several times.

3. Add the carrots, celery, onions, bouquet garni and salt to the stockpot. Simmer, partially covered, for 3 hours; strain through a fine-mesh sieve. If there is more than 8 cups, boil to reduce. *(The stock can be made up to 2 days in advance and refrigerated, covered.)*

—*Lydie Pinoy Marshall*

• • •

FISH STOCK

When cleaning whole fish, save the heads and frames for stock; or, inquire at your local fish market. Use this stock for a variety of sauces.

—— Makes About 2 Quarts ——
4 pounds fish bones and trimmings
  (heads, tails, skin)
3 tablespoons vegetable oil
1 medium onion, cut into eighths
1 large celery rib, cut into 1-inch
  lengths
1 large carrot, cut into 1-inch
  lengths

Bouquet garni: 3 sprigs of parsley, ½ teaspoon thyme, 1 bay leaf and 8 to 10 peppercorns tied in a double thickness of cheesecloth

1. Rinse the fish bones and trimmings under cold running water to remove any blood; drain.

2. Heat the oil in a large, heavy stockpot. Add the fish bones and trimmings and sauté over moderate heat for 5 minutes, breaking them up occasionally with a wooden spoon. Cook, partially covered, for 5 minutes longer.

3. Add the onion, celery, carrot and bouquet garni. Pour in 3 quarts of cold water. Bring the mixture to a boil over high heat, skimming off any foam from the surface. Reduce the heat to low and simmer, uncovered, for 30 minutes. Strain through a fine sieve lined with several layers of dampened cheesecloth.
—*F&W*

• • •

VEGETABLE STOCK

——— *Makes About 1½ Quarts* ———
3 celery ribs, cut into 2-inch lengths
2 large carrots, cut into 2-inch lengths
2 small onions, unpeeled and quartered
1 large boiling potato, cut into 1-inch slices
½ pound mushrooms, roughly chopped
4 small leeks (white part only), split lengthwise
2 small white turnips, peeled and quartered
6 garlic cloves, unpeeled
1½ teaspoons salt
1½ teaspoons Hungarian sweet paprika

Bouquet garni: 10 sprigs of parsley, 1½ teaspoons marjoram, 2 bay leaves and 8 peppercorns tied in a double thickness of cheesecloth

1. Place all the vegetables in a stockpot. Add the garlic, salt, paprika, bouquet garni and 3 quarts of water and bring to a boil over moderate heat.

2. Reduce the heat to low and simmer the stock, partially covered, until reduced by half, about 1½ hours.

3. Strain through a double thickness of dampened cheesecloth, pressing lightly on the vegetables with the back of a spoon.

—*F&W*

• • •

SEAFOOD BOIL

In the Deep South, recipes for boiling shellfish invariably call for a commercially prepared "boil" such as McCormick's, Old Bay's or Zatarain's, plus added salt. My mix combines herbs, spices and salt. To use, allow 2 teaspoons per quart of water, plus half a lemon. You will need one quart of water per pound of shrimp.

——— *Makes About 1 Cup* ———
¼ cup mustard seeds
2 tablespoons whole black peppercorns
2 tablespoons crushed hot red pepper
6 bay leaves
1 tablespoon celery seeds
1 tablespoon coriander seeds
1 tablespoon ground ginger
A few blades of mace
¼ cup coarse (kosher), sea or pickling salt

In a blender, combine all of the ingredients except the salt and blend until evenly ground. Add the salt and blend briefly to incorporate. Transfer the mixture to a well-sealed jar and store in a cool, dark, dry place for up to 2 months.
—*John Martin Taylor*

• • •

TOMATO SAUCE

This makes a good, all-purpose tomato sauce lightly flavored with tarragon and sweetened with the addition of a roasted red pepper.

——— *Makes About 4 Cups* ———
1 large red bell pepper
2 tablespoons unsalted butter
2 tablespoons olive oil
3 medium onions, coarsely chopped
1 garlic clove, crushed through a press
1 can (35 ounces) Italian peeled tomatoes, with their juice
1¼ teaspoons salt
1 teaspoon thyme
10 or more large fresh tarragon leaves, chopped, or ½ teaspoon dried
⅛ teaspoon cayenne pepper
¼ cup minced parsley

1. Roast the red pepper directly over a gas flame or under the broiler as close to the heat as possible, turning, until charred all over. Enclose the pepper in a paper bag and set aside for 10 minutes to steam. When cool enough to handle, peel the pepper and remove the core, seeds and ribs. Coarsely chop the pepper.

2. In a large saucepan or flameproof casserole, melt the butter in the olive oil over moderate heat. Add the onions and sauté until wilted, about 5 minutes.

3. Add the garlic and cook for 1 minute. Add the tomatoes with their juice, the salt, thyme, tarragon and cayenne. Simmer over low heat until the sauce is thickened, 25 to 35 minutes.

4. Transfer to a food processor. Add the roasted pepper. Turn the machine quickly on and off to puree coarsely. Return the sauce to the pan and stir in the parsley. Simmer over low heat for 10 minutes to blend the flavors.

—Lee Bailey

• • •

TOMATO-OLIVE SAUCE

You could toss this sauce with pasta or serve it alongside the Beef, Sausage and Spinach Loaf (p. 60) for which it was designed.

——— *Makes About 3 Cups* ———
3 tablespoons olive oil
1 medium onion, chopped
3 garlic cloves, minced
½ teaspoon basil
½ teaspoon oregano
½ teaspoon thyme
¾ teaspoon crushed hot red pepper
1 can (35 ounces) Italian peeled
tomatoes, with their juice
½ teaspoon salt
⅓ cup finely chopped Italian flat-leaf
parsley
12 brine-cured black olives, such as
Calamata, pitted and chopped

1. In a large nonreactive saucepan or flameproof casserole, heat the olive oil. Add the onion, garlic, basil, oregano, thyme and hot pepper. Cook over low heat, covered, stirring once or twice, until the onion is very soft, about 20 minutes.

2. Add the tomatoes, breaking them up with a spoon; add their juice and the salt. Simmer, uncovered, stirring occa-

sionally, until the sauce is reduced to about 3 cups, 45 to 50 minutes.

3. Let the sauce cool slightly, then force through the medium blade of a food mill or puree coarsely in a food processor. Return the sauce to the pan and stir in the parsley and olives. *(The sauce can be prepared up to 3 days ahead and refrigerated, covered.)* Reheat before serving.

—Michael McLaughlin

• • •

FRESH PLUM TOMATO SAUCE

This sauce is best made with fresh tomatoes and herbs. Serve it with small pasta shapes or homemade stuffed pasta, such as the tortelli on page 106.

——— *6 to 8 Servings* ———
⅓ cup olive oil
1 medium onion, chopped
2 garlic cloves, minced
1 tablespoon chopped fresh basil or 1
teaspoon dried
2 tablespoons chopped parsley
1½ teaspoons chopped fresh
oregano or ½ teaspoon dried
2 pounds fresh plum tomatoes—
rinsed, dried and cut into ½-inch
dice—or 2 cans (35 ounces each)
Italian peeled tomatoes, drained
and chopped
1½ teaspoons sugar
1 teaspoon salt
Pinch of freshly ground pepper

1. In a large nonreactive saucepan, heat the olive oil over moderate heat. Add the onion and cook, stirring occasionally, until softened but not browned, about 5 minutes.

2. Add the garlic, basil, parsley and oregano and stir to combine. Cook until fragrant, about 1 minute. Stir in the tomatoes, sugar, salt and pepper.

3. Cover the pot and simmer, stirring occasionally, for 30 minutes.

—Fred Ferretti

• • •

SAVORY TOMATO-CARROT SAUCE

This sauce was inspired by a recipe of Marcella Hazan's. It's delicious with pasta, pork chops, grilled chicken or fish. A pleasant, coarse texture is obtained by using a food mill. You can use a food processor but the consistency will be slightly different.

——— *Makes About 2¼ Cups* ———
3 tablespoons olive oil
1 large carrot, halved lengthwise
and thinly sliced into half-rounds
1 medium onion, chopped
2 large garlic cloves, sliced
1 can (28-ounces) Italian peeled
tomatoes, crushed and juice
reserved
1½ tablespoons minced winter
savory
¼ teaspoon salt
¼ teaspoon freshly ground pepper

1. In a heavy medium nonreactive saucepan, heat the olive oil over moderate heat. Add the carrot, onion and garlic. Reduce the heat to low and cook, stirring occasionally, until the vegetables are soft, about 15 minutes.

2. Add the tomatoes and their juice and increase the heat to moderate. Simmer briskly, stirring occasionally, until slightly thickened and most of the juice has evaporated, about 20 minutes.

3. Pass the sauce through a food mill and return it to the saucepan. Stir in the savory, salt and pepper and heat through. *(The sauce can be made up to 2 days in advance; cover and refrigerate. Add a little more savory after reheating.)*

—Marcia Kiesel

• • •

STOCKS, SAUCES & CONDIMENTS

CREME FRAICHE

—— Makes About 2¼ Cups ——
2 cups heavy cream
⅓ cup active-culture buttermilk

1. In a small saucepan, gently heat the cream and buttermilk to just under 100° (higher will kill the culture).

2. Pour into a clean glass jar, cover and place in a saucepan filled with warm (100°) water; or put in a thermos bottle. Allow to stand for 8 to 36 hours, or until thickened, replenishing the warm water from time to time. The longer you culture the cream, the tangier it will become.

3. Refrigerate until chilled. Crème fraîche will keep in the refrigerator for a week to 10 days.

—*F&W*

• • •

BASIC MAYONNAISE

Mayonnaise works best if all the ingredients are at room temperature before you begin. The emulsion (the suspension of the particles of oil within the yolk) will not form if the oil or the yolks are too cold. On a chilly day, warm the bowl in hot water, then dry well before starting.

—— Makes About 1½ Cups ——
3 egg yolks, at room temperature
1 teaspoon Dijon-style mustard
½ teaspoon salt
Pinch of white pepper
1 tablespoon fresh lemon juice
½ cup olive oil mixed with ½ cup
*   light vegetable oil (see Note)*
1 tablespoon white wine vinegar
1 tablespoon boiling water

1. In a medium bowl, whisk the egg yolks until they lighten in color and begin

to thicken. Beat in the mustard, salt, pepper and lemon juice and continue whisking until the mixture thickens enough to leave a trail when the whisk is drawn across the bottom of the bowl.

2. Very gradually, begin whisking in the oil by droplets. The emulsion will not form if the oil is added too quickly at this stage.

3. Once the emulsion forms and the mayonnaise begins to thicken, you can add the oil more rapidly, but never faster than in a thin stream.

4. After all the oil has been incorporated, whisk in the vinegar and the boiling water. (The vinegar will lighten and flavor the sauce, the boiling water will help stabilize it.) Taste the mayonnaise and adjust the seasonings according to your taste and the planned use. Cover and refrigerate for up to 5 days.

NOTE: We find this combination of oils produces the perfect balance of flavor and lightness for an all-purpose mayonnaise. You can adjust the proportions according to your taste and particular use.

—*F&W*

• • •

LEMON GRASS DIPPING SAUCE

Serve this dipping sauce with Fried Chicken Drumettes with Lemon Grass (p. 19).

—— Makes About ⅓ Cup ——
1 tablespoon peanut oil
1 stalk of lemon grass* (bottom third
*   only), finely minced*
1½ teaspoons minced fresh ginger
2 tablespoons soy sauce
2 tablespoons rice wine vinegar

1 tablespoon Oriental sesame oil
1 teaspoon hot chile oil
½ teaspoon sugar
*Available at Asian markets

In a small saucepan, heat the peanut oil over moderate heat. Add the lemon grass and ginger; sauté until fragrant, about 30 seconds. Remove from the heat and add the soy sauce, vinegar, sesame oil, hot oil and sugar. Stir to dissolve the sugar. Pour into a small bowl; let stand at room temperature for 1 hour before serving.

—*Bruce Cost*

• • •

THAI BASIL DIPPING SAUCE

This sauce is based on one generally served with Thai egg rolls, but we've reduced the sweetness and added fresh basil for a summery taste.

—— Makes About 1½ Cups ——
⅔ cup distilled white vinegar
½ cup light corn syrup
¼ cup fish sauce (nuoc mam)*
6 medium garlic cloves
2 large serrano peppers or other hot
*   chiles, seeded*
2 tablespoons sugar
¾ cup (lightly packed) fresh basil
*   leaves, chopped*
*Available at Asian markets

1. In a small nonreactive saucepan, combine the vinegar, corn syrup, fish sauce and 3 tablespoons of water. Bring to a boil over high heat, stirring to blend well. Remove from the heat and let cool to room temperature.

2. In a food processor, combine the garlic, chiles and sugar. Puree to a paste. Add the cooled syrup to the paste and process briefly just to blend. Add the basil leaves and process until minced.

—*Linda Burum & Linda Merinoff*

• • •

PEANUT DIPPING SAUCE

Serve this dipping sauce with various satays, such as Lamb Barbecue on a Stick (p. 80).

—————— Makes About 1²/₃ Cups ——————
1 cup crunchy peanut butter
¼ cup ketjap manis, storebought or
*   homemade (p. 256)*
3 garlic cloves, crushed through a
*   press*
1½ tablespoons brown sugar
2 tablespoons fresh lemon juice
1 teaspoon crushed hot red pepper
¾ cup boiling water

In a medium bowl, combine the peanut butter, *ketjap manis,* garlic, brown sugar, lemon juice and hot pepper. Add the boiling water and stir until smooth. *(The sauce can be made up to 3 hours in advance. Set aside at room temperature; do not refrigerate. If the sauce thickens too much, thin with a little more water.)*
—Copeland Marks

• • •

NUOC CHAM DIPPING SAUCE

This indispensable dipping sauce is served with every Vietnamese meal.

—————— Makes About 2½ Cups ——————
1 teaspoon crushed hot red pepper
1 tablespoon distilled white vinegar
*½ cup fish sauce (nuoc mam) ***
¼ cup fresh lime juice
1 small carrot—finely shredded,
*   rinsed and squeezed dry*
2 small garlic cloves, minced

½ cup sugar
*Available at Asian markets

1. In a small dish, soak the hot pepper in the vinegar for 2 minutes.
2. In a small bowl, combine the fish sauce, lime juice, carrot, garlic and sugar. Stir in 1½ cups warm water and the hot pepper–vinegar mixture. Stir until the sugar dissolves. Serve at room temperature. Store the sauce in a jar in the refrigerator for up to 3 days.
—Marcia Kiesel

• • •

CREAMY HORSERADISH SAUCE

Serve this delicious fresh horseradish sauce with roast beef or hamburger.

—————— Makes About 1³/₄ Cups ——————
2 tablespoons unsalted butter
1 shallot, minced
2 garlic cloves, minced
2 cups heavy cream
¾ cup grated fresh horseradish
½ teaspoon salt
¼ teaspoon freshly ground white
*   pepper*
Pinch of cayenne pepper

1. In a medium skillet, melt the butter over moderate heat. Add the minced shallot and garlic and sauté until softened but not browned, about 2 minutes.
2. Add the heavy cream and the horseradish. Bring to a boil, reduce the heat to low and simmer until the sauce is thick enough to coat the back of a spoon, 12 to 15 minutes.
3. Season with the salt, white pepper and cayenne.
—Commander's Palace, New Orleans

• • •

LEMON MAYONNAISE

—————— Makes About 1½ Cups ——————
3 egg yolks, at room temperature
½ teaspoon salt
¼ cup fresh lemon juice
1 cup olive oil

1. In a medium bowl, combine the egg yolks, salt and 2 tablespoons of the lemon juice. Whisk until smooth.
2. Slowly drizzle in the oil, a few drops at a time, until the mayonnaise begins to thicken. Whisk in the remaining oil in a slow, thin stream. Whisk in the remaining 2 tablespoons lemon juice.
—Jeremiah Tower

• • •

SWEET RED PEPPER REMOULADE

Serve this red pepper-flavored mayonnaise as a sandwich spread or in a seafood salad.

—————— Makes About 1½ Cups ——————
1 large red bell pepper
1¼ cups mayonnaise

1. Preheat the oven to 350°. Place the red pepper on a pie pan, set it uncovered in the oven and roast until the pepper is soft and its skin crinkles, 40 to 45 minutes.
2. Remove from the oven, cover loosely with a cloth and let cool to room temperature, about 1 hour.
3. Peel, core and seed the roasted pepper; cut into 1-inch pieces. Place in a food processor with ¼ cup of the mayonnaise and puree until smooth. Add the remaining mayonnaise and blend. *(The recipe can be made up to 1 day in advance.)*
—Sandy Hollander,
45 South Restaurant, Savannah

• • •

STOCKS, SAUCES & CONDIMENTS

CUCUMBER-YOGURT SAUCE

This refreshing and tart sauce goes well with grilled meats and especially lamb. Serve it with Fragrant Lamb Shish Kebabs (p. 80).

——— *Makes About 1½ Cups* ———
2 tablespoons olive oil
2 tablespoons dry white wine
1 tablespoon minced fresh dill
1 garlic clove, crushed through a press
¾ teaspoon salt
¼ teaspoon freshly ground pepper
1 cup plain yogurt
2 medium cucumbers—peeled, seeded and finely diced

In a medium bowl, combine the olive oil, white wine, dill, garlic, salt, pepper and yogurt. Whisk to blend well. Add the diced cucumbers. Cover and refrigerate for up to 3 hours before serving.
—*Jim Fobel*

• • •

HERB BUTTER

This can be used in the '21' Club Hamburger (p. 59) or tossed with steamed vegetables.

——— *Makes About 1 Cup* ———
1 stick (4 ounces) unsalted butter, at room temperature
1 tablespoon finely chopped fresh thyme
1 tablespoon finely chopped fresh basil
1 tablespoon finely chopped fresh parsley

In a small bowl, combine the butter, thyme, basil and parsley. Beat until well blended. Place on a sheet of waxed paper, roll into a 1-inch-thick log and freeze until firm, about 1 hour. *(The herb butter can be prepared up to 1 month ahead.)*
—*'21' Club, New York City*

• • •

ITALIAN PARSLEY PESTO

This pesto will keep covered in the refrigerator for up to one week.

——— *Makes About 1 Cup* ———
¼ cup pine nuts or blanched almonds
3 medium garlic cloves
2 cups (packed) Italian flat-leaf parsley leaves, rinsed and dried
⅓ cup extra-virgin olive oil
3 tablespoons freshly grated Parmesan cheese
½ teaspoon salt
½ teaspoon freshly ground pepper

1. Preheat the oven to 325°. Place the nuts on a baking sheet and bake for 8 minutes, or until lightly toasted. Let cool.
2. In a food processor, mince the garlic. Add the parsley and nuts and process until minced. With the machine on, add the oil in a thin stream and process until well blended. Add the Parmesan and the salt and pepper and process to mix.
—*The Riviera, Dallas*

• • •

SALSA VERDE

This tart, piquant sauce is good on anything, but is often served with chicken and sour cream. If you can't find tomatillos, increase the chopped chiles to one cup, but use a milder green chile for the additional half-cup so that the salsa will not be overpowering.

——— *Makes About 2½ Cups* ———
1 can (13 ounces) tomatillos, drained
1 cup chopped scallions (white and tender green)
½ cup chopped hot green New Mexico chiles (roasted and peeled fresh or frozen) or 1 can (4 ounces) chopped hot green chiles, drained
1 large garlic clove, minced
½ teaspoon salt

Combine all the ingredients in a blender or food processor and puree.
—*Jane Butel*

• • •

SALSA FRESCA

This fresh hot sauce will keep for one week in the refrigerator or can be frozen for several months.

——— *Makes About 1½ Cups* ———
½ cup finely chopped red onion or scallions
4 fresh hot green chiles—roasted, peeled and chopped (about ½ cup)—or 1 can (4 ounces) chopped hot green chiles, drained

*1 large tomato, peeled and finely
   chopped*
1 large garlic clove, minced

Combine all the ingredients in a bowl
and let stand for at least 15 minutes before
serving.

—*Jane Butel*

• • •

TOMATO SALSA

Serve this fresh tomato salsa with Black-
Eyed-Pea Cakes (p. 130).

——— *Makes About 2¾ Cups* ———
*3 medium tomatoes—peeled, seeded
   and coarsely chopped*
¼ cup finely diced red onion
2 tablespoons thinly sliced scallions
1½ teaspoons minced garlic
*1 jalapeño pepper, seeded and finely
   minced*
*2 tablespoons chopped fresh
   coriander*
¾ teaspoon cumin
*½ teaspoon freshly ground black
   pepper*
½ teaspoon salt
2 tablespoons olive oil
1 tablespoon cider vinegar

Combine all the ingredients in a large
bowl and toss well. *(The recipe can be
prepared up to 1 day in advance, covered
and refrigerated. Drain off any excess
liquid before serving.)*

—*Donald Barickman, Carolina's,
Charleston, South Carolina*

• • •

GOLDEN TOMATO, PEPPER AND ONION SAUCE

Yellow tomatoes and peppers have a
much sweeter flavor than the other varieties, so use them here if you can. This
sauce should be made a day ahead to let
the peppers and onions marinate.

——— *6 Servings* ———
*½ cup coarsely chopped yellow bell
   pepper*
½ cup coarsely chopped onion
¼ cup white wine vinegar
¼ cup extra-virgin olive oil
2 dashes of hot pepper sauce
½ teaspoon honey
*2 cups small yellow pear (or cherry)
   tomatoes, cut in half*
¼ teaspoon salt
*⅛ teaspoon freshly ground black
   pepper*

1. In a medium heatproof glass bowl,
mix the pepper and onion together.

2. In a medium nonreactive saucepan,
combine the vinegar, olive oil, hot pepper
sauce, honey and ¼ cup of water over
moderate heat. Bring to a boil and boil for
3 minutes.

3. Pour over the pepper and onion; stir
well. Let cool for about 15 minutes, then
cover with plastic wrap and refrigerate
overnight.

4. To serve, drain the onion and pepper well. Add the tomatoes and toss at the
last minute. Season with the salt and
pepper.

—*Lee Bailey*

• • •

PEAR SALSA

I have made this same recipe with peaches, and it is equally good. However, I'd
save that for summer when peaches are at
their best. If you prefer your salsa very
zesty, add more scallions and jalapeño
pepper.

——— *Makes About 3 Cups* ———
2 plum tomatoes
*2 firm pears, preferably Bosc—
   peeled, cored and cut into ¼-inch
   dice*
1 tablespoon fresh lemon juice
6 large scallions, chopped
*1 tablespoon minced, seeded
   jalapeño peppers*
*¼ cup plus 2 tablespoons extra-
   virgin olive oil*
2 tablespoons sherry wine vinegar
1 teaspoon honey

1. Blanch the tomatoes in a medium
saucepan of boiling water for 1 minute.
Rinse under cold running water to cool.
Slip the skins off, cut the tomatoes in half
and scoop out the seeds. Slice the tomatoes into ¼-inch julienne strips.

2. In a medium bowl, toss the pears
with the lemon juice. Add the tomatoes,
scallions and jalapeño; toss to mix well.

3. In another medium bowl, whisk
together the oil, vinegar and honey. Drizzle over the pears and toss to coat. *(The
recipe can be prepared ahead to this point.
If you are having it within 3 hours, set
aside at room temperature; up to 1 day
ahead, cover and refrigerate.)* Serve with
a slotted spoon, allowing most of the juice
to drain off.

—*Lee Bailey*

• • •

PLUM SAUCE

The texture in our duck sauce is similar to chutney. You can either process the sauce in canning jars and store it for at least a year or keep it in the refrigerator in a tightly closed bottle for several weeks.

——— *Makes About 4 Cups* ———
2 pounds ripe plums—peeled and coarsely chopped
1 pound ripe apricots, coarsely chopped, or 2 cans (15 ounces each) apricot halves, drained and coarsely chopped
1 cup finely chopped fresh or canned unsweetened pineapple
1 cup distilled white vinegar
1½ cups sugar
1¼ teaspoons minced fresh ginger

In a large, heavy nonreactive saucepan or flameproof casserole, combine all the ingredients. Bring to a boil over high heat. Reduce the heat to low and simmer, stirring occasionally, until most of the liquid has evaporated and the sauce thickens, about 3 hours. (It will firm up more when chilled.) Taste and add more sugar or vinegar if desired. Refrigerate until well chilled before using.

—*Linda Burum & Linda Merinoff*

• • •

CHILLED BOURBON CUSTARD

This custard is a clone of the English syllabub, a rich, frothy beverage for which the English designed beautiful serving cups the size of demitasse cups but with two handles. You can serve this wonderful custard southern-style in small cups, or use it as a sauce, like a crème anglaise. It is delicious with the Old-Fashioned Brandied Pumpkin Pie (p. 220).

——— *Makes About 3½ Cups* ———
6 egg yolks
¼ cup sugar
1 teaspoon all-purpose flour
Pinch of salt
2 cups milk, scalded
1 to 2 tablespoons good bourbon, to taste
Lightly sweetened whipped cream, as accompaniment

1. In a medium nonreactive pan, beat the egg yolks with the sugar, flour and salt until the yolks turn pale, about 5 minutes. Gradually beat the warm milk into the egg mixture.

2. Set the saucepan over moderately low heat and cook, stirring constantly, until the custard thickens enough to lightly coat the back of the spoon, about 5 minutes.

3. Pour the custard into a well-chilled serving bowl. Cover the surface directly with a piece of plastic wrap and refrigerate until cold.

4. Just before serving, stir in the bourbon. Serve in small cups with whipped cream on top if desired.

—*Camille Glenn*

• • •

RASPBERRY COULIS

Serve this raspberry sauce with fresh fruit, or toasted pound cake, or as part of a dessert called Peanut Butter Ice Cream with Chocolate Sauce (p. 207).

——— *Makes About 1 Cup* ———
1 package (10 ounces) frozen raspberries, thawed, with their juice
2 tablespoons raspberry jam
1½ teaspoons arrowroot or cornstarch
1 tablespoon lemon juice

1. In a food processor, puree the raspberries with their juice and the jam by pulsing on and off for 30 seconds. Strain the mixture into a small nonreactive saucepan through a fine-mesh sieve.

2. In a medium bowl, whisk ¼ cup of the raspberry puree with the arrowroot until blended. Stir in the remaining puree and return the mixture to the saucepan. Cook over moderate heat, stirring constantly, until the mixture bubbles up, thickens and clears, 2 to 3 minutes. Remove from the heat and add the lemon juice. Let cool to room temperature.

—*Marcelo Vasquez, Morton's, Charleston, South Carolina*

• • •

BUTTERSCOTCH-BOURBON SAUCE

In addition to complementing the Pecan-Almond Tart (p. 229) for which it was designed, this dessert sauce would make a good ice cream topping.

—————— *Makes About 2⅔ Cups* ——————
⅔ cup light corn syrup
1½ cups (packed) light brown sugar
4 tablespoons unsalted butter
⅔ cup heavy cream
2 to 3 tablespoons bourbon, to taste

In a small heavy saucepan, bring the corn syrup, brown sugar and butter to a boil over moderately low heat, stirring frequently with a wooden spoon. Remove from the heat and blend in the cream. Let cool to room temperature. Stir in the bourbon.

—*Elizabeth Terry, Elizabeth*
on 37th, Savannah

• • •

CREME ANGLAISE

This thin, rich custard sauce is a wonderful accompaniment to all manner of desserts, from fresh fruit to cake.

—————— *Makes About 1 Cup* ——————
1 cup milk
3 egg yolks
3 tablespoons sugar
1 teaspoon vanilla extract

1. In a small heavy saucepan, scald the milk over moderately low heat.

2. Meanwhile, in a medium bowl, beat the egg yolks, sugar and vanilla until thick and pale, about 5 minutes. Gradually beat the hot milk into the yolk mixture in a thin stream. Return to the saucepan and cook over moderately high heat, stirring constantly, until the custard coats the back of a metal spoon, 5 to 6 minutes. Do not let boil.

3. Strain the custard through a fine-mesh sieve and let cool to room temperature, stirring frequently to prevent a skin from forming on the surface.

—*Marcelo Vasquez, Morton's,*
Charleston, South Carolina

• • •

CHOCOLATE SAUCE

Serve this chocolate sauce over ice cream, such as Peanut Butter Ice Cream (p. 207).

—————— *Makes About 2½ Cups* ——————
2 sticks (8 ounces) unsalted butter
1 pound bittersweet chocolate, grated
½ teaspoon vanilla extract

1. In a medium saucepan, melt the butter over low heat. Remove from the heat and let stand until the milk solids have settled. Strain the butter through cheesecloth or a fine-mesh sieve.

2. In the top of a double boiler over hot—but not simmering—water, combine the chocolate and the clarified butter. Cook over low heat, stirring, until absolutely smooth, 3 to 4 minutes. Remove from the heat and stir in the vanilla. Keep the sauce warm by leaving it in the double boiler but *off* the heat.

—*Marcelo Vasquez, Morton's,*
Charleston, South Carolina.

• • •

KETJAP MANIS WITH FRESH GINGER

Stored in a tightly capped bottle at room temperature, this sauce will keep almost indefinitely.

—————— *Makes About 1½ Cups* ——————
½ cup granulated sugar
½ cup (packed) brown sugar
1 cup soy sauce
2 star anise pods*
½ teaspoon minced fresh ginger
*Available at spice shops and Asian markets

1. In a medium saucepan, combine the granulated and brown sugars with ½ cup of water. Bring to a boil over moderate heat, stirring constantly. Reduce the heat to low and simmer, stirring, until the sugars are completely dissolved, about 3 minutes.

2. Stir in the soy sauce, star anise and ginger. Stop stirring and bring to a boil over high heat. Reduce the heat to low and simmer for 10 minutes. Let cool, then strain.

—*Linda Burum & Linda Merinoff*

• • •

KETJAP MANIS

Although *ketjap manis*, Indonesian sweetened soy sauce, is available at Asian markets, I much prefer the flavor of homemade.

——— Makes About 1½ Cups ———
1 cup sugar
1¼ cups light Chinese soy sauce*
2 garlic cloves, bruised
2 large star anise pods*
*Available at Asian markets

1. In a heavy medium saucepan, cook the sugar over moderately low heat, stirring occasionally, until it melts and caramelizes to a rich brown.

2. Add the soy sauce, garlic, star anise and ¼ cup of water. Cook, stirring, until the caramel and soy are blended. Simmer until slightly thickened, about 15 minutes. Let cool, then pour into a widemouthed jar. Cover and refrigerate for up to 2 years.

—Copeland Marks

• • •

RASPBERRY KETCHUP

This flavorful ketchup is delicious with hot or cold duck, turkey, chicken or pork, and it makes a tasty dip for broiled chicken wings or barbecued ribs.

——— Makes About 2 Cups ———
3½ cups raspberries (about 1 pint)
½ cup sugar
1½ cups minced onions (about 2
   large)
½ cup white wine vinegar
2 garlic cloves, minced
1½ teaspoons allspice

1. Place the raspberries in a heavy, medium, nonreactive saucepan with 2

tablespoons of water and 1 tablespoon of the sugar. With a wooden spoon, mash the berries while bringing the mixture to a boil over moderate heat. Reduce the heat, cover and simmer for 5 minutes.

2. Press the mixture through a fine sieve to remove the seeds.

3. Return the sieved mixture to the saucepan and add the onions, vinegar, garlic, allspice and remaining 7 tablespoons sugar. Bring to a boil, reduce the heat to low and simmer uncovered, stirring occasionally, until the onions are tender and the mixture is reduced to 2 cups, 10 to 15 minutes.

4. Puree in a food processor or pass through a food mill. Store in a covered jar in the refrigerator for up to 1 month.

—Diana Sturgis

• • •

PORTUGUESE ROASTED
GARLIC PATE

Serve this spread with crackers, as a topping for baked potatoes or tossed with well-drained hot fettuccine or linguine. Store the pâté, covered, in the refrigerator for up to a week, but let it return to room temperature before serving. If the pâté is still too firm, return it to the food processor and beat in one to three tablespoons of water.

——— Makes About 2 Cups ———
2 large heads of garlic
1 pound mozzarella cheese, cut into
   1-inch cubes
1 teaspoon freshly ground pepper
2 to 3 tablespoons extra-virgin olive
   oil

1. Preheat the oven to 300°. Wrap the unpeeled garlic heads individually in a double thickness of aluminum foil and roast in the middle of the oven until soft, 40 to 45 minutes.

2. Set aside until cool enough to handle, about 15 minutes. Remove the foil and separate the cloves.

3. Working over the bowl of a food processor, pinch the garlic cloves, one by one, letting the roasted garlic fall into the bowl and discarding the skins.

4. Add the cheese and pepper and process for 30 seconds. With the machine on, gradually add the olive oil, 1 tablespoon at a time, until the mixture is the texture of softly whipped potatoes. Transfer to a serving dish.

—Jean Anderson

• • •

STRAWBERRY VINEGAR

Ripe, juicy berries are a must when making fruit vinegar. It adds a nice change of flavor to a salad dressing. I like to save the bottle from the white wine vinegar used in the recipe and then pour the strawberry vinegar into it when it is ready.

——— Makes About 1½ Cups ———
1 cup small ripe strawberries (about
   ½ pint), quartered
1 bottle (12 to 14 ounces) white wine
   vinegar (about 1 pint)

1. Place the berries in a 2-cup glass jar and pour in the vinegar. Cover and set aside at room temperature for 3 days.

2. Strain the strawberry vinegar through a fine sieve. Pour into a clean bottle, using a funnel if necessary, cap tightly and store in a cool dark place.

—Diana Sturgis

• • •

GINGER-SPICED CUCUMBER

The method of salting the cut cucumber softens it just enough to remove the raw quality while leaving the fresh taste in. The effect of the hot ginger sauce on the cool cucumber is surprising and sublime. It goes well with almost any grilled meat.

4 to 6 Servings
as an Accompaniment

1 European seedless cucumber (about 1 pound)
¾ teaspoon salt
1 teaspoon vegetable oil
1 teaspoon Oriental sesame oil
1 garlic clove, minced
1½-inch-long piece of fresh ginger, peeled and minced
⅓ cup sugar
⅓ cup distilled white vinegar

1. Rest the cucumber lengthwise against the handle of a wooden spoon or chopstick, and cut on an angle into ¼-inch slices, stopping at the spoon so that you do not cut all the way through. Turn the cucumber over. Again resting it against the spoon, cut straight down into ¼-inch slices without cutting all the way through.

2. Sprinkle the cucumber all over and in between the slices with the salt. Wrap in a clean kitchen towel and refrigerate for at least 2 hours and up to 24 hours.

3. In a small saucepan, heat the vegetable oil and sesame oil over high heat. Add the garlic and ginger and cook, stirring, until aromatic, about 1 minute. Add the sugar and vinegar. Bring to a boil and cook, stirring, until the syrup is slightly thickened and reduced to about ⅓ cup, about 3 minutes. *(The sauce can be made up to 24 hours in advance; cover and refrigerate. Reheat before proceeding.)*

4. Arrange the cucumber on a platter and spread to open up the slices slightly. Pour the ginger syrup over the cucumber.

—*Marcia Kiesel*

• • •

PICKLED PEARS

The southern fondness for making preserves with spices of all kinds goes back to the days when the East India Company first brought the spices from the Orient and the West Indies to South Carolina and Virginia. We southern cooks have known and loved ginger for several hundred years.

Makes About 2 Pints

3 pounds firm Bosc or Anjou pears— peeled, quartered and cored
1 tablespoon fresh lemon juice
3 cups sugar
2 cups cider vinegar
2 thin slices of lemon
1 tablespoon whole cloves
1 tablespoon allspice berries
2 pieces of dried stem ginger or 3 quarter-size slices of fresh ginger
2 cinnamon sticks

1. Put the pears in a bowl with cold water to cover. Add the lemon juice to prevent discoloration.

2. In a large nonreactive saucepan, combine the sugar, vinegar, lemon slices, cloves, allspice, ginger, cinnamon and 3 cups of water. Bring to a boil over high heat, stirring to dissolve the sugar.

3. Drain the pears and add them to the spiced syrup. Bring to a boil, reduce the heat to moderate and simmer until the pears are tender but still firm, about 3 minutes.

4. Remove from the heat and let the pears macerate in the syrup overnight. The next day, using a slotted spoon, transfer the pears to 2 clean pint canning jars. Boil the syrup over high heat until it registers 200° on a candy thermometer and is almost at the thread stage, about 35 minutes.

5. Pour the syrup over the pears. Let cool, then cover and refrigerate until ready to serve. (The pears will become a more beautiful color after 2 or 3 days in the syrup. They keep well in the refrigerator for up to a month.)

—*Camille Glenn*

• • •

OLIVE-OREGANO RELISH

This relish will complement all grilled meat, vegetables and the more unctuous fish, such as tuna, swordfish, pompano and salmon.

Makes About 1½ Cups

2 tablespoons dried currants
2 tablespoons boiling water
1½ tablespoons chopped fresh oregano
1 tablespoon fresh lemon juice
¾ teaspoon grated lemon zest
1½ teaspoons anchovy paste
1 teaspoon honey
1 cup Calamata olives (about ½ pound), pitted and chopped
2 garlic cloves, peeled and bruised
¼ cup olive oil

1. In a small bowl, cover the currants with the boiling water. Let soften for about 5 minutes.

2. Meanwhile, in a medium bowl, combine the oregano, lemon juice, lemon zest, anchovy paste and honey. Stir well to dissolve the anchovy paste.

3. Drain and coarsely chop the currants. Add the currants, olives and garlic to the lemon mixture and stir to combine. Add the olive oil and stir well. Cover and refrigerate overnight. Before serving, bring to room temperature. Remove the garlic and stir well.

—*Marcia Kiesel*

• • •

STOCKS, SAUCES & CONDIMENTS

TIME-HONORED PEPPER RELISH

This is a delicious, typically southern condiment, which is compatible with turkey, chicken, braised beef, veal or ham.

——————Makes About 2 Pints——————
2 large red bell peppers
1 medium green bell pepper
1 medium Bermuda onion
1 tender celery rib
1/4 cup plus 2 tablespoons sugar
3/4 cup cider vinegar

1. In a food processor, combine the red and green bell peppers, onion and celery. Process until the vegetables are coarsely chopped. Transfer to a colander and let drain for 10 minutes.

2. In a medium nonreactive saucepan, combine the sugar and vinegar. Bring to a boil over moderate heat and cook for 2 minutes. Add the drained vegetables. Return to a boil and cook for 2 minutes.

3. Ladle the relish into impeccably clean or sterilized pint jars; cover. Let cool, then refrigerate.

—Camille Glenn

• • •

FRESH CRANBERRY AND ORANGE RELISH

The southern Thanksgiving table would not be complete without relishes, including perhaps a fresh relish, such as this one made with cranberries and oranges.

——————Makes About 2 3/4 Cups——————
3/4 cup sugar
1 large navel orange with the peel on, cut into 8 wedges
2 cups (1/2 pound) cranberries, rinsed and picked over

1. In a food processor, combine the sugar and orange wedges. Turn the machine on and off quickly for 30 seconds to chop very coarsely. Add the cranberries and continue to pulse for 45 seconds, or until all the ingredients are coarsely chopped and well mixed.

2. Transfer the relish to a serving bowl. Refrigerate until chilled before serving.

—Camille Glenn

• • •

SPICED CRANBERRY JELLY

It is not uncommon to find cranberries in more than one form as part of a southern Thanksgiving, including this molded cranberry sauce spiced with cinnamon, allspice and cloves.

——————Makes About 3 Cups——————
4 cups (1 pound) cranberries, picked over, stems removed
2 cups sugar
2 cinnamon sticks
8 allspice berries
20 whole cloves

1. In a large nonreactive saucepan, bring 2 cups of water to a boil over high heat. Add the cranberries, sugar, cinnamon sticks, allspice and cloves. Return to a boil, reduce the heat to moderately low and boil for 20 minutes.

2. Transfer the mixture to a coarse sieve set over a bowl. Press the cranberries through the sieve with a spatula. Discard the spices.

3. Return the strained cranberries to the saucepan. Bring to a boil over moderately high heat. Cook for 5 minutes, stirring constantly.

4. Pour the cranberry jelly into a 3-cup ring mold and set aside to cool. Cover the jelly and refrigerate overnight.

5. To unmold, invert the ring mold onto a serving plate and press a damp hot kitchen towel on top. Carefully lift off the ring mold and serve.

—Camille Glenn

• • •

THREE-BERRY PRESERVE

Here's a wonderful way around the rigamarole of pressure canning. Make fruit preserves in small batches and keep them refrigerated.

——————Makes 1 1/2 Cups——————
1 1/2 cups raspberries or loganberries (about 1/2 pint)
1 1/2 cups strawberries (about 1/2 pint), halved or quartered if large
1 1/2 cups gooseberries (about 1/2 pint), ends trimmed with scissors
1/2 cup sugar

1. In a medium nonreactive saucepan, combine the raspberries, strawberries, gooseberries and sugar. Bring to a boil over moderate heat, stirring to dissolve the sugar. Cook for 20 minutes, stirring occasionally.

2. Press the cooked berries through a sieve to remove the seeds. Measure the berry mixture. If you have more than 1 1/2 cups, return to the saucepan and boil until reduced to 1 1/2 cups.

3. Pour the preserves into a heatproof glass jar and cover. The preserves will keep in the refrigerator for up to 3 weeks.

—Diana Sturgis

• • •

INDEX

Q-R

S

W-Y-Z

CONTRIBUTORS

Claude Alviry is chef at Le Chardonnay in Los Angeles.

Jean Anderson is a food and travel writer and cookbook author whose most recent books are *The Food of Portugal* (Morrow) and the upcoming *The Doubleday Microwave Cookbook* to be published in 1990.

Lee Bailey is the author of the *Entertaining with Lee Bailey* column for *Food & Wine*. The author of numerous cookbooks, he is currently working on *Southern Food & Plantation Houses* (Clarkson-Potter, 1990) and *California Wine Country Cooking* (Clarkson-Potter, 1991).

Donald Barickman is chef at Carolina's in Charleston, South Carolina.

Sarah Belk is Food & Entertaining Editor of *House Beautiful* magazine and the author of a book on southern cooking to be published by Simon & Schuster.

Jean-Pierre Bose is chef at Fennel in Santa Monica, California.

Mimi Ruth Brodeur is a former member of *Food & Wine*'s test kitchen staff.

Linda Burum is a food writer and cookbook author whose most recent book is *Frozen Delights* (Scribner's).

Jane Butel is a food writer, cooking teacher, cookbook author and president of Pecos Valley Spice Company. She is currently planning to open a restaurant in New York City called Pecos River Cafe.

Nora Carey is former associate director of La Varenne cooking school in Paris and the author of the upcoming *Perfect Preserves* (Stewart, Tabori & Chang, 1990).

Irena Chalmers is a food writer, cookbook publisher and the author of, most recently, *First Home Cookbook* (Prentice-Hall) and *Alphabet Soup* (Doubleday).

Bob Chambers, food stylist, caterer and food consultant, is currently executive chef for American Express Publishing Corporation.

Julia Child, renowned cooking teacher and cookbook author, has most recently published *The Way to Cook* (Knopf).

Bruce Cost is a cooking teacher and the author of *Bruce Cost's Asian Ingredients* (Morrow) and *Ginger East to West* (Aris Books), which has recently been revised and expanded. He is also working on a new restaurant (Monsoon in San Francisco) scheduled to open in late 1989.

Mark Cox is executive chef of Tony's Restaurant in Houston.

Marion Cunningham is a cooking teacher, restaurant consultant and the author of *The Breakfast Book*, *The Fannie Farmer Cookbook* (revised edition due out in 1990) and *The Fannie Farmer Baking Book* (all from Knopf).

Diane Darrow is a food and wine writer and the co-author, with Tom Maresca, of *La Tavola Italiana* (Morrow) and the upcoming *Seasonal Italian Cooking*, to be published in 1991.

Robert Del Grande is executive chef and co-owner of Cafe Annie in Houston.

Anne Disrude is a food stylist and food writer.

John Egerton is the author of *Southern Food: At Home, On the Road, In History* (Knopf) and the upcoming *Side Orders: Small Servings of Southern Cookery and Culture* (Peachtree, 1990).

Fred Ferretti writes the *A Gourmet At Large* column for *Gourmet* magazine.

Janet Fletcher is a food and wine writer and the author of *Grain Gastronomy* (Aris Books) and the upcoming *French Home Cooking*.

Jim Fobel is a food journalist, artist and author of *Jim Fobel's Old-Fashioned Baking Book* (Ballantine), *Beautiful Food* (Van Nostrand Reinhold) and *Jim Fobel's Diet Feasts*, to be published by Doubleday in 1990.

Camille Glenn is a food writer and cooking teacher (Camille Glenn's School of Gourmet Cooking in Louisville, Kentucky), whose most recent cookbook is *The Heritage of Southern Cooking* (Workman).

Joyce Goldstein is chef/owner of Square One in San Francisco, food columnist for the *San Francisco Chronicle* and the author of *The Mediterranean Kitchen* (Morrow).

Ken Haedrich is a food writer, columnist and cookbook author. His latest book is *The Maple Syrup Cookbook* (Garden Way Publishing).

Sandy Hollander is chef at 45 South Restaurant in Savannah, Georgia.

Marcia Kiesel is Associate Director of *Food & Wine's* test kitchen.

Johanne Killeen is chef at Al Forno in Providence, Rhode Island.

Evan Kleiman is a cooking teacher, food writer, chef/owner (Angeli Caffè, Los Angeles) and co-author, with Viana La Place, of numerous cookbooks (see La Place).

Viana La Place is a cooking teacher, food writer and co-author, with Evan Kleiman, of *Cucina Fresca* (Harper & Row), *Pasta Fresca* (Morrow) and *Cucina Rustica*, to be published in 1990 by Morrow. She is also working on a book tentatively titled *Italian Vegetable Cooking* (Morrow) for publication in 1991.

Bruce Marder is owner and executive chef at West Beach Cafe in Venice, California.

Tom Maresca is a wine and food writer and the author of *Mastering Wine* (Bantam) and the upcoming *The Right Wine* (Weidenfeld & Nicolson, 1990). He has also co-authored two cookbooks with Diane Darrow (see Darrow).

Galina Mariani is a cooking teacher (Galina Mariani's Cooking) in Tuckahoe, New York.

John F. Mariani is a food writer and the author of *The Dictionary of American Food & Drink* (Ticknor & Fields). He is currently working on *Mariani's History of American Restaurants* to be published in 1991.

Copeland Marks is a food historian, cooking teacher and cookbook author whose most recent book is *The Exotic Kitchens of India* (M. Evans). He is currently working on a book on the ethnic kitchens of Jewish communities in North Africa, India, the Middle East and Asiatic Russia.

271

Lydie Pinoy Marshall is a cooking teacher (A La Bonne Cocotte in New York City) and the author of *Cooking with Lydie Marshall* (Knopf) and an upcoming potato cookbook to be published by Harper & Row.

Elin McCoy & John Frederick Walker are contributing editors of *Food & Wine* and co-authors of *Thinking About Wine* (Simon & Schuster).

Michael McLaughlin is a food writer and the author, in collaboration with Julee Rosso and Sheila Lukins, of *The Silver Palate Cookbook* (Workman). He is currently working on *The New American Kitchen* (Simon & Schuster, 1990).

Linda Merinoff is a food writer and cookbook author whose latest book is *Gingerbread* (Fireside Books).

Mark Militello is chef/owner of Max's Place in Miami, Florida.

David Millen is chef at Rebecca's in Los Angeles.

Molly O'Neill is a style reporter for *The New York Times* and co-author, with Stanley Dry, of a forthcoming book entitled *New York's Cooking* (Workman).

Jean-Louis Palladin is chef/owner of Jean-Louis in Washington, D.C.

Jacques Pépin, renowned cooking teacher and cookbook author, has most recently published *The Art of Cooking, Volumes I & II* (Knopf) and he is working on a "shortcuts" cookbook to be published by Morrow in 1990.

W. Peter Prestcott is *Food & Wine's* Entertaining & Special Projects Editor.

Carl Quagliata is chef at Giovanni's in Beachwood, Ohio.

Michel Richard is chef at Citrus in Los Angeles.

Felipe Rojas-Lombardi is executive chef/owner at The Ballroom in New York City and the author of numerous cookbooks, including, most recently, *Soup Beautiful Soup* (Random House) and the forthcoming *Felipe Rojas-Lombardi's South American Kitchen*.

David Rosengarten is a cooking teacher, wine and food writer, and the publisher of "Wine & Food Newsletter." He is also the author of *Red Wine with Fish: The New Art of Matching Wine with Food* (Simon & Schuster) and the upcoming *The Simon & Schuster Pocket Guide to Wine with Food*, to be published in 1991.

Julie Sahni is a chef, consultant, cooking teacher (Julie Sahni's Indian Cooking School in New York City) and cookbook author.

Richard Sax is a cooking teacher, food writer and author of five cookbooks. He is currently at work on a dessert cookbook.

Leonard Schwartz, co-owner and executive chef of 72 Market St. Oyster Bar & Grill (Venice, California), is working on a book of salads to be published by Harper & Row.

Michele Scicolone is a cooking teacher, wine and food writer, and the author of *Shellfish* and *Fish Steaks and Fillets* (both from Harmony Books) and the upcoming *The Antipasto Table* from Crown (1991).

Tracey Seaman is Recipe Tester-Developer at *Food & Wine* magazine.

André Soltner is chef/owner of Lutèce in New York City.

Diana Sturgis is Test Kitchen Director at *Food & Wine* magazine.

John Martin Taylor is a food writer and owner of Hoppin' John's, a culinary bookstore in Charleston, South Carolina. He is currently at work on *Hoppin' John's Foods of the Lowcountry*, to be published by Bantam Books in 1991.

Elizabeth Terry is chef/owner of Elizabeth on 37th in Savannah, Georgia.

Jeremiah Tower is a cooking teacher, chef and restaurateur (Stars, Stars Cafe and 690 in San Francisco) and the author of *Jeremiah Tower's New American Classics* (Harper & Row). He is currently working on plans for Stars' Wine Bar and Stars' Wine School & Shop.

Marcelo Vasquez is chef at Morton's in Charleston, South Carolina.

Patricia Wells is the restaurant critic for *The International Herald Tribune* and the author of *The Food Lover's Guide to Paris*, *The Food Lover's Guide to France* and *Bistro Cooking* (all from Workman).

Eileen Yin-Fei Lo is a cooking teacher, food writer and the author of *Eileen Yin-Fei Lo's New Cantonese Cooking* (Viking Penguin), *The Chinese Banquet Cookbook* (Crown) and *The Dim Sum Book: Classic Recipes from the Chinese Teahouse* (Crown).

We would also like to thank the following restaurants and individuals for their contributions to *Food & Wine* and to this cookbook:

Amerigo's in New York City; **Auberge du Soleil** in Rutherford, California; **Commander's Palace** in New Orleans; **Jilich's on East Bay** in Charleston, South Carolina; **John Makin**; **Montrachet** in New York City; **Jim Nassikas** at The Stanford Court hotel in San Francisco; **Opera** in Los Angeles; **Pazzia** in Los Angeles; **San Domenico** in New York City; **Jean-Michel Savoca** and **Boyce Brawley** of New York Parties in New York City; **The Riviera** in Dallas; **'21' Club** in New York City.

PHOTO CREDITS
Cover: Jerry Simpson. **Page 33:** Anthony Johnson. **Page 34 (top):** Jerry Simpson. **Page 34 (bottom):** Jerry Simpson. **Pages 34-35:** Mark Thomas. **Page 36:** Michael Skott. **Pages 69-71:** Jerry Simpson. **Page 72:** Mark Thomas. **Pages 72-73:** Jerry Simpson. **Page 74:** Mark Thomas. **Page 75 (top):** Mark Thomas. **Page 75 (bottom):** Jerry Simpson. **Pages 76, 109:** Jerry Simpson. **Page 110:** Dennis Gottlieb. **Pages 110-111, 112:** Jerry Simpson. **Page 145:** Steven Mark Needham. **Pages 146-148, 181:** Jerry Simpson. **Page 182:** Elizabeth Watt. **Page 183:** Jerry Simpson. **Page 184 (all):** Dennis Galante. **Pages 185-186:** Mark Thomas. **Page 187:** Steven Mark Needham. **Pages 188, 221:** Jerry Simpson. **Pages 222-223:** Mark Thomas. **Page 223:** Jerry Simpson. **Page 224:** Steven Mark Needham.